D1144791

The Unnatural Alliance

The Unnatural Alliance

James Adams

Q
Quartet Books
London Melbourne New York

To Patricia

First published by Quartet Books Limited 1984
A member of the Namara Group
27/29 Goodge Street, London W1P 1FD

Copyright © by James Adams 1984

British Library Cataloguing in Publication Data

Adams, James
    The unnatural alliance.
    1. South Africa—Foreign relations—Israel
    2. Israel—Foreign relations—South Africa
    I. Title
    327.6805694   DT779.7

    ISBN 0-7043-2373-7

Typeset by MC Typeset, Chatham, Kent
Printed and bound in Great Britain
by Mackays of Chatham Ltd, Kent

Contents

Acknowledgements

I would like to thank my two researchers, Zaira Steele and Muriel Grieve, as well as David Blundy, Sam Hemingway, the Humboldt State University Library, the Library of Congress, Cal McCrystal, Yossi Melman, the Institute for the Study of Conflict, the International Institute for Strategic Studies, Peter Wilsher, Tana de Zulueta, and many others who wish to remain anonymous. Special thanks to Eric Marsden for his help at a difficult time, and to Toby Eady for his kind and constant encouragement.

Charlotte Nicholson made sense out of my drafts and managed to type a perfect manuscript; she has my thanks for doing such a difficult job so cheerfully.

Nancy Duin painstakingly edited the manuscript. Her incisive questions improved the finished product immeasurably.

PART ONE

1 Mutual Security

During the last ten years, Israel and South Africa have felt more and more isolated and surrounded by enemies. Both are united in their hatred of Communism and feel directly threatened by its followers; both also feel threatened by guerrilla groups on their borders. In this isolation, they have drawn increasingly closer together for mutual security and, as a result, have used every means at their disposal to equip themselves with modern weapons from the open market and from each other, and to build up their own independent arms industries, combining Israel's innovative technology and South Africa's rich supplies of raw materials and its relatively full coffers. However, their joint production and shared research and development (R&D) costs have not only been applied to sophisticated missiles, tanks, aircraft and naval vessels, but also to nuclear weapons.

This book is an account of the marriage between the needs and capabilities of Israel and South Africa, and the repercussions that their joint military production has had on themselves, on other countries such as Argentina and the United States and, in particular, on the Third World. The book also sets out to show how the political influence of both countries has increased as a result of their mutual alliance and dependence, making both increasingly resistant to outside pressures.

Most of this story takes place between 1975 and 1983; however, in order to understand the strength of the mutual feeling between Israel and South Africa, the problems and the tensions, it is first necessary to explain briefly the historical basis for their close union, for they make strange bedfellows.

In 1836, some of the Boers, the Dutch-speaking people of South Africa, became disenchanted with British interference in their affairs and trekked inland across the Vaal River, wresting land from local tribes in order to set up their own independent farming state. For much of their journey, these people took inspiration from the Israelites of the Old Testament: they were, they thought, called by God, and their goal was to find a land flowing with milk and honey.

Later, diamonds and gold were discovered in Boer territory and people, including many Jews, some with strong Zionist ideals, flocked in from all over the world. Many of the Boers regarded these newcomers as interlopers, a dissolute crowd who would pollute their high moral Calvinistic ideals. These disenchanted Boers – or Afrikaners as they came to be called – later formed themselves into the Nationalist Party. However, the country's main political group during the early twentieth century was the South African Party led by Jan Smuts. He was initially an Anglophile who encouraged immigration; he also had a great liking for Chaim Weizmann, President of the British Zionist Federation, whom he met in 1917. The friendship between the two men helped to lay the foundations of the Jewish state and to cement a growing relationship between South Africa and the Zionists. It is probably fair to say that, without the help of Jan Smuts – who had access to, and was respected by, the leaders of the British Empire – the founding of the State of Israel might well have been delayed for some time. He was a powerful ally and a formidable friend whom Weizmann valued highly.

Smuts found in Weizmann everything that his nation admired in the Zionists: Weizmann believed in a continuing relationship with the British, which coincided with Smuts' convictions; Weizmann also believed that the Zionists were pioneers who could bring civilization to a desolate region, something every South African felt he was doing for the African continent. There was an additional, albeit negative, factor which naturally bound the two men: Smuts had little sympathy for the Arab cause. The Arabs, in his view, were merely an extension of the very people against whom his own followers had fought in the course of their expansion northwards from the Cape. As far as Smuts was concerned, the Arabs were an uncivilized and backward people who did not deserve support, contrasted with the intelligent, civilized and educated Jews, many of whom had helped to build South Africa.

Finally, as a fervent Christian, Smuts (along with members of the British government, including Foreign Secretary Arthur Balfour) believed that the Jews had been treated disgracefully throughout history. He felt strongly that the Diaspora was a crime that it was every Christian's duty to correct. It was natural that he should fight hard for the Zionists, believing as he did that only the establishment of a State of Israel would atone for what he saw as the continuing crime against the Jewish people.

Smuts played a prominent part in ensuring the passing of the

Balfour Declaration in 1917 which committed Britain to the concept of a Jewish homeland in Palestine; throughout the difficult political battles of the next thirty years, he continually fought in the Zionist corner, in South Africa and by using his influence with the British Cabinet. On several occasions, the British tried to dilute their commitment to the Balfour Declaration and, on every occasion, Smuts intervened. When Smuts died two years after the founding of Israel, the Israeli acting Prime Minister, Joseph Sprinzak, marked the occasion by proclaiming: 'General Smuts is written on the map of Israel and in the heart of our nation.' These sentiments took a more practical form two years later when, on the southern slopes of the Judaean hills, the Smuts Forest (overlooking the Weizmann Forest) was dedicated.

The rise of the right-wing South African Nationalist Party naturally caused considerable concern among the Jewish community. Writing in *South Africa International*, Martyn Adelberg quotes Benjamin Pogrund, the deputy editor of the Rand *Daily Mail*, on his recollections of the 1948 Nationalist victory:

> I recall it very vividly in 1948 when I was fifteen and very interested in life around me . . . in Cape Town. The morning newspaper, the *Cape Times*, used to put a billboard in St George Street across the road from the *Cape Times* building. The election results were displayed on this board . . . It was during the night when the astonishing defeat of the Smuts government was coming through. I recall, in the next couple of days, in this fairly close-knit Jewish community, the tremor of fear that ran through it because the Nationalists had come into office. I had grown up in this community simply accepting that the Nationalists were Nazi supporters and God help the Jews if they came to power.

But, in his fight to win re-election and to undercut Smuts' reputation as a tolerant leader, Dr Daniel Malan, head of the Nationalist Party, had privately reassured Jewish leaders prior to the election that he would not allow discrimination of any kind against them. This private assurance was repeated publicly immediately after the election and the Nationalists have since stuck to their promise. Moreover, in a gesture of solidarity and under pressure from the highly influential Jewish population in South Africa, Malan immediately offered financial and logistical support to Israel. South Africa was also the first country formally to recognize the State of Israel after its foundation on 14 May 1948, and Malan was eventually to be the first foreign head of government to visit there.

Even before this, South Africa had made considerable efforts to smuggle food, medical supplies, money, arms, uniforms, fighter aircraft and two Bonanza transports to the Zionist insurgent force, the Haganah, and several hundred Jews from South Africa went to Israel to fight. According to an official Israeli government account of the time, South Africa 'contributed more to the Israeli war effort, in terms of skilled volunteers, than any other country in the world'. The first pilot to be killed in action in the Israeli Air Force (IAF) was a South African volunteer, and it was Sid Cohen, a Vrystater from Bothaville and a former Western Desert squadron leader, who helped found the IAF, with some German ME-109 fighters. This first offer of aid provided the foundations on which has been built one of the great military relationships in the world today.

The arrival of the Nationalists led to a fundamental shift in the nature of South African politics but a continuation in the government's support for Israel. The Nationalist Party had come to power in 1948 on a platform of 'apartheid', or racial separateness. Although there had been visible signs of racial segregation for some years before, with whites being given preferential treatment in jobs and housing as well as in wages, the apartheid policy of the Nationalists attempted to advance and mythologize this policy as a justification for segregation and (ironically) a solution to increasing world criticism. They wanted to establish tribal homelands, or Bantustans, where the blacks from the major tribal groups would be allowed to create their own governments and levy their own taxes. Only in the homelands would blacks have the right of residence, and under no circumstance would they be allowed to seek representation in the South African parliament.

Superficially, this seemed to solve many of South Africa's problems: the vast majority of the people (the blacks) would be allowed to develop their own political infrastructure without in any way interfering with the rights and needs of the (minority) whites. To enforce the new policy, the Nationalists introduced a series of legislative measures that set back racial integration by several decades and enshrined the broad policy of apartheid on the statute books. These laws established the legal segregation of public accommodation, ordered that whites be hired in preference to blacks and that marriages between blacks and whites be outlawed, established residential and territorial separation by race and specifically excluded blacks from white universities. It should be emphasized that these were all new laws. Certainly, before the arrival of the Nationalist Party, there had been segregation and discrimination, but nothing on the scale of that which was suddenly introduced in the late 1940s and early 1950s.

The relationship between South Africa and Israel is not just based on the friendship between Smuts and Weizmann. The South African Jewish population, many of whom had a staunch Zionist Lithuanian background, were ardent supporters of the establishment of a homeland in Palestine, and it was generally recognized among the Diaspora that South African Jews were the most united behind the concept of *Eretz Israel* ('The Land of Israel' or 'Greater Israel') of any group among the worldwide community.

In 1948, there were around 118,000 Jews in South Africa (a figure that has remained virtually static ever since), and they made up the largest percentage of Zionists in the Jewish population of any country in the world. Their contribution to Zionist funds was second in the world only to that of the United States, and proportionately was three times larger. Again, this figure has remained remarkably consistent and it is one of which the South African Jewish population is very proud. In addition, many Israelis have taken up residence in South Africa. It is estimated that as many as 25,000 Israelis are living in South Africa at any one time, representing the largest proportion of Israelis to a local Jewish population anywhere in the world. Few of this great number have emigrated through pure political conviction or dissatisfaction with the Israeli way of life. On the contrary, many have been seconded to work on intergovernment contracts, especially in the fields of arms and energy.

The reverse has also occurred: between 1948 and 1966, an average of 200 South African Jews emigrated to Israel each year. This figure held steady, with the exception of 1961, when the number of emigrants quadrupled in the aftermath of the Sharpeville shootings. By 1967, nearly 4,000 South Africans had settled in Israel, and by 1975 the figure had reached 6,000. Today, nearly 8,500 South Africans are resident in Israel – which may not seem an enormous figure but, when considered as a proportion of the total Jewish population in South Africa, is the equivalent of 400,000 US Jews emigrating to Israel.

According to Howard Sachar's *A History of Israel*, during the period 1948–75,

A fourth of the South African immigration settled on the land, established a chain of *kibbutzim* and *moshavim* and joined other collective farms in large numbers. Many hundreds of South Africans resumed their medical and dental practices in Israel. A large minority entered the diplomatic and military services. Two South Africans were members of the cabinet, another a member of the Knesset; two were mayors. Most were businessmen, however. Indeed, a number of Israel's most important companies owed their growth and development to South African capital and leadership, among them El Al, the national airline, Ata, a leading clothing manufacturer, as well as a variety of dress factories, banks, mortgage and insurance companies and scores of other middle-sized businesses, ranging from cold-storage plants to foundries. Perhaps the most visually impressive South African contribution was the Mediterranean resort of Ashkelon, founded in 1953 by private investors in partnership with the South African Zionist Federation and the Israeli government. Within ten years, the results of this enterprise could be seen as a handsome garden city of 15,000 inhabitants, one of the showpieces of Israel, and a vivid talisman of Diaspora loyalty.

From Israel's point of view, this steady flow of wealthy and highly qualified immigrants was deeply gratifying – a constant example of the power of the homeland to draw real talent from the Diaspora.

There is no doubt that many of those Jews who left South Africa, particularly in the early days, did so because they wanted to play a part in the growth and development of the new state. However, as time went by, the Nationalists grew more entrenched, and as their policy of apartheid became more visible, there was increasing disenchantment within the South African Jewish community. They began to leave in increasing numbers, and today this group of emigrants forms the core of opposition to the new Israel–South African *rapprochement.*

It should be remembered that South African Jews were considered to be among the best educated and most liberal members of South African society. They had none of the repressive instincts of the Boer, their whole strategy as an ethnic group being based on pragmatism and an intellectual appreciation of the liberal standpoint, and therefore apartheid and the resulting suppression of freedom for the black people in South Africa were anathema to many of them. Aside from a simple feeling that the suppression of a people by a privileged minority would only store up trouble for the future and threaten the stability of everyone, the Jews felt distinctly uncomfortable being involved with a country that practised oppression towards another group. The whole Jewish experience over centuries had centred around their own repression, and they had every sympathy for those similarly threatened.

For the majority of the Jewish community that remained in South Africa, the choice was difficult. They could either fight their own government that had promised them freedom from any form of discrimination, or they could compromise and bend to accommodate the injustices of apartheid.

In a shrewd move, in 1948, the Nationalist government granted the Jewish community the unique privilege of being allowed to export funds to Israel. In effect, this bought off the Jewish hierarchy who were now faced with a very delicate issue of divided loyalty. Although the threat was never mentioned specifically, the Jews were well aware that a vociferous campaign against apartheid might well result in the Malan government or its successors abandoning previous agreements and not only cancelling the flow of cash to Israel but possibly introducing discrimination in some form against the Jewish population. With hindsight, it would have been extraordinary for the Malan government to have done anything very radical to upset the Jewish community. The Nationalists were only at the beginning of their term of office and were struggling to make sense of a complex economy and prove themselves to a watching world. Any move against the Jews would inevitably have led to a flight of both capital and people out of the country, and could possibly have done irreparable damage to the Nationalist cause.

Many of the younger and more militant Jews felt it was impossible to remain silent about the injustices of apartheid. More socially aware and often better educated than other white Europeans in South Africa, the young Jews who did not leave for Israel provided a useful source of recruits to the more militant underground movements that carried out a campaign of sabotage within the country in the 1950s and 1960s. Many Nationalists, who had always remained deeply suspicious of the Jewish influence on South African affairs, took the view that these militant Jews were representative of the total population and, while this was not so, it tended to produce some measure of social tension – although not enough to disturb the generally cosy relationship. (South Africans today remain proud of their relationship with the Jewish population and scorn any suggestion of discrimination, claiming that there is more anti-Semitism in the United States and Europe than in South Africa.)

When Hendrik Verwoerd was made Prime Minister in 1958, a measure of alarm spread through the Jewish community. Verwoerd was well known for his violently anti-Semitic sentiments – he had marched in protest against Jewish immigration before the Second World War – and there were fears that the agreements that had been reached with the Malan administration would be abandoned on his election. This fear was compounded when Verwoerd appointed, as his Foreign Minister, Eric Louw, the author of anti-Jewish legislation before the war. In the event, however, Verwoerd reassured the Jewish community that nothing would alter the status quo, and he kept his word. A curious aspect of the relationship between the Jews and the

Nationalists has been that those who are known to be anti-Semitic out of power are forced to adapt when holding office. As each government has come to power, it has found the Jewish community completely entrenched, and it has fully appreciated that any attack on the Jews would seriously undermine the economy of the country as a whole.

The founders of Israel – sharing the same sentiments with the anti-apartheid Jews of South Africa – always argued that the state must be established on the grounds of freedom and justice for all without regard to race, colour or creed, the very oppression that the Jews had suffered over the centuries making them determined to prevent discrimination whenever possible and to fight for the advancement of the common man. The imposition of the policy of apartheid was anathema to all liberal Jews, and certainly Israel's founding fathers would have been appalled at any suggestion that Israelis should support such an unjust social system.

The principles on which Israel was established have made the strong bonds between that country and South Africa all the more surprising, and this has produced a wealth of contradictions which those South Africans who have chosen voluntary exile rather than stay and live with apartheid have had somehow to overcome. Some of the exiles have found themselves training South African soldiers in counter-insurgency warfare, and those soldiers have then been able to fight more effectively against anti-government guerrillas and thus perpetuate the apartheid system. Similarly, those South African exiles who have joined the Israeli labour movement, the Histadrut, found an organization that has repeatedly expressed its violent opposition to apartheid. On a number of occasions, Histadrut leaders have banned South African sports teams from playing in Israel, and there is no question of their anti-apartheid views. Yet the Histadrut is the main backer of the giant Koor Industries which produces (among other things) substantial quantities of arms for sale to South Africa.

As a result, there has always been a degree of uneasiness among Israelis regarding their close ties with a country that the rest of the world has vilified. Even now, it is impossible to get any senior official in Israel to talk in detail about the relationship, and any criticism is met with a degree of defiance that borders on guilt.

Although the South Africans are naturally well aware of the Jews' general support of liberal causes, the Pretoria government is unwilling to conceal a relationship that directly contradicts liberal views in the West. The South Africans are prepared to talk perfectly frankly about the relationship (with the exception of any military links). There is a certain amount of boastful pride among South African leaders that they can point to one pro-Western country and say without fear of contradiction that here is one government that still supports them despite the problems of apartheid.

Although individual Jews in both South Africa and Israel may have their doubts about the connections between the two countries, and some South Africans still harbour anti-Semitic sentiments, as with any long-term relationship, there have been times of great harmony and others when the partners have had serious disagreements, the period following the rise to power of the Nationalists in 1948 until the beginning of the 1960s having proved to be particularly harmonious. However, from then until the 1973 Arab–Israeli war there was considerable tension. South Africa was faced with both a rapid rise in racial unrest within its own borders and increasing international support for guerrilla groups. In 1974, the United Nations condemned apartheid, and the process of isolating South Africa from the world scene began to get under way. This was a time when South Africa felt acutely the need for friends – and Israel chose that particular moment to look elsewhere for new allies, settling on black Africa as the focus for overseas diplomacy. The developing African nations represented a sizeable political bloc; they had considerable unexploited natural resources, and could do much to counter Arab attempts to isolate Israel. However, South Africa viewed Israeli ambitions on the continent with alarm and felt for a time that the Israelis – for their own ends – were trying to cut off South Africa from what little support it still had in the world.

In 1961, at the beginning of Israel's campaign to win friends in black Africa and expand its sphere of influence on the continent, Israel openly criticized apartheid. When the President of Upper Volta, Maurice Yameogo, visited Israel, the government issued a statement condemning apartheid as 'disadvantageous to the interests of the non-white majority in the land'. However, the South African government was quite prepared to forgive such blatant political engineering as it was partly in their own interests that a pro-South Africa, anti-Communist country like Israel should win new friends on the continent. If it had ended there, nothing further would have been said to interrupt the harmony. In October 1961, however, the Israelis in the UN voted to prevent the South African Foreign Minister, Eric Louw, from speaking and presenting South Africa's case for apartheid. The Israeli action provoked outrage in South Africa and, for the first time, the government attacked Israel's policy towards the Arabs. Verwoerd and his ministers felt a genuine sense of betrayal that a country that they had supported and helped bring into existence should have turned on them so suddenly.

By a large majority, the Jews in South Africa itself opposed Israel's stand in the UN, the Jewish Board of Deputies and the Jewish press uniting in their condemnation of Israel and assuring the South African government of their continued support. Verwoerd took the easy option, and accepted that Jews in South Africa could not be held responsible for the actions of the Israeli government. However, following the government's criticism of the Israeli vote, there were isolated outbreaks of anti-Semitism: a number of violent anti-Jewish articles appeared in the press and an even greater number were suppressed by the government; there were also sporadic attacks on Jewish property and daubing of anti-Semitic slogans, both the Great Synagogue in Johannesburg and the Jewish cemetery in Pretoria being desecrated.

At the same time, the government was concerned at the growing amount of sabotage and the circulation of underground literature calling for the overthrow of white rule. Two repressive Bills were brought before Parliament: the Publications and Control Bill and the Sabotage Bill. When passed, the former introduced radical censorship which has remained in force, while the Sabotage Act increased both the power of the police and the penalties for those caught committing attacks against the state. Because of the outbreaks of anti-Semitism, the Board of Deputies supported the passage of both pieces of legislation on the purely chauvinistic ground that Jews would be better protected from terrorist attacks after their passage through Parliament.

The behaviour of the South African Jews in supporting increasingly repressive apartheid legislation was in direct contrast to the attitude of Israel, which had taken a strong anti-apartheid stand in the UN, was actively courting African leaders and was anxious to distance itself from any close association with South Africa. Even as recently as 1966, Israel supported a UN resolution revoking South Africa's mandate over South-West Africa (Namibia). Among the pragmatists in the South African government, it was felt that there could be considerable long-term advantages to having as a friend an Israel that was closely allied with some of South Africa's most vociferous opponents. The more hard-line Nationalists were not in a position to force Israel into changing its foreign policy, and the government decided to do nothing.

Israel had been astonishingly successful in its overtures to the emerging black African nations. Since the end of the 1950s discreet approaches had been made to a number of black African states and had, in almost every case, proved successful. Africa was the major focus of Israeli foreign policy at this time, and of the 3,948 Israeli experts serving abroad from 1958 to 1970, 3,483 were in Africa; of the 13,790 foreign students in Israel during the same period, more than half were from black Africa.

Israel's military prowess proved very attractive to the African leaders, most of whom presided over unstable governments and armed forces whose loyalty could never be guaranteed. As a result, Israel became involved in the training of military personnel in the Ivory Coast, the Central African Republic, Dahomey, Cameroon, Senegal, Togo, Tanzania, Uganda, Ethiopia, Nigeria, Sierra Leone, Somalia and Mauritania. Following hard on the heels of the military men were the agricultural experts and the developers. Israelis set up joint companies and helped to manage ailing businesses that were threatened with collapse in the post-colonial era.

In addition, of course, the Israeli secret service, the Mossad, lost no opportunity in setting up a highly efficient intelligence network which spread throughout the continent. Aside from training the secret services in Ghana, Uganda and Zaïre, Mossad gathered recruits in every country that Israel supplied with aid. It was a good investment in that it has led to Israel having invaluable intelligence, and this in turn has proved very useful to the South Africans who generally have access to all Israeli intelligence relating to guerrilla activity on the African continent.

Part of the Israeli involvement in Africa was intended to have political dividends. The Israelis have always been anxious for the UN to pass a resolution calling for direct talks between themselves and the Arabs, but this was repeatedly defeated by a combination of Arab and Communist bloc votes. In 1963, when the resolution was again placed before the UN General Assembly, it was sponsored by nineteen nations, including ten from Africa, but again unsuccessfully.

If Israeli ambitions in Africa had been allowed to proceed without interruption, the logical result could have been a vast bloc of pro-Western, anti-Communist nations stretching from Israel in the north to South Africa. Such a grouping would have virtually guaranteed the security of the two most vulnerable nations at either end of the African continent and reduced the ability of the Soviet Union to expand its sphere of influence in the region.

However, the 1967 war interrupted the calm development of Israeli interest in Africa. Although the Arab nations were defeated, two factors began to put some distance between Israel and black Africa.

The first was South Africa's marked support of the Israelis. Within a week of the outbreak of war, the Vorster government in South Africa had allowed Jews to transfer an emergency fund of $20.5 million to Israel to help in the war effort. Several hundred South African Jews went to Israel – on their own initiative – to fight or help keep essential services operating. Arms and aircraft were also shipped from South Africa to replace damaged equipment.

In June 1967, when the UN General Assembly debated the Six Day War, forty-two developing nations voted in favour of a resolution that would have linked the Israeli withdrawal from Arab territories to an agreement by the Arabs to stop attacks on Israel. Significantly, South Africa voted for the motion and abstained from another attacking Israel and criticizing its annexation of East Jerusalem, which even the United States had voted for. It was the last time Israel was treated so kindly by the UN and the last occasion when it was able to muster so many votes for a moderate resolution. The visible support received from South Africa did considerable damage to Israel's relations with the Africans and began the distancing that was to culminate in the final severing of relations six years later.

The second factor affecting black Africa's dealings with Israel stemmed from a general disenchantment with the level and quality of aid that had been received from the West. There was a feeling that the West had not been delivering the aid 'goods' and had merely been paying lip-service to post-colonial responsibilities; in particular, the standard of Israeli aid, which had been high, began to fall after the 1967 war. While the developing African nations might have been prepared to be grateful for what little they *were* getting, the Arabs were just beginning to realize the power their vast reserves of oil gave them, and began to use their oil money to buy influence all over the world. They saw black Africa as a prime and a vulnerable target.

After the 1967 war, black Africa began to import substantial quantities of cheap oil from the Middle East nations, particularly from the Gulf states. It was hoped by the Arabs that this would be the beginning of a vast rearrangement of capital from the oil producers to the oil consumers of the Third World, which would help to bail out the ailing economies that were a symptom of nearly every emerging African nation. In fact, that expectation has never been realized but, at the time, black Africa looked on the newly rich oil producers as a possible source of salvation. When the 1973 Arab–Israeli war broke out and Israel crossed the Suez Canal into Egypt, the last ties between the developing African nations and Israel were broken, with the Arabs promising to give cash and other aid to fill in any holes left by the departing Israelis.

The result of both natural indignation and Arab aid was an outpouring of criticism from those African nations that had hitherto supported Israel. Typical was Tanzania, previously one of Israel's staunchest allies in Africa. In 1964, when Tanzania's regular army distintegrated after an unsuccessful rebellion, it was the Israeli-trained paramilitary troops that had remained loyal to President Julius Nyerere. Israel became even more closely involved in Tanzania's affairs after that and even trained the presidential bodyguard. However, in response to Israel's crossing of the Suez Canal, Nyerere declared that the war was

> the direct result of the insolence and the deliberate and continuing aggression of Israel against the Arab people. Israel therefore is fully responsible for this dangerous development and Israel bears the blame. Israel has repeatedly and openly defied United Nations resolutions demanding her to withdraw from the Arab territories which she occupied as a result of her own aggression of June 1967.

Such anti-Israel sentiments struck a sympathetic chord in the rest of black Africa, and twenty-nine out of thirty-two states (the exceptions being Swaziland, Lesotho and Malawi) severed all official ties with Israel. It was a major blow to Israeli ambitions in the region and was a setback to nearly twelve years of careful diplomacy.

This may have upset the Israelis, but there was considerable rejoicing in Pretoria. Jews in South Africa had been unstinting in their support of the Israeli war effort in 1973. More than $30 million in contributions from the Jewish community had poured out of South Africa, and more than 1,500 Jewish volunteers had left South Africa either to fight in the war or to run essential services.

The combination of rejection by the African states and support provided by South African Jews to the Israeli war effort with government agreement led to a renewal of the previously close alliance. As both countries felt themselves becoming increasingly isolated in the world – Israel because of the growing power of the weapon of Arab oil and South Africa through the increasing influence of Third World countries in international forums – so they drew closer together. Since the 1973 war, nothing has disturbed the even tenor of a relationship that has grown stronger with every passing year.

The South African government was not prepared to leave the newly restored friendship to simple goodwill. Instead, from the beginning of the 1970s until 1978, as part of a worldwide propaganda campaign masterminded by Interior Minister Connie Mulder and Information Secretary Eschel Rhoodie, the South Africans began pouring millions of dollars into such covert activities as the purchase of newspapers and magazines, the planting of misleading stories and the bribing of dozens of people who might be able to influence international policy against South Africa. The operation, which became known as 'Muldergate', involved any country that South Africa had dealings with, and naturally included Israel. (The whole project is dealt with in more detail in Chapter 7.) The division of Muldergate that concerned Israel was code-named 'Project David' and involved the funding of tours by Israelis to South Africa and visits by South African sports teams to Israel.

One of the central collaborators in Project David was Oscar Hurwitz, a prominent Jewish architect based in Pretoria. He helped found Thor Communications which was used to channel a great deal of money to Israel and other parts of the world. In addition, Hurwitz used his contacts in Israel to help organize a secret visit by Connie Mulder and Eschel Rhoodie in June 1975, when they met Prime Minister Yitzhak Rabin, Defence Minister Shimon Peres and six other Cabinet ministers.

Les de Villiers, at that time the Deputy Minister of Information, was with Mulder and Rhoodie when they visited Israel. In his book, *Secret Information*, he described how the visiting South Africans were each given silver replicas of a statuette, designed by a local artist, that depicted David and Goliath in battle. Mulder was said to have remarked: 'This I will always treasure because it symbolizes not only Israel's struggle for survival but also our own fight against the world. Our opponents may look bigger and stronger, but we have the will on our side. And faith.'

Before the South Africans left, Rabin extended a formal invitation to Prime Minister John Vorster to come to Israel on a private visit. The invitation caused some difficulty in Pretoria, as the South Africans received much of their oil from the Arabs, in particular Saudi Arabia, and were concerned that a visit to Israel might interrupt the flow. In the event, quiet representations were made to the Arabs, and the South Africans were given reassurances that their oil would continue to come through as normal. Although it may seem surprising that the Arabs took such a relaxed view about the proposed visit, South Africa has always paid over the odds for its oil supplies, and the Arabs have always been most anxious to maintain a stable pro-West regime in the country that guards the Cape of Good Hope and ensures the free passage of oil tankers from the Arabian Gulf to Europe and the United States.

While the South Africans hesitated before accepting the Israeli invitation, the UN stepped in to make up their minds for them: the post-1973 alliance between black Africa and the Arabs had produced a powerful new lobby and they lost no time in flexing their muscles. On

10 November 1975, the UN General Assembly adopted a draft resolution describing Zionism as 'a form of racism and racial discrimination'. The operative part of the draft read:

> The General Assembly recalling . . . that in its Resolution of 14 December 1973, the General Assembly condemned . . . the unholy alliance between South African racism and Zionism; . . . taking note also of Resolution 77 . . . of the Organization of African Unity [OAU] which considered that the racist regimes in occupied Palestine and . . . in Zimbabwe and South Africa have a common imperialist origin . . . determines that Zionism is a form of racism and racial discrimination.

The passing of this resolution and others that constantly linked condemnation of apartheid with the Zionism of Israel led both countries to feel that there was little reason to keep the relationship quiet any longer.

In April 1976, Vorster arrived in Israel for a week's visit. It was the first time a South African prime minister had officially visited the country (Malan's trip in 1948 having been described as a 'courtesy visit') and was public affirmation that the coolness in the relationship that had existed prior to the 1973 war was finally over. By any standards, it was a remarkably successful visit. Vorster met with all the important political leaders, toured military installations, factories and *kibbutzim*. A wide range of joint projects were discussed, on the general basis of South African raw materials and Israeli manpower. These projects were said to include an extension of Israel's railways into the Negev desert and the development of three additional ports, as well as South African aid to help build an oil and coal power station between Haifa and Ashdod. Military co-operation was also discussed, including the joint financing of a new generation of fighter aircraft and missile-carrying patrol boats. After the visit, full diplomatic relations were opened between Israel and South Africa and a formal exchange of ambassadors took place. Regular visits by senior government ministers followed, and these continue today.

The visit generated considerable criticism among black African nations. An African diplomat in Nairobi was quoted as saying that, as far as Africa was concerned, Israel was 'finished', and Kampala Radio condemned the visit as a 'calculated move by two racist states to consolidate their hold and repressive measures on the indigenous people they rule'.

However, despite such strong talk, Africans were already growing disenchanted at the level of Arab aid, and secret talks had begun between a number of African states including Kenya and Uganda concerning the possibility of reopening formal relations with Israel. The Vorster visit seems to have done nothing to interrupt those discussions; delicate negotiations have continued for seven years and Israeli diplomats are now actively talking to some seven African nations in the hope of establishing full diplomatic relations in the near future. In 1983, both Zaïre and Liberia re-established diplomatic relations with Israel. Zaïre, which has always been staunchly pro-West, has traditionally maintained close covert ties with Israel (*see* pp. 98–101). However, Liberia's behaviour was more of a surprise. It appears to have been dictated by a fear of the ambitions of Libya's Colonel Muammar Qaddafi for Liberia. General Samuel Doe, Liberia's head of state, has been promised intelligence and military support from Israel in return for diplomatic recognition.

Still, the campaign against South Africa and Israel in the UN and elsewhere grew more fierce every day. In many people's minds, apartheid and Israel's policy towards the Palestinians have become synonymous; joint assaults on their national integrity have become increasingly frequent. But it seems that the more the world has attacked them, the more they have come to depend on each other.

2 A Marriage of Money

While there is an obvious political dimension to the relationship, economic forces have played a major part in drawing Israel and South Africa closer together. They may be extremely reluctant to disclose any details concerning the arms trade between them, but both countries do publish annual statistics of imports and exports, listing the trade between the two nations in exhaustive detail.

According to the International Monetary Fund (IMF) South African trade with Israel represented only 0.6 per cent of the former's total exports and only 0.5 per cent of its total imports, which is small in comparison with South Africa's trade with the United States, West Germany, the United Kingdom and Japan. It has also been suggested that South Africa's trade with the Soviet Union in gold and diamonds is greater in value than the total trade with Israel. Exports to South Africa represent only about 1 per cent of Israel's total exports, and imports from South Africa are only around 2 per cent of the total. Israel has the same major trading partners as South Africa and, in comparison with these, the trade with South Africa seems hardly significant. The trading relationship can be further put into perspective by examining the volume of South Africa's trade with the rest of Africa, which at the moment is currently six times South Africa's current published trade with Israel.

These statistics reveal that the level of trade between the two countries is very small indeed; given what will be shown to be their close relationship in other fields, this is surprising. However, all is not quite what it seems. The official figures take no account of the trade in diamonds and military equipment. Military sales are considered too sensitive to be discussed publicly, while all diamond sales by South Africa to any country are kept confidential. While it is impossible to place an accurate figure on the true total volume, it is probable that, when *all* trade is taken into account, Israel may be South Africa's biggest trading partner.

It is believed that Israel currently gets 50 per cent of its diamonds from South Africa. The trade with Israel was originally begun by the Oppenheimer family, the founders of the giant Anglo-American Corporation that dominates much of South Africa's economy, including gold and diamond mining. Through a subsidiary, De Beers, which in turn controlled the marketing of diamonds through the Central Selling Organization, the Oppenheimers were responsible for regulating and selling the production of diamonds all over the world. In his absorbing book, *The Diamond Invention*, Edward J. Epstein detailed how De Beers managed to control the high prices of diamonds artificially by bringing under its wing all the individual producers around the world, including such diverse countries as the USSR and Zaïre (which has now left the cartel).

One of the first industries to be established in the State of Israel was the cutting and polishing of diamonds; it has since become a vast business employing some 15,000 people and is now the second largest export-earner for the country (military sales being the first). Israel has specialized in the manufacture of industrial diamonds, which are generally of smaller size and lower quality than the gems that go to make up jewellery. Through their representative in Israel, the appropriately named Joseph Goldfinger, South Africa currently exports in excess of $100 million of uncut gems to Israel each year, and it has been a steady and lucrative market for both parties. However, there are signs that the closely monitored cartel of diamond producers – and the diamond market itself – are beginning to collapse.

Since 1980, the price of an average one-carat flawless diamond has fallen from $60,000 to $20,000, and many experts believe the price has yet to bottom out. Ironically, according to Epstein, much of the blame for this dramatic fall in the price and image of the diamond as a secure investment must rest with the Israelis, who showed for the first time how vulnerable the might of De Beers was to market forces.

In 1948, when the Israeli state came into being, there was very little industry that the government could encourage except diamonds. Even before Palestine became Israel, Jewish immigrants had been engaged in the diamond cutting and polishing business, and the new government was anxious to see this small industrial base expand. As a result, the banks extended virtually unlimited credit to the diamond merchants, a practice that continued even after the country came on to a sound economic footing. This worked perfectly satisfactorily as long as diamonds maintained their steady upward spiral and the market remained firm. De Beers had happily divided the world diamond market into two major centres, Antwerp and Tel Aviv, with the former concentrating on the larger gems and the latter looking after the small and less valuable industrial diamonds.

However, in the early 1970s the Israeli economy began to fall apart. Successive wars and defence costs that ate up over 40 per cent of the total budget all took their toll. Inflation headed inexorably upwards and the government were forced repeatedly to devalue the Israeli pound (now the shekel). Devaluations made Israeli products very competitive, and Tel Aviv firms were able to undercut Antwerp dealers savagely. This in itself might have been bearable if the Israelis had not become greedy: the merchants began to move into the large-gem market and buy up substantial quantities whenever they became available. For De Beers, this could have spelled disaster. If the Antwerp outlets had shut down – and many of them were already facing bankruptcy – then Israel would have a monopoly of the cutting and polishing end of the market. With such strength, the Israelis could match De Beers in a fight that could see the traditional control of the market fall to the Tel Aviv interloper.

De Beers acted in a way that had become almost second nature: they used muscle. Emissaries were sent from Johannesburg to Tel Aviv to inform the Israeli dealers that De Beers would not tolerate Israeli domination of the market at the expense of Antwerp's trade, and then, just to show who was really boss, the South Africans cut Israel's supply of diamonds by 20 per cent.

Far from cowing the Israeli merchants, this only drove them to more unconventional methods to obtain their supplies. Paying a premium sometimes as high as 100 per cent, Israeli diamond buyers fanned out all over the world to vacuum up any uncut gems that came on to the market, whether smuggled or legitimate. To fund this massive buying spree, the diamond dealers had to rely heavily on the traditionally generous Israeli banking system. Dealers were able to obtain 80 per cent of the total price of diamonds as loans from the banks, using the gems as security; in addition, the interest charged on these loans was pegged at 6 per cent, far below market rate. By 1978, the banks had loaned $850 million to diamond dealers who had stockpiled over six million carats.

De Beers was seriously concerned that, if the trend continued, the Israelis could flood the market at any time, which would force prices downwards and destroy for ever the myth of diamonds as a solid investment. In a ruthless exercise in power, De Beers unilaterally imposed a 40 per cent surcharge on all diamond sales worldwide. They also warned the Israeli banks, with which De Beers had close connections, that the surcharge – in effect, an artificial price increase – might be withdrawn at any moment, thus leaving the banks over-exposed. This argument persuaded the banks to increase their lending rates and cut off supplies to forty or so major dealers who had been supplying Israel with uncut gems. As well as putting up their interest rates, the banks were also forced to call in more collateral for loans. The result was a huge rise in the interest rates charged to dealers and, as they were forced to liquidate their stocks to pay the charges, heavy losses for many firms.

This savage attack by De Beers had the immediate effect of stopping Israeli purchases on the open market and of shoring up the price of diamonds. However, the action was to cost De Beers its international credibility.

Many of the Israeli diamond dealers had been unable to meet their debts and had paid the banks with their collateral of diamonds; others had held on to their stocks of diamonds but, because of outstanding loans, these remained promised to the banks. In the spring of 1981, De Beers received word that more than $1.5 billion (thousand million) in diamonds were being held by three Israeli banks. This sum was nearly equal to total annual world production, and the Israeli banks were threatening to dump the lot on the open market. The average price of a one-carat flawless diamond had already fallen by 50 per cent in the previous year, and the Israeli banks were concerned that, shortly, their collateral would not be worth enough to cover debts. De Beers bought in some $500 million of diamonds from the Israeli banks and persuaded the Israeli government to stretch the banking laws to allow them to trade, although their liquidity was highly questionable. This tiny finger in the huge dam prevented disaster for the moment, but the confidence of the international community in De Beers' ability to control the market had gone for ever.

The spectre of over $1 billion in diamonds stored in the vaults of Israeli banks still hangs over De Beers. The world diamond market now knows that all those diamonds are sitting there; it also realizes that the Israelis could attempt to dump them on the market at any time. It is generally recognized that a rescue effort such as De Beers launched in Israel could never work again, and so the stability of the diamond price will always remain vulnerable. It is an ironic end to what was once the world's most powerful and successful cartel. In a quietly philanthropic way, De Beers did much to encourage the growth of the Israeli diamond industry and with it the State of Israel by channeling diamonds to Israel and ensuring the Jewish nation regular access to a constant stream of uncut stones, but the child became a greedy adult and brought the whole house of cards tumbling down.

Jews were prominent in the early development of South Africa, first as small traders and travelling salesmen, then as pioneers of industry. Many of the men associated with South Africa's early development – such as Barney Barnato, Alfred Beit and Ernest Oppenheimer – were Jews and, although their numbers were small, their contribution to the South African economy was enormous. The South Africa Jewish community consistently supported the Jews in Palestine (and, later, Israel) with money and men, and a number of companies – such as Africa–Palestine Investments (later Africa–Israel Investments) – were set up on a joint basis, but none of these measures was particularly significant in terms of trade or finance.

Then in January 1968, after the Six Day War of 1967, the Israeli–South African Friendship League was set up; this was intended to encourage general relations, with particular emphasis on business, and counted among its members senior politicians in both countries, as well as business executives and local councillors. In similar vein, the South Africa Foundation established the Man-to-Man Committee in the same year; under its auspices, business executives were, in theory, able to contact their opposite numbers in the other country directly. The Man-to-Man Committee helped organize and participated in the Millionaires Conference, held in Jerusalem in 1968. That meeting not only introduced executives, powerful in their respective countries, to each other; it also resulted in the formation of the Israel–South Africa Trade Association which today plays a very prominent part in promoting trade between the two nations. By the beginning of the 1970s, South Africa was importing from Israel manufactured items such as chemicals, textiles, rubber goods, pharmaceuticals, electronic equipment and specialized machinery, and was exporting steel, cement, timber and sugar to Israel.

Israel's relations with black Africa were now beginning to sour, following Arab pressure on developing African states to sever relations with Israel in exchange for increased aid. The 1973 war resulted in all but three black African states breaking off relations with Israel. This eliminated the need to keep Israel's growing relationship with South Africa secret, and trade was conducted much more openly. In January 1974, the Israel–South Africa Chamber of Commerce was founded in Tel Aviv. Nearly a hundred firms in Israel joined, and its success led to the formation of its Johannesburg counterpart, the South Africa–Israel Chamber of Commerce. Vorster's visit to Israel in 1976 then paved the way for a whole new range of deals that have built on Israel's need for investment in industry and South Africa's raw materials and Israeli-trained manpower.

Following the visit, the South African Foreign Trade Organization held a seminar entitled 'The South African–Israeli Pact', at which opportunities in Israel were explained to potential South African investors, including such joint projects as the building of a railway link between Eilat and Beersheba, the supply of steel and tanks for the underground storage of oil, the processing of Dead Sea chemical products, the manufacturing of special cutting and tool steel, and the supply of coal for the new power station then being built north of Tel Aviv. All the projects have since proceeded, but it is the coal agreement that is of the most significance today. When Vorster visited Israel, he had broached the subject of South Africa supplying Israel with coal; subsequently this idea was eagerly taken up by the Transvaal Coal Owners Association, and this has resulted in an agreement for South Africa to supply all of Israel's coal needs, originally scheduled for 500,000 tons a year, eventually rising to one million tons.

This agreement is illustrative of how the needs of the two countries could coincide, making a deal perfectly suited to both parties. Before the agreement, Israel had traditionally used oil to fuel its non-nuclear power stations; however, the constant threat of embargo, combined with the Arab nations' apparent willingness to use oil as a weapon against Israel's supporters – particularly the United States and Western Europe – forced Israeli energy experts to look at other options. The South Africans appeared to provide a perfect solution. Coal already supplied over 75 per cent of South Africa's total energy needs, and her reserves are sufficient to last well into the next century. A firm agreement with South Africa would secure Israel against embargo threats and guarantee a regular source of supply for the power stations.

Israel decided to convert the Hadera oil-fired power station north of Tel Aviv, due to come on line in 1980, to run off coal. With a possible production of 1,400 megawatts (at full capacity in 1983), the station eats up 3.5 million tons of coal a year. South Africa is contracted to supply up to a million tons per annum, with Australia and the United States making up the difference; under present contractual arrangements, South Africa will supply all of Israel's coal needs by 1986. Although the price negotiated by the Israelis has never been officially confirmed, it is understood that they agreed to pay the South Africans $23 a ton. The effect of this massive export will almost double the visible trade between the two countries. It seems likely that Israel will make up this apparent imbalance by substantially increasing the export of arms to South Africa.

The two governments have continued to concentrate on expanding trade into other areas. There were two ministerial visits following Vorster's 1976 trip to Israel, and in 1980 it was agreed that the finance minister in each country would meet his opposite number at least once every year. When, in February 1978, Israeli Finance Minister Simcha Ehrlich visited South Africa, it was agreed that a special dispensation would be granted to waive the very stringent laws governing the export of capital from South Africa, and allowance was made for business executives to export a maximum of $41.14 million over a three-year period for investment in Israeli manufacturing, construction and tourism. South Africa also granted Israel a $42.5 million line of credit to pay for imports from South Africa, eased import restrictions on Israeli goods and, in a unique dispensation, allowed Israel to sell dollar-denominated government bonds to South African citizens.

The success of the Ehrlich visit encouraged members of the Israeli business community: later that year, a delegation of Israeli executives went to South Africa to sell electronics, textiles, chemicals, furniture and agricultural products. A regular exchange of business groups followed, culminating in the visit, at the end of 1981, of the South African Finance Minister Owen Horwood. In meetings with his Israeli opposite number, Yigael Hurwitz – which, according to Horwood, 'could not have been more friendly' – it was agreed that Israeli bonds to a ceiling of $25 million could now be sold in South Africa and that contributions to the United Jewish Appeal could be deducted from tax. In addition, an increase in the permissible level of South African investments in Israel to $60 million was agreed, and the range of projects in which South Africans could invest was widened to include rented flats. South African investors were also allowed to conduct business in Israel at Pretoria's official rate of exchange for the rand, which is 30 per cent higher than the world rate, having the effect of giving South Africans a far better return on their investments than would normally have been expected. The trading agreement also led to South Africa extending easy credit to Israeli imports to the tune of $165 million, and allowing a bigger catch for Israeli fishermen in South African waters.

Trade has increased markedly. According to the IMF, in 1970 Israel exported $10.7 million to South Africa and imported $10.2 million. In 1978, after Vorster's visit, South Africa exported some $80 million worth of goods to Israel, and in 1980, this amount had risen to nearly $117 million, while Israel's exports to South Africa jumped from $38 million in 1978 to just under $80 million in 1980.

At a Tel Aviv meeting of the Israel–South Africa Chamber of Commerce in March 1982, the former Israeli Counsellor (Trade and Commercial) in South Africa, E. Raviv, detailed the current trading position between the two countries, and of the four categories that he outlined, three were not being fully used by Israeli and South African

businesses. According to Raviv, the investment allowance for South
Africans to put money into Israeli projects 'has not been fully
exploited yet . . . We are experiencing a lot of difficulty in
implementing' the agreement to sell Israeli government bonds in
South Africa. Efforts to increase the fishing quota from 2,500 to 5,000
tons 'have failed so far'. The only good news was that the extended
credit for Israeli importers bringing in South African goods had been
completely taken up. Raviv told the meeting:

> The biggest problem is that we have no overall trade agreement with
> South Africa. There are no concessions or reductions in duties.
> While Israel has liberalized its foreign trade with most countries, we
> still have to battle with restrictive measures and import permits in
> South Africa. Every day we are witnessing applications to the Board
> of Trade for increased duties. Fighting such an increase might be
> successful, but it could take many months to get results. Meanwhile
> the importer is reluctant to buy because he does not know when and
> to what extent these new tariffs will hit him. Thus a bilateral trade
> agreement is an absolute necessity.

Israel has some very advantageous trading arrangements in the West,
and South Africa has very healthy ones with much of black Africa, as
well as a growing and upwardly mobile black population. To exploit
this, the result, as in many other facets of the relationship, has been a
marriage of needs.

Israel has preferential access to both the EEC and the United
States: goods manufactured in Israel, or with an Israeli added value of
40 to 50 per cent, are eligible for duty-free entry into the EEC; 2,700
Israeli-manufactured products are permitted free entry into the United
States under the Generalized Preference System. These two schemes
have obvious attractions to South Africa. Aside from diamonds and
coal, steel is the biggest export from South Africa to Israel, and when
this is passed on by Israel to the EEC, such steel avoids EEC import
restriction. According to Dr Tamir Agmom, Professor of International
Finance at Tel Aviv University, semi-processed iron and steel is
shipped to Israel, finished at the jointly owned Iskoor factory near Tel
Aviv, and then shipped abroad either as refined steel or in completed
products such as heating units or household items complete with a
'Made in Israel' stamp. Such an arrangement is perfectly legal and
particularly suited to the two nations.

There has been considerable encouragement for Israel to invest in
South Africa in order to use that country to gain access into black

Africa. As Piet Kieser, General Manager of the South African Foreign Trade Organization, told a group of Israeli business executives in Tel Aviv:

> South Africa's trade with black Africa . . . constitutes about 10 per cent of our exports – mainly food products, clothing and household goods. South Africa has good transport connections with the African countries and has gained a lot of experience in trading with them over the years. There are opportunities here for Israeli companies to start trading with southern Africa via Johannesburg.

An additional attraction to the Israeli investor is the growing black market within South Africa itself. As Kieser pointed out:

> The black market is a vast one that can be tapped by the Israeli exporter. The huge wage gap in South Africa is starting to close and the black market is rapidly developing. It demands clothing, shoes, furniture, housewares and other consumer goods. But the black does not buy trash; he purchases carefully and selectively. The size of the market is some 20 million and growing rapidly.

While South Africa retains some import restrictions, the trading relationship will never realize its full potential. However, there is a great deal of pressure from businesses in South Africa and Israel to relax the rules, so some improvement can be expected.

In recent years, South Africa has battled with rising inflation and an apparent reduction in the level of growth. The battle appears to have been partially successful and there is a new air of optimism in the financial centre of Johannesburg, with a realization that consistent growth in the South African economy is dependent on tapping the growing market of the increasingly affluent black population. In turn, this is dependent on producing locally a large quantity of material goods at competitive prices. Historically, Israel has managed to supply the technology required and has appeared willing to invest in South African industry.

Israel has been swift to take advantage of the fresh markets that have opened up in the Bantustan homelands established by the South African government. Alone among foreign countries, Israel has invested millions of dollars in the homelands and its support has done much to underpin the homelands both economically and politically. Both Bophuthatswana and Ciskei have accredited representatives in Israel and several Knesset members, including at least two from the ruling Likud party have ties to the new homelands either through industrial or military contracts. Israeli interest has been particularly strong in Bophuthatswana which includes the Sun City entertainment centre.

President Charles Sebe of Ciskei visited Israel three times in 1983. On his first visit he completed negotiations for the purchase of six Mooney TX-1 aircraft for the homeland's fledgling air force. Seventeen Ciskeian pilots are training at the Dror pilots school in Herzliya, near Tel Aviv. When he returned from his last visit in November 1983, President Sebe said his tour, which coincided with an international tourism exhibition at which Ciskei had a stand, had strengthened formal relations. Asked if it was fair to say that Israel recognized Ciskei as an independent state, he replied: 'For the sake of diplomacy and speaking in parables, I would say that it is an ad hoc recognition.'

Israel's de facto recognition of the legitimacy of the homelands makes her the only country outside of South Africa to give such status to what even South Africa's closest friends believe are puppet regimes established by the Pretoria government. Israel's independent stand is causing her some difficulty in consolidating her new-found influence in black Africa. The more militant African states argue that while Israel deals so openly with the homelands a closer relationship with their own countries is impossible.

The result of this pressure has been a very delicate tightrope walk by the Israeli government. In December 1983, Prime Minister Yitzhak Shamir let it be known that his government would actively discourage Israeli official and unofficial contacts with the Bantustan homelands. This public posture may be sufficient to reassure the black African states. However, it is highly unlikely that any realistic steps will be taken to curb a growing and profitable outlet for Israeli exports.

There are additional pressures in Israel to expand the economic relationship between Israel and South Africa, including the homelands. Inflation in Israel continues to hover at well over 100 per cent per annum (1983's figure was over 190 per cent), and there is an urgent need to expand the economic base. South Africa will provide a ready outlet for Israel's manufacturing industries and a potentially vital source of foreign earnings.

The Israeli economy is in such a shambles because of the need for the country to devote so much of its annual budget to defence. Here, too, South Africa can help. Joint defence projects are growing every year and Israel is anxious to develop the relationship further to relieve some of the research and development costs which have proved so crippling. South Africa, of course, is keen to get access to the latest defence technology without the troublesome problems of sanctions busting.

3 The Military Alliance

South Africa's military strategy has been developed with the help of Israeli officers, her armed forces are equipped by Israel and their counter-insurgency tactics have evolved almost entirely as a result of lessons learned by the Israelis in their fight against the Palestine Liberation Organization.

At the same time as the new apartheid laws were introduced in South Africa in the early 1950s, there was a campaign to undermine the influence and authority of the non-Afrikaner white who was distrusted as a product of imperialism and also as a source of potentially subversive liberalism. Immigration was discouraged and the waiting period for South African citizenship was extended from two to five years. Such a wholesale policy of disenfranchisement of blacks and (some) whites was to have severe domestic and international repercussions eliminating overt support from the West, and it is this which has solidified the alliance between South Africa and Israel.

Until the arrival of the Nationalist Party government under Malan in 1948, and the worldwide condemnation it earned during the next decade, the defence of South Africa and the evolution of its armed forces had been part of the British imperial umbrella. As a legacy of its colonial days, South Africa remained a member of the Commonwealth and, in an unwritten treaty, agreed to supply troops to help Britain in time of need. Thus, in the Second World War, South African troops fought with considerable distinction on the Allied side and their armaments industry supplied large quantities of small arms and explosives to fuel the war effort.

For its part, Britain and, by implication, its Western allies agreed to help secure South Africa's borders from any external threat and guarantee the vital sea-lanes around the Cape of Good Hope. Such a bilateral arrangement served both parties and, until the late 1950s, everyone remained very happy with the agreement. South Africa helped in the Berlin airlift and the UN military intervention in Korea, and came out on the side of Israel and Britain during the Suez crisis of 1956.

There is every reason to suppose that this symbiotic relationship could have continued for some considerable time. Indeed, the Simonstown agreement of 1955, which gave Britain certain rights to bases in South Africa, tended to reinforce the South African government's view that a close strategic arrangement with the West was an historic and future fact. However, the Nationalist Party policies led to a rapid rise of militant black nationalism which in turn helped mobilize world opinion against the South African government. Meanwhile, South Africa watched with dismay as country after country was handed over to black rule. Of particular concern was the freedom given to Botswana, Lesotho and Swaziland, all of which had long common borders with South Africa and presented an obvious avenue for guerrilla infiltration.

In 1961, South Africa was forced to leave the Commonwealth, deserted by its ever-pragmatic ally, Britain. Following the Sharpeville massacre in 1960, there had been a growing movement within the Commonwealth to expel South Africa. Finally, in March 1961 when the South Africans reapplied for membership, they refused to sign a joint declaration binding all members to a policy of multi-racialism and withdrew their application. There were several votes criticizing the South African government in the UN, culminating, in August 1963, in a vote for an arms embargo. Under Resolution 181, the Security Council called upon 'all States to cease forthwith the sale and shipment of arms, ammunition of all types and military vehicles to South Africa'. This was passed, although both France and Britain abstained on this resolution. There was a further successful vote in December calling for (in addition to that covered by Resolution 181) an embargo on 'the sale and shipment of equipment and materials for the manufacture and maintenance of arms and ammunition in South Africa'. Although France, Britain and the United States have not kept to the substance of the arms ban, the South African government began to realize that it would have to fight on without the continued and automatic support of the Western powers.

The government also faced an increasingly serious threat in the shape of black militancy which was channelled through the banned African National Congress. The ANC was formed in 1912 to champion black rights, and in its long history, it has largely concentrated on civil disobedience campaigns and political pressure, both of which have proved remarkably ineffective. However, in recent years, in response to the Sharpeville and Soweto massacres as well as to competition from the more militant Pan African Congress (PAC), the ANC has turned to armed action.

Until 1963, the South African Defence Force (SADF) had little in the way of modern armaments; they had largely second-hand tanks, armoured cars and small arms with a few outdated aircraft. As the South African navy was expected to operate in conjunction with the British navy and others, its few vessels were aimed at minesweeping and anti-submarine warfare and were in no way co-ordinated with the rest of the SADF. However, the development of a militant guerrilla group operating both within South Africa and just across neighbouring borders, as well as the rise of anti-white militancy in Rhodesia and Angola, forced the South African government to alter its defence posture. Instead of simple concern for maintaining internal security, there was recognition that a threat to the country could come about from a neighbouring country or from a well-armed and trained guerrilla force operating within its borders but supplied from outside.

In 1961, armed opposition was launched in Angola, in 1964 in Mozambique and in 1966 in Namibia; in that year Rhodesia began to feel the impact of guerrillas inside its borders coming from bases in neighbouring countries. Although the forces of the Zimbabwe African National Union (ZANU) and the Zimbabwe African People's Union (ZAPU) operating in Rhodesia complied exactly with the South African defence strategists' view of an incompetent, badly led and poorly trained band of highly motivated amateurs (the Rhodesian army could reckon on a 'kill ratio' of at least 50 to 1), through a policy of intimidation combined with a significant measure of local village support, the guerrillas were beginning to gain control of large areas of the countryside. In 1967–8, a joint force of ZAPU and ANC began operating in Rhodesia. This showed the South Africans that co-operation among guerrilla groups – which previously had often operated on tribal lines – was possible. The South Africans sent members of their own paramilitary police force north to Rhodesia to fight alongside their neighbours and to gain some first-hand experience of counter-insurgency warfare.

That same year (1967), the Israelis became embroiled in the second of their wars with the Arabs. Unlike the South Africans, Israel had always recognized the threat posed by its neighbours, and since its inception, a concentrated effort had been made to build a modern and effective armed force. Supplied mainly by France and the United States, Israel was superbly equipped and, although outnumbered and outgunned, was able to defeat the Arab nations. Again, South Africa was not slow in coming to Israel's help. The South African reaction to the war showed that its support for Israel went beyond a national affiliation of Jew for Jew but extended into the heart of the South African psyche. Writing in the magazine *Armed Forces*, Brigadier Penn has confirmed that South African Mirages were used in the 1967 war:

> General Dayan indicated to me that 100 Mirages, ordered from France and paid for, were not sent to Israel . . . South Africa also had Mirages and spare parts, and Dayan wondered whether he could get spares from South Africa. I told him I felt confident he would get co-operation but it would be advisable for Mr Tekoah at the United Nations not to bark against South Africa louder than the rest of the pack, and that his own advice on Russian equipment might be useful to the South African army. I need hardly tell you that both sides kept to this bargain.

Until this time, co-operation on a military level had been limited to a direct exchange of materiel. The South Africans, for example, had the licence (via the Belgian Fabrique Nationale factory) to manufacture the Israeli Uzi submachine-gun which is still standard issue in the SADF. South Africa – which was manufacturing tanks to the British Chieftain design – had also exported an undisclosed number of these to Israel. But the war of 1967 led to a firming of the relationship, both militarily and politically, that was to have a profound effect on the development of both Israel's and South Africa's defence capabilities.

Until June 1967, the character of the Israeli nation had largely been determined by the quality of its Jewish immigrant population. A large number of these people were well-educated liberals who were firmly dedicated to the concept of a democratic state that they were determined would be an example to the world. It was a fine ideal and much had been done since 1948 to transform an inhospitable land into a model of agricultural and technological advancement.

Israel's conquest of Arab lands in the 1967 war meant not only a vastly expanded state, but also the presence of over one million Palestinians. Like South Africa, Israel was faced with a serious dilemma: the Palestinians could be given full democratic rights, as would be expected in a society pledged to democracy; however, it was expected that they would outnumber the Israelis by the end of the century and would thus take over the State of Israel. Equally, to allow them to operate freely within the society would compromise the

Jewish ideal of having Jews develop their own society.

Although the Israelis in no way approached the problem with the extremism of the South African Nationalists, they nevertheless kept the Palestinians disenfranchised and helped give birth to a guerrilla movement on the West Bank that has graduated from espousing terrorism to favouring democratic solutions to the question of Palestinian rights. Much more alarming to Israeli conservatives has been the transformation of the Palestinian Liberation Organization (PLO) into a moderate voice accepted in world forums. The change in status has been a considerable coup for the PLO and one which the South Africans are anxious to prevent happening with the ANC.

The June war also served to fuel the anxieties of those who feared another holocaust. The Arab armies, although defeated on this occasion, would always be there waiting to pounce should the Jewish state ever drop its guard, and for the Israelis, it was a chilling reality to have to accept as a permanent facet of Israeli political and military strategy.

Of course, this concept of secure borders, with predators lurking on the other side, was perfectly familiar to the South Africans, and they admired the efficient fashion in which Israel had launched its pre-emptive strike against the Arabs that June. Not only had Israel shown that it possessed a sophisticated and effective armoury; its tactics of rapid attack and high mobility also exactly suited the South Africans. Immediately after the end of the war, the first of several high-level military missions flew to Israel to study the tactics of the Israeli Defence Force (IDF) and the Chief of Staff of the Israeli Air Force (IAF), Mordechai Hod, explained the air tactics of the June war to the students at the South African Staff College in October of the same year. (In April 1968, when South African Minister of Defence Botha warned the Zambian government about the danger it ran by supporting terrorist raids, he drew the analogy of the Israeli reprisal raids against PLO bases, such as the attack on Kerameh in March 1968.) This was the beginning of a regular exchange of information, expertise and materiel that has remained consistent for the past fifteen years.

When the arms embargo was passed by the UN in 1963, the South African government reviewed its arms-purchasing policy and decided that, instead of relying on what was obviously going to be a highly uncertain import market, strenuous efforts would be made to establish an indigenous industry. In 1964, with assistance from private industry, two state organizations were established: the Armaments Board (for purchasing arms and maintaining quality and cost control in production) and the Armaments Development and Production Corporation (Armscor), which would look after arms manufacturing. In addition, the National Institute for Defence Research (NIDR) had been formed in the 1950s under the umbrella of the Council for Scientific and Industrial Research to be responsible for all arms research and development. Both NIDR and the Armaments Board were later absorbed into Armscor, which now controls all purchasing, manufacture, research and development for the South African arms industry. Although in 1968 the turnover of Armscor was a mere R32 million, only one year later the SADF was being supplied by the company with most basic armaments including rifles, mortars, ammunition, grenades, bombs and mines. Their first jet aircraft, the Impala, also had begun to roll off the production lines.

Both South Africa and Israel began to understand that there might be a mutual need in the field of arms. For the Israelis, South Africa had a large stock of Mirage spares, particularly engines, and the prospect of a substantial manufacturing capacity using cheap labour. The South Africans, admiring the training and tactics of the IDF, were naturally eager to benefit from Israel's war experience. Both sides also recognized that their problems were likely to worsen. For Israel, as a smaller country with hostile borders and with the PLO having few problems with arms supply and training, these were more immediate.

In October 1967, the deputy director and chief engineer of Israeli Aircraft Industries (IAI) toured South Africa's Atlas Aircraft Industries and discussed the possibility of joint fighter production. That fairly low-key meeting laid the foundation for a very close linking of the aircraft industries of the two countries that will soon result in the world's most advanced fighter rolling off the production lines in Israel. While relations between the aircraft industries were developing, so the other two arms of the military came together as well. For the past fifteen years, men of staff rank from both armed forces have been visiting their opposite numbers; this has been particularly helpful to the Israeli military, as it is common practice for senior officers of that country to go into the arms business on retirement. Thus, an Israeli serving officer can help train a South African unit, retire and then use friendships and contacts to sell Israeli arms.

This was a difficult time for the Israelis. While they had almost every sympathy with South Africa and were under some pressure from the Jewish community there, they were forced by the demands of international politics to maintain a highly ambivalent attitude. Their relations with black Africa were still developing and, while there was a chance of keeping the diplomatic channels open, the Israeli government was unwilling to declare its support openly for South Africa. For example, in November 1967, Joel Barromi, the Israeli representative at the UN, walked out when the South African representative rose to defend apartheid. In a fierce editorial, the Nationalist newspaper *Dagbreek* stated: 'The suspicion of dual loyalty, to Israel and South Africa, cannot be talked away. An attitude of disapproval [from the South African Jewish community] towards Israel's UN actions is long overdue. And forget the smokescreen of anti-Semitism.'

The Israeli military, which had of course benefited most from South Africa's support during the war, were not slow in coming to its defence. For example, Brigadier Chaim Herzog wrote in the Hebrew newspaper *Ha'aretz*: 'Why should Israel adopt this stand towards South Africa for fear of losing support among African states, when France continues to supply tanks and planes to Pretoria without endangering its influence in black Africa?'

Aside from the licensing of the Uzi to South Africa in the 1960s, the arms trade was still in its infancy. However, it began to gather pace and in January 1970, the Jewish Telegraph Agency announced that South Africa had finalized arrangements to sell tanks to Israel: 'The South African government has begun to organize the export of tanks to Israel, marking a new stage in their co-operation. The South African tank is a 65-ton giant, armed with a heavy gun, and designed according to the model of the new British tank.' This is an apparent reference to the Chieftain tank, which Israel has been trying to buy from the UK.

While Israel maintained its ambivalent attitude about Africa, the relationship was not able to develop fully; however, the Yom Kippur War in 1973 changed all that. When Egypt launched its attack across the Suez Canal, the Israelis were caught completely by surprise. Despite the six months of preparation orchestrated by President Anwar Sadat of Egypt, Israel's fabled Mossad had been unable to pick up a hint of what was about to occur. When Syria joined in the fray on the northern front, it appeared for a while that Israel was going to be overwhelmed.

True to form, South African Jewry rushed to Israel's aid, and there were also unconfirmed reports that South Africans may have been flying fighters for the Israelis, for the Egyptians claimed that a Mirage jet that they had shot down was of South African origin. However, it seems unlikely that South Africans were actually flying for the Israelis: Israel has always operated a sophisticated tactical air force which is highly trained both for squadron integration and to work with other divisions of the armed forces, so that the introduction of a willing interloper in a sky thick with fighters would do more damage to the Israelis than to the enemy.

Perhaps the most significant fallout from the war was the change in Israel's relations with the rest of black Africa. Pressure from the Arab states compelled all but three African nations (Malawi, Lesotho, Swaziland) to sever relations with Israel, and its carefully nurtured and enormously expensive scheme to win allies on the African continent collapsed in failure. For Israel it was a rude awakening which was radically to affect its global strategy and its relations with South Africa.

As Yosef Lapide, writing in the Tel Aviv newspaper *Ma'ariv*, put it:

> Well, the so-called liberated African states are, with a few exceptions, a bad joke and an insult to human dignity. They are run by a bunch of corrupt rulers, some of whom, like Idi Amin of Uganda, are mad according to all the rules of psychiatry. I feel unburdened when I say this; I've wanted to say this all these years, and all these years I had the feeling that we fool the public when, for reasons of diplomacy, we do not tell them that the majority of black African states are one nauseating mess . . . For the life of me, if I must choose between friendship with black Africa as it is today, and friendship with a white state that is orderly and successful, and contains a blossoming Jewish community, then I prefer South Africa. The only pity is that we waited until the blacks threw us out.

While not voicing such views publicly, privately the Israeli government reacted in similar vein. It now consciously tried to build a closer relationship with South Africa; and the most visible sign of this was in the UN, where on all votes relating to apartheid, Israel either abstained or was absent for the vote, a direct reversal of previous policy.

In an article entitled 'Time for Initiatives', published in *Ha'aretz* on 7 December 1973, Haim Herzog – later to be Israel's UN ambassador – outlined his plans for Israel's foreign initiatives following the war, including the strengthening of relations with South Africa, 'the strongest power on the African continent', which he suggested, because of its 'gold power', was impervious to economic pressures from the Arabs and the Third World. The Herzog recommendations were carefully noted by the government, and in 1974 the Israeli delegation to South Africa was promoted to embassy status; the following year, South Africa opened an embassy in Israel.

It may not, of course, have been so much to do with Herzog, for a number of factors now occurred within a very short time to alarm the

South African government seriously. In 1974, the coup in Portugal took place which was eventually to lead to the independence of Angola. Although the Vorster government attempted to open some sort of dialogue with the new regime, the latter did not seem receptive and, looking around, Vorster must have realized that the Afrikaner dread of a black onslaught on South Africa was in danger of becoming a reality. To the east, Mozambique was achieving its independence, and although slightly more stable than Angola, it was still a radical black government. To the north, Rhodesia was beginning to crumble under the persistent assaults of black guerrilla groups. The South Africans saw for the first time that, in a few very short years, they would be completely surrounded by independent black countries and that two of the three most important governments (in Angola and Mozambique) had come to power through the actions of armed guerrillas who had overthrown a minority white government.

The lessons for South Africa were obvious. She must be prepared to fight a high-level guerrilla war on or near her own territory.

4 South Africa, Israel and the Nuclear Howitzer

The South African invasion of Angola in 1975 was intended to be a sweeping victory against the Popular Movement for the Liberation of Angola (MPLA) and the guerrilla forces of SWAPO (South-West African People's Organization). In fact, after a long and costly campaign, the South African army was forced into a humiliating retreat. In the aftermath of the invasion, South Africa's defence analysts placed much of the blame for the defeat on superior Soviet artillery – particularly Katyusha rockets – that were part of the Angolan armoury: the Katyusha was able to pin down the advancing South African forces, who had no comparable weapons. The military strategists decided that priority must be given to acquiring, by whatever means possible, an artillery system that would give the army an unbeatable edge over any opposition that existed in Africa.

Israel, South Africa's long-standing ally, was able to demonstrate a new artillery system they had recently employed successfully against the Syrians in the 1973 Arab–Israeli war. The system had been sold to the Israelis by Space Research Corporation (SRC), a US-based arms manufacturing company. Under the guidance of their brilliant founder, Dr Jerry Bull, SRC had devised an artillery system that could deliver a shell 30 per cent further than any comparable howitzer anywhere in the world. In addition, the howitzer could double as a nuclear delivery system.

In an extraordinary example of international co-operation, the Israelis, the CIA, the Pentagon and the US State Department all united in a concerted three-year. secret effort to ship illegally the artillery and the technology for its manufacture to South Africa. In defiance of US arms export laws and UN embargoes, the artillery left the United States with frightening ease, and has now filled a large hole in South Africa's armoury.

The South Africans have made good use of the technology: the artillery system is now at the forefront of a major international arms sales campaign that the country hopes will reap substantial earnings in foreign exchange and help to make new friends in the developing Third World countries.

The story must really begin with the man at the centre, Dr Jerry Bull, then a Canadian citizen. Now fifty-five years old (1983) and a balding, overweight lover of ice cream and hockey, Bill was once the great white hope of the US army. Born in Ontario, Canada, he was the youngest person ever to be awarded a doctorate from the University of Toronto. He then became a professor of engineering science at McGill Univeristy and, while still in his twenties, began building a formidable reputation as an expert in aeroballistics. But Bull was frustrated; he wanted to translate some of his theories into hard reality. More particularly, he wanted to pioneer a new type of gun that could launch meteorological satellites into space. The system he had in mind would save money by cutting out the need for expensive rocket-launchers and would have considerable flexibility.

Both Canada and the United States were impressed. With initial funding of $2,000 (which rose rapidly into the millions) Bull and his company, SRC, set up the High Altitude Research Project (HARP) with the blessing of the US army and the Canadian government. In the early days, the Canadians and Bull concentrated on the peaceful applications of his innovative system, but the Canadians became increasingly concerned about its possible military applications and, in 1967, withdrew their support. By that time, however, Bull was already well down the road. He had been loaned a test site in Barbados in the Caribbean and had constructed an enormous 118-foot-long gun for vertical test firings. He remained convinced that his project was viable and went hunting for cash in the commercial market.

There was obviously still considerable backing from the US government, since Bull managed to set up an operation almost certainly unique in international law. He purchased several thousand acres of woodland on the Vermont–Quebec border, and SRC's headquarters straddled this, with the majority of the property in Canada. However, the company was registered in the United States, and so was considered American in law. The blurring of the commercial distinctions plus the suggestion of high-level support helped SRC to achieve what was effectively a 'most favoured nation' status. Employees were allowed to move freely from one country to the other; goods and services could be supplied from either side of the border with little or no checking. This relaxed attitude was vital for Bull's future plans.

The SRC headquarters was equipped with every modern surveillance device known to man, as well as extensive genuine research facilities. Bull lived on the site and personally supervised the development of his space gun. The gun itself evolved into a monster, 172 feet long with a sixteen-inch bore which, Bull once boasted, could shoot a shell as far as Mexico and would have no problems in lobbing a satellite into space. There was no doubting Bull's creative genius but, like a lot of brilliant men, he had no head for figures and his obsession with research and pushing back the frontiers of science ate up every penny of the SRC budget. There was no real effort at cost control and the company gradually slipped deeply into debt.

In the late 1960s, in exchange for administrative and technical assistance which primarily consisted of strict financial controls, the American Arthur D. Little Company took a 50 per cent share in SRC, and in September 1968, four Arthur D. Little executives joined the SRC board. In 1969, Little turned over its interest in SRC to its own majority holding company, the multi-million-dollar investment firm, Memorial Drive Trust, and Jean de Valpine, its chief executive officer, became chairman of the SRC board until 1977. The Trust finally severed its links with SRC in 1978, when a federal grand jury began investigating Bull's activities.

Even though others were now becoming involved in the administration of SRC, it continued to be Bull's brainchild; the focus remained on aeroballistics, with the winning of subsidiary government contracts providing the cash for the enormously expensive research. Bull's links with the US army and some portions of the government were such that special dispensation was made when, in 1972, the army realized that Bull, to get access to top-secret material, would have to become an American citizen.

A member of the Senate Armed Services Committee, Republican Senator Barry Goldwater of Arizona, sponsored a rare private Act of Congress that waived any further residency requirement and made Bull eligible for naturalized citizenship. The Bill was passed through Congress and, just in case there might be any future questions about Bull's ready access to top-secret material while still a Canadian citizen, his naturalization papers were backdated to 1955, the year when Bull first came to the United States. In only two other cases in the entire history of the United States has honorary American citizenship been given to individuals: the Marquis de Lafayette and Winston Churchill. At this distance, it is difficult to comprehend either the sense of urgency that then obtained or the degree of influence that Bull obviously had. Even the mandatory appearance before a judge was specially organized: an Appeals Court judge from New York was flown in especially for the occasion.

The Canadians' argument (that Jerry Bull's plans for using his gun to launch meteorological satellites had a military application) was beginning to sound right. Bull had managed to convince the Pentagon that orbiting nuclear warheads launched into space using his specially developed gun would provide a cheap and highly effective deterrent against any Soviet advances in conventional warfare. The Pentagon agreed, and the money continued to pour in. However, when the project was taken beyond the theoretical and experimental stage and Bull went to his paymasters to ask for funding in order to go into full-time production, he was turned down and the project was abandoned.

Bull was later to argue that the rocket manufacturers had too powerful a lobby in Washington and that their conventional outlook had prevailed. He may have been partly right – although there is no doubt that the Pentagon, when it came to investing the hundreds of millions of dollars that would have been necessary, were reluctant to risk such large sums on a company with an appalling financial track-record and no real evidence of an ability to deliver the goods.

Without the funds and major backing for the space project, Bull had to direct SRC elsewhere. In the course of the research into aeroballistics, Bull had developed an extended-range 155-mm artillery shell that was, without doubt, the finest in the world for range, accuracy and destructive power. In addition, SRC had developed a conversion kit for howitzers that would otherwise be unable to take the heavier and more powerful shell. Bull had decided that the future of his company lay in the development of this conventional weaponry, and his Pentagon supporters agreed. He was also urged to develop a more modern version of the 155-mm howitzer, both as a mobile and a fixed unit, to replace a design that had been around for years.

Like South Africa, Israel faces a number of serious problems in designing an effective defence strategy. Surrounded on three sides by the Arabs and on the fourth by the sea, in the north there stands a range of hills, the Golan Heights, that commands enough of Israel to threaten its very existence. In the south-west lies the Sinai desert, flat country that is excellent for fighting if you have large numbers to throw into the fray. The potential for swift defeat has always existed and explains in some measure Israel's consistently huge investment in defence.

More particularly, a strategy has been evolved which, over the years, has proved remarkably effective against Israel's enemies. The first priority for Israel has consistently been to obtain or to manufacture equipment that is better than anything the Arabs have in their armoury – when superior training and a lower 'down-time' (periods when equipment is not actually being used in combat) then gives them the edge – as they acknowledge that they will always have to face superior numbers. Control of the air and tactical superiority are therefore essential.

In the 1973 Yom Kippur War, it appeared at first that Israel would lose, particularly when the Syrians joined in on the northern front but, a nuclear alert (*see* Chapter 8) and several counter-attacks later, the tide had turned and Israel moved towards another victory. Part of Israel's success was due to the skilful disposition of Bull's new 155-mm extended-range artillery which boosted the firing range from thirty to fifty kilometres – well in excess of anything the Arab armies possessed.

The deal to get the artillery had been made in 1972 when Yitzhak Rabin, then Israeli ambassador in Washington, approached the US Secretary of State, Henry Kissinger, for a strategic shell which would give Israel command of the Golan Heights. Kissinger came up with SRC and Jerry Bull's innovative 155-mm extended-range shell. In a government-to-government deal, Israel bought several thousand of these shells, and proved their effectiveness for the first time during the 1973 war. So impressed were the Israelis with the shell that they sent their most successful arms salesman, Shaul Eisenberg, to Vermont to meet Jerry Bull in order to discuss possible Israeli purchase of the company. Bull, who was just beginning to see the cash come in for his revolutionary artillery, was unwilling to hand over the controls and turned him down, but the two men remained firm friends and Bull often visited Tel Aviv to stay with Eisenberg.

Arms deals in Israel work rather differently from elsewhere in the world. In the early years, dealers who could get the armaments that Israel needed were given special dispensation by the government, and since much of the arms dealing was done in secret and often contravened international law, arms dealers had very close contact with the government and the intelligence community, as well as with their prospective purchasers in the military. In fact, over the years the links have grown even stronger: it is now common practice for former senior serving officers to go into the arms business on retirement. (As one retired general said: 'I am in the import–export business; I export arms and I import money.')

Eisenberg is a legend in the field. He has sold everything that Israel produces, from grenades to fighter planes, and even managed to sell a

Canadian atomic reactor to Korea. In addition, he had been involved during the early days of selling arms to South Africa and had built up extensive contacts in that country. Although he failed to buy SRC, Eisenberg felt there might be a potential market in passing on Bull's shells and artillery system to friendly governments. He received the go-ahead from the Israeli government, and the South Africans were issued an official invitation to come to Israel and see the artillery in action. Israel's offer of the extended-range shell was somewhat premature, as they had no right to market the materiel. However, the South Africans – who had nothing so sophisticated in their own army – were most impressed by the demonstration in the Negev and agreed to pursue the matter as and when Israel's negotiations with SRC were completed.

For the South Africans, 1974 was a particularly upsetting year since their last great colonial ally in Africa, Portugal, was beginning to dismantle its empire following a military coup. More particularly, this gave control of Angola, on South Africa's north-west frontier, to a grab-bag of guerrilla groups, almost all of which were hostile to the apartheid regime.

Although it was under pressure to do so, the United States government had not deserted South Africa. As early as 1969, Kissinger had prepared National Security Study Memorandum 39 which suggested that the United States had five options for dealing with the instability in southern Africa:

1 Closer association with the white regimes to protect and enhance [US] economic and strategic interests.

2 Broader association with both black and white states in an effort to encourage moderation in the white states, to enlist the co-operation of the black states in reducing tensions and the likelihood of increasing cross-border violence, and to encourage improved relations among states in the area.

3 Limited association with the white states and continued association with blacks in an effort to retain some economic, scientific and strategic interest in the white states while maintaining a posture on the racial issue which the blacks will accept, though opposing violent solutions to the problems of the region.

4 Disassociation from the white regimes, with closer relations with the black states, in an effort to enhance US standing on the racial issue in Africa and internationally.

5 Disassociation from both black and white states in an effort to limit US involvement in the problems of the area.

The somewhat dispassionate nature of NSSM 39 disguised the fierce argument that was going on in the government at that time; it was only resolved by both Kissinger and Nixon agreeing to adopt the second option, which has been the cornerstone of US policy in Africa ever since.

Independence for Angola from their western ally, Portugal, meant that the United States was forced to look elsewhere for allies on the continent, and South Africa foresaw the onset of a Communist onslaught supported by the left-wing governments in Mozambique and Angola. Of the two, Angola represented the far more serious threat. Mozambique had a largely ineffective central government and an ailing economy; the Angolans, however, were rich in oil and other natural resources and were well supported by the Eastern bloc. South Africa was also concerned at the activities of Angolan-backed SWAPO who were fighting for the independence of Namibia.

As well as supporting Unicio Nacional de Independencia Total de Angola (UNITA), the guerrilla group run by Jonas Savimbi in south-western Angola, the South Africans, through cross-border raids and subversion, launched a campaign to undermine the Angolan government. The most significant South African military action began on 14 October 1975. Around 1,000 SADF troops – supported by UNITA forces and armed with mortars, Panhard armoured cars and artillery – swept rapidly north along the coast, rolling up the MPLA forces with astonishing ease. Within a month, the SADF was operating on a 400-mile front and had conquered well over half of Angola. The opposition had been so light and the inefficiency of the Angolan armed forces so apparent that the South African high command decided to press north for the Angolan capital of Luanda, with a view to capturing the city and installing a UNITA government.

However, now the tide began to turn, and what had seemed an inexorable advance and a brilliant campaign was to turn into a ragged and humiliating retreat. For the first time, outside the coastal town of Benguela, the SADF came under heavy artillery fire from the MPLA's solitary 122-mm Katyusha rocket-launcher. Although the South Africans had some light artillery, they had nothing that could match the range of the Katyusha; they were therefore placed in the unenviable position of retreating or sitting it out. They decided to sit it out while bigger guns were brought up. Four 88-mm guns eventually arrived but their range was still not enough, and the high command then ordered that the 155-mm M-109 recently supplied from the United States be sent forward.

The SADF were pinned down for nearly three weeks, a vital period that gave the MPLA enough time to consolidate and its allies time to begin to muster world opinion, particularly against the United States. In November, Cuban troops began to arrive in Angola, and the MPLA, operating in a much smaller area than the SADF, received supplies of ammunition which had run dangerously low. For their part, the South Africans had a very extended supply-line and even the regular airlifts by C-130 transports had not solved the problem.

Although neither the Cubans nor the MPLA were serious adversaries for the superbly trained and equipped South African forces, the war – far from being a quick and clean surgical operation – was in danger of becoming a long-drawn-out campaign with mounting casualties on both sides and considerable political gains for the MPLA (as the victim) and losses for the South Africans (as the aggressor).

The original intention of the SADF had been to capture Luanda by 11 November, the date of independence when the new government was due to be sworn in. However, the period during which the SADF had been pinned down by the MPLA had proved critical. Although the South Africans did manage to advance slowly north, they were met by stiff resistance and, as casualties began to mount, the objective of Luanda was abandoned. The SADF consolidated and reinforced throughout November and December; when the Cubans and MPLA counter-attacked in the middle of January, the South Africans began a rapid retreat south, blowing up bridges behind them as they went. The campaign had been a serious failure for the South Africans.

P.W. Botha, then South Africa's Defence Minister, had believed that he had a firm commitment from the US government that, if his country moved north into Angola, the United States would back the action in international forums and would offer material support. In fact, no such support appeared and South Africa was left to fight alone. The only exception lay in the activities of the CIA, which was allocated $14 million to deliver weapons and fuel to right-wing guerrillas and, later, to pay for mercenaries, arms and fuel for the SADF. The South Africans were further disappointed when Senator John Tunney won Senate passage for his amendment to prevent the use in Angola of any funds from the Defense Appropriations Bill of fiscal year 1976. As this Bill contained the budget of the CIA, the Senate vote effectively hamstrung those within the organization who believed that South Africa should be supported at all costs.

Before their move into Angola, the South Africans had consulted with the leaders of Zaïre, the Ivory Coast and Senegal, who all feared the advent of a radical government in Angola and gave quiet encouragement to any attempt to oust President Neto. However, once

South Africa had moved north, all support evaporated and the
countries that Vorster had thought would at least provide some
measure of support within the Organization of African Unity (OAU)
lined up alongside the shriller voices of opposition. The invasion
taught the South Africans quite clearly that they could not rely on their
allies in the West for support in a crisis and confirmed their view that
African nations, who might fear the arrival of radical governments on
the continent, did not have enough courage to support the outlawed
apartheid regime in even the gravest of circumstances.

At this stage, the concept of 'Fortress South Africa' – a nation
alone, surrounded by enemies but strong enough to survive any attack
– began to evolve. Some have argued that the fortress concept is a
natural evolution of apartheid philosophy, but there is no doubt that,
after the Angolan débâcle, considerable efforts were made to make
South Africa as independent militarily and economically from her
neighbours and her Western allies as possible.

The post-mortem following the Angola affair led to two major
decisions by the South African government: every effort would be
made to render South Africa's arms industry self-sufficient, and the
quest for arms and allies would rely not on political expediency but on
the need to survive. It was then that South Africa turned to its two
most stalwart allies, the CIA and Israel, to achieve its aims.

Immediately after the SADF had been pinned down by Katyusha
rocket-fire in Angola, defence chiefs in Pretoria began an anxious and
urgent reappraisal of their weapons systems. They recalled the
demonstration by the Israelis the previous year and decided to try and
obtain the extended-range artillery shells and the concomitant
technology, to use with their 155-mm artillery.

The South Africans approached the normally co-operative CIA
chief in Pretoria and asked for his help. The request, which had
immediate CIA backing, then filtered back down the line to
Washington, where it was brought up at a meeting of the joint State
Department/CIA Africa working group which devised strategy and
reported to the National Security Council. According to John
Stockwell (a former CIA agent who had been involved in the Agency's
activities in Angola), Jim Potts, the CIA representative in the working
group, proposed shipping the artillery shells, along with some fuel and
additional supplies to the guerrillas in Angola. When Potts mooted
this, he encountered strong opposition, as delivery of arms to South
Africa was banned by US law. Although in the past, this had not
stopped a fairly steady flow from reaching South Africa (with the US

government aiding the transfers with official certificates and permission), on this occasion the whole matter was too sensitive for the United States to be seen providing highly sophisticated weapons to the South Africans. Despite some fast talking by Potts, Edward Mulcahy, then Assistant Secretary of State for African Affairs, threatened to resign if the deal went through, and the plans for an immediate shipment were shelved.

However, as is so often the case with the CIA, there was a second and much more important operation running alongside the official proposition that had just been blocked by Mulcahy. In the summer of 1975, the CIA officer in charge of raising arms for South Africa and the guerrillas in Angola, Major John Clancy III, who was also a representative of the Joint Operations branch of the Joint Chiefs of Staff, approached a former CIA-operative-turned-arms-dealer known by the code-name 'Gunman/1'. This was Colonel John (Jack) Frost who, after retiring from the Agency in the early 1970s, had gone into business as an independent arms dealer.

Frost and Clancy were old friends who had worked together in the CIA and had kept in touch since then. If ever Clancy needed a front man to channel arms or other sensitive material around the world, he would come to Jack Frost. In return, Frost would keep Clancy informed of any gossip in the arms business and of any major arms deals that he had heard about that might be indicative of new friendships or strategic alliances. Ironically, in a letter that he had written to Clancy on 4 February 1975, Frost had complained of Israeli interference in his deals with SRC and he had also crossed swords with Eisenberg, the man who was eventually to mastermind the SRC deal with South Africa:

SUBJECT: Israeli External Sales
There is a group identified as the 'Eisenberg' group which is selling materiel purchased ostensibly for Israel to Iran and other nations. They are closely associated with IMI [Israeli Military Industries] and, in particular, Dov Peleg [IMI salesman].

Recently they got info, backdoor, of my offer for 155-mm and 175-mm extended-range to Iran and may have pulled off a deal to manufacture in Israel inasmuch as Israel has the rights after a purchase of 10,000 from SRC.

They appeared also to be selling a wide range of Russian stuff captured; however, I'm of the opinion PRB [SRC's Belgian agents] has acquired the Russian stuff from Egypt and is selling through the Israelis.

For Frost, the deal now proposed by Clancy was a substantial one and apparently had the official blessing of both the CIA and the Joint Chiefs of Staff. The arms dealer felt that if this one went right, there must be the prospect of further large orders in the pipeline.

While it is not necessarily so unusual for such a large order to be placed through one small company, it was certainly extraordinary that Clancy should ever have approached a company that, in the past, had been, under US law, illegally trading in arms. From the founding of Frost's company – FFE International – in 1968, he had failed to register with the Office of Munitions Control (OMC) as demanded under US law. Although he did finally register in 1974, Frost had been operating illegally, and Clancy and his CIA colleagues had previously been channelling apparently illegal business through an illegitimate company.

Clancy told Frost that the materiel was destined for Zambia. and included 10,000 7.62-mm assault rifles, 50 million rounds of NATO 7.62-mm ammunition, ten 81-mm mortars, 5,000 rounds of 81-mm mortar ammunition, ten 106-mm recoil-less rifles and 1,000 rounds of 106-mm recoil-less ammunition. Frost placed a preliminary order with three US companies – Heckler & Koch, Tampella and SIDEM – as he was quite confident that, with government backing, the deal would pass off without any difficulty over export permits.

However, according to a classified tape recording of an interview with Frost by the OMC, which took place on 16 December 1975, it began to dawn on Frost that the arms were not destined for Zambia at all. In fact, at a meeting in Madrid on 30 September, where he met Denys Zeederberg, the Head of Development of Armscor, he realized that the arms were destined for South Africa. Even so, Frost was not worried as he remained convinced that the deal had official US backing. To pay for the arms, Zeederberg handed over a $13 million letter of credit drawn on the Credite Bank of Brussels, the one normally used by South Africa for such transactions.

Once Frost was certain that the ultimate destination was South Africa, he decided that a more circuitous route was necessary for the shipping of the arms in order to avoid detection. According to the evidence Frost later gave to the OMC, the original order with the US arms companies was cancelled and placed with a Belgian-based firm called Commerce International, which had been run from Connecticut Avenue in Washington before it had been moved to Brussels; it was headed by Thomas Drago, a US citizen. Commerce International told Frost that they would accept the order and that the materiel was available in Thailand and would be moved to Taiwan. Although the paperwork would show that the materiel had been moved out of

Taiwan under an order signed by the Supreme Command, authorizing disposal of the arms by dumping at sea, in reality the arms would be shipped direct to South Africa.

Frost felt that the deal was not as secure as it had appeared to be, and he arranged with Clancy and Armscor representatives to meet Major General Lay Ying, the Chief of Staff of the Taiwanese Combined Service Force, to discuss the project. General Lay indicated that the proposed arms deal could be arranged, provided the US government consented. Both Frost and Clancy promised to push for an early agreement, but at this stage, the deal began to go sour. Frost, having found that Armscor was secretly dealing with his contacts, suspected that he was being set up by one or all of the parties involved. Both he and the Taiwanese realized that if the arms were shipped to South Africa without US government approval, they would both be in serious trouble. Taiwan would put its extensive arms trade with the US in jeopardy, while Frost would lose any future chance of government sponsorship in the arms business. All along he had assumed that this was a straightforward international arms deal; it was only very late in the day that he realized that he had been put up as front man for a sanctions-busting arms-smuggling operation to South Africa.

Although Frost and the Taiwanese appeared to have the same honourable concern for complying with US law, Frost had been in the intelligence world long enough to know how to cover his tracks. Although he was scheduled to visit South Africa at the beginning of December to finalize arrangements for the onward shipment of the arms, he cancelled, pleading high blood pressure (which may well have been true). However, in his letter to General Lay (later submitted to the Grand Jury investigating SRC), he left open, like any good businessman, the possibility of having future dealings with the Taiwanese government and suggested that they might wish to purchase arms from South Africa.

On 3 December, as Frost began to realize that he had been duped by his old friends in the CIA, he wrote to Drago of Commerce International: 'A meeting was arranged by and between [two other officials of Commerce International], Mr Smith [Piet Smith, Chief of Procurement of Armscor], Mr Zeederberg and myself to discuss the status of our purchase programme . . . I was certainly misled as to who if anybody controlled the materiel [causing] me to expend time and funds on a will-o'-the wisp. So therefore I have no alternative but to terminate.'

It is not clear exactly what happened to the arms because Frost backed out of the deal and the CIA have refused to comment. There is every reason to suppose that they were eventually delivered as, throughout the negotiations, Clancy had been representing the Joint Chiefs of Staff: even if the Taiwanese had been holding out for official US government sanction, Clancy was close enough to the central authority in the United States to arrange authorization. Certainly, Frost never cashed his $13 million letter of credit which automatically expired in December 1975; he had backed out and the arms had not been delivered by that time.

Although the deal did not go through, the Frost/South African connection had been made. During the course of one of their meetings, Zeederberg had asked Frost if he knew where he might obtain 155-mm artillery. Among other companies, Frost had mentioned SRC and their revolutionary artillery system. Having already been informed of the successful demonstration of the SRC system in Israel, and reflecting the enthusiasm of the South African military, Zeederberg and his colleagues had then expressed an interest in buying it. Both Frost and Clancy had promised to do what they could to expedite the deal.

As a preliminary exercise, the South Africans decided to try a formal approach to the US government for permission to purchase the SRC system. Although this formal approach had the backing of the CIA, Edward Mulcahy, then Assistant Secretary of State for African Affairs and the State Department's representative on the committee that considered the deal, vetoed a proposal that would involve breaking US arms embargoes against South Africa.

However, with their customary thoroughness, Armscor had also been dealing with the Israelis, in an attempt to use their experience to get the shells and the technology to South Africa. On previous occasions, Israel had been used as a conduit to smuggle arms to South Africa, and relations between both governments and their arms industries were very close. What was particularly important in this case was that, when Israel had wanted to buy additional artillery shells, following their successful deployment in the Yom Kippur War, they had managed to circumvent normal, US government regulations.

In an apparently uncommercial deal, SRC had agreed to sell Israel 15,000 shells and, if the purchase was successfully completed, hand over manufacturing rights to IMI. Such a deal is very unusual in the arms business, as the manufacturing company is writing off the prospects of future earnings and royalties with no residual benefit. It was highly unusual in one other crucial aspect. Under US law, private military sales to a foreign government are specifically prohibited and have to pass through the US government's sales machine. Two special dispensations were therefore required: the first to export the technology of the shell-manufacturing process, and the second for the sale of the shells. In the former case, no licence had been obtained; in the latter, subtle pressure by both SRC and IMI had resulted in the first known case of bending the rules.

The first stumbling block had come when SRC requested the use of the manufacturing facilities at the Army Ammunition Plant in Scranton, Pennsylvania, operated under contract by the Chamberlain Manufacturing Corporation. SRC did not have the facilities to forge the vast volume of shells that Israel wanted, and so had to turn to the government for help. However, this had remained a private deal and, under existing law, US government plants cannot be used by private companies. This had been emphasized by a legal memorandum produced by the Army Materiel Command (AMC) in March 1975 which said that requests by private contractors for use of government facilities had been 'consistently denied', and added that only Congress had the power to dispose of government property. The memorandum concluded: 'All requests must be disapproved.'

Within a month, by a process that is not altogether clear, SRC, using former army officers as lobbyists, had managed to get the AMC to agree to reverse its initial opposition. The Israeli government had then applied direct to have the shells supplied to them, suggesting that SRC was acting as their agent. (At no time had SRC been registered as an agent, as required by law, at the Foreign Agents Registration Board at the Justice Department.) Under US Government Regulation ASPR-13-406, government plant is to be provided rent-free, but in this instance, although ASPR-13-406 had been cited as the explanation for the army's change of heart, SRC had been charged $39,891 for use of the Scranton facility.

When all had seemed to be going so well, the US government had introduced a ban on all arms sales to Israel. According to President Gerald Ford's autobiography, *A Time to Heal*, relations with Israel at this time had been exceptionally strained, with the Israeli government refusing to move on any suggestions of compromise with Egypt that might avert another Middle East war. Ford, essentially a simple and decent man, could not understand Israel's intransigence and had become increasingly frustrated. In a memorable speech, he had suggested that he would have to 'reassess' American–Israeli relations and that this would include arms sales. Part of this new coolness towards Israel had resulted in a US army 'Security Assistance' memorandum which queried the necessity for any additional supplies of US military ammunition to Israel. Such a memorandum should have raised flags in all the relevant government agencies, to ensure that any application went through a rigorous checking process. In this instance, there is no evidence that checks of any kind had been made. Swiftly adjusting to the new circumstances, IMI had announced that 10,000 of the shells would, in fact, be passed on to Iran. There is no evidence that any of the shells were ever actually delivered to the Shah's army, but the ruse had been enough to give the army a big enough loophole to pass the authorization through.

In a catalogue of errors, the final mistake was to prove particularly helpful to SRC and Armscor. The Israelis had discovered how incompetent the US State Department's Office of Munitions Control was when it had issued the wrong export licences for the shells. The forgings (unfinished shell casings) made at Scranton had been exported to Canada for finishing, then shipped back into the United States before being exported to Israel. Attachments to the OMC licences had noted that 'US army production facilities were required [by SRC] for use in the manufacture of the projectiles', but although the shells had clearly required an export licence, OMC had simply issued an in-transit licence on the assumption that the shells had originated in Canada and were merely passing through the United States on their way to Israel.

The Meridien Hotel lies at the southern end of the magnificent Cococabana Beach in Rio de Janeiro. Its white, square, multi-storey façade comprises the outer boundary of one of the world's most famous tourist playgrounds, and its five-star luxury attracts a constant stream of American package tours. In many respects, the Meridien – or even Rio itself – was an unlikely setting for the hatching of a plot that would involve the CIA, the US Chiefs of Staff, the Pentagon and the governments of Israel and South Africa – an extraordinary story of intrigue, incompetence and international fraud that, in terms of the potential damage to world security, is unparalleled in modern times.

Certainly, none of the men who arrived at the Meridien on 20 March 1976 exactly resembled the average tourist. To any curious onlooker, they would simply have been dismissed as businessmen, in Rio to put the seal on a deal and take advantage of the country's rapidly expanding economy. On this occasion, however, there was no question of discussions with the Brazilian government. Rio was a mere convenience, of easy access to both the United States and South Africa.

Among those present at the meeting were: Dr Jerry Bull, the founder, chairman and chief scientist of SRC; Louis Palacio, joint inventor of the revolutionary shell and manager of Space Research International, the overseas division of SRC; Paul Rigo and Joseph Severin, both SRC employees; and a representative from SRC's

Belgian agents PRB – a subsidiary of the vast Fabrique Nationale (FN), the Belgian-government-owned arms industry (Israel also produces the FN rifle under licence). They had gathered together to put their signatures to a deal to sell SRC's artillery system, complete with ammunition, to South Africa in defiance of UN embargoes, the US Arms Export Control Act and a US arms embargo on shipments to South Africa which had been in force since 1964.

The meeting was harmonious, since all those present were agreed on the objectives, and all that was left to the small group was to sort out the logistics. According to one of those who had been present, Bull was able to explain that, although the deal was officially against the law, the CIA and others had unofficially given their blessing and would smooth over any problems in official channels. It was agreed to try and speed up the transfer of the shells and technology to South Africa, using a process similar to that which proved so successful for Israel. Under the agreement reached in Rio, one plan called for the supply of 65,000 howitzer shells, and the other for delivery of a number of howitzer conversion kits.

Reassured, and after a hard and successful day's work, the men discussed the possibility, with one of the hotel's porters, of a little evening's relaxation. As always on such occasions, the porter provided exactly what was required, this time a willing local girl named Elana. So charming and so willing did Elana prove to be to all the businessmen that they decided to name the project in her honour. Thus, the shell-smuggling operation became known as Elana I, and the smuggling of the artillery, Elana II.

On 28 March, Denys Zeederberg, Armscor's Head of Development, checked into the Hotel Jay in Jay Peak, Vermont, five miles from SRC headquarters. He was joined by Colonel P. M. Lombard, who had headed South Africa's artillery effort during the invasion of Angola in 1975, and Piet Smith, another Armscor official. They subsequently met with SRC's Jerry Bull, and as a result of that meeting, the project was begun. As part of the deal, SRC and PRB set up two shell companies – Paragon Holdings Ltd (named after SRC's testing station in Barbados) and Colet Trading Establishment, representing the South Africans – to handle the transaction. The formal agreement between Colet and Paragon was signed on 7 April 1976.

As a result of a series of investigations conducted by different newspapers led by the Burlington (Vermont) Free Press, a Senate subcommittee was already investigating arms smuggling. According to

evidence submitted to them, Jack Frost had spoken to Clyde G.
Bryant, Jr of the State Department's OMC as early as 16 December
1975, and had told him how he had been recruited by Clancy of the
CIA to organize some arms for Zambia, and of his later realization
that the destination was to be South Africa. Frost also named
Zeederberg, Lombard and Smith as the Armscor representatives he
had been dealing with.

Such a detailed confession should have alerted the OMC, other
parts of the State Department and various enforcement agencies as to
exactly what was going on – but by all accounts Frost's allegations were
completely ignored. Certainly when, immediately after the formal
signing of the Colet/Paragon contract, Jerry Bull visited the OMC, he
could not have received a warmer or more reassuring welcome.

Bull's visit to the OMC was inspired by his fear that the expensive
financing for the South African deal might not be forthcoming if SRC's
bank felt that US government regulations might prohibit the sale of
the shells. Bull had reason to be worried because, since late 1972, in an
attempt to keep the company going, their main supporters, First
Pennsylvania Bank of Philadelphia, had held all the SRC assets,
including the buildings and land at the SRC headquarters, in exchange
for rolling over a $5 million debt. In the intervening three years, the
situation had worsened and, by the end of 1975, SRC owed First
Pennsylvania around $11 million, of which $1.1 million was in arrears.
The SRC contract was very tempting to First Pennsylvania. Although
it was required to guarantee further advances of $14.5 million in letters
of credit over the next ten months, the potential profit was enough to
wipe out all SRC's debts and leave the company in a very healthy
financial state. However, before giving the go-ahead, the bank had to
be certain that SRC was not committed to purchasing the raw
materials and then having nowhere to sell them legally.

The main problems facing SRC lay in establishing: whether the shell
forgings could be considered to be arms; whether they were of
American origin; and if they were sold first to a Belgian subsidiary of
SRC, and then passed on to a third party, whether an export licence
was needed. The answer in every case appeared to be reassuring.
Following Bull's meeting at the OMC, he wrote to James D.
Hathaway Jr, Deputy Director of the OMC, on 21 April 1976, asking
for confirmation that US approval was not needed for exports by the
Belgian subsidiary and that the 'rough non-machined nosed forgings'
did not require export permits. Two days later, OMC director William
Robinson replied:

This is to confirm that your interpretation is correct that US government approvals are not required with regard to contracts of your international company acting as a marketing agent under Canadian export license to Belgium. Similarly, exports of rough, non-machined, nosed forgings from the United States are not considered as falling under the purview of the UN munitions list so long as they are not clearly identifiable as parts or components of weapons or sub-systems covered by that list. Hence no license is required from this office for exports of such raw materials from the United States.

With hindsight, it is difficult to comprehend how the OMC could have arrived at such a judgement. Although Bull had suggested that the shell forgings would be exported under Canadian law, SRC was considered by the Canadians, the US Customs and the Canadian Customs to be a US corporation. In addition, by any reasonable yardstick, rough, non-machined, nosed forgings can only be used as shells. They have no other industrial use and, indeed, look exactly like what they are: unpolished, unshiny artillery shells, unmistakable even to the layman. The OMC's own regulations, the International Traffic in Arms Regulations (ITAR), state that 'items in a partially completed state, such as forgings . . . which have reached a state in manufacturing where they are clearly identifiable as arms, are covered exports'. When he later appeared before the Senate subcommittee, a somewhat embarrassed Director Robinson told the subcommittee staff that he 'didn't know' if there could be any 'rough, non-machined, nosed forgings' that were not arms.

Encouraged by the response from the OMC, the first of the complicated financial arrangements were put into effect. At the end of April, Colet Trading was given a $3.7 million letter of credit from the Société Générale de Banque, a Belgian bank which owns 22 per cent of PRB. The letter was guaranteed by the Canadian Imperial Bank, and that, in turn, was covered by the First Pennsylvania on behalf of SRC. Such an arrangement is normal and reassures the purchaser that the seller has the assets to fulfil his side of the bargain.

Using their Israeli experience, SRC then contacted the Chamberlain Manufacturing Corporation in Scranton and asked if they could complete an order for 50,000 artillery shell forgings to be delivered to Israel and unnamed NATO countries. Again SRC said that it was acting as an agent for the recipients, although at no time did any US government agency ask for evidence to support this statement.

On 3 May 1976, Chamberlain asked the US Army Armament Command (Armcom) to approve the deal; at the same time they learned that if the contract was not allowed to go through, the corporation would have to lay off sixty-five skilled personnel and would lose $182,000 in rental fees. Chamberlain gave Armcom four days to make a decision; after that, it was said, SRC would take its business elsewhere.

In what was later described as an astonishingly swift decision, Armcom verbally approved the deal the same day and forwarded its recommendation to superiors at Army Material Command (AMC) for formal approval. AMC gave its verbal approval on 7 May, and the manufacture of the shell forgings began. At the heart of the swift authorization was General Howard Fish who had been a member of the committee that had considered South Africa's request for artillery at the time of the Angola invasion.

In the contract with Chamberlain, Israel was listed as the assignee, which meant that it would step in to take over the contract and honour it if, for any reason, SRC backed out. Under the secret Colet/Paragon agreement, IMI was subcontracted to supply Armscor with the propellants for the shells which would be filled in Israel and then shipped to South Africa. Two days after the agreement was signed, John Vorster paid his official visit to Israel. In the event, IMI supplied only 300 propellants before backing out of the deal; PRB then stepped in to fulfil the contract.

Jack Frost, who was still fluttering around the periphery of the scheme, heard in July 1976 that the deal had been signed and the shells were going to be transferred to South Africa. He now became seriously alarmed as he was under the impression that official clearance had not yet been granted and, if the deal was ever discovered, he might be implicated. He sent letters to Piet Smith and Denys Zeederberg of Armscor, warning them of the danger he thought they were running. The tone of the letters seems to indicate that Frost was in something of a panic; this stream of abuse must have finished any chance he may ever have had of dealing with the South Africans:

Dear Peet [sic],
It is indeed amusing and disheartening to discover the amateurish security practices and the lack of ethics as practiced by members of both [the Armaments] Board and Corps [Armscor]. I have now plotted the complete itinerary of my 'good friends' based on my previous conversations and correspondence. You, collectively, are treading on very thin ice and, at the same time, placing some naive people in a very precarious position.

It is evident that I have exposed some companies to serious consequences if knowledge of their proposed co-operation becomes public. As you know, there was an approved and proper manner for accomplishing your requirements. Since I have been pre-empted and, at the same time, am responsible for opening the door, I feel I have only one valid option.

Before I'll allow these companies to get into trouble, I must force them out of any direct or indirect co-operation. I will be calling each and every one to advise them of the general nature of the consequences. After this, and to prevent further contact, I shall have those known to me from the Board and Corps placed on a watch list.

You know there are elements in the North American governments who would make capital of the violation of the law to the detriment of some very nice people. The stupidity by which this program has been prosecuted is only exceeded by my personal affection for the people of your country. If it were any other country, I would have blown the whistle long ago. I would suggest that Denys [Zeederberg], Gibbon, David, [Magnus] Malan *et al.* [South African government employees] cease coming this way and that you cease to invite Allen, Bill N., Gerry [Jerry Bull], Dave and Ed *et al.* [SRC employees] to experience the wonders of the south.

I trust you will use good judgment and discontinue the US program before it becomes a national issue.

Dear Denys,
How stupid can you people get? You know well enough that there is a security leak in your own organization, apropos the leaks to the Far East on your and Pete's [*sic*] travels; but now you try to exploit the leads I have given you and Pete without regard for whom you talk to or the consequences.

Well, get this through your head, I won't allow you or anybody else to exploit these people . . . You and your associates are placing [them] in a precarious position which could result in them being barred from future US business and a probability of criminal prosecution. Your big mistake was contacting one group which is under continuous surveillance for violations and unfortunately has some very mouthy individuals. You could not have done a better job of exposing your activity if you had published it in the newspapers.

Right now, the anti-RSA groups would give their right arms to have this type of incident to exploit.

At this point, I don't know the appropriate course of action. I am considering the establishment of a watch list. It is evident that you have done your job well and my people are willing, nay anxious, to take more than a calculated risk for money. That's really a dirty trick. It now looks like I'll have to lose friends at both ends of the circuit, but be assured the sacrifice won't be too great.

I still view the actions of your group with incomprehension. You are unreal. Is the threat that great that you flush your ethics down the drain?

It is not clear whether Frost ever carried out his threats but, if he did, absolutely no action of any kind was taken to prevent the manufacture and export of the steel forgings that were now proceeding at a steady pace.

By February 1977 the first batch of 740 shells was ready for shipping to Israel. Unfortunately, in the nine months since the contract had been signed, the political situation in Israel had changed drastically. Prime Minister Rabin was beset by scandal: his housing minister had been accused of corruption and had committed suicide, his nominee for Governor of the Bank of Israel had been accused of taking bribes; then it was revealed that Rabin and his wife had maintained an illegal bank account in the United States. In addition, President Jimmy Carter, only a month in office, wanted to implement one of his campaign pledges and make some mark in the area of human rights. While Ford and Nixon had been prepared either to turn a blind eye or not to acknowledge the relationship between Israel and South Africa, Carter felt that the Israelis should do all they could to withdraw from it. The President let it be known that he expected Israel to take a strong position against South Africa if Israel wanted US aid and economic assistance to continue at the same level.

In a memorandum to his Belgian partners PRB, Jerry Bull reported that 'Israel is without an effective government . . . it is clear that political chaos and turmoil have spread from Washington. While the Israelis hesitate, the shells continue to await shipment from Canada.' Finally, on 17 February 1977, Bull told PRB he had received 'somewhat of a bombshell': 'The [Israeli] Cabinet has denied permission to IMI to enter into the filling contract unless (1) no Zim [the Israeli national shipping company] ships are used (we are loaded on Zim containers), (2) no SRC subsidiary, affiliate, etc. is involved.' As far as SRC was concerned, this was the end of the possibility of shipping the shells to Israel and then on to South Africa.

Some inkling of the Israeli climb-down must already have reached the ears of the South Africans and SRC, because only three days later, on 20 February, the vessel *Lady Scotia* left New Brunswick for

Antigua with at least 740 shells, followed by two other vessls on 7 March and 10 May, carrying, respectively, 7,468 and 2,688 shells.

In 1975, when Israel had bought artillery shells direct from SRC, they had been shipped via SRC's Caribbean testing station in Paragon, Barbados. SRC had established an extremely privileged position on the island and were able to avoid all Customs duties for goods coming to or going from Paragon. The initial plan called for the South African shells to be offloaded in Barbados, then transferred to an Israeli vessel and carried to Haifa. However, not only did the Israelis back out, but the Barbadian Prime Minister, Errol Barrow, with whom SRC enjoyed such a close relationship, had been swept out of office and Tom Adams had taken power. SRC were not prepared to take unnecessary risks with such a delicate contract, and the search began for another compliant government with a suitable staging post.

Fortunately, they did not have to look very far: Antigua lay 250 miles north of Barbados. Bull approached Prime Minister V. C. Bird and offered him a deal: in return for SRC establishing an army for Antigua, Bird would allow SRC to operate a test site that would be free from local interference. Bird readily agreed, especially when his son Lester, the Deputy Prime Minister and a lawyer, was retained at an undisclosed fee as SRC's legal representative on the island. It was a cosy relationship since the 'army' was in reality a private security force operating independently of local controls to keep the SRC operation secure from prying eyes.

The compound, situated on a remote peninsula called Crab's Point, was the ideal secure testing ground. In early 1977, both South African and Israeli military personnel arrived there for a demonstration of the 155-mm shell. All parties were completely satisfied and the South Africans gave the go-ahead for the deliveries to proceed.

On 27 May, the motor vessel *Tugelaland* sailed from New York for Cape Town. Although apparently registered to a German company, Globus Reedesey, and flying the German flag, the vessel was in fact owned by South African Marine, a New York-based company controlled by the South African government. After leaving New York, the *Tugelaland* made an unscheduled stop in Antigua and loaded on board thirty-six SRC containers and two radar vans, telling curious dockers who helped with the loading that they were destined for Canada – where, of course, they had originated earlier in the month. In fact, the vessel sailed for South Africa and arrived there on 7 June. The first load of SRC's extended-range artillery shells had been delivered on schedule.

While SRC was supplying the hardware through its Antigua test site, the company had also embarked on a smuggling operation that was to have far more serious long-term consequences.

In October 1976, the first of several planeloads of highly sophisticated technical equipment relevant to artillery performance and manufacture was flown out of Canada to South Africa. The initial shipment on Sabena Airlines on 21 October from Mirabel Airport, Montreal, to Johannesburg contained cardboard spacers and cavity liners which are used to separate propellant components inside the shells. Later that month, Visco Transgear Industries Ltd of Johannesburg received several shipments by air, one of which included 'seven 155-mm inert filling models which are used to demonstrate the loading of a shell'.

SRC continued to send shipments, the most significant occurring on 4 February 1977, when SRC delivered what was apparently a complete ballistics instrumentation testing system. The shipment was carried by South African Airways Flight 210 out of New York City's Kennedy Airport. Included in the shipment were such items as a 'Kistler Piezzotonic Gauge', and a 'textronic scope'. A Kistler gauge measures the interior ballistics of a gun; the textronic scope records a picture of the pressure inside the barrel. All the material that was shipped is highly sophisticated testing gear that is used to measure the performance of artillery shells and the converted howitzers firing them. At this time, South Africa had nothing comparable in its inventory, and such equipment set Armscor well along the path to developing its own artillery system. At no time did SRC make application in an official capacity to any US government agency to get permission to export material which quite clearly had only a military application.

So far then, South Africa had managed to obtain illegally both testing equipment and shells. All that were now needed were the guns to fire them – and, almost inevitably, SRC had that little problem well in hand.

As part of a $600,000 contract with the US army, SRC was to be loaned Gun Barrel No. 3147 by the Picatinny Arsenal. This barrel came from a 155-mm howitzer bored to take the extended-range shell designed by SRC. On 15 February 1977, SRC trucks picked up the cannon at Aberdeen Proving Grounds in Maryland, and the following day it was exported from the United States to the Canadian side of the SRC compound. An SRC receiving report dated 17 February bore the notation 'to be shipped to Antigua'. The gun barrel joined the containers of shells in Antigua to be shipped to South Africa aboard the *Tugelaland*.

According to the Senate subcommittee, two years after the original loan Customs investigators examined Picatinny Arsenal's file on Gun Barrel No. 3147 and found no paperwork beyond the initial loan authorization. The subcommittee report then cited an amazingly relaxed attempt to recover what at that time was one of the most advanced artillery pieces in the world.

In February 1979 a Picatinny official told a Customs agent that he had checked with SRC and learned that the cannon was then in Antigua, and would be shipped back to Vermont in the next six or seven weeks. In August 1979, an official at Aberdeen Proving Grounds told Customs that he had checked with SRC and learned that the weapon would be returned 'in approximately six weeks'. In May 1981, the Defense Contract Administrations Services Office noted that it had been delegated the responsibility for retrieving the gun barrel and had been trying to accomplish this since March 1980. Three individuals had been contacted – an SRC Paragon official, a Barbados clergyman and a Defense Property Officer – but they had been unable to help; in fact, the SRC Paragon representative had declared that the Gun Barrel No. 3147 was 'in possession of the Antigua Government Defence Forces'. On 25 August 1981, the US Defense Department gracefully surrendered: 'The property in Antigua is obviously not available for disposal at this time. Therefore above clearance case has been closed.' Of course, none of this really mattered four years after the event. SRC have never denied, and the overwhelming weight of the circumstantial evidence suggests, that the gun barrel went from Antigua to Pretoria. The equipment had apparently been allowed to pass to South Africa with such incredible ease and in total disregard of all normal precautions relating to equipment on the US secret list.

SRC – which had so far taken care of the gun, the shells and the testing equipment to make sure everything worked – completed the deal by providing the trained personnel to help the South African artillery experts make the best use of what they had got. Several representatives from SRC secretly travelled to South Africa and based themselves at a small town known as Schmidt's Drift on the edge of the Vaal river, some sixty miles west of Kimberley. This is the main artillery testing range for the South African army, and here SRC personnel were able to give vital insights into the working of the new howitzer.

The man in charge of the SRC contingent was Steve Adams, who had been project manager for the company's development of their 155-mm extended-range howitzer. He resigned from SRC in early 1978 and now lives in South Africa. The new artillery was first tested in the autumn of 1977 with the aid of SRC personnel and equipment, and the South Africans pronounced themselves completely satisfied. And so they should have been. SRC had provided everything that the South Africans could have wanted, even flying Tom Colgin, a range photographer who specialized in taking pictures of shells in flight, out to Schmidt's Drift.

By now, South Africa had in its possession everything required to develop its own artillery system, but setting up the manufacturing capacity would take time, and SRC were anxious to fulfil the complete contract and deliver the remaining 54,104 shells. Although the production of the shells appeared to be proceeding smoothly, SRC's financial problems continued to cause difficulty with the First Pennsylvania Bank. As collateral for a $2.2 million letter of credit issued by the First Pennsylvania Bank in June 1976, SRC had given the bank all its patents for its shells. South Africa had paid around $7 million in early June immediately after the first shells had arrived in South Africa, but SRC were having to pay their suppliers and the debt to First Pennsylvania showed no signs of being cleared off. However, as the estimated total value of the contract was $30 million excluding the technology or additional equipment, the cash-flow problem was only temporary. But a problem there was, and Bull turned to his willing South African friends for help in resolving the difficulty.

The South Africans dreamed up a perfect solution that embraced First Pennsylvania's money worries, SRC's cash-flow problems and their own need for continuing access to SRC research. In June 1977, Jerry Bull and his wife formed a company called Canadian Technical Industries, and another firm – Space Capital International NV, registered in Amsterdam – purchased 19.9 per cent of the Canadian Technical stock. The wrinkle in what became a fairly complicated financial transaction appeared in the form of J. S. Coetsee, the chief commercial salesman for Armscor and a director of Space Capital. At a meeting in London on 6 June 1977, the South Africans bought a 20 per cent share of SRC through the front of Space Capital and Canadian Technical.

The South Africans, using Space Capital as a channel, invested $10 million in Canadian Technical Industries. Of this, $3 million was converted into 545,970 preferred shares in Canadian Technical Industries, while the rest was secured by a $7 million debenture. Canadian Technical then made four transfers, totalling $6.3 million, to the First Pennsylvania Bank. It also released the bank from the initial $3.7 million letter of credit issued to back the purchase of the shell forgings from Chamberlain. In return, the bank agreed to transfer all SRC mortgages, collateral agreements, patents and company shares held by the bank. The bank also returned the assignment of the original shell contract with South Africa agreed on 7 April 1976.

For the South Africans, the deal was a dream. They now controlled all the technology relating to the new weapons systems. They controlled the patents and could thus manufacture and sell the artillery and reap substantial profits. In addition, they had access to SRC's top-secret research for the US government. With the deal wrapped up and the first batch of shells plus a gun, radar monitoring equipment and personnel already in place in South Africa, it must have seemed to the South Africans that nothing could go wrong. But the whole deal now began to unravel and, as with all the most complicated arrangements, it was a simple error that exposed the whole affair to an astonished world.

On 22 August 1977, the trusty vessel *Tugelaland* picked up 10,560 shells at New Brunswick and headed for the SRC base in Antigua. While taking on some additional cargo, a crane dropped its load into the hold, splitting open one of the containers holding the shells. That might not have been too alarming in itself, particularly as the vessel was cleared to go to Barbados, but then one of the dockers, in a casual conversation with the skipper of the *Tugelaland*, discovered that they were actually headed for South Africa. Although they allowed this cargo to leave, the trade unions on Antigua then refused to handle any further shipments by SRC and began to publicize the case. In particular they informed Joshua Nkomo, then leader of ZAPU, a Rhodesian guerrilla group based in Zambia. On 17 October, at a news conference in Ottawa, Nkomo charged Canada with having been the main shipping route for artillery shells destined for South Africa.

Alarmed at the growing attention on the SRC/South Africa link, plans to ship a further 21,000 shells to Antigua from New Brunswick were abandoned. Instead, SRC applied for a Canadian export licence to ship 35,000 shells to the government of Spain. The licence was granted. On 2 March 1978, a Dutch ship, the *Nordfarer*, picked up 21,624 shells in New Brunswick and transported them to Barcelona under the official Canadian export licence. They were stored there for three months; then on 26 June they were transferred to the South African-owned *Breezand* and eventually arrived in Durban on 19 July. On 27 July, SRC shipped a further 12,648 shells from Canada to South Africa under the Spanish licence. The ship stopped in the Bay of Cadiz on 10 August and bunkered at Las Palmas, the Canary Islands, on 14 August before arriving in South Africa on 10 September.

Astonishingly, even after Nkomo had brought the attention of US law-enforcement agencies to the SRC violation of the arms embargo and the Antigua route for smuggling the shells, that route was kept open with the support of the US navy. For two months, from December 1977 to January 1978, a convoy of trucks shipped more than 1,700 shells from SRC to the port at Cape Canaveral, Florida. Under its army contract with the Picatinny Arsenal, SRC persuaded the US navy to charter vessels especially to ship the shells to Antigua, where they were again collected by the South Africans and shipped direct to Durban. Because the shells were shipped by US government vessels, they did not need an export permit. Although dock workers in Antigua refused to unload the shells, the local army (paid and trained by SRC) did the unloading and then carried the containers aboard the South African vessel that arrived immediately after the US government ships had departed.

Inevitably, South Africa did not waste its investment in SRC. Some sixteen artillery experts from South Africa made regular trips to the Vermont headquarters of SRC in order to clarify details that were not clear on the patent drawings; meanwhile SRC continued to supply personnel to help South Africa develop an independent artillery system. Among those who visited South Africa from SRC were Robert Mortensen and John Ward, computer experts; John Alsop, a computer consultant; Sam Bailey, a photo-technician; Denis Lyster, a ballistics analyst; Bruce Smith, a range officer; George Tangen, a radar specialist; Louis Palacio, joint inventor of the shell and manager of SRC's international operations; and Jean Vezina, a propellants expert. Also, in January 1978, Cementation Engineering Ltd bought P. & E. Eustice Ltd, a drop-hammer and die-forging firm near Johannesburg which, according to the Johannesburg *Financial Mail*, began 'shelling out the profits'.

Cementation, aside from that delivered by SRC, bought equipment from various European companies including Hambrook Co. of Zandam, Holland, and Suid Durch Press of West Germany. Among its purchases were a double-action extrusion forge, automatic annealing equipment, swaging hydraulic presses, and a driving bank swage. All this equipment goes towards producing a shell-manufacturing capability.

On 28 April, South Africa announced that it had developed its own 155-mm shell and artillery system. Prime Minister Botha denied suggestions that the technology had been smuggled from the United States – 'Devoid of all truth. Armscor developed and is manufacturing it and its ammunition' – but in a subsequent interview in the Johannesburg *Times*, Commandant P. G. Marais, head of Armscor, confirmed that its own artillery system had been developed with some help from SRC. Marais argued, however, that all Armscor ever did was use the SRC computer to check its own estimates of its artillery's performance and made use of the testing range in Antigua. 'No one could supply us with the weapon we required so it was decided to produce the 155-mm locally. We were told by a defence consultant in Belgium, Mr John Frost, that the best man to assist us would be Mr Gerald Bull of the Space Research Corporation of Canada,' said Marais.

In evidence to US government investigators, Frost contradicted Marais' statement. If the South Africans said the artillery system had been developed in their own country, they were 'full of crap', claimed Frost. 'There's no question where the package came from.'

Marais said he was concerned that Armscor's involvement with SRC could be interpreted as breaking the embargo and feared an international outcry if the arrangement became public. 'I became even more concerned when a prototype gun system was developed from the tests [at SRC] and it was time to try the system out. Mr Bull refused to come to South Africa to assist with the tests because of the arms embargo, so it was agreed they would be conducted in Antigua,' Marais told the newspaper. But in fact Bull did travel to South Africa several times during the smuggling operation; although Marais claimed that the first tests on the system were not carried out until 1979, there is no doubt that preliminary test firings were made at Schmidt's Drift in 1977.

By early 1978, after most of the shells had reached South Africa and Armscor had already begun setting up its own shell production line and howitzer-manufacturing plant, officials in the United States belatedly began to grow concerned that there may have been violations of the standing US embargo against arms sales to the South Africans. A twenty-three-month Justice Department investigation followed, which resulted in Gerald Bull and former SRC president Ronald L. Gregory each being sentenced to one year in jail with six months suspended for having defied the UN arms embargo; this was later reduced on appeal to their being jailed for four and four-and-a-half months respectively. SRC was fined $25,000 on the same charge, and a further $20,000 on four counts of filing false information on US Customs Service documents.

SRC has now virtually disappeared, although part of the operation remains as Saber Industries, specializing in the sale of electronic equipment to the US government.

At the same time as the Justice Department was conducting its investigation, a Senate subcommittee began to look into the whole

SRC saga. It finally reported in March 1982, its major conclusions being:

1 From 1976–78, Space Research Corporation of Vermont broke the US and UN arms embargoes against South Africa by selling and shipping to the South African government approximately 60,000 155-mm extended-range artillery shells, at least four 155-mm guns including three advanced prototypes*, technology and technical assistance to establish its own 155-mm gun and ammunition manufacturing and testing capability, and other military equipment. Almost all of the equipment sent to South Africa was acquired in the US, mainly from US Army plants and supply stocks.

2 The SRC/South Africa transactions led to South Africa's acquisition and development of advanced 155-mm artillery systems which have made major contributions to its regional military capabilities.

3 The SRC case shows that while there has been an official US policy of embargoing arms to South Africa since 1963, the relevant US government agencies have thus far failed to adopt procedures to effectively implement the embargo. Had such procedures been in place, the SRC violations would have either not occurred or been promptly detected and halted.

4 The State Department's Office of Munitions Control gave SRC a letter which misapplied its own regulations and thereby encouraged SRC and its financier, the First Pennsylvania Bank, to proceed with their plans to ship arms to South Africa. The letter indicated that it might be legally possible for SRC to ship unfinished artillery shell forgings out of the US without an arms export license. It also accepted without investigation SRC's tenuous claim that its technology was not of US origin and therefore did not need a license to be exported abroad. The effect of this mistaken letter was to minimize the corporation's legal risks in exporting arms and arms technology to South Africa. Without the letter, the First Pennsylvania Bank would probably not have approved [the letter of credit which enabled] SRC's use of US manufacturing facilities to produce its shells, and might well have reconsidered the entire project. OMC's mishandling of SRC's questions was part of a pattern of errors and carelessness in dealing with the corporation's arms exports.

5 Acting under loose and ill-defined procedures, the US Army

---

*There is only clear evidence of one barrel being supplied to South Africa. However the subcommittee had access to other information – not made public – which led them to conclude that four barrels had actually been delivered.

approved two SRC requests to use a government-owned ammunition plant to manufacture 65,000 artillery shell forgings, nearly all of which went to South Africa. The Army made no attempt to independently verify the supposed destination of the shells.

6 According to the preponderance of evidence, it is probable that a US defense consultant who was assisting the CIA's covert action program in Angola – and was under the supervision of a CIA officer – planned with South African government officials shipments of US-origin arms to South Africa for use in Angola. He also informed the South Africans (representatives of Armscor, the state defense production and procurement agency) that they could obtain superior 155-mm artillery from SRC. Much of this planning and discussion took place after the US government had decided not to ship arms for Angola via South Africa and not respond to an official South African request for 155-mm artillery from SRC. At the very least, this episode suggests serious negligence on the part of the Agency. At most, there is a possibility that elements of the CIA purposefully evaded US policy. Although the probable CIA agent was one channel of information about SRC to South Africa and was subsequently approached by Armscor to act as an intermediary in concluding a deal with SRC, there were two other channels which seem even more important.

7 SRC's extensive and long-term violations of the arms embargo were made possible by the absence of a co-ordinated US enforcement system to detect and prevent such violations. The State Department and the CIA, respectively, did not follow up on reports of South Africans seeking US-origin arms from a US citizen or share information on South Africa's efforts to obtain 155-mm shells from the US government. No US foreign policy agency monitored the visits of at least eight Armscor-led arms buyers to the US in 1976–77 or the often multiple trips of sixteen high officials and technicians from SRC to South Africa in 1976–78. No US agency was aware of the role of . . . Israeli third parties in the development of the SRC–Armscor contracts. As news reports began to expose the SRC violations, no US foreign policy agency felt responsible for investigating the specific allegations being made. After a US Customs investigation was launched, the emphasis was on the slow, careful construction of a criminal prosecution and not on the detection of continuing SRC violations and the prevention of future ones. Thus no co-ordinated action was taken to follow up on information that SRC had a Canadian export license for 35,000 artillery shells for the 'government of Spain' and that the shell forgings came from a US munitions plant. As a result of these

enforcement lapses, SRC was able to ship over 32,000 US-forged artillery shells to South Africa, via Spain, eight to nine months after the initial allegations and four to five months after the Customs inquiry began.

8 The poor performance of US foreign policy agencies in the SRC case seriously weakened the Justice Department's 1980–81 criminal case against SRC, the First Pennsylvania Bank, and their officers and associates. Of particular concern to government lawyers in a potential trial was the appearance of possible US government authorization of SRC shipments to South Africa. The upshot was Justice's acceptance of a plea bargain in which only the two top officers of SRC paid a price – four and four-and-a-half months at a minimum security prison – for a $19 million illegal arms deal.* Although there was some minority sentiment in Justice for attempting more vigorous prosecution, no State Department representatives (and thereby no US foreign policy interests) participated in the decision to accept the plea bargain.

9 The causes of the government's failure to adequately implement the arms embargo were structural rather than accidental in nature. OMC's failures reflected the organization's lack of capacity to adequately enforce arms licensing regulations. OMC officials acknowledged their lack of sufficient technical expertise to make reliable judgements on applications of their own regulations and lack of sufficient staff resources to properly process their workload. The Army's slip-ups were due to loose and ill-defined procedures, some of which have been tightened in the backwash of the SRC affair. At the CIA, a preoccupation with the immediate bureaucratic need to move arms efficiently into Angola through South Africa appeared to supersede the larger US policy of enforcing the arms embargo against South Africa. Finally, SRC's successful implementation of its plans revealed that there is a 'non-system' of enforcing the arms embargo in the US government. US foreign policy agencies did not interrupt this scam because collecting information on the embargo's operation was not high on the list of any agency's priorities; procedures for sharing and centrally assessing relevant information did not exist, and – most fundamentally – there was no clear delineation of organizational responsibilities for obtaining relevant intelligence, evaluating it and acting upon it.

10 In order to strengthen the US arms embargo against South Africa (and arms restrictions aimed at other countries), the

---

*This figure is a substantial reduction on the true $30 million value of the deal.

following steps are recommended:

(a) The Secretary of State should promptly designate a lead office, logically the Bureau of Politico-Military Affairs, to supervise US implementation of arms embargoes and restrictions. The lead office should have a formal, written mission and authority to represent the Department in inter-agency discussions. A Deputy Assistant Secretary of State should be made formally responsible for implementing arms export restrictions. At the time of these designations, the Secretary of State should clearly and vigorously express the rationale for the arms embargo against South Africa and other arms-export restrictions.

(b) Under the aegis of the lead office, the Executive should reassess the current system for implementing US arms-export restrictions. Following this review, and in consultation with Congress, the Executive should:

*delineate formally and in writing organizational responsibilities for implementation, including preventative action;

*re-evaluate existing organizational procedures in light of newly assigned responsibilities;

*take steps to ensure that each organization has the resources to do its job;

*require increased intelligence collection on illegal international arms transactions and install formal communications procedures to make sure that intelligence is utilized.

(c) Pending completion of this reorganization:

*the Office of Munitions Control should be given increased resources in staff and technical training to perform its existing functions;

*the House and Senate Intelligence Committees should investigate the possible roles of employees, agents and contacts of the CIA in efforts to evade the US arms embargo against South Africa during the Angola conflict, and in the development of the SRC/South Africa relationship.

To date, none of the recommendations of the subcommittee has been implemented.

With their undoubted brilliance for innovation and modification, the South Africans have taken the SRC system and improved a highly efficient artillery system until it is now the world's most effective mobile battlefield artillery.

On 26 September 1982, Armscor gave a champagne breakfast to

launch the marketing of a new mobile artillery system. According to Pieter Marais, the G5 gun (an adaptation of SRC's G4) is capable of firing a nuclear warhead and 'is the most sophisticated artillery piece in the world'. For its export version, Marais explained, South Africa had refined the product even further, calling it the G6. Mounted on a self-propelled armoured chassis, the vehicle is capable of travelling at 50 mph on a highway and 25 mph across rough terrain, smashing down trees, climbing over rocks, riding through deep sand and firing its 155-mm howitzer within one minute of stopping, moving off again one minute later. The vehicle, which is also fitted with grenade launchers and a light anti-aircraft machine-gun, has a range of 250 miles and is very accurate over a twenty-five-mile range.

One reason for the South African howitzer's longer range is its 'base bleed' system that generates gas at the rear of the shell to destroy the partial vacuum restricting flight length. The G5 or G6 can also use a standard 155-mm NATO shell and, like a similar device in service in the United States, can be converted to take a nuclear shell. However, according to Marais, there is currently no intention of converting the G6 into a nuclear delivery system.

There is no doubting that the acquisition of the G5 and its enhancement into the G6 has placed South Africa at the forefront of modern artillery development. Not only has the gun system given South Africa a nuclear delivery capability that could easily devastate its neighbours, but it has also provided the means for South Africa to gain valuable foreign exchange and, perhaps more importantly, considerable influence among Third World countries. For Marais and his government, the sales of sophisticated armaments abroad are a very valuable way of gaining friends in an increasingly hostile world. Certainly, the potential income from arms sales is attractive; however, this pales into insignificance when set alongside the value of a few friendly votes in the UN.

There is an overwhelming weight of evidence that, without the help of the CIA in originally putting the South Africans in touch with former Agency personnel who set up the deal and smoothing the way through potential opposition at the Pentagon and the State Department, South Africa would have had to wait many more years before her equipment could hold its own in the highly competitive international arms market. Nearly all the recent developments by Armscor have been derivatives of Israeli products or improvements on vintage material supplied by Western countries before the arms embargo came into force. The conventional military opposition in Angola is now faced with a weapon of immense power that, in the next major hot-pursuit operation over the border, could well turn the balance in the South Africans' favour.

Perhaps the ultimate irony of this tale is that South Africa has been in discussions with Israel in an attempt to sell them the technology for the system that Israel first tried to sell to South Africa.

5 Israel and the Fortification of South Africa

The adventure into Angola in 1975 had two important effects on South Africa's military posture. It showed the government that strikes across South Africa's borders were perfectly practicable but that the right equipment was essential. A heavy investment in artillery and armoured vehicles followed – including the 155-mm howitzer – as well as a realization that continued peace both internally and with its neighbours was no longer a viable aim. Major-General Neil Webster declared in 1976, 'South Africans, like the Israelis, must get used to the idea of living with a warlike situation for some years to come.' But more particularly, South Africa, which had been promised aid from the United States in international forums, was left to fight on alone. This was a heavy blow, as South Africa had always maintained that she was Africa's last bastion against Communism and that, in Angola, her troops were actually engaging in combat against Cubans sent in by the Soviet Union. Worse was to follow: immediately after South Africa withdrew from Angola, some 20,000 Cuban troops began to arrive in the country, reinforcing the few hundred who were already in the country to bolster the battle-weary and largely incompetent troops of President Neto.

Otto Krause, a leading South African commentator, has declared that South African relations with the West – and particularly with the United States – were permanently damaged: 'The feeling of having been let down, or even of having been taken for a ride, by Washington in that attempt to exclude a Soviet/Cuban Communist presence from Africa still persuades South Africans that they should "not put thine trust" . . . even in Republican administrations.'

Finally, the Soweto riots of June–November 1976 gave clear warning to the South African government that security within the country was at best uncertain. For four months, thousands of blacks and whites demonstrated against both the apartheid laws and the general economic conditions in which non-whites were being forced to live. The demonstrations, often violent, spread across the whole country into white suburbs and black townships. Controlling such a spreading bush-fire proved extraordinarily difficult for a police force that did not possess the required sophisticated training. When the fighting and the riots died down in November, 600 were dead and thousands injured, with several thousand more in jail. In the year that followed, an estimated 3,000 young blacks left for neighbouring Angola and Mozambique, to provide willing and motivated recruits for the growing guerrilla army marshalling just outside South African territory.

In detailed defence studies undertaken in South Africa in 1975, it was realized that the country would have to go on a total war footing. As the Defence White Paper pointed out: 'The collapse of support in neighbouring states will undoubtedly encourage the radical elements in revolutionary organizations inside and outside South Africa and incite them to greater efforts. They regard Angola and Mozambique as new allies and potential new operational bases for action against Rhodesia and the Republic.' The danger to South Africa would come, not from a conventional military attack by the armies of the black African countries in the north, but rather from the guerrillas of the ANC who were already beginning to grow active in the bush and in urban areas, building up an extensive network of informers and supporters.

In the first of what was to become a regular series of Defence Amendment Bills, on 28 January 1976 the South African Parliament agreed that troops could be made to serve anywhere in the world; previously they were only required to serve within the country's borders. The Bill also said that the State President could decide whether any armed conflict outside South Africa posed a threat to its security and would need to be prevented or suppressed by the SADF. In addition, it provided that no proceedings, civil or military, could be taken following any act committed in good faith in preventing or suppressing terrorism in any operational area. In other words, for the first time the Defence Amendment Bill passed into law a legal provision to conduct hot pursuit across borders in the hunt for guerrillas.

As Julius Nyerere admitted candidly in August 1977, 'Not a single African country is really a military threat to South Africa. No combination of African states can really be a threat to South Africa.' In terms of conventional warfare, he was undoubtedly quite correct. None of the neighbouring regimes has a very stable government and their relatively small armies would be no match for the well-equipped and highly disciplined SADF. In addition, no black African country has ever been proved in battle, and the prospects of them uniting for a lengthy ground war against South Africa are remote. However, South Africans are well aware that a modern industrial society is particularly vulnerable to a wearing campaign by relatively small numbers of well-armed, politically motivated individuals.

The Ministry of Defence's own estimate was that only 20 per cent of the onslaught came from the military; the remaining 80 per cent was political and psychological. As a restricted SADF handbook issued to senior officers in 1976 pointed out, '*The Guide to Psychological Action* represents the application of a well co-ordinated combination of assistance designed to improve the living conditions of the population and raise its cultural level. It contributes to winning the hearts and minds of the population . . . making it more receptive to psychological action.' But, as neighbouring Zimbabwe found out, a hearts-and-minds campaign, particularly in rural areas, depends to a large extent on who the people believe is going to win the fight. The Rhodesian army found that they were never able to win the village battle, that there was always a network of spies and safe houses for the roving guerrilla patrols to contact. The local people believed (and they were, of course, proved right) that the government had no prospect of winning the war. South Africa recognized that, while the military threat in a conventional sense might not be immediately serious, for the hearts-and-minds campaign to have any chance of success the military machine would have to become the most effective in Africa. That entailed not just a total modernization campaign but also a new approach to training and a new aggression in their anti-guerrilla activities. This was to involve all aspects of the country's economy which was to be effectively placed on a permanent war footing.

South Africa had several immediate requirements: defence spending had to be increased; the necessary manufacturing expertise had to be acquired; the manpower for the armed forces had to be increased; and the army, navy and air force had to be supplied with the most modern and suitable equipment for fighting a counter-insurgency war.

One of the first results of the new wind of change in South Africa's defence posture was the visit of Vorster to Israel in April 1976. Officially, economic projects were discussed; however, behind the scenes, agreement was reached on future co-operation in arms sales, manufacture and distribution. This would enable Israel and South Africa, in the space of seven years, to become a prime force in the world arms trade . . . all in defiance of international opinion and UN sanctions. This co-operation also went directly against public statements made repeatedly by senior Israeli officials to the effect that they would comply with the UN arms embargo imposed in November 1977. For example, in a note to Secretary-General Kurt Waldheim in December 1977, Israel said it would be 'guided' by the embargo resolution, and in April of the following year, the Israeli government announced it would 'comply' with the embargo.

Although Israel had always been prepared to spend a huge proportion of its gross national product (a fairly constant 30 per cent in the past five years) on military spending, the big military budget is a relatively new phenomenon for South Africa. In 1976, South Africa's defence expenditure was a mere $1,332 million; by 1983 this had risen to just under $2.99 billion (3.48 per cent of the GNP) and a proposal to raise $3.47 billion for the fiscal year 1983/84 has been passed by Parliament. In presenting the 1981 budget (which eventually resulted in an expenditure of $2.76 billion), Finance Minister Owen Horwood said that the allocation would make it 'perfectly clear . . . to our enemies that the government is in earnest with its commitment to the proper protection of our country'.

The heart of the South African arms manufacturing effort is Armscor. In the words of its chairman, Commandant Piet Marais, the organization

> is part of and exists only to render a service to the SADF. The aim, of course, is to procure and manufacture arms at the lowest possible cost . . . The Defence Force is responsible for determining new types of weapons that it requires to defend South Africa, and expansion of existing lines. After these have been defined, we come into the picture. Through a joint committee, they state their needs relative to the external threat, then we state our capabilities of meeting their needs within cost and time limits.

Armscor was formed in 1968, and in ten years its turnover soared from £17.8 million to £543 million; it is expected to spend in excess of £600 million in 1983. It employs 25,000 people, mostly in the Johannesburg and Pretoria areas, and the business is channelled through a number of major subsidiaries. These are:
*Atlas Aircraft Corporation, based at Kempton Park, Waterkloof and Ysterplat (aircraft design and manufacture).
*Aloptro, Kempton Park (design and manufacture of electro-optical systems).

*Kentron, Pretoria (design and manufacture of guided missile systems).
*Lyttleton Engineering Works, Verwerdburg (largest weapons manufacturer, including artillery).
*Musgraves, Bloemfontein (rifles).
*Naschem, Braamfontein (explosives, propellants and ammunition).
*Pretoria Metal Pressing, Pretoria (ammunition).
*Somchem, Somerset West (explosives).
*Swartklip Products, Cape Town (chemical research).
*Sandock Austral, Cape Town, Boksburg and Durban (Panhard armoured cars, Ratel armoured personnel carriers, naval shipyard).
There are an additional 900 companies involved in defence work, nearly all of them in private hands. A total of some 32,000 workers (11.5 per cent of the workforce) are employed in the defence industries. The equivalent figure for the United States, the world's biggest arms supplier, is 10 per cent.

Ultimately, of course, the intention is for South Africa to become entirely self-sufficient. Although it has not yet totally achieved that aim, considerable advances have been made, particularly in the field of heavy engineering. Little of the country's arms manufacturing has been innovative, but like the Israelis, South Africa appears to be very efficient at adapting existing designs for its own use, and is also able to set up sophisticated production lines in a relatively short space of time.

Ten years ago, South Africa produced a mere 10 per cent of its armaments requirements, but that figure has now climbed to 90 per cent. According to a military White Paper published in April 1982, South Africa is now self-sufficient in artillery, guns and rockets, armoured and other operational vehicles, as well as arms, ammunition and land mines. According to Marais, there is now surplus production in some areas and South Africa is launching a major export drive, aiming at annual sales of R100–150 million to Third World countries.

The major push towards an independent Israeli weapons and aerospace industry came with the French arms embargo in 1967 and 1968. When the French government halted the delivery of fifty Mirage-Vs in 1967, Israel decided to proceed with the development of the Kfir combat aircraft. The Reshef fast-attack craft was built in Israeli yards after five finished boats were prevented from leaving the Cherbourg shipyards (they were eventually illegally smuggled to Israel), and the decision to build the Merkhava main battle-tank came when the British cancelled an almost completed deal for the supply of Chieftain tanks.

The Israeli Aircraft Industries (IAI), the nation's largest defence company with over 20,000 employees and a production capacity for all areas of the armed forces, is organized into five intersupportive divisions: engineering, aircraft manufacturing, electronics, combined technologies and Bedek Aviation. The two other major companies dealing with defence are IMI which produces the Merkhava tank, and Tadiran which specializes in electronics.

The building up of the Israeli electronics industry came about only in the 1960s when the armed forces listed their requirements for weaponry and systems that could not be obtained abroad. Because the West had no tactical answer to the Soviet Styx missiles which were in use with some Arab navies, the anti-ship Gabriel missile was developed. Another example is the Israeli EL/M 2001B aircraft radar, which resulted when the French Cyrano system proved inadequate.

Michael Schor, managing director of IMI, has pointed out that his organization produces 450 items through eighty major programmes, and that about 60 per cent of production is home-grown: 'We are unconditionally compelled to keep our superiority over the enemy who has been supplied by a superpower with the most modern equipment.' Schor attributes the success of IMI to three main factors:

[The first is] the very close collaboration between industry and the military. We [also] have less bureaucracy than other countries in that respect. A third factor is our practice of developing projects using engineers with extensive production experience who guide an entire project through all the development phases to production. And so, right from the start, the product is designed in terms of ease of production, and there is no real break in continuity between development, preparation of prototypes and series production.

For Israel, the main thrust of their weapons development has been aimed at maintaining a qualitative edge over their potential enemies. The government officially lists Syria, Jordan, Iraq, the Lebanon and Saudi Arabia as 'confrontation states', or potential aggressors. These have a combined population of 39.79 million as against Israel's 4 million, and a combined GNP of $145 billion against Israel's $23 billion. The combined armies facing Israel approach 700,000 while Israel has a regular army of 172,000, augmented by reservists who can be in the front line within seventy-two hours, bringing total strength up to 400,000. Similar figures reflect a substantial equipment imbalance, with Arab aircraft totalling 1,334 against Israel's 602; 8,450 tanks against 3,500; and 5,430 artillery pieces against 1,688.

On paper then, Israel would be in serious trouble if war broke out.

However, there are several factors which have so far given it a considerable advantage in any conflict. The Israelis consider themselves to be fighting for survival. Troops put up much stiffer resistance when defending their homeland than when they are on foreign sorties. In addition, the Israelis have always managed to maintain a highly effective technological and training edge over the Arabs. Although outnumbered, they have reduced the downtime for all moving equipment, particularly aircraft. During the 1973 war, it took the Arabs six hours to change the engine on a fighter, but the Israelis only three hours; their tank breakdowns were cut by 25 per cent, and the actual time while broken down on the battlefield was reduced by the effective use of mobile repair teams.

However, personnel is extremely expensive to train and, as one senior Israeli intelligence officer pointed out: 'If it takes six hours to change an engine on a Mirage fighter, we can reduce that to three. But the engine on the F16 only takes six-and-a-half minutes to change – and even if we cut that by half, it is not going to make any real difference to the course of battle.' Thus, Israeli defence officials are convinced that they have already lost the battle, in terms of personnel and efficiency advantage. What remains is equipment that simply does the job better. As a result, Israel devotes a very large percentage of its budget to research and development in an attempt to produce equipment that will not be available to its potential enemies.

To a large extent, she has succeeded in that aim. The US and Soviet governments were astounded at the performance of the Israeli fighting machine in the Lebanon in 1982. While the PLO was not a conventional opposition, the Syrian armed forces had been very well equipped by some of the best that the Soviet Union had to offer. In the event, it was no real contest and, to the astonishment of the superpowers, Israel was shown to be employing equipment that in many cases (tanks, fighters, electronic warfare) was far superior to anything they had in their own armouries.

While the Israelis have fairly regular reminders of their vulnerability, the situation in South Africa is rather different. Certainly there is a running sore in Namibia, but that does not threaten the destruction of the country. The ANC occasionally manages to plant a few bombs but, so far, these have been aimed at 'hard' targets such as police stations, power stations and government buildings; there have been only very infrequent attacks on 'soft' targets such as farms, private houses or schools. Security problems have been confined and there is still no feeling among the local population that the country could collapse

tomorrow. Inevitably, changes will occur, but a highly effective
security arm has ensured that the people believe that these will be at
some unspecified period in the future.

This belief has led to some serious problems for the armed forces
and the intelligence service. Without the need for a greater sense of
urgency that the generals and the politicians believe exists, it has
proved difficult to convince people that the funding for a bigger and
better defence force is necessary. It has also become difficult to attract
personnel into the armed services. According to the International
Institute for Strategic Studies (IISS), in 1975/76 the total strength of
the South African armed forces was only 50,500 – with 35,400 of those
being conscripts whose battle qualities are always questionable. The
country's thousands of miles of border – with only a hard core of
14,600 troops trained in conventional warfare to protect it – began to
look very vulnerable to the country's defence chiefs. The problem was
exacerbated by the steady drain of highly trained officers into the
better-paid private sector. As the 1975 Defence White Paper pointed
out: 'The officers' strength is moving towards a potential danger
point.' In other areas, too, trained personnel were leaving the armed
forces, and there was a net loss in manpower over the year.

The manpower shortage was given added importance by the
problem of Angola. By 1975, South Africa had already embarked on
several cross-border expeditions including the ill-fated CIA-backed
invasion that ended in such a humiliating defeat. However, the South
Africans discovered that their fighting methods were not only
outdated, but they were also suffering an unacceptably high casualty
rate. As in Israel, the ruling class in South Africa – the whites – is very
small, and for every soldier killed at the front, there are generally
several dozen grieving relatives back home, all of whom are in a
position to bring pressure and influence to bear on their political
leaders.

The South Africans recognized that they faced a long defensive
operation that may last up to thirty years; to have any chance of
succeeding, the armed forces had to be strengthened, fighting tactics
improved and border security tightened. In all three fields, the advice
and experience of the Israelis was to prove essential. Following
Vorster's visit in April 1976, military relations between the two
countries were put on a much firmer and more regular footing. Where
there had previously been frequent informal exchanges of information
and technology, there were now formal agreements; where Israeli
servicemen might have gone on lecture tours to South Africa,
specialists were now formally seconded for service there.

In May 1976, Marcia Friedman, an opposition member of South

Africa's Parliament, suggested that 'hundreds' of Israeli troops were
attached to South African army units as instructors. This was denied
by the Israeli defence ministry: 'There are no IDF personnel in South
Africa.' In fact, Friedman was correct. Senior army officers in Israel
have confirmed that IDF personnel have been seconded to all
branches of the South African armed forces, and according to senior
sources in the Israeli defence establishment, there are currently some
300 active Israeli servicemen and women on secondment in South
Africa. These include army, navy and air force personnel who help
train the South Africans, border security experts who advise on
improvements to restrict guerrilla activity, counter-intelligence experts
who have information relating to guerrilla activity worldwide and help
in training South Africans, and defence scientists who co-operate on
the development of new weapons systems. In addition, there are
several hundred South Africans in Israel at any one time, being trained
in weapons systems, battle strategy and counter-insurgency warfare.
As both countries are particularly discreet on all matters relating to
defence, it has always been difficult to obtain exact figures, but
certainly the direct relationship (aside from general trade co-
operation) is far greater than anyone had previously suspected.

With the South Africans promising a greatly enlarged budget, the
Israelis, with their considerable experience of manpower problems
and guerrilla warfare, argued that the regular and conscripted
branches of the armed services would have to be expanded greatly.
Perhaps more importantly, the Israelis pointed out that, if the
apartheid government was to survive, colour discrimination in the
armed forces would have to be abolished. There are only about one
million white South African males between the ages of eighteen and
forty-five; the maintenance of an enlarged standing army comprising
whites only would be an impossible drain on the country's resources,
emasculating industry and the business community, even if enough
recruits could be persuaded to join – which was very doubtful.

It was General Magnus Malan, then head of the armed forces and
now Defence Minister, who most strongly supported the Israeli line.
Malan has always taken the view that South Africa faces a two-
pronged assault, one from Communist-backed troops based in
neighbouring countries and the other from guerrillas, again
Communist-backed, operating inside the country. He devised the
phrase 'total war' which was and is his estimation of South Africa's
position, and in 1977, he called for a 'total national strategy' to face the
security threat.

Both Malan and his senior advisers realized that the key to victory in
an unconventional war lay not with military might but in persuasive

psychology. While the senior army men were in no doubt that a tough foreign relations policy was essential, they advocated a much more moderate policy at home. The experience in Rhodesia had taught them that without the support of the vast majority of the blacks, there would be no chance of a white-dominated security force winning a hearts-and-minds campaign. To that end, Malan began slowly to introduce reforms into the armed forces that are opposed to the spirit and letter of the apartheid laws.

A major recruiting drive was launched among blacks and coloureds, with the result that there are now substantial numbers in the army and in the police force which is responsible for most counter-terrorist activity within South Africa. In the army, out of a total of 67,400 personnel, there are 10,000 whites, 5,400 black and coloured regulars, 2,000 women (black and white) and over 50,000 conscripts. In the police, out of a total of 35,000, 19,500 are white and 16,000 non-white.

This radical development in a government that still believes in apartheid is not mere tokenism. There are now black officers in both the army and the police, and it is a quite common sight to see black policemen with submachine-guns patrolling white residential areas in Johannesburg or Cape Town. In the navy, which is perhaps the most integrated of the three services, coloureds and Indians account for more than 80 per cent of its complement of 5,000. Non-white officers are often in charge of lower white ranks and, in defiance of some of the basic tenets of apartheid, blacks and whites bunk and eat together, as well as draw the same pay. One senior naval officer has been quoted as saying: 'There is no room for apartheid on ships. We break the race laws of this country every day, but we don't make a big noise about it, to avoid embarrassing the Prime Minister.'

In the army, the same pattern emerges although, because of its vastly greater size, there has been room to establish black regiments as part of a policy of actively encouraging blacks to defend themselves against guerrilla activity. The eventual intention of the army and government policy is to extend the self-help thesis into the homelands where independent defence forces are being trained and equipped by the South African government. As the white South Africans withdraw into a central enclave, so the black homelands will rise up to act as the first redoubt against either a conventional ground attack or guerrilla infiltration.

It is an interesting – if risky – policy that, so far, while guerrilla activity is relatively light, has proved quite successful. It is uncertain how much the South African government can depend on the loyalty of the homeland troops if or when the fighting gets tough. If the homeland government, at some time in the future, feels that South

Africa is losing or if the war against the ANC escalates into a full-scale confrontation between South Africa and its black neighbours, the white government may well find itself facing its own well-trained and equipped black homeland troops. If the experience in Namibia is anything to go by, the black troops are formidable fighters and far more battle-hardened than the soldiers of the large but poorly trained armies of Angola, Mozambique, Zimbabwe and Botswana. However, whatever the longer-term risk, the government has determined that an integrated armed force represents the only realistic hope for survival against the 'total onslaught' which they are convinced is bound to escalate over the next few years.

For some blacks, this policy of integration is totally unacceptable as they are being asked to fight for a country in which they have no political rights and are forced to accept a role as second-class citizens. As Zulu chief Gatsha Buthelezi has said: 'While blacks do not enjoy citizenship or share political power, we will not urge [them] . . . to participate in the military defence of the apartheid regime.'

Under present South African policy, blacks will eventually lose their South African citizenship once their homelands are truly established. As Chief Buthelezi has pointed out, that will make blacks even more reluctant to co-operate with the South African government: 'They expect us to be "patriotic" foreigners. We are called on to offer our lives in defence of the borders of our country in which we will now be foreigners . . . I have never seen such insensitivity in my whole life.'

So far, the black leaders have failed to influence very large numbers of their followers, and recruitment has been steady enough to see the raising of seven non-white battalions in Namibia; several others are planned, with recruitment aimed at those who live in, and have extensive knowledge of, the border areas. The white soldiers fighting in Namibia and Angola have been particularly impressed with the performance of a battalion formed entirely from Bushmen, who have proved formidable trackers and very skilful fighters. As Rhodesia discovered, the guerrillas were often more frightened of the black soldiers fighting in Ian Smith's army – they were far more ruthless and naturally had unrivalled knowledge of guerrilla strategy – than they were of the white soldiers. Indeed, right up to the fall of the Smith government, Rhodesia had no trouble in recruiting blacks even for the élite undercover Selous Scouts or the Special Branch. But it is also true that, throughout the guerrilla war in Rhodesia, the insurgents had excellent political and military intelligence, much of it leaked by blacks who were ostensibly fighting for the Smith government.

Although recruitment has improved, the estimates of future guerrilla activity are so gloomy that, in mid-1982, Defence Minister

Malan announced that the government planned to double its armed forces by altering the conscription laws. However, plans to include coloureds and Indians in the conscription net were dropped after both the liberal and the right-wing opposition voiced strong objections. At present, all white South African men must serve two years in the armed forces and one month a year in active-duty reserve for the following eight years. Under the new scheme, military obligations will be increased from 240 days spread over two years to a full two years less ten days. After this, all white males will be transferred to the active reserve for at least twelve years; they will then serve in commando units until they are sixty and then be kept on the national reserve until aged sixty-five. It is estimated that the new rules will affect some 800,000 men and will give South Africa a total mobilized armed force in excess of that of the combined African states south of the Sahara.

The expansion of the army has gone ahead remarkably smoothly and has resulted in the formation of a formidable fighting force. According to the IISS, the total armed forces strength is now 81,400, up from 50,000 in 1976. In addition, the commandos (equivalent to the British Territorials or the US National Guard) have been increased from 75,000 to 90,000. The South Africans claim a total mobilized strength of 404,500 which could be used to repel a conventional armed attack from one of its neighbouring countries. (However, for general security, the government depends entirely on the regular armed forces and, more particularly, on the South African Police. The armed forces deal with border security and hot-pursuit operations into Mozambique and Angola, while the South African Police both mastermind intelligence gathering and operate against guerrillas within the country's borders.)

Although regular serving soldiers can be subjected to rigid army discipline to some extent, the same does not apply to the conscripts who now number 53,100, compared with 35,400 in 1976. Should the present trend continue, more and more white conscripts will face the prospect of being commanded by a black or coloured officer.

Of course, while this pragmatically liberal approach may have gone a long way towards solving the armed forces' problems with recruitment, it has begun to attack the very foundations of apartheid. With such a large army of men – both black and white – living together, drawing the same pay and in some cases dying together, the concept of racial segregation is difficult to sustain. It is ironic indeed that the attempts to prevent the activities of guerrillas by the army is bringing about exactly the changes that the ANC are fighting for – albeit as a by-product of an increasingly violent war.

The pressure for change introduced by General Malan while he was operating as head of the armed forces has also led to what some in South Africa have described as an effective military coup.

South Africa's Prime Minister Botha has long been an admirer of Malan who had served under Botha while the latter was Defence Minister in the Vorster government. Like Botha, Malan is a hard-liner in foreign relations but tends to be more pragmatic in internal politics. Certainly under the Botha government, the more extreme examples of apartheid have been modified, at least for public consumption. Malan's success at integrating the army and beefing up its fighting strength are the cornerstones of Botha's government, as without a strong military machine, the guerrilla bush-fire would quickly grow into an urban conflagration. With the escalation in guerrilla activity, the political machine has inevitably been brought into such close contact with the military that it is difficult to distinguish which is the tail and which the dog. In early 1980, Botha acknowledged the pre-eminent role that the military now plays in South Africa's affairs, by bringing Malan and his top aides into the highest levels of government policy-making.

Central to the revised structure are the State Security Committee and the Prime Minister's Office. The State Security Committee brings together the heads of the SADF, the police and the national intelligence service, along with the secretaries for foreign affairs and justice and their respective ministers, all under Botha's chairmanship. Although in theory the Committee is responsible to the Cabinet and its decisions have to be officially endorsed by it, there are recent instances of the Cabinet over-ruling a Committee proposal. In effect, the military and law-enforcement leaders, their ministers and the Prime Minister operate an inner cabinet that runs the government of South Africa.

Of course, this does have very tangible benefits. South Africa now has a clear and coherent voice within the country and in world forums. Decision-making in a rapidly changing situation of crisis is also considerably streamlined. However, critics argue that, because of its very close co-operation with the military, the Botha government is drifting towards becoming a totalitarian state. The criticism is realistic. As guerrilla activity and general restlessness among blacks continue to escalate, so must the Malan philosophy of 'total war' become the basic philosophy for South Africa's maintenance of the status quo. As Malan explains that philosophy, 'It means the formulation of national objectives in which all the community's resources are mustered and managed on a co-ordinated level to ensure survival. Every activity of the state must be seen and understood as a function of total war.'

While Malan and his defence chiefs will do what they can to influence the government to bring about a more liberal interpretation of apartheid within South Africa and thus blunt much of the propaganda appeal of the ANC, they will use every technique and stratagem in their armoury to minimize the military effectiveness of the guerrilla forces. In 1982, South Africa claimed to have killed 1,268 guerrillas, while losing only 77 of its own soldiers, and because of their tighter border security, thus far there has been very little ANC action in urban areas, and most guerrillas infiltrating from their bases over the northern borders have been captured within a few miles of entering South African territory.

However, there have been a few notable successes by the ANC, which managed to penetrate not only the tight border security screen but also the net placed around sensitive government installations. Although these attacks represent considerable propaganda coups, they achieve little in the way of significant damage. In fact, in its near seventy-year struggle against South Africa, neither the ANC nor its sister organization, the Pan-African Congress, (PAC) has managed to make a significant impact through guerrilla action.

Much of the efficiency of the South African security services must be placed at the door of Israel, for both army experts and specialists in counter-intelligence operations and interrogation from the Mossad have been based in South Africa in a permanent advisory capacity since 1976. Links between the Mossad and South Africa have always been very strong. A secret CIA analysis of Israel's foreign intelligence and security services, prepared in March 1979 and captured by Iranian students at the US embassy in Tehran, said, in part:

> Israeli liaison in Africa has varied considerably from country to country, depending on the exigencies of the situation. Israeli intelligence activities in Africa have usually been carried out under the cover of military and police training, arms sales to national military forces and aid and development programs. The Arab nations, in conjunction with the Organization of African Unity, have brought great pressure to bear on most African nations to break all formal ties with Israel. Despite the break in diplomatic relations between Israel and many African nations, the Israelis still maintain good intelligence liaison with the Kenyan service. In central Africa the Israelis are still active in Zaïre. In west Africa, the Israelis trained the Liberian Security Service and police. They also helped establish the Ghanaian Military Intelligence Service. In

southern Africa, the Israelis have a relationship with South African intelligence and security services.

For South Africa, such a relationship has obvious value. With the Mossad spanning the African political spectrum and wielding considerable covert influence as well as gathering excellent intelligence, the Israelis are a valuable ally. Their intelligence service has a high reputation which has been frequently used for long-term political gains, and at various times, the Mossad has co-operated with all the Western agencies as well as with Iran. Such unlikely partnerships have often paid considerable dividends. For example, during the Shah's reign, Israel maintained a full diplomatic staff in Tehran although without full embassy status. After the fall of the Shah, enough contacts had been made among the Khomeini regime to enable a mutually beneficial relationship to survive, and since the accession of the Ayatollah Khomeini, Israel has supplied the Iranian regime with arms in exchange for both cash and oil.

A similar trading agreement exists with South Africa. Israel and South Africa, as part of their expanding relationship, in 1976 agreed on a pooling of intelligence information. For South Africa, this meant access to Israel's unrivalled sources in the United States and Africa, while Israel had access to South Africa's monitoring operation at Silvermine. Silvermine is one of the world's most advanced communications centres, situated near Simonstown and established with technology supplied by the United States, Italy, West Germany and France, and its electronic surveillance system monitors the movements of all ships and aircraft within a huge area extending from west Africa to the South Pole and from South America to the Mozambique Channel.

Perhaps more important is the pooling of terrorism intelligence. When the Israelis pushed north into the Lebanon in June 1982, the initial thrust came as a complete surprise to the PLO. This had an immediate twofold impact: Israeli armed forces captured the cities of Tyre and Sidon with minimal loss of life and discovered a hoard of PLO documents. According to a very senior source in the Mossad, their haul was an unprecedented intelligence coup. The captured documents will take at least ten years to analyse and collate, but a preliminary search of the papers has revealed to the Israelis the degree of international co-operation that exists between different intelligence services of the PLO and other groups and the help that the PLO has given others, including the ANC. Also included in the haul were details of training, funding, equipment, safe houses and agents around the world. South Africa was an early recipient of all the information relating to terrorist activity that the Israelis had managed to sift out of the mass of captured information.

In Israel, there is a harmonious relationship between military intelligence and the other branches of the information-gathering network. Most Israeli intelligence and security personnel, especially on the policy and co-ordination level, realize that their very existence depends on an efficient intelligence community. In addition, most serving intelligence officers have been battle-hardened and have known one another for a long time, in both peace and war. This has so far not been the case in South Africa, and it is interesting that Botha has recently reorganized his intelligence network along Israeli lines to improve efficiency and cut inter-departmental rivalry.

In 1969, the CIA, then headed by James Angleton, helped South Africa set up the infamous Bureau of State Security (BOSS) under General Hendrik Van Den Bergh. In theory, BOSS was supposed to work alongside the security police who, until the early 1960s, had been almost entirely responsible for intelligence work aimed at countering the rising threat of black militancy. BOSS's initial successes in the early 1970s, achieved by heavy infiltration of the guerrilla movements followed by a wave of arrests, expulsions and imprisonments, forced the ANC, PAC and lesser groups to go underground or out of existence altogether. The success helped raise Van Den Bergh's prestige and power, particularly as he was a close confidant of the then Prime Minister, John Vorster. BOSS became so confident of its own immunity from interference that it enlarged its area of operations to include all aspects of state security – which was interpreted to involve members of the parliamentary opposition, the churches, the media and anyone else who might conceivably hold views that differed from those of Van Den Bergh or Vorster. In addition, much of the credit for South Africa's détente policy of the late 1960s must go to BOSS. Covert contacts made by their agents (with introductions furnished by the Mossad) resulted in dialogues between South Africa and Zambia, Liberia, the Ivory Coast, Ghana, the Malagasy Republic, Uganda, Malawi and the Central African Republic.

The intransigence of the South African government combined with the black South Africans' demand for 'one man, one vote' led to the collapse of détente, and BOSS's star began to sink. The failure to predict or counter the Soweto uprising, the disaster of the Muldergate scandal (*see* Chapter 7) and, above all, the change of prime minister that resulted, provided an opportunity for change. The new Prime Minister, P. W. Botha, had an intense dislike of the extremist policies carried out by BOSS under Vorster, which he viewed as counterproductive, and he lost no time in curbing the organization's power:

Van Den Bergh was fired and the intelligence agency renamed, first as the Directorate of National Security, and then (as now) the National Intelligence Service (NIS). A purge, similar to that carried out in the CIA under President Carter, followed. Many of the old guard departed with their leader and a new, younger element was brought in under the leadership of thirty-one-year-old Dr Neil Barnard.

Although the NIS remains largely responsible for external intelligence operations, it has nothing like the independence that BOSS had. Liaison is much closer with both the military and the police, with the SADF press officer handling all inquiries relating to intelligence. In addition, Dr Barnard now has to report to the State Security Committee.

The net result of all the changes has been to curb some of the wilder actions of South African intelligence and, at the same time, to improve its efficiency. It is hoped, for example, that there will be no repetition of Muldergate, which would not have been sanctioned under the Botha regime – but spying on ANC activities in Britain or the United States by NIS agents remains perfectly permissible.

Relations between the South Africans and Western government agencies are still very intimate. Senior military officials from the South African armed forces are now able to visit the United States officially and do so regularly, while co-operation between the intelligence services of the West and of South Africa remains remarkably close. There is a regular exchange of information, with the South Africans supplying the West with details of shipping movements, terrorist activity both in Africa and abroad and with hard intelligence from the Soviet Union where, perhaps surprisingly, South Africa has extremely good sources to rival the more conventional operations of the United States and Britain. Both the CIA and Britain's MI5 regularly carry out informal vetting of local residents at the request of the South African police or for the NIS. Such information exchanges might surprise some members of Western governments, but there remain strong factions in every intelligence service and all the armed forces of the West which believe that a strongly pro-West, white-ruled South Africa is essential to halt the advance of Communism in Africa and to secure the free flow of oil around the Cape of Good Hope.

While the activities of BOSS (and subsequently of the NIS) have contributed substantially to the counter-terrorist successes of the South African government, the guerrilla groups have had their successes, too. In particular, there has been a steady flow of guerrilla recruits crossing the border into Botswana, Mozambique and Angola and small numbers of trained and armed guerrillas do manage to evade the security forces and infiltrate South Africa.

For both blacks and whites in South Africa, the rise of the ANC or, more particularly, the ascendancy of black power is now viewed as almost inevitable. It is difficult to find anyone, either black or white, who does not accept that some form of radical transformation will come within a few years. The difference comes over the definition of 'few'. For some black rule will occur within the next five years, while the more cautious will talk of a slow change over the next twenty-five. The latter seems more likely.

The increase in support for the ANC has placed the government in a difficult position, for it must be seen by both black and white to be firmly in control and yet change must occur at a fast enough pace to convince the majority of blacks that their interests are best served by following the white establishment line. So far, this does appear to be working, and although there have been more visible signs of support for the ANC inside the country (public demonstrations, clandestine newspaper distribution, poster displays), there is little evidence of any sign of a popular revolution.

Such apathy is very frustrating for the ANC hierarchy and is very difficult to counter. In the Rhodesian war, the guerrillas won many willing volunteers but also overcame the lack of interest shown by the rural population by a ruthless programme of intimidation, indoctrination and kidnapping of potential recruits. In the end, this proved remarkably successful, particularly after the whites, who saw the end of white rule as a foregone conclusion, began to leave their farms. But there is no sign yet that the ANC are going to embark on a similar recruiting campaign among the blacks. What is much more likely is an intensified campaign of sabotage within South Africa. Indeed, at the end of 1982, ANC leaders based in Mozambique predicted an increase in the level of violence in the coming year. This prediction has been realized and 1983 saw a serious increase in violent actions. Also, for the first time the ANC appear to have decided to hit 'soft' civilian targets which, for example, resulted in explosions in Pretoria and Bloemfontein. Certainly this violence will continue to escalate over the next few years, and the low level of overt support that now exists for the ANC will increase, as will the numbers of young recruits flowing across the borders to the training camps. To meet the threat, and to pre-empt cross-border strikes by guerrillas into the highly vulnerable urban areas, the security forces will take the fight to the ANC bases in neighbouring countries.

From the beginning of the bush war in Namibia, Israeli counter-terrorist experts have been training the SADF and the South African police. In a two-way exchange, Israeli experts have visited border areas and passed on the benefit of their experience with the PLO in Israel. In addition, several hundred of the more senior members of the South African police have been to Israel to make a detailed study of the law-enforcement techniques there. It is hardly surprising, therefore, that South Africa has adopted many of Israel's tactics in countering the guerrilla threat.

The South Africans have learned two important lessons from their Israeli tutors in counter-insurgency warfare: the gathering of good intelligence from within guerrilla movements, and taking the initiative to force the guerrillas to fight on South Africa's terms on the guerrillas' territory. With twenty years of warning, and viewing the current escalation of the fighting as inevitable, the security services have had plenty of time to infiltrate the ANC up to a high level. While this has given the South Africans access to ANC long-term strategy, they have not been as successful in countering the small guerrilla gangs that infiltrate from their cross-border havens.

In the early years of the guerrilla war with the PLO, the Israelis decided that interception was not enough and that the fight had to be taken into the enemy's camp. This resulted in extensive commando operations, particularly in the Lebanon, aimed at both pre-empting PLO strikes and retaliating for guerrilla activity inside the Lebanon. These did not act as a complete deterrent, but the Israeli invasion of the Lebanon in 1982 seriously put the PLO back as a military force for the present. There remained the problem of isolated acts of terrorism, particularly those outside the borders of Israel.

The ascendancy of PLO chairman Yasser Arafat and his decision to pursue a diplomatic rather than a military solution to the problem of establishing a Palestinian state led to a notable decline in international terrorist incidents. Despite Israeli propaganda to the contrary, there is no doubt that Arafat was a very moderating influence on a movement that has always been wracked with dissension. However, the ruthless way in which the Israelis dealt with the PLO military arm has weakened Arafat's hold over the more militant groups that fall under the PLO umbrella, and both Israelis and Palestinians expect a serious escalation in international terrorism over the next few years.

Somewhat surprisingly, the ANC has not yet engaged in any international terrorism, apparently preferring to concentrate exclusively on targets within South Africa. This soft approach to terrorism is causing increasing dissatisfaction within the guerrilla movement, especially now that many of the young blacks who joined the ANC after Soweto have completed their training and have risen to positions of some authority within the ANC.

It is in the area of training that the Israelis have been able to help the South Africans monitor the ANC. According to Israeli intelligence, several hundred ANC members have been trained by the PLO either in the Lebanon or at training camps in South Yemen. The Mossad has managed to infiltrate the camps to an astonishing degree and has unfailingly passed back relevant data to the South African authorities, giving the latter early warning of changes in strategy and tactics as well as detailed lists of recruits, their specialities, units and even their performance on the training courses. South African sources indicate that such Israeli information on the ANC will severely hamper any planned action of the guerrilla group for at least eighteen months while they attempt to reorganize to counter the threat posed by the Israeli intelligence. This may well have pre-empted any pressure from the more militant ANC members to take the war abroad.

South Africa owes much to Israel for its successes against the ANC. It is a (to them) fortunate coincidence that both countries have a very similar experience of guerrilla warfare. Israel, with its early background of the fight against the British in Palestine followed by its long-running conflict with the PLO, probably has more knowledge than any other nation in the art of counter-insurgency warfare.

Although any murder of a Jew by a Palestinian in Israel is considered a barbarous act and is usually punished savagely, it is the threat posed by subversion that is considered more worrying. The political assessment suggests that, as long as the Arab population under Israeli control remains quiescent, guerrilla attacks by the PLO and their satellites will continue to be annoying, often tragic, but no serious threat to the body ·politic. However, should the Palestinian population begin to mobilize *en masse*, then the situation would be very different. There are over one million Arabs living on the occupied West Bank; even a small percentage of them organized into an armed civil-disobedience campaign would offer a very serious threat to stability in Israel.

A secret study made by the US State Department in late 1982 suggested that there would be no real settlement of the Palestinian problem, or the prospect of the Palestinians being given a state, in the foreseeable future. Instead, the specialists looking at the problem surmised that as the next generation of young Palestinians who have been educated under the Israeli administration reach adulthood, they will realize that they will never gain the wealth, stature and freedom of Israeli citizens, and so they will become more vociferous and more united. At the same time the only serious voice of the Palestinians, the PLO, will be reduced in power and influence. The theory then runs that a situation will arise similar to that of Algeria during its civil war which culminated in independence from the French in 1961. Of course, both the US government and others elsewhere in the world maintain that a peaceful settlement of the Palestinian question is possible, but the pessimists suggest that nothing short of a bloody civil war will persuade the Israelis to hand over any part of the state to the Arabs.

Such vulnerability to internal subversion has led the Israelis to develop what is perhaps the most sophisticated border surveillance system existing anywhere in the world. As Amiram Nir of the Centre for Strategic Studies at Tel Aviv University has pointed out:

> A category of special measures has been designed to facilitate the prevention of infiltration by small forces intent on carrying out acts of terror or limited military actions. This is 'blind' prevention in which the preventive means passively 'await' the intruder and are operated at the point of infiltration without pre-identifying him.
>
> These measures include: anti-personnel minefields scattered along the border; varying configurations of barbed-wire fencing congruent with the minefields; night ambushes (aided by special night-vision equipment) laid at locations where infiltration is made possible and even probable by the lie of the land and the enemy's tactical logic; and motorized recce units patrolling all border sectors day and night.

In addition, Israel has installed an electronic fence along the whole length of its border. While this does not prevent infiltration, a guerrilla has to cut – or at least touch – the fence to get through the border, and electronic circuits within the fence relay the information to nearby army posts which can swiftly mount an interception. To complement the fixed ordnance, mobile patrols allied with regular border posts manned with anti-personnel radar and night sights cover the whole length of the border. These posts and patrols both act as an immediate deterrent and provide a very swift reaction to any discovered penetration. In recent years, it has become extraordinarily difficult for Palestinian guerrillas to cross the Israel/Lebanon border and greater efforts have been made to approach by sea. As a result of their border protection measures (in some ways similar to those in place along the Berlin Wall), Israeli defence strategists feel they have managed to undermine severely the military threat of the PLO.

South Africa's problems are very similar to those of Israel. There is the threat of considerable cross-border infiltration from Angola and Botswana in the north, Zimbabwe in the north-east and Mozambique in the north-east and east. All, at one time or another, have acted as hosts to anti-South African guerrillas, but at the moment, Angola and Mozambique alone provide all the infrastructure, including bases, supply routes and training facilities, that is essential for a growing army. Zimbabwe does offer some help to the ANC, but so far this has been kept at a very low level, while Botswana tries (so far fairly successfully) to remain quietly neutral. There has, however, been an increase in the number of guerrillas using Botswana as a transit country to South Africa, since the tiny 3,000-strong Botswana army is in no effective position to enforce the normal entry and exit requirements of visitors.

As part of the informal arrangements that existed before 1976 and the formal military and economic agreements that came about after that date, Israel has taken a prominent role in setting up an effective border-policing unit for the South Africans. Israeli security specialists have been permanently based in South Africa on secondment for at least ten years, and at the present time, more than fifty are working along the borders and advising the South Africans. This has not been an example of simple philanthropy. As a result of Israeli advice, millions of dollars in orders have been placed with Israeli firms, and the South African border is now equipped with Israeli fencing, night sights, microwave protection and detection systems, electronic fences, barbed wire and anti-personnel mines.

Mirroring the advice of the Israeli advisers, in March 1978 a report prepared by Kobie Coetsee, then the country's Deputy Minister of Defence and now a justice minister, recommended that South Africa build a 'ring of steel' around the country's border areas. Again in an exact copy of the Israeli system, the fence and the strategic bases would all be linked into the military network to enable a swift reaction to any infiltration. Work on much of the fence has now been completed and, in the areas where it is possible to travel, the fifteen-foot-high fence is clearly visible with a *cordon sanitaire* running alongside. Privately, the South African military has conceded that much of the border area, particularly near Angola and Mozambique, is riddled with anti-personnel mines manufactured in Israel. Similar mines, used by the Argentinians, have proved difficult to detect and remove in the Falkland Islands. In addition, South Africa has installed an intricate network of detection systems, including ground sonar which is activated by the vibration of people walking or running over the ground, microwave which detects movement, and infra-red which enables the security forces to see in the dark. All this equipment has been supplied by the Israelis, with the exception of some radio and electronics which have been manufactured locally.

However, the cocooning of all the border areas is an enormous task that will considerably stretch the resources of the armed forces who are already engaged in a running war in Namibia. It was inevitable, therefore, that the government has concentrated its resources in the most common areas of guerrilla infiltration and has relied on random patrols and reliable intelligence to sweep up those guerrillas who choose to come into South Africa the hard way.

This policy has not pleased many of those who live in the border areas, and over one thousand farms have been abandoned in the past five years, particularly those on the border with Botswana (although this is primarily because of economics, not fear). This situation is causing considerable alarm to the South Africans, who are aware that, in Rhodesia, the farmers and their 'Agric Alert' communications system played a vital role in giving early warning of guerrilla movements. As Hendrik Schoeman, a former agriculture minister, has pointed out, because of the farming exodus from the region, 'A terrorist can walk from the Limpopo river through to Pietersburg without having to set foot on a farm occupied by whites.' (Pietersburg is the industrial capital of northern South Africa and lies 100 miles south of the border with Zimbabwe.)

Such vulnerability, which is increasing week by week, is obviously extremely worrying for the South Africans. The Coetsee report also considered the question of the white exodus. Coetsee suggested that South Africa adopt the 'strategic hamlet' concept – used successfully by the British in Malaya but which was a failure for the United States in Vietnam – whereby government forces control the local population by shepherding them into protected villages. In Zimbabwe, this system had isolated the black population from the influence of guerrillas but had also alienated the very villagers it was aimed to protect, because it interfered with farming, interrupted the normal progress of village life and put a tremendous strain on the economy which had to pay for policing and for the additional food supplies which the villagers were unable to produce for themselves.

As a result of the Coetsee recommendations, in May 1980 Prime Minister Botha announced new steps to improve border security, including the formation of black regional units at strategic points, the formation of a number of area headquarters for counter-insurgency and the creation of strongpoints on a decentralized basis. Four ethnic battalions have been formed:

111 Battalion: Swazis trained at Amsterdam, Eastern Transvaal.

112 Battalion: Vendas trained at Madimbo, Venda.

113 Battalion: Shangaans trained at Impala, near Phalaborwam, Eastern Transvaal.

121 Battalion: Zulus trained at Jozini, Northern Natal.

Although there is no doubt that the formation of the ethnic battalions will go some way to increasing the policing of border areas, the South African government realizes that, without additional measures, guerrilla infiltration will increase from a trickle to a flood.

A research paper prepared by a strategy expert in 1979, but kept secret until the beginning of 1983, predicted that, by 1984, a major assault will have been launched on border farms by the ANC and other guerrillas and that 80 per cent of all whites killed could comprise farmers and their families. Certainly, that was the initial experience in Zimbabwe, and there is no reason to doubt that the tactics used in that successful guerrilla war will be used in South Africa. The research paper, drawn up to investigate the market potential for security devices in the Transvaal border areas, stated that the bush war will develop in the same way as in Rhodesia: the guerrillas will cross from neighbouring states to infiltrate farming areas, starting by intimidation of farm labour in the north and east of the Transvaal and northern Natal, and then escalating to destruction of property and farms. The black independent and self-governing homelands would thus be a target for attacks, with the homeland areas becoming possible bases for the guerrillas.

Much of the exodus from the white farms has occurred because farmers are finding it very difficult to make a profit in South Africa's depressed economy. There has been no real evidence of intimidation so far, and in bush wars, farmers generally prove to be the most obstinate of all groups in resisting guerrilla activity. None the less, on the Zimbabwe border, 39 per cent of border farms are lying idle, on the Botswana border 43 per cent and on the Mozambique border 14 per cent. These figures are rising monthly.

The government is in a dilemma, as it is anxious to encourage the development of black homelands, many of which take away farmland from whites, but also to ensure that white farmers maintain a prominent presence along the border. As a result, the government has offered farmers money as an inducement to stay, but both the offers and the response have been very patchy and have done little to stem the exodus. As more and more land is turned over to the blacks in the form of homelands, so the security problems will increase. The homelands are now allowed to form their own armies (and most of them are doing so) but South Africa does maintain control over security, and the worries over guerrilla infiltration remain the same.

However, experts from Israel are using their considerable experience in establishing settlements in sensitive areas to help the homelands in their agricultural developments, increase food production and do something about the security problem. In 1967, when Israel first occupied the West Bank, the settlement question became central to the government's strategic thinking. The result was a series of armed forts in border areas that made infiltration by guerrillas more difficult and provided a first line of defence against any conventional attack.

In the mid-1960s, the government of Prime Minister Eshkol decided to establish communities with as few as forty families, generally composed of religious zealots who were enthusiastic about moving to a high-risk security area because they saw the move as a return to their natural heritage. This settlement programme was expanded under Begin in order to prevent the establishment of a Palestinian state on the West Bank. For every settlement that springs up, the less likely is a negotiated agreement for handing over to the Palestinians a region that is increasingly populated by Jews. No Israeli government is going to be able to justify the existence of a Palestinian government ruling over Jewish settlers, while the economic and political costs of settlement repatriation seem prohibitive. In addition, the more settlements that are in place, the easier it will be to defend the occupied territories. Those that have sprung up so far are uniformly ugly, some of the greatest architectural monstrosities of the twentieth century in a region that has one of the finest traditions of building in the world. However, they are all functional, with high walls, generally constructed on hills with a wide field of fire and an easily defended perimeter. There is nothing in the settlements that will help to integrate the Jews with the Arab community. Indeed, the fortress-like construction will only serve to heighten the divisions that exist and further the impression of ruler and ruled, rather than of one society.

The situation is rather different in South Africa. A nucleus of hard-core, right-wing Afrikaners exists which might form a basis for a white settlement policy, but this would be directly opposed to the current policy of doing everything possible to win over the Africans who might possibly be influenced by the guerrilla movement. In a synthesis of the needs of both the military strategists and the government psychologists, the Israelis have been doing their bit for the past eight years to try and solve the problem for South Africa.

Under a joint project between the Israeli military, the Ministry of Agriculture and local youth movements, Israelis have been training thousands of young black people in Swaziland, Botswana and the homeland of Bophuthatswana to establish their own settlements in rural areas. (This is in addition to a $45 million Israeli investment in Bophuthatswana agriculture announced in 1981.) The scheme is modelled on the Israeli *Nahal* (an acronym for 'fighting and pioneering youth') which, in 1948, pioneered Israeli agricultural development through the establishment of settlements. Nahal gave young Jewish immigrants three months' basic army training, followed by six months on a *kibbutz*, then a further six months in the army. At the end of that time, they were provided with sufficient funding from the Israeli government to go into the wilderness and establish their own *kibbutz*.

The policy in South Africa, Swaziland and Botswana has been very successful and with the aid of Israeli and South African cash, all the homelands and black nations under South African control have experienced an explosion in agricultural development, an expansion of their citizen reserve and an early warning of any serious guerrilla activity.

While Israel has helped to train a buffer army and security force to protect the heartland of South Africa, it has not been able to do much about instability and Communist subversion in the rest of Africa. The apartheid government desperately needs support in the OAU and in the UN in their fight against this, and such support has far greater credibility if it comes direct from black Africa.

Fortunately, South Africa and Israel have virtually identical perceptions of the problem. In December 1981, the then Defence Minister, Ariel Sharon, spoke of 'Israel's strategic problem in the 1980s', listing three major factors that would influence Israel's security: the national ideology of radical Arab regimes, the PLO, and the Soviet policy of expansionism.

Sharon argued that Soviet expansionism presented a threat to the security of the Israeli nation, particularly as he considered the USSR to be a primary influence – both political and military – on the PLO. Sharon also expressed concern that Soviet influence was rapidly growing in black Africa, a region that was a prospective major sphere of influence for Israel. In his speech, Sharon suggested that Israel had to take the initiative in countering Soviet actions in Africa and the Middle East. Central to this policy was a strengthening of links with the United States and South Africa as well as the reopening of diplomatic relations with black Africa.

Sharon's speech struck exactly the right note in Pretoria, as an open expression of what both countries have privately felt for a number of years. The speech was also the first public affirmation of a major Israeli drive to win new friends in black Africa, a drive that had been in the minds of both Israelis and South Africans since that unhappy post-1973 period when all of black Africa, under pressure from the Arabs, severed relations with Israel.

The campaign launched by Sharon has been successful, and Israel is now stronger in Africa than it was before 1973 and its influence is growing daily. The black African states of Zaïre, Kenya, Ghana, the Ivory Coast, Gabon, Nigeria, Lesotho, Swaziland, Liberia and Malawi now all have close relations with Israel, involving both military assistance and agricultural programmes. What is extraordinary about this growing strategic alliance is that it has taken place in tandem with increasing public links between Israel and South Africa.

The Sharon speech followed the signing, on 30 November 1981, of a Memorandum of Understanding between the United States and Israel which, for the first time, would allow Israel to supply military aid to black Africa, paid for by the United States. A new and interesting strategic equation had thus been established, the effects of which are only just beginning to appear. The United States is now able to use Israel, through aid money, as a vehicle for influence in Africa. The Memorandum, was, in effect, a new subsidy for the Israelis and formal permission to begin equipping and training sympathetic black African armies. Although Israel had already been providing arms and training to some states, there was now virtually no limit to the power the Israelis might wield in selling guns to buy influence.

However, two weeks after the Memorandum was signed, Prime Minister Begin annexed the Golan Heights, and in retaliation and under pressure from world opinion, President Reagan suspended the MOU. This formal censure was a useful public-relations exercise – but in reality, business has continued very much as usual, with the United States supplying aid to Africa and to Israel as well as military sales to Israel, and doing nothing to stop Israel selling arms or equipment to black Africa.

When the twenty-five black African countries severed diplomatic relations in 1973, commercial contacts with them remained and have steadily increased; there are now some 4,000 Israeli experts working in African countries, and the value of contracts has increased from $30 million in 1973 to $100 million today. But these commercial deals are small compared with potential arms exports, and for some years Israel has been trying to get a bigger share of the lucrative arms market in combination with a firming of political relationships.

One of the places in which Israel managed to keep a tenuous toehold after 1973 was Zaïre. General Mobutu Sese Seko, the country's head of state, has long had an affection for Israel. Before independence, Mobutu was a staff-sergeant in the Belgian colonial army and was sent to Israel for parachute training. The friends he made on that trip remained with him when he was made chief of staff after independence, and it was Mobutu who asked Israel to set up an efficient secret service for Zaïre (as well as for Israeli agricultural experts to ensure the smooth running of his private estates). That secret service is now one of the most feared in Africa, and Mobutu without doubt is one of the most corrupt and despotic leaders on the continent. However, Mobutu is also staunchly pro-West and anti-Communist, and his vast country occupies a crucial position in the centre of Africa and has access to vast mineral wealth. All this has made it very attractive to the Israelis, while for the United States and the South Africans, there is the additional bonus in that Zaïre's borders to the south and west run alongside Angola.

In November 1981, General Sharon went on a rapid tour of five African states: Zaïre, Gabon, Togo, Nigeria and the Central African Republic. Mobutu and Sharon took a two-day cruise on the Congo river and discussed the problems of Soviet expansion in Africa, and they also agreed that Zaïre would reopen diplomatic relations with Israel as soon as the withdrawal from Sinai was complete.

The foundations of Sharon's trip to Zaïre had been laid by David Kimche, Director General of Israel's Foreign Ministry. But while Kimche was particularly anxious about the reopening of diplomatic relations, Sharon was much more interested in drumming up some arms business. The official announcements of the meeting did not mention any discussion of security matters, but Sharon had taken with him Arye Ganger, the man in overall charge of overseas weapons sales, and a broad-ranging agreement for future arms deals was signed. Sharon finished his trip with a visit to South Africa; he reported on his apparent success to the Botha government, and then made a tour of SADF positions on the border with Namibia.

As a result of his trip, during his stay in Washington the following month to sign the Memorandum with the Reagan administration, Sharon made a special plea for more arms to be given to South Africa. He argued that South Africa needed more modern weapons to combat Soviet-supplied guerrillas and that the West should be doing more to help such an important country in a vital region. The Memorandum, signed by Sharon and US Defense Secretary Caspar Weinberger, was a clear indication that the United States agreed with much of what the Israelis had been saying. While the Memorandum may not have referred directly to arms sales to South Africa, Israel's ability to operate freely on the continent could do nothing but help bolster the South African government.

Sharon returned to Zaïre in December 1982 to finalize arrangements for the arms deals. This time, he took with him Brigadier General Avraham Tamir who was deputed to handle the detailed arrangements. Under the agreements so far signed, Israel will hand on to Zaïre those arms captured from the PLO that have not already been sold to Iran in exchange for oil. These are being supplied free as a gesture of goodwill and mark the start of an Israeli-designed five-year plan to modernize the Zaïre armed forces. In addition, Zaïre will purchase $8 million worth of military equipment to outfit the presidential guard, and this will be followed by purchases for the remainder of the armed forces for an undisclosed amount.

For South Africa, perhaps the most important aspect of the Israel–Zaïre treaty was Sharon's agreement to organize the retraining of the 12,000-strong Kamanyola Brigade, based in Shaba province on the borders with Angola. Ostensibly this army will be used to deter Katangese exiles from invading as they did in 1977 and 1978, but others believe that the retraining programme is all part of a plan, orchestrated by the United States, Israel and South Africa, to encircle and destabilize the Angolan government. Nguza Karl-I-Bond, leader of the Brussels-based Front for the Restoration of Congolese Democracy, has claimed that there is a 'secret plan involving Zaïre, Israel and South Africa'. While there is little solid evidence of such a conspiracy, it is true that a strong pro-Western military influence in moderate Africa would be of considerable benefit to all concerned.

Both the United States and South Africa are preoccupied by the estimated 20,000 Cubans in Angola and look forward to their early departure. There seems little prospect of the Cubans doing this voluntarily, but the beleaguered government in Luanda, with an Israeli-trained army in the north and a South Africa-trained army in the south and east (Jonas Savimbi's UNITA), may have to compromise.

Sharon again visited Zaïre in January 1983 to satisfy himself that the retraining programme was working smoothly. Mobutu and Sharon seem to get on exceptionally well; on this occasion they went fishing on the Congo and Sharon, with unusual diplomacy, caught only two fish to Mobutu's three. Mobutu pronounced himself well satisfied with the progress that has so far been made. There would have to have been fairly comprehensive results from the Israeli involvement in Zaïre's affairs, as the renewing of relations – particularly the opening of an embassy in Tel Aviv in 1982 – has cost Zaïre dear.

Predictably, the Arabs were furious at Zaïre's change of position, and Saudi Arabia and Oman immediately broke off diplomatic relations. All Arab aid, valued at $36.8 million in 1981, was cut off, and any other country which opens diplomatic relations with Israel was threatened with the same fate. With foreign debts estimated at $4.8 billion and an economy in tatters because of widespread corruption and incompetence, Zaïre badly needed all the money it could get.

However, the threat of the withdrawal of oil money is not as powerful as it once was. The Reagan administration is determined at almost any cost to prevent Soviet expansion in Africa and, while its covert activities may be restricted by Congress, there is still considerable leeway in the budget coffers. In May 1982, after Zaïre had recognized Israel, the Senate Foreign Relations Committee cut $25 million from the President's requested $36.3 million budget aid for Zaïre as a penalty for Mobutu's appalling human rights and corruption record. However, at the same time, it altered the Reagan request for Israel ($500 million in grants, $1.2 billion in loans) and made the grant and the loan figures equal, $850 million each. The senators then added $125 million to the President's request of $525 million for 'security-related economic grants to the Israelis'. In the past, the Israelis have often been used as conduits for US cash to countries whose identity needed to be disguised. It is difficult to believe that President Mobutu, who is renowned for both his greed and his paranoia, would have easily given up millions of dollars in Arab aid. What is more logical is that the United States government promised him that his aid would be increased if he reopened diplomatic relations with Israel, and that aid has now been paid, using the Israeli government as middleman.

With Zaïre having been the first to take the plunge, later followed by Liberia, other countries are expected to announce the resumption of diplomatic relations with Israel: these include the Central African Republic, the Ivory Coast and Kenya. The condemnation that greeted the opening of a Zaïrois embassy in Tel Aviv was not echoed by any of these nations. Kenya's response was typical: an editorial in the Kenyan *Standard* welcomed the establishment of the embassy and said that other African nations should follow suit as Israel had been 'a good and dependable friend of Africa'. The military takeover in January 1984 by Nigerian army officers is likely to prove of considerable benefit to both Israel and South Africa. Although the government of ousted President Shagari had been particularly vociferous in its opposition to the Pretoria government, the military has very close relations with Israel, with many of the general staff having visited Tel Aviv in the past year.

Immediately after the Zaïre decision became known, Israeli Foreign Minister Shamir told friends that he confidently ·expected more announcements in a similar vein 'within months'. In fact, this has not yet happened, but the delay has largely been Israel's doing. The annexation of the Golan Heights followed by the invasion of the Lebanon made the climate for a thaw in relations particularly difficult. However, officials in the Israeli foreign ministry remain quite confident that they are well on their way to becoming one of the most influential nations in Africa, a state of affairs which will certainly please both South Africa and the United States.

6 The Arms Business

Officially, Israel no longer has any dealings with the South African military following the UN arms embargo in 1977. However, defence officials, including the then Foreign Minister Moshe Dayan, insisted that Israel would honour its contractual obligations with South Africa. This insistence on honouring commitments has been a major part of the sales pitch of Israeli arms dealers. The Israelis themselves have often been hit by political embargoes interfering with arms sales: during the 1973 war, for example, Britain refused to supply Israel with shells for its Centurion tanks, despite written contracts to the contrary. Thus Israel, with its rapidly growing arms exports to the Third World, is justifiably able to say that contracts are always fulfilled, whatever the political circumstances – a major selling point to many insecure world leaders.

This was amply illustrated during the Falklands War of 1982 when Britain eventually reoccupied the Falkland Islands which had been captured by the Argentinian government of General Galtieri. During a bitter diplomatic campaign, mainly waged through the UN in New York, Britain managed to win the support of the West (particularly that of the United States) and the neutrality of the Eastern bloc. Argentina had serious problems from the outset in obtaining sufficient spare parts to keep its air force flying. Under a series of wide-ranging military contracts, Israel had already supplied two squadrons of Dagger jet fighters, four Dabur-class patrol boats, Gabriel ship-to-ship missiles, Shafrir air-to-air missiles, mines, 'smart' bombs and more general ordnance. Even before their losses began to mount, the Galtieri junta contacted a number of countries in a desperate attempt to bolster their armoury. During the last week in May, they contacted twelve countries including Israel, South Africa, the Netherlands, Spain, West Germany, France, Venezuela, Peru, Brazil and Romania, specifically requesting Gabriel missiles, Exocet missiles, Mirage spares (which fit the Dagger), long-range fuel tanks, 'smart' bombs, bombs for the A4 fighter and aircraft ammunition. Of all the countries approached, only two, South Africa and Israel, were willing to co-operate. Such has been the close relationship between Israel and South Africa that there is an almost exact duplication in arms, and either country could have filled Argentina's shopping list quite happily.

Aside from fulfilling existing contracts, there was an additional incentive for both Israel and South Africa to comply with Argentina's request. In the early 1960s, when the British Labour government of Harold Wilson allowed the Simonstown agreement with South Africa to lapse, the South Africans secretly formed the South Atlantic Treaty Organization (SATO). Israel, Taiwan, Argentina, Brazil, Paraguay and Uruguay all joined South Africa in the organization, which had the full approval of the United States. Although billed as a mutual defence pact along the lines of NATO, the Americans have always seen SATO as an alliance of Latin America and the West against the USSR, and the two most powerful armies at either end of the African continent against the incursions of Communism. Relations among the members of SATO have grown increasingly close in the last ten years, and the Falklands crisis was the first time the treaty had been called on in time of war. Both South Africa and Israel fulfilled their obligations.

British intelligence was naturally most anxious that no spares should get through to Argentina, as the vulnerability of the British naval task force was fully recognized by the Prime Minister and the chiefs of staff. In an operation reminiscent of MI6 thirty years before, British intelligence called for a worldwide dragnet to try to ensure that no arms slipped through to their enemy. With the aid of the CIA, they were able to track down a number of arms movements but whereas thirty years ago violent deterrent activity might have been permissible, political considerations ruled out any such move in 1982. In a solution that must have been anathema to the old guard in MI6, the aid of the press was enlisted, and a careful leak to the British media was judged to be the most effective way of dealing with the problem. Although it was too late to deal with the arms that had already slipped through, the publicity was such that both South Africa and Israel said that they had stopped shipments to Argentina until after the war. British intelligence has proved, however, that both countries continued to' supply ammunition, Gabriel missiles, spares for the Dagger aircraft and bombs for the A4s during the conflict. Both have officially denied this, but unofficial sources in South Africa have confirmed that the allegations are quite correct.

The British say that four Israeli arms dealers, named as Eli,

Dimayor, Gitron and Rotem, were involved. In a typical trip, a Boeing 727 freighter belonging to Peruvian Airlines arrived in Lima, Peru, on 24 May 1982, having come from Tel Aviv via the Canaries and Manaos in Brazil. There had been two complete crews on board the aircraft so that they could alternate during the journey and thus eliminate the need for long layovers. On arrival in Lima, the aircraft went directly to Fawcett's parking bay, some distance from the main terminal, where it was surrounded by armed guards. There was only one cargo, consisting of fourteen cylinders, each in two halves, bolted together lengthwise like a cigar box. Each cylinder had a diameter of 1·5 metres and was approximately 4·5 metres long, exactly the size of Gabriel missiles. The cargo was unloaded and put aboard an Aerolineas Argentinas aircraft which took off with the security guards on board, heading for Argentina. There were several other similar flights. Another airline, Cargo Lux which has Libyan backing, was also alleged to have been involved and was reported to have flown out of Johannesburg, loaded down with Gabriel missiles and Mirage spares.

While the South Africans continue to deny their involvement in the Falklands War, the Israelis have admitted that they did honour some existing contracts. Ariel Sharon has said that Israel refused to honour Britain's request to halt deliveries to Buenos Aires because of the former's desire to be seen in Latin America as 'a reliable supplier'.

This philosophy of 'sales under any circumstances' is naturally not limited to Latin America, although the Falklands War did provide a useful illustration of the concept in action. If Israel was not put off by a war which isolated Argentina against the full strength of the Western powers, it is hardly likely that it would feel obliged to follow an embargo imposed by the UN, an organization that both Israel and South Africa despise as a tool of the Third World and the Eastern bloc.

The UN's 1977 Resolution 418 called on all member states to immediately cease providing South Africa with arms, ammunition, military vehicles and equipment as well as new licences for manufacturing armaments. It also called on all countries to 'review' existing licences with South Africa, with a view to terminating them. Although Israel agreed to comply – aside from existing contracts – there is ample evidence that arms suppliers have continued to operate uninterrupted since that time, although the official denials continue. Aside from these, there has been a moral response used as a back-up by senior Israeli officials both publicly and privately: the argument runs that, while countries have been banned from selling arms to South Africa because of alleged human rights violations by the white government, the United States and her Western allies have continued to supply arms to countries such as Chile where there are daily abuses of human rights, so why should South Africa be singled out?

The UN resolution may appear clear-cut on paper, but it is full of loopholes that governments and armaments manufacturers have been quick to exploit. While countries such as Britain and the United States do have lists of specific items that are prohibited for export to South Africa, the items vary according to the political inclinations of each administration. It is perfectly understandable that governments will, from time to time, be motivated by political expediency on broad strategic considerations rather than by a purely moral distaste for apartheid, which is what the UN resolution is based on. No government, however moralistic, can avoid being pragmatic on occasion, and pragmatism, like most aspects of political judgement, can be interpreted with an almost infinite degree of flexibility. It is not surprising, therefore, that there have been widespread abuses of the UN embargo involving most of the major Western powers, including the United States, France, Britain, Italy and West Germany. In addition, a growing number of countries, such as Brazil and Taiwan, have appeared on the arms manufacturing scene which are more anxious to make their arms industry profitable than they are to comply with a UN arms embargo.

There is no doubt that there is a powerful lobby working on behalf of South Africa in the West (*see* Chapter 7), and such support is based mainly on a wish to counter Communism rather than on any feelings in favour of apartheid. South Africa has very successfully emphasized the growing spread of left-wing regimes in Africa and has put itself forward as the only loyal friend of the West of any strategic consequence remaining in the southern half of the continent. Such an argument has won a great deal of sympathy and, allied with the considerable profit to be made in the arms business, there is a powerful motive for continuing to sell to South Africa whatever it requires to modernize and improve its armed forces.

Periodically, arms-smuggling cases are brought to light and prosecuted, but there seems to be little enthusiasm for the task among enforcement agencies. One less well-known case illustrates the problems of enforcing any arms embargo. On 3 April 1980, the Italian socialist deputy Falco Accame, an ex-naval officer, raised several questions in Parliament concerning government controls on arms exports. Initially, he queried a government statement issued on 18 March in which the Italian government declared: 'Since 1972, following the adoption of Resolution 311 in the UN, Italy has rigorously applied the arms embargo to South Africa.' Although the

1972 resolution was not mandatory, Italy claimed to have abided by its recommendations and by the mandatory embargo imposed in 1977. However, Accame pointed out, the South Africans themselves had announced publicly in their arms trade magazine *Interconair* (January 1980) that they had obtained weapons from Italy via Israel. Accame also described how the Italians had supplied guns to South Africa via France, as well as torpedoes via an Italian front company, and plans for Oto Melara guns and torpedoes through the same front company via India.

In a further question in the Italian parliament on 17 September 1980, Accame asked the government to explain why the guns manufactured at the Oto Melara plant at La Spezia were sold without end-user certificates. (Under international law, all weapons have to be sold with a certificate indicating the final destination of the product. This is supposed to cut down illegal shipments of arms and to facilitate Customs examinations; however, forgery of end-user certificates is widespread and the provisions are often ignored.)

The article published in *Interconair* and written by Julius Kroner was headlined 'A Navy for South Africa'. It argued that, since South Africa is defending the Cape route for the benefit of the West, it should be allowed to equip its navy by buying from Western countries. The article added:

> . . . Luckily we had and still have friends who, possibly secretly, are glad to supply us with the items we need or, far more simply, like making good deals. Thanks to the friendship which binds us to Israel, a friendship strengthened by the fact that we are seen, both as South Africans and Israelis, pretty badly by the rest of the world, we have succeeded in creating a nucleus of modern ships based on fast-attack and missile craft derived from the Israeli Reshef.

While the Reshef is an Israeli vessel, the guns on it are Italian. The Oto Melara 76-mm single-barrel gun is designed for use on ships of any type from hydrofoils upwards, and is one of the most advanced of its type in the world. When the Italians first supplied them to the Israelis, the guns were adapted specially to handle shore bombardment; subsequently a modified fire control unit was introduced, enabling the gun to track and hit surface targets as well as engaging incoming aircraft in line of sight. When the Israelis allowed the South Africans to produce the Reshef under licence in Durban, it was agreed with the Italians that they would supply the armaments via Israel. In his article, Kroner added, 'It is well known that in business there are infinite ways . . .' but he was not getting anyone into trouble when he said that 'thanks to a few friends, the Italian firms were able to sell equipment we were interested in to some intermediaries who then transferred it to us.'

The smuggling of the arms was in flagrant violation of the UN embargo and was part of an international operation that has gone on virtually unchecked for the past five years. South Africa now has one of the most modern forces in the world designed for counter-insurgency warfare and, while there are certainly some gaps in its armaments inventory, the general high level of sophistication can be accounted for by the ineffectual nature of UN embargoes and the refusal of member states to adhere to either the spirit or letter of UN resolutions.

Although it is generally the West that gets the bad press for repeated breaches of the UN arms embargo, the Eastern bloc has also been heavily involved in supplying arms to South Africa. The matter is understandably highly sensitive, since the Soviet Union and other members of the Warsaw Pact have all, at one time or another, supplied liberation groups in Africa. At the present time, the USSR, Czechoslovakia and Bulgaria are all supplying arms and munitions to SWAPO in Namibia and to the Angolan and the Mozambique governments.

However, what is not generally appreciated is that Communist arms have also been reaching the South African government regularly – arms that are mostly employed either by UNITA fighting against the Angolan government or by the army of the Mozambique National Resistance which is waging a guerrilla campaign inside Mozambique. For example, between 1976 and 1980, the South African government received five large consignments of arms from Bulgaria varying in value from $8 million to over $20 million. The deals involved people at the highest levels of Bulgarian political life, and it is certain that none of the arms could have been shipped without the full approval of the Soviet government. Charles Canfield, the South African who originally dreamed up the deal, is now back in Pretoria working for Armscor, and no one has ever been censured for involvement in the affair.

There is a curious ambivalence about South Africa's relations with the Eastern bloc. In public, the Pretoria government maintains that South Africa is the last bastion in southern Africa fighting the Communist menace; in private, the Soviet Union is one of the country's biggest trading partners. South Africa markets the entire diamond production of the USSR, and there are regular meetings between them to discuss the future of gold on the international market. At the same time, there is no doubt that the Soviets are doing everything they can to expand their sphere of influence on the African

continent, and this would naturally include the overthrow of the South
African government to establish a pro-Soviet black one.

South Africa's nervousness of the USSR's intentions was amply
illustrated in January 1983 when Commodore Dieter Gerhardt of the
Simonstown naval base and his wife were arrested and charged with
spying for the Soviet Union. Gerhardt was in charge of the dockyard
repair facility and had access to the most sensitive intelligence in the
South African armed forces, all of which he presumably passed to his
Soviet masters. The press in the West, and in South Africa, reported
the arrest and speculated that Gerhardt may have given the USSR
details of contingency plans for the West to use South African port
facilities in the event of an East–West confrontation. This may well
have been true, but the major concern about Gerhardt's successes lay
elsewhere – in Tel Aviv.

Hurried meetings of the Israeli defence staff were called immediately following Gerhardt's arrest, in an attempt to assess the damage that
had been done to Israel. The conclusion was that Gerhardt's spying
may well have been a devastating coup against Israel. Security within
the Israeli defence industry and in the armed forces is very tight. There
have been occasional spying successes by the Arabs or by the Eastern
bloc – the USSR does not actually conduct any espionage activities in
Israel; the East Germans do it on their behalf – but these have been
concentrated on isolated events (monitoring radio traffic or discovering the design of a new missile) and have been of strictly limited value.
However, because of Israel's extremely close relations with South
Africa, the government in Tel Aviv believes that Gerhardt supplied
the Soviets with details of strategy and tactics as well as with
information on all the arms that Israel has delivered to South Africa,
including the designs for the Reshef fast patrol boat, the Gabriel
missile, the new Israeli/South African submarine project and the latest
electronics for both fighter aircraft and ground troops, and the designs
and uses of counter-insurgency equipment.

It is believed in Tel Aviv that the USSR will waste no time in
inventing counters to Israel's new equipment, particularly in the light
of the serious Soviet equipment failures during the Israelis' invasion of
the Lebanon in 1982. While there is no immediate threat from the
Soviets themselves, it is expected that Moscow will pass on new
equipment and details of Israeli strategy to her Arab allies. Syria is the
country most likely to benefit, as it is the most pro-Soviet of all the
Arab confrontation states and represents the most immediate threat to
Israel. In every Arab–Israeli war so far, the Syrians have been
defeated by Israeli equipment which has always proved more
sophisticated and reliable that the Soviet-supplied ordnance in the

Syrian inventory. With the information supplied from South Africa, the Israelis fear that such superiority may well be a thing of the past.

While their arms relationship has mushroomed during the last ten years, Israel and South Africa remain extraordinarily sensitive about any discussion concerning the trade. For example, the South Africans, in common with all other embassies, have senior officers from the army (a brigadier), navy (a captain) and air force (a group captain) acting as defence attachés in Tel Aviv. However, the three are not listed as defence attachés, and other Western diplomats – all listed under their correct titles – have great difficulty in discovering who their opposite numbers actually are in the South African embassy, particularly as the South African officers insist on driving cars with special number-plates untraceable to the South African embassy.

While the Israelis have insisted on this anonymity, there is equal secrecy about their own officials visiting Pretoria. In March 1980, the then Defence Minister, Ezer Weizmann, went on a covert visit to Pretoria to discuss, among other things, the joint Lavi fighter project. Journalists in Israel picked up the story and Israeli Radio planned to broadcast a news bulletin on the subject. As is normal, the story was submitted to the government censor for approval and, through some oversight, was passed. The story of the visit went out at 11.00 a.m., and Weizmann, who by this time had returned from South Africa, was horrified to hear details of the trip being broadcast to the world. He immediately telephoned the censor's office who, in turn, got in touch with Israeli Radio; by 11.15, the story had been killed.

The Weizmann visit was just one of several that have taken place in recent years to discuss joint defence ventures. The cost of developing a major new weapons system can be prohibitive to any country that does not rely on exports to spread the unit costs; joint production and, particularly, shared R&D costs make good sense to any arms producer. For Israel and South Africa, who have almost identical defence needs, this has been quickly appreciated by their respective governments, and there is now co-operation in the manufacture of a new generation of tanks, a revolutionary fighter, naval vessels and submarines, as well as artillery and small arms.

The South Africans have recently announced an export drive aimed at increasing arms sales from $8.6 million to $130 million a year. Spearheading the new sales drive is the 155-mm artillery system that was smuggled from the United States to South Africa with Israeli help (*see* Chapter 4). The South Africans are also offering missiles, armoured cars, troop-carrying vehicles, missile patrol boats and sophisticated electronic equipment. The missiles, patrol boats and communications equipment are all made either under licence from Israel or with direct Israeli help. Israeli advertisements for weaponry generally stress that every item for sale has been proved in combat. South African arms salesmen are stressing that their goods have seen service in Namibia or Angola and have had all their teething troubles ironed out in battle. It is an effective sales pitch that, like the Israelis', is likely to prove very successful.

In launching an export drive, the South Africans are merely following the example of their mentors. For some years, Israel has been selling equipment to countries as diverse as Iran, the United States and Chile, and has found that the sales provide a very useful supply of much-needed foreign exchange earnings, as well as the ready cash to finance more R&D – which is essential if Israel is to maintain its current qualitative edge over the Arab nations.

IAI, the biggest division of the country's armaments industry, reported total exports of $520 million for the fiscal year ending in March 1982. The previous year, IAI exports had totalled a mere $340 million, with 1982 marking the first time that IAI had cracked $500 million. Israeli defence officials hope that 1983 will be the first year that total arms exports will break the $1 billion mark.

Prior to the visit of Vorster to Israel in 1976, the arms business between the two countries had been growing steadily. The visit took place before the implementation of the UN arms embargo, when South Africa was still receiving arms from some Western countries, particularly from France who had been delivering Mirage fighters and helicopters. Vorster asked Israel to help in the delivery of new naval vessels, fighter aircraft, counter-insurgency equipment and missiles, and perhaps more important for the long term, he also discussed the setting up of joint manufacturing projects in South Africa, as well as South African investment in the Israeli arms industry. An immediate result was a plan to overhaul the armour on the tanks and personnel carriers of the SADF. Iskoor, a company based just outside Tel Aviv and 51 per cent owned by Koor Industries in Israel and 49 per cent by the South African Steel Corporation, was at the heart of the deal.

For the past ten years, Israel has been working on the production of the Merkhava main battle-tank. In the two wars of 1967 and 1973, the Israeli army found that the US-produced tanks – the M-48 and M-60 – were neither powerful enough nor sufficiently protected. In the fast-moving war over open territory that Israel has traditionally fought, tanks are at the forefront of the land battle and can win or lose the war. After the British refused to supply Chieftain tanks, the Israeli defence planners decided that they would have to build a tank to suit their own special needs, and the Merkhava project was launched. By 1976, plans were well advanced, but they needed special steel which was not available in Israel. However, South Africa, which has a vast and very sophisticated steel industry, was happy to oblige and, in return, Israel has supplied the formula for a new type of armour plate that experts believe is the finest on the market today.

The Mark 1 Merkhava entered service with the Israeli army in 1977, by which time development of an upgraded Mark 2 tank had already begun. The Mark 2 version was developed primarily with Israeli funds and some help from the United States but again using the armour produced in South Africa. The US army wanted Israel to press ahead with its own tank development so that information gained during the programme could be fed into US plans for a new main battle-tank, code-named XM-1. (An interesting device, developed by the Elta Electronics Division of IAI, has been deployed in the Mark 2 Merkhava which takes over normal, and often difficult to understand, communication between tank driver and commander. The commander uses a manual control handle mounted on the turret; its movements are converted into understandable audio commands for the driver. The Israelis have found that this has improved both efficiency and reliability under stress conditions.)

The Merkhava Mark 1 tanks were first deployed during the invasion of the Lebanon in 1982 and have proved a success. Although the detailed performance remains classified, it is known that a number of rounds fired from the Merkhava 105-mm gun penetrated the armour of the Syrian T-72 at its weakest point on the frontal arc. The Israeli tank does have its problems, however: it did not prove as immune to Syrian anti-tank missiles as had been hoped, and the Merkhava Marks 2 and 3 will have bigger engines and more powerful 120-mm guns. One of the main design strengths of the tank was proved satisfactory, however: even if the tank was hit, the crews had time to escape and did not burn alive inside the hull – as happened during the 1973 war.

While Israel was developing its new tank, South Africa embarked on a major modernization programme for its ground forces: personnel carriers, tanks and scout cars have all been strengthened with the Israeli-supplied armour, and the 150 Centurion tanks that form the main complement of South Africa's heavy armour have all been modernized by Israel as part of the steel-for-technology deal. The modernization of the Centurions was a simple stop-gap measure while the Israelis were completing the development of the Merkhava. Now that this has been done, sources in Israel suggest, an agreement has been reached for Israel to suppy substantial quantities of the tank to South Africa. If the deal goes through, South Africa will have arguably the most sophisticated and deadly main battle-tank in the whole of Africa, and with sufficient quantities, the threat of a successful conventional assault against the South African armed forces is considerably reduced.

Helicopters play an increasingly important role on the battlefield as reconnaissance aircraft, troop carriers and gunships. In this area, too, South Africa has established a joint deal with Israel. The two-seater 'Scorpion' helicopter, a lightweight aircraft based on a US design, is now produced as part of a joint venture between Rotoflight Helicopters of Cape Town and the Israeli company, Chemavir-Masok. The helicopters are built in South Africa and assembled in Israel for both home use and export. Again, while the EEC imposes a boycott on South African goods, Israel provides a useful and covert conduit to the outside world.

In the recent war in the Lebanon, Syrian MiG fighters relied on ground control to direct them towards their Israeli enemies who were using mainly the American F-16 and their own Kfir fighter. Although Israel was using E-2C Hawkeye aircraft as floating radar above the battle, it was mainly the Kfir (in its ground-attack role) and the F-16 (in air-to-air combat) that proved far superior to anything the Syrians had. In addition, superior Israeli electronics were able to block the transmission of Syrian radar crews guiding the fighters who were thus rendered almost blind and became easy targets for the Israelis. Similarly, electronic counter-measures blocked the guidance system of Syrian and PLO anti-aircraft missiles.

As Israel can never rely on numerical superiority in battle, it is essential that her military technology is more advanced than anything in the hands of the Arab nations. In the case of the war in the Lebanon, where the only serious opposition came from Syria, this was not so much of a problem, since Syria employs only Soviet equipment, and this is generally believed to be five to ten years behind the West in microtechnology and electronics. Israeli defence experts are confident, however, that their own electronics industry is more than a match for anything the Arabs have in the armoury. This confidence is a measure of how far the Israelis have developed their indigenous arms industry, since the majority of the Arabs are now supplied by members of NATO with equipment that is similar to that available to Israel. However, Israeli engineers have managed to corrupt and improve systems that have been supplied to them, as well as having invented a few of their own.

To help South Africa take advantage of this increasingly sophisticated range of products, Israeli technicians from the country's three main electronics companies – Tadiran, Elbit and IAI – combined to help South Africa design and build its own electronics manufacturing capability. So successful has this been that South Africa is now able to produce a wide range of articles for home consumption and export, including radios, field telephones and surveillance systems. At the recent arms show, Defence Expo 82, in Athens, the South Africans were able to offer for sale a radio transceiver system complete with frequency hopping which, they say, is one of the most modern available and virtually immune from interception.

While Israel has assisted South African manufacturing, the ideal that both countries appear to be working towards is the development of a complementary arms programme that neatly dovetails to suit the needs of both countries. Israel remains the inventive partner, while South Africa has both spare cash and excess manufacturing capacity.

In the Lebanon war, Israel put this inventive streak to particularly effective use through the creative deployment of Remotely Piloted Vehicles (RPVs). An RPV is basically a large model aircraft, crammed with as many electronic gadgets as possible, that is sent up to reconnoitre enemy lines or act as a decoy for ground forces, who then can be pinpointed by the more sophisticated 'Spies in the Sky' which loiter safely out of range. The usefulness of the RPV was first recognized during the 1973 war when they were used to overfly missile positions. They drew fire and betrayed enemy positions, and were also able to jam the Sam missile guidance systems and make them inoperative. Following the 1973 war, the IDF ordered the development of more sophisticated RPVs and this has resulted in the deployment of two main types, the Scout and the Mastiff.

The Scout is manufactured by IAI and, when launched by catapult from a truck-mounted ramp, has a range of 100 kilometres. On board the aircraft are two cameras mounted in the belly for zoom and panorama photography, and other payloads, such as jamming devices, can be inserted when necessary. The aircraft is controlled in a similar way to a conventional model aeroplane, with the operator handling a joystick that directs it. However, the controller also has automatic map-plotter, video and telemetry signal reception, and minicomputer processing and display of received data for immediate or later analysis. In addition, the Scout controller has a video screen complete with light-pen to enable automatic corrections of artillery fall of shot. The Mastiff, produced by Tadiran, possesses a similar package to that of the Scout, but can carry thirty kilograms as opposed to the Scout's twenty-two. The additional load gives it a shorter range, however – around seventy kilometres and four hours' flying time. Both aircraft are recoverable for recycling: the Scout by means of a vertically mounted net set up just above the ground, and the Mastiff by an arresting wire on a road or flat field.

In the Lebanon war, the Israelis deployed the RPV for the first time as a replacement for the more conventional reconnaissance by ground forces. RPVs were flown by local battalion commanders, and the resulting photographic information was relayed directly to the commander's field headquarters who was then able to make immediate decisions on troop deployment without risking casualties among his scouting parties. Israeli officers in the field were astonished at the success of this tactic, since it revolutionized their ground strategy. RPVs were able to photograph in great detail every single enemy position, they could outflank dug-in forces, avoid ambushes and call up deadly accurate artillery fire. The implications of the success of the RPV for the South Africans have not been lost on either side, and the South Africans have already taken delivery of both types, and have been deployed in Namibia and Mozambique. An Israeli Scout RPV was shot down over Mozambique in mid-1983.

At present, forward reconnaissance in Namibia is carried out by scouts composed of local people and members of the South African version of the SAS. In addition, in 1978 a crack anti-terrorist unit, known as the South-West African Specialist Unit (SWASU), was formed specifically to operate in bush conditions at the border and to cut down on terrorist infiltration. SWASU uses horses and motorcycles for mobility and dogs to help track guerrillas in the dark. The unit has reportedly had the same psychological effect on guerrillas as the Selous Scouts had in Rhodesia, and rumour has endowed them with almost superhuman prowess. While this might make useful propaganda, such operations are expensive in highly trained personnel and cannot adapt to a swiftly changing conventional battle.

The RPV takes care of all those problems. Using an RPV, the South Africans can see a long way forward of their front lines and cover an enormous area of bush country without risking a scout, thus reducing casualties and drastically increasing the effectiveness of the South African troops in Namibia.

To back up the forward reconnaissance of the RPV, the South Africans have been discussing the purchase of two different makes of aircraft that provide early warning and highly sophisticated ground monitoring. For some years, they have been interested in the short-take-off-and-landing (STOL) aircraft, the Arava, manufactured by IAI. A STOL aircraft is very useful for the SADF in Namibia as it facilitates resupply to forward troops and swift communication and reinforcement in areas that would otherwise be inaccessible. In fact, it is understood that the SADF has tried out the Arava in both Israel and Namibia; and there have also been reports of purchases, but this has been impossible to confirm. What will make the Arava even more attractive to the SADF is its conversion for electronic warfare. As well as surveying enemy aircraft heading for the battlefield, the Arava Early Warning (EW) can hover over the combat area and both scan and jam enemy radio transmissions. The system employed in the aircraft can scan 100 channels per second and detect the output of a manpack on the ground in seconds. The Arava's EW capability is primarily intended for use over land; it has been supplemented by the Sea Scan aircraft, a derivative of the Westwind executive jet which can scan 100,000 square miles in a few hours through its bulbous nose, as well as detect submarines. Although this directly rivals the Brazilian Embraer EMB-111 Maritime Patrol aircraft, being jet-powered it is more powerful; it could thus prove more attractive, particularly as the South Africans are making a major push for sales in Latin America.

It is not, however, with the fairly general field of transport and strike aircraft that South Africa is particularly concerned. At the present time, South Africa has only two light-bomber squadrons composed of five Canberra and six Buccaneer aircraft. Both are coming rapidly to the end of their useful lives and, as opposing armies re-equip with increasingly sophisticated anti-aircraft missiles and fighter interceptors, those two squadrons appear very vulnerable. South African defence strategists are working on the assumption that their need for long-range penetration attacks against guerrilla bases is going to increase over the next few years. They also recognize that a revised fighter/bomber arm would give the South African Air Force (SAAF) a much-needed update and bring its equipment more in line with the modern ordnance available to the navy and the army. A similar pattern exists among the air force's fighter aircraft. The South Africans do have the right to build French Mirage fighters under licence, but even the Mirage is now beginning to look a little dated and will have a hard time matching the more advanced Soviet aircraft that are beginning to appear in other African armouries.

Aircraft development demands an exceptionally long lead time – often as much as fifteen years – and the South Africans have been thinking for some time about what their needs will be towards the end of this decade, by which time the air force estimates that their prospects of purchasing advanced replacement aircraft on the open market will be virtually nil. By 1990 the concept of 'Fortress South Africa' will have become a harsh reality and even much of the covert support that is currently available from such countries as the United States and Britain will have dried up. While there are always opportunities to purchase goods on the vast arms black market, really sophisticated aircraft are only available on a government-to-government basis, and for at least ten years after an aircraft has first appeared, there will be no prospect of a secret South African purchase. The air force is therefore faced with an ageing inventory that is quickly becoming outdated even by African standards, with few prospects of replacements being found through normal channels.

For Israel, the problems are almost identical. While their air force is equipped with far more sophisticated aircraft than those available to South Africa, the Israelis believe that they cannot rely on the United States to continue to meet their defence needs. The Israeli government has become alarmed at the growing groundswell of argument in the US government, and particularly in the State Department, that the only way to bring about a settlement of the Palestinian problem is to impose some form of arms embargo. While there is no chance of this happening in the immediate future, the Israelis fear that there will be increasing sympathy for such a move, particularly as the size of Arab investments in the US economy continues to grow. Israel will simply no longer be so important to any politician's or president's survival, and will thus become vulnerable. The scenario that haunts Israel's defence planners is an update of the 1973 war. The theory runs thus: if another war breaks out between Israel and the Arabs (which most defence planners view as a virtual certainty), then even the United States may be tempted to cut arms supplies as a way of forcing Israel to the negotiating table. Developing its own armaments would reduce this threat substantially and would provide a much-needed source of foreign exchange. This policy has already proved very successful and has been expanded to include fighter development.

Today the IAF flies mainly American aircraft, including the F-15 Eagle, the F-16 Falcon, the F-4 Phantom and the A-4 Skyhawk. In addition, the IAF has recently acquired the IAI-built and designed Kfir and the more modern Kfir C-2. Both the Skyhawk and the Phantom will be outdated by the end of the 1980s, with the Kfir and the F-15 and F-16 lasting through to the mid-1990s. The Kfir has been used primarily in a ground-attack role and during the war in the Lebanon proved to be more than a match for both Syrian aircraft and missiles.

For the Israelis, the problem is to find an adequate replacement for the Kfir and the even more ancient Skyhawks, while the South Africans have a twofold need to resolve their immediate and short-term air defence and ground-attack needs, as well as bringing on line a fighter that will see them through to the end of the century. The short-term problem has been resolved by the attempted purchase of the Israeli Kfir: there have been unconfirmed reports that South Africa has already purchased thirty-six Kfir, at a cost of $430 million. The deal was reportedly struck secretly in 1980 and the first aircraft can be expected in South Africa after ground crews and pilots receive training in Israel.

Apart from Israel's willingness to sell to the apartheid regime – a co-operative attitude difficult to find among other Western governments for such a highly visible commodity – the Kfir was a very logical choice for the South Africans. Although developed by the Israelis, it is really a hybrid of the French Mirage which South Africa already manufactures under licence, and so South Africa should be able to service the Kfir without any extensive retooling, and there has had to be very little retraining of South African pilots. In addition, with both countries' defence needs matching almost exactly, the Israelis have designed an aircraft that is ideally suited to the somewhat specialist demands of the SAAF. Although primarily a ground-attack aircraft, the Kfir can also double as an interceptor in an air defence role, so the SAAF will have the capability to penetrate outside its own borders and defend territory against air attack.

The Israelis have extended their help beyond simply supplying sophisticated armaments. IAF officers have regularly lectured South African pilots on tactics. This is particularly important for South Africa as they see their only serious air threat as coming from Soviet-equipped forces – and only Israel has had recent combat experience against Soviet aircraft and Soviet-trained pilots. In addition to helping with equipment and training, Israel has rounded off the package by assisting in the development of more modern air bases for the SAAF, including aid in the construction of the most modern of the bases, at Hoedspruit in the Eastern Transvaal. (It is interesting to note that, following the lead of the Israelis, to try to help in manpower shortages the SAAF has decided to train its ground crew for a number of duties. It was pointed out to the SAAF by Israeli defence officials that, during the 1974 war, Israeli fighters were able to reduce down-time considerably because aircrews were themselves able to carry out a number of servicing functions while the aircraft was on the ground. Radar technicians, for example, refuelled aircraft while engine mechanics changed tyres and helped to rearm them. The SAAF has adopted a similar training strategy which they hope will improve their turn-around of aircraft during operations.)

Although the delivery of the Kfir will undoubtedly fill the gap in the SAAF fighter and ground-attack complement, it is only a short-term solution, and the need for a sophisticated fighter, complete with state-of-the-art avionics, remains. Such a harmony of need between

Israel and South Africa has naturally resulted in a deal that will bring to both air forces a fighter that should lead the world when it comes on line towards the end of the 1980s.

Since the late 1970s, Israeli designers have been looking at the possibility of producing a new and more sophisticated fighter to replace the Kfir. Code-named the Lavi (or 'lion'), the project was finally given the go-ahead by Ariel Sharon in 1982, somewhat to the surprise of many since the scheme was thought to have run out of funds and all work halted.

Originally, the IAF had hoped that a co-production could be organized with the United States which would have both helped with R&D costs and attracted substantial amounts of US aid. When the Israelis had produced the Kfir, they had been able to modify technology and production methods developed abroad, principally in France. This had resulted in an aircraft what was highly competitive at around $5 million per unit, but this price did not reflect a realistic R&D cost spread over each aircraft. The Kfir has, in fact, been a huge loss-maker, largely because the United States, which supplied the jet engines, has refused to allow exports to such sensitive countries as Ecuador. Any new aircraft development will present a similar set of problems; although a US Republican administration can be expected to be more sympathetic to Israeli requests for export permission.

The R&D costs for the Lavi will be enormous and, unlike the situation in the United States or any of the other major arms manufacturing countries, the production run will be relatively small, so the spread cost per unit will be that much higher. While the aircraft may employ state-of-the-art avionics and be a highly efficient and versatile machine, it is likely to be very much more expensive than its nearest competitors. This problem would have been readily resolved by Israel agreeing to a co-production programme with another manufacturer. The most likely candidate would have been the United States as it already supplied most of Israel's arms needs, but the Pentagon proved to be an unwilling partner. In any major project, the United States is certain of a high level of sales at home and almost guaranteed large exports which generate much-needed revenue. Co-production with any country would not be a realistic economic option, although politically it might have some attractions. However, it now seems that the political benefits are not very high: Israel asked for co-production on the F-16 fighter, but the United States offered to help with only 5 per cent of the cost. Such a contribution to a major project such as the Lavi would have been quite insignificant in the grand total, and far greater participation was needed to spread the financial load and make the scheme viable. Israel has also been rebuffed over co-production of the F-18 Hornet. One of the options initially explored by the IAF was to manufacture the Hornet, but this has now been abandoned: a team of Pentagon analysts visited Tel Aviv in 1980 to look at Israel's fighter programme and the options for the future; it is believed that they reported unfavourably on the prospects of co-production.

The Lavi project was originally approved by the Israeli Cabinet in 1980 after the preliminary costings and design had been worked out; it was estimated then that R&D for the aircraft would cost in excess of $2 billion, with each aircraft selling at $11–13 million. There was considerable enthusiasm among senior air force officers for the Lavi which, most believe, will put them years ahead of their Arab neighbours and give them a better edge in air combat – which, in every Middle East war since 1948, has proved crucial. However, the decision would have to be, in the end, a political one and there was considerable concern in the Israeli Cabinet about whether the country could actually afford the enormous investment required.

The Lavi is by far the most ambitious programme ever undertaken by the Israeli armaments industry and even some veterans are nervous of the risk and the financial burden. The President of IAI, Gavriel Gidor, has admitted: 'We cannot afford it economically but we cannot afford not to do it . . . Who has not imposed an embargo on us at one time or another? IAI can provide all the technology except the engines, although that does not mean that we have to do it all in-house. If it is economical and safe to do so, we can have some production carried out somewhere else.' Gidor added that negotiations are under way with twenty-five companies in different countries that may be able to provide parts for the project at competitive prices. Certain basic designs have already been agreed. The canard delta aircraft will be single-engined and powered by an American Pratt & Whitney PW-1120 engine manufactured under licence in Israel.

The Lavi concept is for a lightweight advanced-attack aircraft which will replace the Skyhawk and Kfir C-2 fighters currently employed by the IAF. At the present time, the IAF is budgeted to take 300 of the Lavis at a cost of £10.8 million each. Much of the design work and technology will be carried out with the aid of companies in the United States, and informal approval has already been given for the transfer of technology relating to the Pratt & Whitney engines that will be used in the aircraft, as well as technology relating to the fuel system, electronics, and airframe. Officially, the Reagan administration has been suggesting that final approval for the technology transfer will only be given if there is some move by the Israeli government on the question of West Bank settlements and the Palestinians. Privately, however, few in the administration or outside believe that any serious attempt will be made to block the deal.

According to the authoritative magazine *Aviation Week*, the Lavi design is based on medium- and close-range air-to-ground sorties for close air support, and the design also provides a secondary mission as an air defence interceptor and doubles as a two-seat trainer. The IAF have specified that the Lavi must be capable of high-speed penetration to target, have high manoeuvrability and low-drag ordnance. *Aviation Week* suggested that the Lavi would be armed with two infra-red-guided, air-to-air missiles and eight MK 117 general-purpose 750-pound bombs, and would penetrate to a target at a speed of 538 knots; configured with two AIM-9L Sidewinder missiles and two MK 84, 2,000-pound bombs, this speed would increase to 597 knots. The ground attack range of the Lavi would be 244 nautical miles.

In 1981 Sharon called a halt to the project while he looked more closely at the finances. No agreement on sharing development costs had been made with the South Africans after the Weizmann visit the previous year, so during the temporary hiatus, urgent talks were held with the South African government (and possibly the Taiwanese government) to see if there was the potential for a joint development programme. R&D costs would be shared, each country would manufacture some of the aircraft parts and, aside from ultimately purchasing the Lavi for their own air forces, would share in the export earnings generated by the aircraft. The South Africans have provisionally agreed to help with the development of the Lavi and, although exact figures are not available, its commitment must run into several hundred million dollars, spread over the three years that it is expected to take to put the first Lavi into the air.

The first prototype is expected to be flying by 1985, the first production aircraft will be running off the lines in 1990 and the IAF is scheduled to take delivery of the first Lavi in 1992 when, presumably, under the terms of the co-operation agreement between Israel and South Africa, the SAAF will be re-equipping. If the project goes ahead as planned and the delivery of the thirty-six Kfirs continues on schedule, South Africa will have the most modern air force south of the Sahara for the foreseeable future. Any realistic conventional military threat to South Africa will be doomed to failure, and the guerrilla camps will become increasingly vulnerable to air strikes following the pattern of the lightning Israeli retaliatory raids against the PLO refugee camps in Lebanon.

In late 1982, a senior member of the board of British Shipbuilders was approached by a shipping company operating out of New York. 'Although based in New York, everyone in the business knows they are an Israeli company,' said the board member. 'They were looking for naval vessels which they wanted us to build for them. It was made quite clear that these were for passing on to South Africa.' Such a visible breach of the embargo would have been highly embarrassing to the British government, as British Shipbuilders is a nationalized industry, the chairman of which frequently liaises directly with the Cabinet. The offer was turned down.

Before 1970, five of the eight principal ships in the South African navy predated World War II. The entire navy had been geared to operate as part of a Western fleet protecting the Cape route and the oil supply to the West. However, the abandonment of the Simonstown agreement by Britain and the increasing isolation of South Africa meant that the navy had to radically rethink its role in the country's defence plans. If the navy re-equipped with large ocean-going vessels for realistic patrol and protection of the Cape route, a vast integrated network of vessels and aircraft would have been needed. The vintage long-range naval-reconnaissance Shackletons would have to be replaced, and the navy would require a far larger support fleet than it then had.

In 1978, P. W. Botha, then Minister of Defence, said that the international arms boycott had forced South Africa to change its strategy on naval defence. 'From now on, South Africa's navy will be specially geared and designed to coastal defence for protecting the sovereignty of home waters. The West will have to conduct its own patrols of the shipping lanes to, from and around the Cape, and will have to look after its own interests.' The navy had decided to draw in its horns and, in keeping with the rest of the defence force, developed plans to handle guerrilla infiltration or a conventional assault by other African armed forces; it was not realistic to attempt to counter the enormous Soviet naval presence in the Indian Ocean, and it was hoped that, in the event of a conventional East–West confrontation involving the superpowers, there would be some support for the South African navy, given its strategic importance.

While the navy accepted its role as a coastal patrol and harbour protection service, it was faced with the problem of finding the equipment to do the job properly. Although Britain had supplied three frigates before the ending of the Simonstown agreement, these were neither suitable for coastal work nor sufficiently up to date to integrate with the modernized army and air force. However, Israel had been thinking along similar lines and had developed its own solution to the problem in the shape of the Reshef patrol boat.

During the Six Day War of 1967, the Israeli destroyer *Eilat* had been sunk when two Soviet Styx missiles were fired from an Egyptian ship at anchor in Port Said, twelve miles away. The Israelis decided that they needed a fast and well-armed patrol boat that would be able to counter any enemy missile system, pack a powerful punch and act as support or transport for commandos operating beyond the country's borders. The result was the Reshef, a 415-ton, 32-knot, missile-carrying patrol boat, built by the Israeli shipyards at Haifa. At the time of its original deployment in 1973, the Reshef was perhaps the finest small patrol craft available in the world and it quickly showed its mettle. Using a home-produced missile – the Gabriel – the Israelis sank ten Syrian and Egyptian missile boats during the war, suffering no losses themselves. The Gabriel also managed to intercept and down fifty-two Styx missiles, thus somewhat redressing the humiliation of 1967. In addition to Gabriel missiles, the Reshef is also equipped with Harpoon ship-to-ship missiles, one 76-mm gun and one 40-mm gun, both manufactured by Oto Melara of Italy.

At the time of Vorster's visit in 1976, it was agreed that Israel would supply South Africa with three of the Reshef-class vessels, and would allow South Africa to manufacture a further nine under licence in the Sandock-Austral shipyards in Durban. As has already been shown, while the armaments for the vessels have not been supplied directly by Israel, the Israeli government has acted as middleman in negotiations between South Africa and the Italian company Oto Melara, and supplies and spares have continued, despite the UN arms embargo. To disguise the relationship between Israel and itself, South Africa has renamed the Reshef the 'Minister' class and the Gabriel missile the 'Skerpioen'; for public consumption, it insists that both are entirely locally produced.

It seems to be part of the licensing agreement between Israel and South Africa that the former will provide details of any modifications that are made to a weapons system, so that the latter can incorporate the changes in its own production lines. The South Africans originally began manufacturing the Gabriel II missile after they had taken delivery of the first Reshefs; now that the Israelis have developed the Gabriel III, the South Africans have begun altering their production lines. The Gabriel III is a copy of the sea-skimming French-designed Exocet missile that was used with such devastating effect during the Falklands War. The Israelis project that the Gabriel III will remain effective well into the 1990s and will defeat any anti-missile missiles or jammers, be they currently deployed or on the drawing board.

While the initial order of three Reshefs was being filled at the Haifa shipyards, the Israeli government helped train several hundred South

African sailors in the operation of the vessel. In addition, the Haifa shipyard helped establish South Africa's virtually non-existent ship-building industry by supplying personnel to the Sandock-Austral yard and advising on the organization of an efficient production line. South Africa has also taken delivery of at least six Dvora-class fast patrol boats which, Israel claims, are among the most advanced in the world. Although they displace only thirty-five tons and can be transported on the backs of lorries, they can travel at 50 knots and are armed with two Gabriel II missiles, two 20-mm guns and two 12.7-mm machine-guns.

Following the sinking of the *President Kruger* (which was already obsolete) in February 1982 after a collision at sea, South Africa lost its one remaining vessel capable of deep-sea work and offshore patrols. While a similar vessel, the *President Pretorius*, has been brought out of mothballs and is undergoing a major refit, the South African navy is keen on finding a longer-term solution. The possibility of a joint South African–Israeli development of a corvette first arose following the successful delivery of the Reshef in 1977. The Israelis were keen on developing their own corvette, which they felt would suit their local needs and have a ready market among the growing navies of Third World countries. South African cash and Israeli technology have resulted in the development of an 850-ton guided-missile corvette, code-named Q9, which will carry a helicopter to provide over-the-horizon target data for the Harpoon missile system. There are no figures available for the number of vessels due to be delivered to either country, but as the first keel was laid down in 1981, it is expected that the Israeli navy will take first delivery in early 1984, and the South Africans should have their first vessel shortly afterwards.

South Africa has also expressed interest in purchasing the newly developed Aliyah-class guided-missile patrol boat from Israel. The first of these vessels has only just entered service (1983), and it is understood that South African naval officers have been on sea trials and have stated their requirements, with only the price and the quantity still to be agreed. Delivery of the Aliyah would usefully fill the gap between the Reshef and the corvettes, and sources in South Africa state that a licence deal has now been agreed and that construction will shortly begin in South Africa.

South Africa and Israel each have three submarines. In South Africa's case, these are three ancient Daphne-class submarines bought from the French, the first having been delivered in 1970 and the other two in 1971. To all intents and purposes, they are completely outdated and the South African navy would like to phase them out as soon as alternatives become available. With their new coastal defence strategy, the South Africans have always expected the submarines to take a vital part in aggressively enforcing territorial claims. Aside from acting as a delivery system for commandos, the South Africans believe that a modern submarine force could be extremely useful in blockading enemy ports in time of war. The Israelis have three Gal-class submarines built by Vickers which, by the time they were delivered in 1977, were already obsolete. For a country such as Israel which relies on a qualitative edge in all its armed forces, its antiquated submarines are something of an embarrassment, particularly as they were used extensively during the war in Lebanon to land commandos and there are plans for them to play a prominent role in any future conflict in the region.

It is the estimate of defence experts that the submarines of neither navy are adequately equipped to fight in a modern war and the expectation is that, if they were deployed aggressively against a reasonably modern anti-submarine navy or air force, they would quickly be sunk. Well aware of their own limitations, the South Africans have offered to help the Israelis out. Although neither country has ever built a submarine before, South Africa has recently trebled the capacity of the Simonstown dockyards. It is difficult to understand why the South Africans should have carried out such a major refit unless there were plans to manufacture a submarine to take advantage of such facilities. While the basing agreement with the British was in force, submarines would regularly dock for servicing at Simonstown, and the South African navy has considerable experience in looking after vessels superior in size and technology to their own Daphnes. The Simonstown base can now hold submarines of up to 3,000 tons, well in excess of the 1,000-ton submarines currently in service. There have been reports, particularly among opposition groups in South Africa, that it is co-operating with Israel in building a nuclear submarine, but what in fact has been agreed is that a number of submarines will be constructed in South Africa to a joint South African/Israeli design.

The effect of the deal (first suggested by Vorster during his 1976 visit) on the South African navy can be gauged by quoting from the IISS statistics for the years 1975–6 and 1982–3. In the first year, the South African navy had three Daphne-class submarines, two destroyers, six frigates, ten coastal minesweepers and four patrol craft. By 1982–3, after a large number of obsolete vessels had been phased out and the whole character of the navy had dramatically altered, the navy had three Daphne-class submarines, one frigate, six Reshefs, seven patrol craft, six minesweepers and two minehunters.

The arms trade between Israel and South Africa now runs into hundreds of millions of dollars and is rising each year. As the new fighter aircraft and navy vessels come into service, the Israeli/South African arms-exporting business will be one of the largest in the world, and with their arms exports will come a high degree of political influence that will increase as each fighter or Gabriel missile is sold to an emerging Third World country.

From both Israel's and South Africa's points of view, the development of a joint arms industry has been a shrewd move. Not only will both countries be less vulnerable to military attack and political pressure, but they will also aim to win a large number of new friends around the world. This orchestrated attack on the vulnerabilities of the Third World has so far taken place almost entirely in secret, and both countries remain acutely conscious of the potential damage of adverse publicity. The longer they can operate with discretion, the greater the arms sales and the more the influence they can hope to gain.

What is perhaps most surprising about the development of their respective armed forces is that it has all taken place without the world either knowing or caring. The enforcement of the UN arms embargo against South Africa has been a farce and there is little prospect of it gaining any improvement. The inadequate nature of the embargo has enabled the concept of 'Fortress South Africa' to become a reality . . . and it is a fortress that is going to be virtually unassailable militarily for many years to come.

7 The US Lobby

Through their trading relationship in arms and other products, both Israel and South Africa have become less dependent on other countries, thus rendering them more able to handle the political pressures brought about by changes in leadership of previously friendly governments. At the heart of the foreign, trading and internal policies of both countries is a fundamental belief that they are battling for their survival. It would be altogether out of character for either country to rely exclusively on a growing trading relationship to shore up their respective economies sufficiently to become immune to outside interference. Such a complacent attitude is directly counter to the almost messianic fervour running through both governments. Both are firmly convinced they have an absolute God-given right to their existence, and that many of the attacks launched against them are Communist-inspired. It is hardly surprising, therefore, that their defence of their territorial integrity is taken far beyond their own national boundaries and into the public and private forums where major decisions affecting nations and global strategy are taken.

Both Israel and South Africa have their own independent foreign policies, and any attempt by critics to suggest that they are so interlinked to be almost indistinguishable is naïve and incorrect. However, there is an informal linking of the alliance that is less an overt pressure group than a subtle interweaving of political and economic interests. There is complete understanding on both sides that there are many occasions when their policy interests coincide . . . or when Israel may be able to use a little influence in the right quarter on behalf of South Africa, or vice versa. Advice and aid are given and taken quite freely. This informal alliance seeks expression through the growing trading relationship between Israel, South Africa and the Third World, and through the increasing prominence of lobby groups working abroad, particularly in the United States.

The purpose of the lobby groups is to gain influential friends who will help pass legislation favourable to either country or prevent unfavourable legislation reaching the statute book. More than $100 million is spent annually by lobbyists from all nations in the United States, and by far the greatest part of that money is aimed at the lawmakers and the government in Washington, D.C. The United States, with its heavily bureaucratic administrative machine and its enormously expensive election campaigns, appears particularly vulnerable to lobbyists. Every would-be senator, congressman or governor relies on the generosity of his supporters for his campaign funds, and those who contribute naturally expect a pay-off should their candidate get elected.

A number of laws have been passed in the United States in an attempt to avoid abuses of the lobby process and to cut down on any suggestion of bribery or corruption buying influence in government:

* The *Foreign Agents Registration Act* requires lobbyists for foreign nations to register with the Justice Department and file semi-annual statements listing clients, activities and services rendered as well as money received and expenses incurred. When making any approach on behalf of clients, lobbyists are obliged to identify themselves.

* The *Federal Election Campaign Act of 1976* prohibits any foreign national from contributing to federal office-seekers and prohibits any US citizen from accepting or encouraging such gifts.

* The *Foreign Gifts and Decorations Act* prohibits public officials or their relatives from accepting gifts worth more than $140, unless it appears that refusing the gift would offend the donor 'or otherwise adversely affect the foreign relations of the United States'.

In theory, these three regulations should do much to discourage the activities of lobbyists. In fact, the industry continues to grow, and while the more extreme activities of the lobby groups may have been curtailed in recent years, foreign governments that really believe they have a point of view to get across will not let mere legislation stand in their way.

The South Africans and Israelis have been remarkably successful lobbyists in the United States, but for very different reasons. Israel has been able to rely on a large and highly motivated Jewish population who can be counted upon to mobilize in any emergency and work on behalf of their spiritual homeland. The rise of the New Right in the United States, embodied in the Reagan administration, has given South Africa unprecedented access to Capitol Hill and, in addition, the Pretoria government is quite prepared to spend a great deal of money to support its beliefs.

On 6 February 1974, a small gathering took place in Vorster's Cape Town office. Seated in the stinkwood chairs surrounding his desk were Minister of the Interior Connie Mulder, the Finance Minister Nico Diederichs, Secretary of Information Eschel Rhoodie, Rhoodie's brother Deneys and Deputy Secretary of Information Les de Villiers.

According to de Villiers' book *Secret Information*, the meeting was opened by Eschel Rhoodie who explained how South Africa had been losing the world propaganda campaign, and argued that it was time for the Vorster government to take the offensive and launch propaganda attacks on a broad front that would win influence and new friends for South Africa. There was no sense, Rhoodie said, in hoping that the rest of the world would change its attitude towards South Africa purely on the basis of right or wrong. 'The truth about our many good deeds towards the black man in this part of Africa would hardly set us free. South Africa had spent millions in the past three decades on orthodox propaganda, to no avail. We were still slipping further into the abyss, despite our well-intentioned efforts, despite speaking the truth,' wrote de Villiers. The time had come, Rhoodie argued, 'for South Africa to embark on a full-scale psychological war, instead of relying on films, brochures and other government handouts. In this unconventional propaganda offensive, no rules would apply, no regulations would stand in our way. Only objectives would count and the end would indeed justify the means – any means.'

Despite the evident risks involved, Vorster gave Mulder the go-ahead for the operation to begin. He also agreed that the scheme should be carried out in total secrecy with a slush fund organized by BOSS. In the following four years, Rhoodie, with Mulder's backing and the support of de Villiers, would mastermind nearly 200 secret projects in the United States, Europe and South Africa at a cost of more than $100 million. (*See* Chapter 1 for details of the 'Project David' aspect of the operation.)

Even before Vorster had given his formal permission for the scheme to proceed, Rhoodie had been testing the water in the United States. Accompanied by de Villiers and Connie Mulder, he had travelled there the previous year and had met Vice-president Gerald Ford and senior members of Congress and the Senate, had met South Africa's allies in the Pentagon and had confronted its critics at the National Press Club in Washington. As well as being a bold propaganda stroke, the trip paid two further dividends. While in California, Mulder met the then Governor of California, Ronald Reagan: de Villiers reported that 'he showed great understanding for the need to have closer relations between South Africa and the United States'. The second bonus was the elevation of John McGoff to the job of principal fixer and professional front man for the South African government in the United States.

McGoff, the son of a Pittsburgh steelworker, was based in Williamstown, Michigan, and had ambitions of being a publishing tycoon. In 1959 he had teamed up with Michael Dow of the Dow Chemical family and, using Dow money and McGoff instinct, the two men had managed to buy up a series of small newspapers centred on Michigan, with a combined circulation of nearly 100,000. Although the total circulation might seem heavyweight, the sales of each individual newspaper were generally below 10,000 and McGoff had dreams of bigger things.

He had first met de Villiers in 1968 when the South African was based in New York looking after the information division. At that time, de Villiers had been impressed by McGoff and his pro-South African views. De Villiers invited him to South Africa and he came back convinced that the country had been receiving an undeservedly bad press. The result was a succession of articles in the McGoff newspapers that were blatantly pro-South Africa. This forthright behaviour quickly endeared McGoff to the South Africans, and frequent visits to Pretoria followed. One such trip occurred immediately after Vorster had agreed with Mulder that the latter's secret propaganda campaign could begin.

At the beginning of 1974, McGoff was running his growing publishing empire through the Panax Corporation in which he held a 4 per cent share worth only about $100,000; his annual salary was $67,507. Notwithstanding the small size of his assets, McGoff approached the ailing *Washington Star* newspaper and offered to purchase it for $20–25 million. *Star* executives discovered that Panax could not possibly afford such a bid, but McGoff insisted that he was acting for himself and had sufficient backing to carry the deal through.

Some months earlier, McGoff had approached the South Africans to tell them that the *Star* was in deep financial trouble and might be available for purchase. He had suggested that Pretoria put up $10 million in seed money and he would find the remaining $15 million. The South Africans, who appear to have been bowled over by McGoff's zeal and apparent entrepreneurial track-record, agreed immediately. While negotiations with the *Star* sputtered on, McGoff suggested to the South Africans that he do something with the interest piling up on the $10 million in his bank account. Again the South Africans agreed and McGoff bought the *Sacramento Union* in California for $7 million. Amazingly, the South Africans did not seem to object too violently to this little extravagance and McGoff continued to front their operations in the United States, becoming, according to de Villiers, 'undoubtedly the single most effective voice for South Africa in the United States'.

With apparently no limit to his spending, McGoff continued on his buying spree. The next target was the London-based organization UPITN. Owned by United Press International News Agency and Independent Television News in England, and Paramount Pictures, UPITN serves over a hundred clients in eighty countries and reports from around the world. Access to such a network would obviously be very useful for any organization wishing to distort the news. McGoff bought 50 per cent of the UPITN shares for $1.7 million from Paramount Pictures and proceeded to make himself co-chairman of the board, elevating another Panax director to board level. Those who worked for UPITN at this time claim that neither McGoff nor his allies tried at any time to interfere with the news or introduce bias into the broadcasts. There is probably more truth in this than might have been expected, given the size of the investment. McGoff seems to have loved the purchase of power but to have had little idea of what to do with it once he had the authority in his hands.

During the next four years, McGoff used Panax to purchase newspapers and magazines all over the United States, and with his acquisition came apparent prosperity: he bought a 100-foot motor yacht and, through a South African front company, obtained the use of a $250,000 luxury house in Miami. At the end of his tour of duty for the South African government, McGoff – either on his own behalf or for the South Africans (the lines of demarcation are often blurred) – had bought six daily and sixty-one weekly newspapers; by 1978, Panax was reporting an annual turnover of $36.1 million. The greatest prize – a newspaper in Washington, the government headquarters in the United States – eluded McGoff. His bid for the *Washington Star* eventually failed when Time Inc. bought the paper for $20 million, and the only other major newspaper in Washington, the *Post*, was not about to sell.

While McGoff had been off on his buying spree, the South Africans had been quietly frying other fish: newspapers were set up in South Africa; a series of pro-South Africa supplements in the US magazine *Business Week* were subsidized to the tune of $300,000; and in the black townships, a comic appeared with a black Superman as hero who was in favour of the status quo prevailing in the country. The latter venture was not as successful as had been hoped because militant blacks kept burning down the newspaper stands where the comic was on sale. Visits by foreign political leaders were also actively encouraged and subsidized by the government. The number of visits by US citizens to South Africa, paid for by the Department of Information, rose from eleven in 1973 to fifty-six in 1974 and continued at that level for the duration of the campaign.

It is hard to believe that visits to a country can convince opponents that they have been grossly ill-informed and make converts out of them; occasionally, however, they can have unexpected dividends: Former Democratic Representative James Symington had been renowned as a civil-rights advocate during his eight years in office, but following a visit to South Africa, he became a lobbyist for the apartheid government. He claims that his job is not to defend apartheid but to 'open lines of communication' that may change South Africa's separatist system: 'There is nothing that I have done or would agree to do on that particular account that I don't deem to be in the interest of the United States and of peace in the world.' Such sentiments from a man who would normally have been in the forefront of criticism against South Africa were considered one of the coups of the Mulder campaign. Symington's conversion to the South Africa cause has paid him, through his law firm of Smathers, Symington and Herlong, very well. In the six months from October 1981 to March 1982, they received $153,612.53 for lobbying on behalf of the South African government. Part of the money was distributed in the form of campaign contributions to selected Republican and Democratic candidates (they were not subject to the Federal Election Campaign Act as they were not foreign nationals), and the balance was taken up by fees incurred by Symington during his lobbying efforts.

South Africa could not rely solely on converts. There was also room for shaking out the middle ground and attempting to move the neutrals towards South Africa's position and giving those who were pro-South Africa encouragement to speak more forcefully on the subject of South Africa's strategic and economic value to the West.

In 1978, Rhoodie hired Donald de Kieffer, a twenty-eight-year-old Washington lawyer, to lobby on behalf of the South African government. Although young, de Kieffer was a staunch conservative who had made good contacts with the up-and-coming Republicans in Washington. On the other hand, his law firm, Collier, Shannon, Rill and Edwards, was well connected among right-of-centre Democrats, so together they made a perfect team. It was Rhoodie's view that de Kieffer was perhaps too young and inexperienced to do the complex selling job required of a lobbyist, so he looked around for someone more suitable to add to his list. In June 1975, Mulder and de Villiers visited Israel as a preliminary to the Vorster visit the following year, and in the course of their discussions, de Villiers asked for the name of an effective lobbyist and was advised to approach Sydney Baron. Although based in New York, Baron has considerable experience of

Washington and is accustomed to difficult customers (he acts for the Japanese electrical industry and Taiwan); he was happy to take on South Africa as a client, particularly in view of his fee which has never fallen below an annual $500,000 since his appointment in 1976.

It is difficult to estimate just how effective these lobbyists have been. Certainly when South Africa wanted to send Admiral H. H. Biermann, chief of the SADF, to Washington to meet with his opposite numbers in the Pentagon, it was the work of McGoff and the lobbyists that wangled him a visa over the objections of the State Department. Since the Biermann visit, there have been regular tours of the United States by senior serving officers in the South African armed forces. Much of the increased sympathy of the present US administration can be traced back to that one visa being granted. The Reagan administration is unduly responsive to the wishes and suggestions of the Pentagon, and South Africa has no shortage of allies in the US armed forces, all of whom are as convinced as the Pretoria government that the Communists intend to take over the world, South Africa included.

It is a logical step from the lobbying of congressmen and senators to attempting to prevent the election of opponents or ensuring that of supporters. When Gerald Ford ran on the Republican ticket against Carter in 1976, the South Africans contributed nearly $4 million to the Ford campaign. Although that particular contribution proved unrewarding, the South Africans had greater success when aiming at slightly less ambitious targets. For example, Rhoodie has claimed that South African cash went into the campaign of Republican S. I. Hayakawa who was running in the California 1976 senatorial campaign against Democrat John Tunney. Tunney, who is an outspoken critic of South Africa's policies and had been responsible for the Senate preventing the use of defence funds in Angola, was defeated.

It was inevitable that the great Mulder masterplan would begin to unravel. In 1978, stories began to appear in South African newspapers about a secret government department that appeared to have access to unlimited funds. The study was teased out bit by bit, and eventually a shocked South Africa discovered that millions of dollars were unaccounted for and had been dissipated by Rhoodie and his friends over four years of uncontrolled extravagance. Rhoodie had warned Vorster at that first meeting in 1974 that he might have to buy 'an important person's wife a fur coat' – but unfortunately he had not only bought too many, but he had failed to keep any sort of record of whom he had been paying and what services had been rendered in return. Vorster was forced to resign, as was Mulder who had been universally expected to succeed Vorster. Rhoodie fled the country, but was extradited from France, tried and sentenced to jail, only to be released immediately on bail.

However, it was not all a tale of misery and woe, from the South Africans' point of view. The $100 million dollars that had been invested around the world is still paying out dividends, and the prominent players who helped South Africa are still there doing their bit. De Villiers resigned from his position as Deputy Secretary of Information to take up a senior position with Sydney Baron's publicity firm in New York, where he works today. McGoff eventually got his Washington newspaper in the shape of a seat on the board of the *Washington Times* which began business in 1982 after the *Washington Star* finally folded. The *Times* is backed in part by the Unification Church of the Reverend Sun Myung Moon, and is published by James Whelan, who used to edit the *Sacramento Union* for McGoff and is a director of Panax. Several of the senior editorial staff have visited South Africa recently and are known for their pro-South Africa views. While there is no direct evidence that the South African government has funds directly invested in the newspaper, McGoff's involvement would certainly indicate some interest. The newspaper has also taken a consistently moderate stand on the question of apartheid in South Africa – in direct contrast to the only other Washington daily paper, the *Post*, which is invariably more liberal in its views.

It might have been expected that, following the crash of the Mulder empire, there would have been a dramatic revision of South Africa's foreign policy and its attitude towards propaganda. In fact, the Erasmus Commission (which investigated the whole affair on behalf of the South African government) did not publish details of many of the projects that had been orchestrated by Rhoodie and Mulder, and after their report had been published, a special government committee recommended that 56 of the 138 secret projects should continue. There is no way of telling where those projects are operating, but the main target will undoubtedly remain the United States which is the controller of Western policy towards South Africa; it must be expected that the Pretoria government will do everything in its power to influence the US administration in its favour.

In the twelve months to November 1980, South Africa paid over nearly $2 million to lobbyists and other groups such as the South Africa Foundation and the South Africa Tourist Office, all of which are charged with projecting a favourable image. South Africa had thus joined a long list of countries (including Japan, Taiwan, China, Britain, West Germany and most of the rest of the developed world) that find it productive to have strong lobbying forces working in the United States.

With the arrival of the Reagan administration, the South Africans expected a change of policy towards their country and, so far, they have been proved correct: there has been a relaxation of the ban on arms shipments and some nuclear fuel is likely to be shipped from the United States to power South Africa's new nuclear power stations at Koeberg. Perhaps more importantly, there is a new air of understanding and sympathy in Washington for South Africa's problems.

The Pretoria government, in common with many other countries, found the Carter administration almost incomprehensible in its obsession with human rights and Christian values which, to the outside world, seemed to bear little relation to the pragmatism required in foreign policy. However, when they had first visited the then Governor Reagan of California in 1973, the South Africans had been convinced that they had a friend in the former film star. They have since used every opportunity to emphasize to the present government the threat of Communism in southern Africa and, in the same way as talk of human rights moved Carter, so the threat of Communism strikes a chord in Reagan and his colleagues.

To put across this point of view, the South Africans have increased their lobbying power in Washington. While still retaining de Kieffer and his law firm, in 1980 they appointed John P. Sears, Reagan's former campaign manager, as their lobbyist. After leaving Reagan's election campaign, Sears had formed the legal firm of Baskin and Sears, immediately winning the South African contract, and in the six months up to the beginning of 1982, it received over $375,000 from the South African government. Sears has visited South Africa regularly and is charged with convincing the Reagan administration that the Pretoria government's policy on Namibia is correct and worth supporting. So far Sears seems to have been remarkably successful: South Africa has received considerable support from Reagan who sees the presence of Cuban troops in Angola as unacceptable. As long as the United States continues to provide that kind of support, South Africans feel that it might be possible to win the war in Namibia.

While the Israelis may find the excesses of the South African lobby campaign rather distasteful, they are faced with exactly the same problem. Without the support of the US government, their country would have little chance of surviving. Of course, there is a general recognition in the United States that Israel has considerable strategic value in an unstable Middle East, particularly as it is staunchly pro-West, and it is generally and rightly considered to be more in tune with Western perceptions of the world than its Arab neighbours. But

Israel remains vulnerable, depending on US aid and military supplies to bolster a shaky economy and re-equip the most modern and effective fighting machine in the world. While the Israeli government has been attempting to reduce this military dependence by manufacturing armaments itself, there is still a very narrow divide between survival and disaster.

During the war in the Lebanon in 1982, a special State Department study group was established to examine ways of pressuring Israel to stop its advance towards Beirut and ultimately to negotiate with the Palestinians. A number of options were examined including cutting military aid, reducing the level of economic support and cutting off diplomatic relations. In the end, the panel decided that cutting off military aid would take too long to have any effect, a reduction in economic support would be politically unacceptable, and the politicians had dithered too long to make the severing of diplomatic relations a viable option. The panel concluded instead that there was nothing that the United States could realistically do to pressure Israel other than make threatening noises. It was a salutary experience for those sitting on the panel, the majority of whom were pro-Israel but concerned at the course of action the Begin government was taking. As one member of the panel privately concluded:

Our inability to act means that Israel can now do virtually what it likes. If the policies were logical that would be fine, but by constantly alienating its friends and infuriating the Arabs, Israel is storing up a lot of trouble for the future. The growing body of Palestinians within Israeli borders are going to want a franchise, and the more that need is suppressed, the more likely it is that there will be an explosion.

After Israel had achieved its objectives in the Lebanon, the United States was allowed to enter the stage as mediator, a valuable but strictly secondary role. Such a demonstration of apparent impotence in a crisis is partly an indication of the complexities of the Middle East and partly an acknowledgement of the special relationship that exists between the United States and Israel.

Jews only make up about 3 per cent of the total population of the United States, but they still exercise an enormous amount of influence on US government policy, a reflection, for the most part, of the astonishing capacity of Jews to rise to positions of prominence and power in industry and politics in almost every country where they choose to live. Much has been made of the power of the Jewish lobby in the United States, and there have been repeated allegations that anything Israel wants gets done and anything Israel's opponents want gets delayed or refused. In the United States at the moment, there are around 300 national groups, 200 local organizations and 5,000 temples and synagogues devoted to fighting for Judaism and the State of Israel. While this is a considerable force, it is not just this Jewish lobby that has brought about the close friendship between the United States and Israel.

When the Jewish state was founded in 1948, it was given immediate backing by the American people. There appeared to be a general sentiment from an unfailingly generous nation that the Jews had had a raw deal and deserved to have their own nation after centuries of struggle. This may be a very simplistic view, but it is one that has largely prevailed over the past thirty-five years. There is no doubt that the largely Jewish-owned media in the United States have done much to perpetuate this view, and Israel has invariably been able to count on the unswerving loyalty of virtually every Jew in the United States in a time of crisis. When this is added to the natural empathy that other Americans feel for Israel, the total is a powerful body of public opinion supporting the Jewish nation, and few political leaders have dared to oppose such a broad consensus.

This support takes two forms: first, political mobilization by lobbying both locally and nationally, and second, financial. Apart from those in South Africa, American Jews are the largest per capita contributors to the State of Israel of all nations on earth. There is an automatic assumption by virtually all the United States' six million Jews that a portion of their income should go towards Israel, and since Jews form the richest ethnic body in America, that contribution has always been substantial.

Politically, it is the role of the different Jewish groups to pressure the US government to adopt policies favourable to Israel. Historically, there was never any question of the line that the lobbyists should take. In his book, *The Triangular Connection: America, Israel and American Jews*, Professor Edward Glick recalled that the Jewish lobby swung into action after the 1975 UN resolution that equated Zionism with racism and apartheid:

On the eve of the Jewish High Holy days and of the 31st [UN] General Assembly. the President's Conference [of major American Jewish organizations] UN Task Force sent letters to eighty-five [specially targeted] UN delegations. Eighteen of the representatives of key nations that had voted for the resolution were asked to 'oppose vigorously all efforts that would, directly or indirectly, malign or assault the Jewish people'. Thirty-three ambassadors who had opposed the resolution were asked to oppose any similar efforts at future UN sessions. Thirty-four ambassadors who had either absented themselves or abstained from voting were reminded in rather rabbinic rhetoric that 'abstention or absence when the issue is profoundly moral, only contributes to strengthening the forces of darkness'. In addition, thirty-seven ambassadors from Asian and black African countries were urged not to tie Zionism to apartheid, especially during the UN's so-called 'Decade against Racism'.

The damage had been done, but the lobby's performance had been what Israel has come to expect from its friends in the United States. Arab nations and the Eastern bloc have tended to emphasize the might and disproportionate influence of the Jewish lobby on American affairs; this is not wholly accurate and is more a reflection of the disorganized and poorly funded Arab lobbying effort.

Jewish lobbyists will point proudly to the fact that, in the seven years after 1973, the US Congress approved more than $11 billion in aid to Israel, $1 billion more than the sum requested by three different administrations and an indication of the pressure that the pro-Israel lobby was able to bring to bear on the government. The Arabs, on the other hand, have never been able to present a united front in the United States. There are a number of organizations, such as the National Association of Arab-Americans (NAAA), which are supposed to represent Arab interests, but the NAAA, like all other Arab groups, is badly funded and suffers from an incoherent policy. Although the Arab nations are collectively enormously wealthy and could do much to counter the influence of the Jews in the United States, each nation wants to have the major say in any joint venture. Jealousies appear in almost every inter-Arab relationship, and Israel has profited from their disunity.

However, the election of Menachem Begin to the position of Prime Minister of Israel did a great deal to erode the almost blanket support that Jews in America have traditionally given to Israel. His uncompromising attitude towards the Palestinians was the main cause of resentment. Few Jews actually support the PLO, the members of which they still regard as terrorists, but equally there was little support for Begin's rigid interpretation of the Bible and his insistence on continually expanding Jewish settlements into Palestinian territory. However, he refused to understand that his actions could alienate the Jews in America as well as the US government.

When the Israelis invaded the Lebanon, television news journalists were able for the first time to record in graphic detail the sufferings of the Arabs rather than the victories of the Israelis. It was a devastating experience for Jews the world over, and ended with a massacre of Palestinians in refugee camps outside Beirut. To many Jews, the whole Lebanese episode brought home the changes that had been taking place in Israel over the previous few years: what were seen as the fine liberal traditions on which Israel had been founded were in danger of disappearing as the Begin government became increasingly isolated from Jewish and world opinion.

The fragile coalition that resulted from Begin's resignation is unlikely to prove any more moderate since, to form his government, Prime Minister Yitzshak Shamir had to draw in the small militant parties of the hard right. The result will be more – not less – expansion of the settlement programme, and following the effective partition of the Lebanon and the emasculation of the PLO, the plight of the Palestinians will certainly not be eased.

As Jews themselves have begun to question the role of Israel in the world, so the power of the Jewish lobby has begun to diminish. In previous years, the great strength of the lobby was its unity; recently, however, the 500 or so Jewish organizations in the United States have examined their previously blanket support. In the past, most have given money unquestioningly to the State of Israel, but many now suggest that the lobbies should become more involved in the politics of Israel and support those groups that will maintain liberal traditions and oppose those individuals who, they feel, are not representative of Jews around the world.

It is an argument that will continue for many years but, while it is going on, others opposed to Israel are able to take advantage of the disunited lobby and a US government that is frustrated by Israeli militancy in the face of calls by the United States for moderation.

For example, during the summer of 1981, the Senate was due to vote on a proposal to sell Airborne Warning and Control Systems (AWACS) aircraft to Saudi Arabia. Israel was opposed to the sale, claiming that AWACS in the hands of a potential aggressor represented a serious threat to the country's security. The Jewish lobby united to try and stop the sale, but simultaneously, and for the first time, an Arab lobby group got themselves sufficiently organized to orchestrate a powerful and highly effective campaign to win support for the AWACS sale in the Senate. The AWACS battle demonstrated that the actual strength of the Jewish lobby was considerably weaker than previous reports might have indicated, and it also illustrated the degree to which support for the Israeli government had declined within the US administration.

The declining influence of the Jewish lobby has compelled the Israeli government to nurture new allies who will back them in the corridors of power. Friends have been found in unlikely quarters, and perhaps the most unusual alliance has been that formed between the Moral Majority and the Israelis, and the Moral Majority and the South Africans.

The Moral Majority is an alliance of various conservative Christian groups, such as Christian Voice and Religious Round Table, which concerns itself with the decline of moral and family standards in modern society. Using television and radio to propagandize their views, the Christian New Right has managed to tap the vast conservative voice that lies deep in the American heartland. These Christian groups are against such 'liberal' measures as the equal rights amendment, homosexual rights and abortion, and argue for the restoration of Bible reading and prayer in public schools. While winning converts, the new evangelists have also become extremely rich. Jerry Falwell, leader of the Moral Majority, claims that his 'Old Time Gospel Hour' raises $1 million a week from 18 million viewers. However, it has never been clear exactly how many people the New Christians really represent. Television audience figures are notoriously inaccurate and none of the religious groups will publish detailed membership lists. Nevertheless, there is no doubt that those who join any of the groups that make up the Moral Majority are fervent and committed supporters and make formidable political campaigners.

Such (reputedly) huge numbers, allied with a substantial income and evangelical fervour, have made the Moral Majority a force to be reckoned with in American politics and it has not hesitated to use its power. For example, in 1980 at the Republican National Convention in Detroit, the evangelical movement brought in several hundred supporters to lobby candidates. Ronald Reagan was sufficiently impressed by their eloquence to make clear from his election platform that he would be standing for traditional family values and the right to life of the unborn child.

There has always been empathy between right-wing Christians in the United States and South Africa, many taking a view directly contrary to the World Council of Churches, which actively opposes apartheid and partially funds guerrilla groups opposed to the Pretoria government. To the Christian fundamentalists, such action borders on heresy. People like Falwell have a fairly straightforward view of the world, with the Bible as the yardstick of performance. Thus all Communists are evil and any nation or group that lives by the standards set in the Bible is good. The South Africans, with their strong Reformed Church background, conservatism and opposition to

Communism, are logical allies, and the ambitions of the South African government and the Moral Majority frequently coincide.

The New Right is now a very powerful force, and although the Reagan administration has proved less pliant to the wishes of the Moral Majority than some might have expected, there is no doubt of its powerful impact upon Republican policies. The South Africans had discovered the usefulness of the New Right early on, during the 1978 re-election campaign of Senator Dick Clark of Iowa, who in the previous election of 1972 had won by a landslide. As Chairman of the Senate's African Affairs Subcommittee, Clark had been the author of an amendment which forbade any direct or indirect US aid to Angola without express congressional authorization – and this had infuriated the South Africans. The Rhoodie slush fund contributed $250,000 to the campaign of Clark's opponent, Republican Roger Jepson, and the South Africans found welcome allies among the Moral Majority. The state's anti-abortion groups took exception to Clark's stand for the liberalization of abortion laws, and they mobilized their forces to ensure his defeat. Churches across the state distributed 300,000 brochures urging them to vote for Jepson, as well as organizing candlelit processions and a savage press campaign. Clark was defeated, and both the South Africans and the Moral Majority were impressed at the influence of their respective groups.

The alliance of the right has not stopped at attempting to influence internal American politics. Since 1979, two aides of Republican Senator Jesse Helms of North Carolina (a star of the New Right), John Carbaugh and Jim Lucier, have regularly visited South Africa and have shown considerable sympathy for the government. In 1979, during the negotiations in London on the future of Rhodesia, the two men turned up and, in secret meetings, tried to persuade Ian Smith, leader of Rhodesia's whites and Bishop Abel Muzorewa, the black leader and favoured child of Britain and the United States, to hold firm against the more militant blacks who eventually took power. The British Foreign Secretary at that time, Lord Carrington, complained to the US State Department and Helms' aides were asked to leave. Their trip to London had been paid for by the Institute of American Relations, another right-wing pressure group.

The South Africans maintain direct liaison with American Christians through an organization called the Christian League which was created as part of the Rhoodie information campaign to publicize the view of South Africa as a God-fearing Christian society in an uncivilized and immoral world, and has sponsored a series of lecture tours by South Africans in the United States. It is based in Pretoria and is primarily backed by John McGoff who, as always, has proved a very useful link between South Africa and his own country.

The vision of South Africa as a God-fearing outpost of civilization is mirrored to some extent by the State of Israel. To the simplistic Christian Right in the United States, at least Israel is more understandable than the Muslims who surround the Jews. Although Jews in America view Christian fundamentalists with deep suspicion, as more middle-of-the-road church groups such as the National Council of Churches have come out in favour of a Palestinian state, these fears have had to be overlooked in the search for new and influential friends.

Israel's closest friend in the Moral Majority is Jerry Falwell. According to Falwell's spokesman, Cal Thomas: 'Jerry has said that as a pastor he believes God deals with nations in direct proportion to how those nations deal with Israel and its people, because the Jews are God's chosen people.' Such sentiments greatly pleased Begin, who counted Falwell among his staunchest allies in the United States.

At the time of the Israeli bombing of the Iraqi nuclear reactor in June 1981, Israel was criticized by the liberal National Council of Churches. Begin ordered Falwell to issue a statement of rebuttal; Falwell did so. Similarly, during the Israeli siege of Beirut in 1982, when Israel was almost universally condemned by friend and foe alike, Falwell spoke to Begin to reassure him that his friends would stand by Israel. At Begin's suggestion, Falwell was presented with a medal for his support of Israel, at a dinner in New York to commemorate the 100th anniversary of the birth of Vladimir Jabotinsky, Begin's mentor and a fervent Zionist.

The growing alliance between Israel and the New Right is causing considerable concern among Jews in Israel and elsewhere. Many believe that the followers of the New Right are nothing less than bigots who have almost no concept of democratic ideals and are at heart anti-Semitic. To counter this, the Israeli government has argued that Israel remains beleaguered and should never turn away a friend. The arrival of Shamir will do nothing to disturb the progress of the relationship. Like Begin, the new Prime Minister is a firm believer in gathering allies wherever and whenever possible, and the Moral Majority represent a strong and potentially very valuable pressure group with close links with the current Republican administration. That argument has also served to cement the alliance between Israel and South Africa. It is an argument of expediency that is serving to isolate Israel further.

PART TWO

8 Israel and the Bomb

In Israel, water is scarce and, without a regular flow, much of the land that is currently crop-producing will revert to desert. To the founding fathers of the fledgling state, atomic power, then also in its infancy, offered the perfect solution. The steam from a nuclear reactor would power a desalination plant which, in turn, would provide enough water to turn the Negev desert into a vast and lush source of food. In 1950, a union was formed between the political and scientific communities, which was to commit Israel to spending billions of dollars over the next twenty years on a nuclear programme that would enable it to join the nuclear club.

This union centred on two men. Recommended by Albert Einstein as one of his most outstanding pupils, Ernst David Bergmann, then in his thirties, was asked by the Israeli government to head the scientific department at the Ministry of Defence. A balding chain-smoker, a workaholic addicted to coffee and a passionate Zionist from an old German-Jewish family, Bergmann was a man of enormous scientific vision, and he brought the first signs of a coherent scientific policy to Israel. His worth was immediately recognized, particularly by Prime Minister David Ben-Gurion. With Ben-Gurion's statesman-like vision and Bergmann's scientific ability, the two made a formidable partnership. It was their strength that gathered to Israel some of the best brains in the world, and the foundations that they laid thirty years ago have placed the country in a position that makes it one of the leading nations in the field of atomic research and arms production.

Unlike many politicians, Ben-Gurion actually recognized the vital role that science and its applications had to play in the survival of Israel:

Scientific research and its achievements are no longer simply an abstract intellectual business, essentially supplying the spiritual and scholarly needs of a few individuals, but a factor of central importance to our everyday lives, a factor which – together with the sweat of our hands – is the first and fundamental condition for the progress of a cultured people.

He realized that, for a small country of Israel's limited resources, atomic energy was the answer, so at the beginning of the 1950s he instructed Bergmann to recruit and train Jewish scientists from all over the world to conduct research into energy, with a view to building or purchasing one or more nuclear reactors in the future.

For four years, Bergmann gathered his troops in total secrecy, convinced that the path Ben-Gurion had chosen was the right one. 'There are those who say,' he wrote, 'that it is possible to purchase everything that we need, including knowledge and experience, from abroad. This attitude worries me. I am convinced . . . that the State of Israel needs a defence research programme of its own so that we shall never again be as lambs led to the slaughter.'

In July 1956, Bergmann, then Scientific Adviser to Israel's Ministry of Defence (and later Chairman of the Atomic Energy Commission in the Prime Minister's Office), presented a lengthy memorandum to Shimon Peres, who was General Director of the Ministry of Defence at the time. According to Peres, the memorandum included a variety of options: Israel could purchase a reactor from the United States, Canada or France, or even build one from scratch. Bergmann also suggested the two following clauses that were to form the foundations of the Israeli nuclear programme:

The small reactor: if the small reactor cannot be established at Rehovot, it will be best to build it close to the sea, for example, at Nahal Sorek.
The large reactor [later to be built at Dimona]: its logical site is the Negev, as the nucleus of a scientific community. An alternative site would be Nebi Rubin.

The memorandum was considered by the Israeli Cabinet and the decision was taken to proceed with the small project at Nebi Rubin, the reactor subsequently being purchased from the United States under the 'Atoms for Peace' programme. The enormous expense for a nation that was still rationing eggs worried the government and a firm decision on Dimona was put off.

Then came the British–French Suez débâcle of 1956. Although the whole affair was a major disaster, Israel over-ran both Suez and Gaza in the first of what were to be several wars over the same piece of ground. To the alarm of the Israeli government, however, they were compelled to withdraw because of international pressure, particularly from the United States and the Soviet Union. Although there were mild reassurances from the United States and an agreement to station a peacekeeping force at Sharm-el-Sheikh, Israel, already highly nervous about territorial security, felt that it had been largely betrayed by its former allies and was being forced to stand alone in an extremely hostile environment. Both Ben-Gurion and his defence experts felt that a rethinking of Israel's strategy was necessary if it were to survive. They argued that if they had been betrayed once, then it could very easily happen again – and on the next occasion they might not be so well prepared. So, in early 1957, the Israeli Cabinet approved the development of the Dimona project. While the world knew that Israel was interested in acquiring one or two nuclear power plants, what the world was *not* told was that, at the Cabinet meeting, it was further agreed to use the facility at Dimona to develop a nuclear bomb.

In the same year, an agreement was reached between France and Israel for the supply of a nuclear reactor and the uranium to run it. Hundreds of Israeli scientists were seconded to the Dimona project, which began to take shape in the desert. At this stage, the project was still secret and officially labelled a 'textile plant', although it was thought that the Americans had a very good idea of what was going on, having flown a U-2 spy-plane over the site in March 1958. When Charles de Gaulle became President of France in 1960, Israel's nuclear development programme suffered a temporary hiccup. The French Foreign Minister Couve de Murville summoned the Israeli ambassador, Walter Eitan, and told him that France would no longer be able to supply his country with the uranium; in addition, the French insisted that Israel make public its nuclear programme.

Two factors had forced the French to jeopardize their special relationship with Israel. First, the US government, alerted by reconnaissance and hard, on-the-ground intelligence, knew full well both what was happening in the Negev and France's role in the project. The United States was seriously concerned that, should the nformation leak out that Israel ws building a nuclear plant, the Arab nations would immediately assume she was building an atomic bomb for use against them; the Americans feared an Arab–Israeli war that might well threaten the very existence of Israel and would certainly drag the United States into direct confrontation with the Soviet Union. Second, the French were concerned that Israel would, in fact, use the facility at Dimona to build a nuclear bomb with which either to threaten its neighbours in the aggressive search for more territory, or to use as a last resort in the face of defeat by the Arabs.

Ben-Gurion flew to Paris in June 1960 for a face-to-face meeting with de Gaulle. The usual sumptuous feast was laid on at the Elysée Palace and, after the meal, the two heads of state went for a stroll through the grounds. A small party consisting of de Gaulle, Ben-Gurion, Peres and Prime Minister Michel Debré sat down at one of the tables in the garden. According to Peres, de Gaulle turned to Ben-Gurion and asked: 'What are your true intentions regarding the frontiers of Israel? Tell me and I promise it will be kept secret. I know that your country is small. Do you want the mountains to the east, or the desert in the south?'

Ben-Gurion replied: 'I am more concerned with the problems of immigration [dealing with the influx of Jews from abroad] and peace than with the question of territory. I am prepared to be content with the existing frontiers, so long as we can achieve peace and bring in more Jews.'

This seemed to reassure de Gaulle, and by the end of the visit, an agreement had been hammered out that gave Israel the uranium while Ben-Gurion promised that he would sanction neither the development of a plutonium separation plant nor the building of a nuclear device. The French government leaked details of the discussions to reassure the Americans who, while mollified, were still not totally convinced that the Dimona project was all that it seemed.

In early December 1960, the United States launched two more U-2 flights over Israel. The photographs they brought back caused considerable alarm: they revealed that the Dimona project was well advanced and, both from analysis that is still classified and from sources with the project, the Americans became convinced that Israel was planning to develop a bomb.

High-level contacts between the two governments were made, with the Americans pressing for a public statement from the Israelis. The Soviets, too, knew about the Dimona project and had been in touch with the Americans to express their concern. As a result of this international pressure, Ben-Gurion was forced to make a statement before the Knesset, on 22 December. He announced that Israel was indeed building a second nuclear reactor at Dimona with a 24-megawatt capacity. The reactor was entirely for peaceful purposes, Ben-Gurion added, and would help in the development of industry and agriculture, as well as acting as a research facility for Israel to plan and develop its own nuclear reactor within the next decade. These reassurances did little to satisfy the Americans, and the confirmation that the Israelis were building a sizeable reactor – for whatever purpose – brought the Arabs close to panic. (The earlier project at Nebi Rubin was so small and with no possibility of a military application that its construction and operation had taken place without any opposition.)

Shortly after taking office, President John Kennedy was told by the CIA that Israel was on the verge of entering the nuclear age. Reportedly furious, Kennedy instructed the US ambassador to Israel to take the matter up with the Ben-Gurion government. In a very firm letter, the ambassador asked the country's then Foreign Minister, Golda Meir, to clarify Israel's own position. The US government demanded to be told exactly how the reactor would operate and what would happen to the plutonium that would be manufactured as a by-product, and perhaps more importantly, the Americans also wanted the Israelis to agree to regular inspection of their Dimona plant.

Ben-Gurion was extremely angry with the United States for the peremptory tone of the letter, and he was also placed in something of a dilemma since he knew that Dimona was being geared up to produce nuclear weapons, but he could not admit this even to his country's closest ally. In the end, he repeated his previous denials and agreed to allow inspectors to enter the Dimona site. Almost unbelievably, the US inspectors who visited Dimona came away convinced that the project was entirely peaceful: in a carefully orchestrated tour, the Dimona scientists managed to conceal the most sensitive areas of the plant from the eyes of the prying Americans. Inspectors from the United States continued to visit the plant annually for six years – and never once did they get a direct indication that Israel was experimenting with nuclear weapons . . . That information came from elsewhere.

Public anxiety in the world at large merely reflected a savage internal debate within the Israeli scientific community and also, more publicly, in the Knesset. Basically, the argument came down to what was voiced by one member of the Knesset: 'We do not have the money to buy wheat, or even rice; are we to squander our resources on a tenuous technological dream?' Seven out of the eight senior scientists at the Israeli Atomic Energy Commission resigned over what they saw as a criminal waste of very limited Israeli resources. They argued that instead of building expensive reactors that might be of use a decade later, it was more important to develop a manufacturing and agricultural base. This left Bergmann to carry on the project alone.

Levi Eshkol, who came to power in 1963, was opposed to the development of the nuclear bomb, and he was supported by Chief of Staff Rabin and General Yighal Allon who was then serving as a cabinet minister. Among the military, too, there was considerable disagreement over the best way to defend the territory against the growing military might of the Arabs. The more conservative generals, among them Allon and Yitzhak Rabin, believed in conventional military strength; they and many other senior officers felt that, with an Arab world permanently divided, the Arab armed forces could never begin to match the Israeli *esprit de corps*. If the best of modern technology in tanks, small arms and missiles was married to the high morale and training of the Israeli armed forces, Rabin and Allon believed they would be unbeatable.

Such a philosophy presumed a static Arab opposition, with the initiative for instigating hostilities resting firmly with the Israelis. General Moshe Dayan, then Chief of Staff of the IDF, disagreed strongly with his colleagues and sided with Ben-Gurion. Dayan recognized that the Arab nations, who were only just beginning to see the benefit of oil, would soon be able to afford the most sophisticated of modern weapons purchased from both East and West. Israel, on the other hand, could not afford another arms race, particularly with an oil-rich and united Arab people who would be able to find an almost limitless supply of petrodollars. United in their common enmity towards Israel, Dayan felt that, in years to come, a well-equipped Arab army launching a pre-emptive strike against Israel would stand a very good chance of winning.

Much later, in 1967 when he was Minister of Defence, it was Dayan who brought the phrase 'bomb in the basement' into the fierce arguments then raging. He suggested that with a nuclear capability, Israel not only possessed a potent final threat that the Arabs already knew about, but that it would also act as a useful bargaining point – unseen but ever-present – in any future negotiations over the size and situation of Israel. In the bomb-in-the-basement theory, the Arabs might be prepared to attack Israel but they would never go so far as to wipe out the country because they knew that, as a last resort, Israel would drop the bomb.

There is little solid evidence that, during the next twenty years, the deterrent philosophy actually worked. After the 1973 war, Dayan argued for an open declaration of Israel's nuclear capability, believing that this would be more effective. At that time, as now, Israel was spending some 30 per cent of its GNP on defence and the economy was beginning to fall apart. Further, the surprise attack by the Arabs in 1973 and the Israeli near-defeat showed Dayan that the bomb in the basement did little to hold the enemy at bay. An open nuclear policy, Dayan argued, would free an enormous amount of defence expenditure for investment in the broad economy and would hopefully act as a real deterrent. Others reasoned that, during the 1973 war, the Arabs had had no intention of eliminating Israel but had merely wanted to recover land for use as a bargaining counter in negotiations over the Palestinians; thus the nuclear deterrent could be said to have worked. This debate goes on in Israel today with no decision yet being made on how the structure of the defence forces should be organized into the 1990s. In any event, the quartet of Ben-Gurion, Bergmann, Peres and Dayan held the line, and Israel continued to develop its nuclear potential.

To produce an atomic bomb, one of two materials can be used, either plutonium or enriched uranium. Whichever is employed, a different type of bomb will emerge, but in each case a highly sophisticated technological process is needed to get the material into suitable bomb-making condition.

At Dimona, the uranium that was fed into the reactor as fuel would eventually be converted into plutonium. The fuel rods used inside the reactor would be bombarded by the neutrons activated in the reactor process, and as the rods were worn down, plutonium would gradually emerge. There are two major drawbacks to the plutonium process. In the first place, it takes a long time to produce enough end-material to make one bomb. At maximum production, the Dimona reactor could only produce around five to seven kilograms of plutonium a year, which at best would be only enough to make one nuclear device. In addition, once the plutonium has been produced by the reactor, it is highly radioactive and still contains some uranium and other waste materials. A complicated chemical process, involving what is known as a 'hot cell' plant, is used to isolate enough pure plutonium for bomb-making.

The alternative method of reaching the bomb stage is to utilize one of two different types of uranium isotope. Uranium-238 makes up some 99.3 per cent of uranium in its natural state and is fairly benign, while uranium-235 makes up the remaining 0.7 per cent. The relatively lighter uranium-235 atoms are the ones that split most readily, causing the fission that starts the chain reaction that is used in both reactors and bombs. In most reactor designs, the proportion of U-235 in the total mass of uranium has to be increased through a process known as enrichment. Typically, reactors for the commercial generation of electricity require about 3 per cent U-235, the reactors in nuclear-powered submarines may require 30 per cent and nuclear explosives require at least 70 per cent, and preferably over 90 per cent.

There are various techniques used for uranium enrichment; these require considerable expertise in nuclear physics and a vast investment in the enrichment plant that has to exploit the different properties of the two isotopes, in order to isolate U-235 and discard U-238. Without the highly sophisticated techniques required to produce enriched uranium, the only alternatives are to buy it or steal it.

The US government had solved their uranium enrichment problem while working towards the bombs that eventually devastated Hiroshima and Nagasaki after completion of the Manhattan Project: they invested over $1 billion and built an enormous mile-long production line at Oak Ridge, Tennessee. Although other enrichment plants were available by the time Israel made its decision to go nuclear, the US government, in company with other countries, had introduced stringent safeguards to prevent enriched uranium from falling into the hands of those nations with nuclear ambitions. Under the auspices of the US Atomic Energy Commission (AEC), the passage of all uranium, enriched or not, throughout the United States was closely monitored. In theory, all uranium that is checked into a factory is weighed, the loss by processing calculated, the production measured – and by simple arithmetic, the totals should always tally. Similarly, raw uranium could only be sold to those countries that already had nuclear power stations, and enriched uranium could only be passed between the exclusive few who had already developed the bomb.

For Israel in the 1950s, the problem was a simple one: how to get enriched uranium to the plant at Dimona without detection. Some time in 1956 there was a meeting between Bergmann, Peres and Isser Harel, Chief Executive of the Mossad. At that meeting the discussion ranged around the various options available, with the emphasis on acquiring the enriched uranium by covert means. By Bergmann's calculations, the Dimona reactor would not be on line before 1963 at the earliest – and more probably 1964 – so the Israeli government had enough time to plan a long-range campaign that would pay steady dividends over the next decade.

The decision was made to take advantage of the apparently weak regulatory system in the United States and siphon off enriched uranium which would then be smuggled into Israel. It was really an exercise on two levels: the first, the acquisition of enriched uranium; the second, the sending of Israeli experts all over the world to be trained in and gather knowledge of the current advances in nuclear physics.

The Mossad's eye fell on Dr Zalman Shapiro. A Jew and a Zionist, he was a research chemist who had been heavily involved in the Manhattan Project and so possessed very useful contacts within the nuclear hierarchy in the United States. In 1957, Shapiro formed the Nuclear Materials and Equipment Corporation (NUMEC), located in Apollo, Pennsylvania, about thirty miles north-east of Pittsburgh, and staffed by Shapiro's former colleagues on the Manhattan Project. In addition, sources within the CIA remain convinced that the company was primarily financed by the Israelis.

At this time, the US nuclear industry was in its infancy. Little had yet been done to regulate those companies involved in the development of nuclear technology, and NUMEC was able to take advantage of the club-like atmosphere that existed. Using his personal contacts, Shapiro was in a position to bid for government contracts to process uranium and produce fuel for reactors and the space programme. For example, Admiral Hyman Rickover, the father of the US nuclear submarine fleet, gave him his division's valuable contracts; with such an official stamp of approval, Shapiro was soon gathering a long string of international clients, mostly in Europe.

At the same time, NUMEC entered into an arrangement with Israel whereby the company agreed to serve as a 'technical consultant and training and procurement agency'. This relationship proved so mutually beneficial that a separate company, ISORAD, was formed, owned half by NUMEC and half by the Israeli government. Officially, according to NUMEC's financial statements, ISORAD was to help develop techniques to preserve fruit through irradiation; in reality, it was to provide a pipeline for uranium and other nuclear technology, one that went straight to Dimona.

This sort of joint venture, on the surface often quite innocent, was to become a hallmark of Israeli operations in the nuclear field. Their early successful experience with NUMEC led them to realize that an appearance of legitimacy was often enough to disguise true intent, since it generally took several years for any official agencies to discover what was happening. The Shapiro plant, with its, by now, long list of top-secret government contracts, was a gold mine for any intelligence agency, and for the young Israeli nuclear programme it presented a wonderful opportunity to obtain a constant update on the latest developments in US nuclear research, at that time the most advanced in the world.

The NUMEC plant in Apollo, Pa. naturally attracted a large number of visitors; however, most alarming to those who were by now beginning to keep a wary eye on Shapiro was the number of visits paid by Baruch Cinai, an Israeli metallurgist, and Ephraim Lahav, the scientific attaché to the Israeli embassy in Washington. Lahav's activities were, in fact, investigated by the FBI, but its report remains classified.

By the beginning of the 1960s, concern about NUMEC was beginning to surface on two levels. Inspectors for the AEC felt that the safeguards supposedly imposed by Shapiro were totally inadequate. In particular, they observed that Shapiro was doing two things to disguise the exact amounts of uranium passing through his plant. Although specifically prohibited from doing so by his government contract, Shapiro was mixing enriched with ordinary uranium, so that keeping track of a particular contract became almost impossible. In any event, to the US government inspectors it appeared that keeping track of the uranium seemed to be the last thing on Shapiro's mind. In addition, sloppy bookkeeping meant that AEC inspectors were unable to trace a particular contract right through the system. The theory of weighing in uranium and then weighing it out again at the end of the line, which was a cornerstone of the regulatory system, was impossible to implement.

The second area of concern lay in security. Both the FBI and the various intelligence divisions of the armed forces for whom Shapiro was now working were increasingly concerned at the apparent ease with which foreigners could get into the NUMEC plant. In particular Shapiro's obvious and close relationship with the Israelis caused alarm. The agencies were worried that visitors had too easy access to the 2,400 classified documents, including 169 'micro-cards' containing descriptions of secret government research and development programmes. Several private and friendly warnings were passed along to Shapiro who ignored them all. In the end, his initial sponsor, Admiral Rickover, wrote Shapiro a letter warning him that, unless he instituted some controls over the aliens who apparently had almost free entrée to the plant, he would be liable for prosecution. None of the warnings seemed to have the slightest effect on NUMEC operations; the foreign visitors continued to pour through the gates and no effective controls were introduced to monitor the flow of uranium.

In late 1964, shortly after the Israelis' Dimona nuclear plant began operation, the Director of the CIA, Richard Helms, received an alarming report: CIA agents had apparently discovered that Israel had managed to obtain a quantity of enriched uranium. Although the Agency was unable to analyse any of the U-235, it was perfectly clear it had been obtained illegally – most probably from the United States which had the largest and most sophisticated enrichment operation in the world. Helms was also told that Israeli fighters had been seen, and photographed, practising a certain type of bombing run. When delivering a nuclear bomb, if an aircraft used a low-level attack and released over the target, it would be destroyed by the explosion; a bomber making a high run is vulnerable to anti-aircraft fire. To get around these two problems the pilot makes a very fast, low-level attack; while still some miles from the target, he climbs steeply upwards and, still ascending, releases the bomb. The pilot then turns away from the bomb, forward momentum taking the bomb to land on or near the target. Obviously this 'loft and toss' is not the most accurate method of bombing, and if used with conventional munitions, it is not very effective; but with a nuclear device, accuracy is not so essential. What the CIA agents had seen were Israeli pilots in US aircraft practising 'loft and toss' runs.

In a preliminary report, Helms concluded that Israel either had already developed a bomb or was on the point of doing so, and he also mentioned NUMEC as a possible source of the uranium. CIA agents had followed Shapiro on his frequent visits to Israel and were sure that he was dealing in both goods and sensitive information.

The bubble burst for NUMEC in April 1965, when a contract obtained from Westinghouse to process some fuel for a nuclear rocket programme began to go awry. Business had been a little slow during the previous few months and there was no other uranium coming into the plant, so Shapiro was unable to disguise the inefficiency of his own monitoring system. Worse was to come, however. Shapiro was forced to tell visiting AEC inspectors that more than 130 pounds of uranium appeared to have gone missing – enough to make at least six atomic bombs.

Such a disaster had not been experienced since the dawn of the US nuclear age. The AEC demanded an immediate explanation. Shapiro reassuringly argued that the uranium was not really lost, merely buried in one of two huge waste pits that had been dug at the plant to bury all the contaminated materials that were by-products of the enrichment process. To prove his point, his workers excavated one of the pits, but analysis revealed only a fraction of the missing uranium concealed among the rubbish.

Following tense negotiations, the AEC persuaded Shapiro to open the one remaining pit; after analysis, it was found that 391 pounds of enriched uranium was unaccounted for. After allowing for natural wastage over the years of processing, the AEC concluded that NUMEC had managed to lose over 206 pounds – more than had ever been lost at any time by any country. The AEC sent another team of investigators into the NUMEC plant in an attempt to trace the records of uranium shipments during the previous eight years. They found that, in the previous year in the course of an overenthusiastic clean-up in the plant, a large quantity of the records had been destroyed (twenty-six of the thirty-two contracts awarded had incomplete records). In the first of many inconclusive reports, the AEC said: 'Although it cannot be stated with certainty that theft or diversion did not take place, the survey found no evidence to suggest these possibilities.'

The problem facing the AEC, the US government's General Accounting Office and the FBI was that Shapiro's records were so thin and the monitoring so haphazard that it was impossible to state decisively where the uranium had gone. As a result, and even with this appalling record, Shapiro stayed in business and went on being awarded government contracts. All this despite the firmly held belief, expressed privately by both the CIA and the FBI, that Shapiro had been the conduit for the uranium that gave Israel her first atomic bomb.

At various times over the next few years, investigations in NUMEC were reopened. Three attorney-generals – Ramsay Clark, John Mitchell and Edward Levi – ordered investigations; President Johnson reportedly refused a request from Helms to reopen the CIA's investigation; and Jerry Ford requested a final – but still inconclusive – inquiry in 1976 after officials of the Nuclear Regulatory Commission (the AEC's successor) were given a briefing on the subject by the CIA.

Perhaps the most interesting of all these investigations was that carried out in 1968 by the FBI at the request of the CIA. By then, the speculation of 1964 had firmed into certainty and the CIA had produced an 'eyes-only' report for the President, alerting him to the fact that Israel had perfected the bomb and the means for its delivery. Partly their rivalry with the FBI and partly their frustration at their inability to nail the culprits prompted the CIA's request for yet another look into Shapiro's and NUMEC's activities.

By all accounts, the FBI devoted a great deal of effort towards an attempt to pin some charge on Shapiro. They received permission from Attorney-General Ramsay Clark to put wiretaps on all Shapiro's telephones, and they tailed him for months. Much to the FBI's annoyance, Shapiro used a scrambler for all his most sensitive phone calls, and the FBI were unable to crack the code. The agency did discover, however, that Shapiro was acting as a high-powered head-hunter for the Israelis, travelling around the United States recruiting scientists of many disciplines, not simply those who were specialists in nuclear energy, to go and work in Israel. According to an AEC file on the case, based in part on the FBI report, the investigation revealed

> very close ties with Israel and a highly organized effort on the part of Israel in this country to solicit substantial technical and financial assistance . . . But the FBI report does not produce any direct evidence of diversion or unlawful activity in connection with performance under AEC contracts.

By this time, NUMEC had outlived its usefulness to the Israelis and was dissolved. In the final accounting, the AEC, who had again gone to the plant in 1967, reckoned that a total of 572 pounds of enriched uranium were unaccounted for, and the CIA have estimated that around 200 pounds of this actually reached Israel during a ten-year period, although the figure may have been much higher. It is interesting to note that little appears to have been done to improve security in other such plants. A US Department of Energy study released in November 1982 revealed that 183 pounds of uranium and plutonium could not be accounted for at five government nuclear complexes. The material had gone missing between 1 April and 30 September 1981.

In ten years, the Mossad had achieved exactly what had been agreed at the secret meeting in 1956. Although suspected since 1960, the Israeli relationship with Shapiro and NUMEC had never been proved, and enough uranium had reached Israel to help her develop a nuclear capability. However, the frustration of the official investigators at NUMEC and the skeletons that seemed to appear with frightening regularity from out of every cupboard compelled the US government to seek a change in the regulatory laws governing the transfer of nuclear technology and materials. Although NUMEC had been fined over $1 million for losing the uranium, officials at AEC felt that this smacked of shutting the stable door far too late. Tough new laws were enacted that would ultimately lead to the disbanding of the old AEC and the establishment of the Nuclear Regulatory Commission (NRC).

The writing was very definitely on the wall for the Israelis' smuggling enterprises. In addition, following the Six Day War of June 1967, various countries imposed a partial or total arms embargo on Israel, and France, its traditional supplier of ordinary uranium, cut off supplies. With its customary aggression, the Mossad decided on a few bold strokes that would give Israel a store of both enriched and ordinary uranium to fall back on while their scientists perfected some highly secret research then under way at Dimona.

According to an article in the US magazine *Rolling Stone*, written by Howard Kohn and Barbara Newman, in 1968 Mossad established an Israeli commando squad that was given the brief of hijacking enriched uranium wherever and whenever they felt they could get away with it; secondly, they established a dummy European company through which uranium would be diverted to Israel. That same year, in France, the Israeli team attacked a truck ferrying uranium, firing tear-gas canisters into the cab, disabling the crew and disappearing with the truck and its contents. The scenario is alleged to have been repeated in Britain – only this time the squad made a mistake and stole a shipment of low-grade 'yellowcake' uranium. Whatever the truth of these relatively sensational stories, Israel was already planning what has so far proved to be the ultimate nuclear hijacking – the lifting of over 200 tons of uranium from Europe.

What became known as the 'Plumbat Affair' was an exercise in deception organized by the Mossad which netted Israel about the same amount of uranium that it had received via Shapiro and NUMEC. Although the theft occurred in 1968, it was ten years before the full story was told, and even then the truth was only revealed by the investigative work of Elaine Davenport and the *Sunday Times* journalists Paul Eddy and Peter Gillman, who described, in their book *The Plumbat Affair*, how the unfortunate capture of a claustrophobic Mossad agent in Lillehammer, Norway, provided the key to the whole affair.

In July 1973, a five-man hit squad was sent by the Mossad to Norway to assassinate a senior official of the PLO, Ali Hassan Salameh, who, it was claimed, had been involved in the massacre of Israeli athletes at the Munich Olympics. In the event, the team botched the job and gunned down an innocent waiter working in a restaurant, and to add insult to injury, the usually efficient Mossad suffered the indignity of their hit team being arrested and locked up in the local jail.

One of their number, Dan Aerbel, had as a child spent part of the Second World War hiding in a cellar. Since then, he had suffered from claustrophobia, and after one night in a jail cell, he was ready to tell all. The following exchange, quoted in *The Plumbat Affair*, must have been baffling to the village police in Lillehammer:

'I owned the *Scheersberg A*,' Aerbel said.
'So what?' the interrogator asked.
'It carried the uranium to Israel.'

Fortunately, the police chief passed the information up the line and Aerbel was soon being subjected to intensive questioning by Norwegian counter-intelligence. The story he had to tell was fascinating and, for the first time, revealed the theft of 200 tons of uranium from Belgium – a theft that had been successfully covered up by the European Commission (the EEC's executive) and Euratom for the previous five years.

As with Shapiro and NUMEC, the Mossad had decided that the best way of getting a substantial quantity of uranium was to set up a dummy company and then, in an apparently legitimate operation, divert the nuclear fuel to Israel. Always on the lookout for useful tools, Mossad had their eyes on a former Nazi pilot called Herbert Schulzen. At the age of twenty, Schulzen had lost an argument with a Canadian Mosquito fighter-bomber and had been forced to crashland. He had suffered a serious head injury, and although the wound healed, it continued to give him pain. Finally, in 1964, he was persuaded to have an operation which apparently solved the pain problem but involved a lengthy period of convalescence. The Mossad had prepared the ground well. Schulzen was a partner in a small chemical company, Asmara Chemie, in the West German town of Wiesbaden. Asmara had at first been involved in the making of soaps and dyes, but as nuclear weapons and power moved into Europe, the firm had moved into the manufacture of cleansers and decontamination creams and ointments. Several lucrative contracts with the US army in West Germany had followed, and the tiny company had thrived.

Immediately after the operation, Schulzen was invited to Israel as part of his convalescence, ostensibly by a furniture manufacturer but, in fact, at the express command of the Mossad. He spent a happy few days being shown the sights, then went home full of memories of the friendly people and the warm hospitality. Several contracts, some direct, others through intermediaries, resulted, and in the course of the next three years, the Israeli government became a major customer of Asmara. But the groundwork was all leading up to one thing: would Schulzen, using Asmara as a front, purchase uranium for Israel? Schulzen had been doing big business with the Israelis until they had become his single most important customer; this uranium deal was the largest and most lucrative so far.

Ever the eager salesman, and with his conscience suitably sweetened, Schulzen readily agreed at the beginning of 1968, and the wheels were set in motion. In March 1968, an approach was made to the Brussels headquarters of the Société Général des Minerais. SGM had large stocks of uranium oxide lying around; this had been shipped out from their mines in Zaïre immediately before independence, and they were anxious to sell. The order fell on the desk of Denis Dewez, the deputy head of SGM's uranium division. Although eager to fill the order, Dewez had never heard of Asmara and was suspicious. However, Schulzen told Dewez that they needed the uranium because they were going into mass production of petrochemicals using uranium as a catalyst. Somewhat reassured, Dewez then checked Asmara's credit references and was pleased to learn that the money for the sale was already lodged in a Swiss bank, just waiting to be handed over.

Before uranium can be used as a catalyst, it has to be processed, and Schulzen told SGM that SAICA, a company in Milan, had agreed to do the work. He also suggested to Dewez that it would be much easier to ship the uranium by sea, even though this would mean that the ship would be outside EEC waters for a brief time – technically a breach of the regulations that insist that traffic going outside the borders of the EEC should be subject to special export licences. Dewez was reassured and eventually gave the go-ahead.

As with NUMEC in the United States, the Israelis were gambling on the incompetence and inefficiency of those designated to carry out the inspections demanded by law. They were only too right. At no time was Asmara, or the Italian company SAICA, checked out or visited by officials. (If they had been, inspectors would have found that Asmara had tiny premises with absolutely no room to store or process even half of the uranium they had agreed to purchase, while SAICA was a varnish factory.)

Another friend of the Mossad, a Turk named Burham Yarisal, purchased a suitable vessel, the *Scheersberg A* for £160,000 cash, registered it under the Liberian flag of convenience and, having dumped the regular crew, sailed for Rotterdam with a skeleton crew of Mossad agents to collect the uranium. A few minutes after midnight on Sunday, 17 November 1968, the *Scheersberg A* sailed from Rotterdam for Genoa, the 200 tons of uranium secure in the hold. She never arrived. The next time she was seen was in December when she arrived at the Turkish port of Iskenderum, her holds empty. In international waters in the Mediterranean, a rendezvous with a heavily escorted Israeli merchant ship had ensured the smooth and easy transfer of the dozens of barrels with the word 'Plumbat' (a typically cryptic Mossad code-name) stencilled on their sides.

It was seven months before Euratom, the European nuclear regulatory agency, realized that the cargo had disappeared. Their inquiries addressed to Asmara and SAICA met a complete stone wall, and Euratom, whose job it is to control the flow of nuclear materials, was unable under its charter to compel anyone to tell them anything. The police in Belgium, Italy and West Germany were alerted but their inquiries were cursory at best. The West Germans actually did board the *Scheersberg A* when it next called at one of their ports, but with a different crew and with the two pages of the log referring to the mystery voyage torn out, there was little they could do. In the end, a secret meeting of the European Commission in 1969 agreed to close the file and keep the whole affair secret. As one EEC official said: 'It would have made our security regulations look a little ridiculous.'

The *Scheersberg A* was actually used again by the Israelis just after Christmas 1969. A special commando squad stole the five gunboats that had been ordered by the Israeli government but had been blockaded in Cherbourg after the French government had imposed an embargo on arms sales to Israel. To make the long journey from Cherbourg to Haifa, the gunboats had to refuel, and a rendezvous north-west of the Spanish town of Corunna with the refitted *Scheersberg A* – now owned by an Israeli front company, Biscayne Traders Shipping Corporation (Dan Aerbel, prop.) – took care of that. This story would never have been revealed if Aerbel had not suffered from claustrophobia and been captured and interrogated by Norwegian counter-intelligence with the Mossad assassination squad in Lillehammer in 1973. By that time, however, the Israeli nuclear industry had made great strides forward.

After its start-up in 1964, American estimates suggested that the Israeli nuclear plant at Dimona was capable of producing enough plutonium to build one 20-kiloton bomb per year. The problem for the Israelis was to convert the plutonium which came out of the reactor as spent fuel into the highly refined product necessary to make a nuclear bomb.

In 1970, two Israeli scientists – Isaiah Nebenzahl, a physicist with the Ministry of Defence, and Menahem Levin of Tel Aviv University – succeeded where scientists with bigger and better facilities in the United States and the Soviet Union had failed. Using a wholly new laser technique, they took ordinary uranium and, by bombarding it with laser beams, managed to extract all the uranium-235. The same process had been researched by scientists at the Los Alamos Scientific Laboratory in New Mexico, the Lawrence Livermore Laboratory in California and elsewhere in the United States, but all had so far failed to come up with an effective method of uranium enrichment that bypassed the old-fashioned and extremely expensive enrichment plants then in use. 'The general reaction appears to have been one of astonishment tinged with disbelief,' said one laser researcher at Los Alamos to Robert Gillette of *Science* magazine after the Israeli success was revealed. 'I guess it means the Israelis are building bombs in their basements.'

The Israelis applied for a West German patent for the technique in March 1972, and this was granted late the following year. Once the papers for the patent were on file, the intelligence agencies naturally got involved. The CIA obtained a copy of the application and were appalled to learn how, in twenty-four hours, the process could produce a yield of seven grams of uranium-235 of 60 per cent purity. The CIA and everyone else who saw the application, which was copied and distributed among an astonished American scientific community, realized that around fifty kilograms of this purity of U-235 would be enough to make a bomb. Moreover, it was clear that Israeli scientists would soon be able to improve both the rate of yield and the purity of the U-235. Israel could now do without the risky expertise of the Mossad; they had their own cheap, highly efficient path to nuclear weapons. Those privy to the laser discovery had absolutely no doubt – if any had still existed – that Israel had joined the nuclear club.

Interestingly, some of the hardest intelligence information at this time came, not from CIA agents or the scientific community, but from a casual conversation between President Richard Nixon and Prime Minister Golda Meir. In 1969, while on a state visit to Washington, Meir had walked alone with Nixon on the White House lawn. The meeting had been a success and the two seemed to get along very well. As Meir reported later to the Israeli Cabinet on her return, Nixon had asked her if Israel had any 'dangerous toys'. Meir had asked what he meant. He meant an atom bomb, he said: did Israel have one? To this, the Israeli leader had replied, 'We do.' Nixon had seemed impressed, Meir said, and had cautioned her to 'be careful' as they had said goodbye. As she wryly remarked to the Israeli Cabinet: 'I was just lucky that he didn't ask how many bombs.'

In May that same year, Meir was reported, in the *International Herald-Tribune*, as saying that Israel had no nuclear bombs, and that Israel had no intention of using them.

General Moshe Dayan's well-argued theory of a bomb in the basement was put to the test sooner than he or anyone else ever expected. When the Egyptians attacked across the Suez Canal in October 1973, Israel was caught totally unprepared. It was a brilliantly planned and executed assault, masterminded by President Anwar Sadat of Egypt. Although the Israeli army managed to hold the Suez front, their counter-attack was repulsed by the Egyptians; in addition, the Syrians were making some progress in an all-out assault on the Golan Heights.

President Sadat's very close relations with the Soviet Union and the latter's friendship treaty with Syria led to Israeli fears that the USSR might send troops to join the war on the Arabs' side. Golda Meir acted to forestall any Soviet move by sending a personal representative to Europe to meet with them. The envoy warned that, should any Soviet troops be moved into the war zone, Israel would not hesitate to launch a pre-emptive nuclear strike.

Then, according to a *Time* magazine article of 12 April 1976 – and since confirmed by other independent sources – Israel prepared for the first time to use its nuclear weapons.

At 10.00 p.m. on 8 October, the Israeli commander on the northern front, Major-General Yitzhak Hofi (later to be head of the Mossad), told General Elazar, the Chief of Staff, 'I am not sure we can hold out much longer.' This message was passed to Defence Minister Moshe Dayan who, at five minutes past midnight, went to Prime Minister Meir and asked for permission to activate the nuclear bombs. 'This is the end of the Third Temple,' Dayan told her. (The first two temples in Jerusalem were destroyed by, respectively, invading Babylonians in 586 BC and the Romans in AD 70.) Until now, the Israelis had always been able, with hands on hearts, to deny that they had an actual nuclear bomb. In their own minds, they had made the distinction between a bomb ready to launch and a bomb which had none of the vital components assembled . . . a fine distinction, perhaps, but one that, in this instance, probably saved the Middle East – and the world – from being plunged into a nuclear war. Once Meir had given permission for the bombs to be assembled, it took some hours before an estimated thirteen bombs were rushed to waiting Phantom F-4 and Kfir fighters. However in the time between the order being given and the bombs reaching the aircraft – some four hours – the tide of battle had turned. The bombs were dismantled and restored to their underground bunkers in the Negev.

However, the story does not end there. The Soviets, through their intelligence-gathering COSMOS satellite, had picked up the frantic preparations for nuclear war, and a few days later, on 13 October, they loaded nuclear bombs suitable for fitting to Egyptian SCUD missiles on to a ship at their naval base of Nikolayev near Odessa, for transportation to Alexandria. The Americans monitored the vessel as it passed through the Bosporus, and an urgent message was flashed to Washington that the Soviets were about to land nuclear bombs in Egypt. Although both the CIA and the White House knew of Israel's nuclear capability, the idea of a Soviet nuclear presence in so sensitive an area, particularly when Egypt appeared to be losing the war, was deemed too dangerous to be allowed.

On the evening of 24 October, Nixon was given a message from Brezhnev relayed via the Soviet ambassador to the United States, Anatoly Dobrynin. In four paragraphs, it accused Israel of 'brazenly challenging both the Soviet Union and the United States' and of seriously violating the ceasefire that had been so painstakingly negotiated by Henry Kissinger. Brezhnev then argued that a peacekeeping force composed of Soviets and Americans should be sent to the Middle East:

I will say it straight, that if you find it impossible to act together with us in this matter, we should be faced with the necessity urgently to consider the question of taking appropriate steps unilaterally. Israel cannot be allowed to get away with the violations.

The United States, anxious both to keep Soviet troops out of the Middle East and to defuse the threat of a third world war, put all US armed forces around the world on 'Defcom B', one stage below red alert. Although the Americans did not mention the increased state of readiness, they were well aware that Soviet monitoring would pick up the signs as the United States got ready for war. By the following day, the Soviets had turned their ship around and had withdrawn the demands for a joint peacekeeping force.

A world war did not break out, but this was the closest it had come since the Cuban missile crisis of 1962. The Israeli government currently feel that a further full-scale war with the Arabs within the next decade is inevitable, and the world may not be so lucky next time.

In 1974, with much of the pretence about Israel's nuclear capability over, confirmation that there were 'bombs in the basement' came from the President of Israel, Professor Ephraim Katzir, an eminent biophysicist and former chief scientist at the Ministry of Defence. He made it clear that his country had assembled the knowledge and equipment to make nuclear weapons: 'It has always been our intention to provide the potential for nuclear weapons development. We now have that potential. We will defend this country with all possible means at hand; we have to develop more powerful and new arms to protect ourselves.' The following day, in a statement of clarification, the President's office added that he had merely 'reiterated past pronouncements to the effect that Israel will not be the first to introduce nuclear weapons into the area'.

Since the 1973 war, both the CIA and the French intelligence service, in separate studies, have concluded that Israel has developed a nuclear arsenal. Both are agreed that Israel now has in excess of thirty nuclear devices and is manufacturing new bombs at a rate of two or more every year.

Seven countries so far have tested atomic weapons: the United States, the Soviet Union, Britain, China, France, Israel and India. For those who already have the bomb, the arrival of a new nuclear power on to the international stage is a matter of grave concern, as the strategic scale is currently so finely balanced that any new weight at either end threatens the stability of the world. It has now been recognized by all the major powers that Israel has joined the exclusive nuclear club, and to some extent that semi-public knowledge may have helped it to survive. However, any attempts by other countries to develop nuclear capabilities are viewed with deep suspicion. In June 1981, convinced that Iraq was on the verge of building a nuclear weapon, the Israelis launched an attack on the Iraqi nuclear reactor outside Baghdad, taking preventive action to ensure that the balance of power in the region was maintained firmly in their favour.

An alliance between Pakistan and other Muslim countries is also co-operating on the development of the Islamic bomb. Using oil money, combined with Pakistani technology – much of it illegally smuggled from Europe – a test blast by the Pakistan government in the province of Baluchistan is expected.

So far, pressure from the superpowers has restricted the spread of nuclear weapons. Countries such as Pakistan or Brazil, who might claim to be contenders for the nuclear club, rely heavily on defence and aid support from the West; others, such as Iraq and Libya, depend equally on the Soviet Union. Neither superpower wants to see atomic weapons in the hands of people who do not understand the complexities of international superpower diplomacy.

Israel has no such qualms. It has developed its own independent nuclear capability and, in the search for friends, has not hesitated to share its experience with its closest ally, South Africa.

9 Atoms for Apartheid

South Africa has one great advantage over Israel in the nuclear race: uranium.

The precious metal can be extracted as a by-product of gold mining; in consequence, it is extremely cheap for South Africa to manufacture, compared with the rest of the world who have to develop uranium mining or acquisition as a separate programme. According to Atomic Industrial Forum Inc., a US-based research group, after the United States and Australia, South Africa has the world's biggest reserves of uranium, with production running at over 6,000 tons per annum. (This excludes the enormous Rossing mine in Namibia which, while producing revenues for South Africa at the moment, has a questionable future.)

It is these massive reserves that have made South Africa so attractive to the Western nuclear powers for so many years. Uranium has also ensured a solid bargaining counter for the government to use against all pressure for sanctions to halt the spread of nuclear technology. From the start of her nuclear programme, South Africa has been able to trade uranium for technology with the United States, Britain, France and West Germany, but although this trade has continued over the years, it has gradually become more embarrassing as international pressure against the apartheid system has mounted.

As a result, South Africa has changed tack and moved towards two other internationally isolated nations, Israel and Taiwan; as the flow of information, personnel and technology from the West began to dwindle, so the gaps were filled by these two countries. In return for a steady supply of uranium, both agreed to keep South Africa fully informed of the state of the nuclear art. In Israel's case, this was part of a much broader package involving arms, diamonds and more general trade. Specifically in the nuclear field, Israel agreed to help South Africa in any way possible, including the development of nuclear power stations for peaceful purposes and helping the South African government develop a nuclear capability. According to officials in South Africa, there are 'several dozen' Israeli scientists working in South Africa at any one time.

South Africa also has a growing relationship with Taiwan, particularly as the country sees the United States drawing closer to mainland China. One of the results of Taiwan's isolation has been a need to find new friends, and South Africa is an obvious choice. In 1980, Taiwan signed a six-year contract to purchase 4,000 tons of uranium from South Africa in exchange for hard cash, arms technology and some help in the nuclear field (although Israel is far more advanced than Taiwan).

There have been unconfirmed reports that the three countries are jointly developing a cruise missile as a nuclear delivery system, but most international strategists tend to believe that the cost of developing an independent cruise system would be prohibitive and of little use, and all three already have very effective nuclear delivery systems that are some way ahead of anything a potential enemy might put against them. By the time China, Saudi Arabia or Mozambique are sufficiently well armed and trained to present a more serious threat, cruise technology should be more readily available.

The decision by the South African government to go nuclear was arrived at in almost exactly the same way that the government of Israel decided to build Dimona. The South Africans saw the stable world that they knew and relied upon crumbling around them, leaving them an isolated nation with few indigenous energy resources. It was natural for the Afrikaner government to think in terms of nuclear power plants for satisfying their energy needs and, as their isolation grew, to expand their ideas to include nuclear weapons as a way of also ensuring their security.

As the 1940s became the 1950s, Britain, Belgium and France began shedding what remained of their empire, and the order that colonialism had brought to the African continent was gone for ever. South African leaders and the ruling Afrikaner élite have inherited a rigid and dogmatic educational and military system that reflects this now-vanished order and leaves little room for flexibility. Only since the late 1960s have the social sciences been treated with anything approaching the openness automatically expected in Europe and the United States, and virtually all those who completed their university education before the early 1960s – the people who by and large are in power today – come from very narrow educational backgrounds. They are committed to the maintenance of traditional values – in this case, to the survival of white Afrikaner rule at all costs. In the military, too, this narrow view of life is perpetuated as there are very few teachers at a senior level who are deemed politically acceptable. Thus the political arm of the government dictates what the military are allowed to learn in the field of international and intercultural relations. This helps to ensure the continuation of the regime but narrows the options for maintaining the security of the government.

The prevailing view was well illustrated in 1942 by D. F. Malan, then a future prime minister:

> It is through the will of God that the Afrikaner people exist at all. In His wisdom He determined that on the southern point of Africa . . . a people should be born who would be the bearer of Christian culture and civilization. He surrounded this people by great dangers . . . God also willed that the Afrikaner people should be continually threatened by other peoples. There was a ferocious barbarian who resisted the intruding Christian civilization and caused the Afrikaners' blood to flow in streams. There were times when as a result of this the Afrikaner was deeply despairing, but God at the same time prevented the swamping of the young Afrikaner people in the sea of barbarianism.

This paranoid view of the world has brought with it two fundamental concepts: total response to total onslaught, and winning the hearts and minds of the people. The hearts-and-minds campaign has been a long-term investment and as yet has not been seen to work, but the total-response philosophy was always simply a matter of technology and logistics and could be arranged without recourse to political debate.

In their excellent study on South Africa's nuclear capability, Kenneth Adelman and Albion Knight of the Strategic Studies Center in Arlington, Virginia, have suggested five main reasons why South Africa believes it needs nuclear weapons:

> *1* At the minimum, a nuclear device could serve as a weapon of last resort in an ultimate crisis. If survival of Afrikanerdom were truly threatened, deployment of such a weapon could give a measure of hope, buy time, or destroy some of the opposition as they destroy the Afrikaner people. Targets in this area would include areas of fiercest combat within or on the borders, enemy camps or bases in neighboring states or capitals of those countries providing sanctuaries and/or forces.
>
> *2* Short of this worst-case scenario, nuclear weapons could help against a large-scale conventional build-up – to break up a

concentration of conventional forces against South Africa's industrial and population centers. While potentially helpful, this contingency is rather remote; such a concentration of enemy forces would be vulnerable to a devastating conventional retaliation by South Africa, without any need for its forces to go nuclear.

3 Relatively small nuclear devices could be used in tactical battlefield situations. Provided the technology was right, this would remove centers of unrest while the fallout would not harm the white population.

4 Nuclear weapons could be set off during combat to constitute a frightening deterrent against further actions which endanger Afrikaner survival. In this instance, the target may be some remote and uninhabited area, such as the Kalahari desert.

5 Nuclear weapons might be employed against Soviet forces, should they get involved in a conflict beyond their current, rather limited role as advisers in Angola, Mozambique and Zimbabwe. This has the added danger of inviting retaliation and escalating the conflict.

In 1949, the South African Atomic Energy Institute (AEI) was founded and given responsibility for research in such fields as chemistry, extraction, metallurgy, isotopes and radiation, physical metallurgy, physics and reactor development. South Africa's uranium brought the big powers sniffing round, and a year after its formation, the AEI signed an agreement with the American/British Combined Development Agency to develop the uranium potential in South Africa. Within ten years, twenty-seven mines had been opened and South Africa was placed in the top rank of world producers. In 1952, the first of seventeen uranium-oxide plants was established, and throughout that decade, the South African government continued to build on the developing relationship between supplier and consumer.

The aim, of course, was to obtain nuclear technology and, following the formation of the Atomic Energy Board (AEB) in 1957 to replace the AEI, the United States and South Africa signed an agreement covering nuclear aid from the United States as well as nuclear co-operation. On the American side, the agreement was part of the 'Atoms for Peace' programme, under which the United States provided assistance to a number of other states (including Israel) in the civil development of nuclear technology for peaceful purposes. The 1957 agreement with South Africa was amended three times – in 1962, 1967 and 1974 – to extend its scope and duration; it now runs until 2007. In 1961, under this agreement, the United States licensed the export of a light-water reactor known as Safari 1, that used highly enriched uranium and was sited at Pelindaba near Pretoria. Safari 1 went critical in 1965; it has a capacity of 20 megawatts, which makes it a small reactor, unsuited to the commercial production of energy, but it has been important for research and the development of technological expertise. In 1962, in the first amendment to the original agreement, the United States agreed to supply the enriched uranium that Pretoria needed to run the Safari 1. The contract called for delivery of 104 kilograms of enriched uranium, and by 1975, 95.32 kilograms had entered South Africa.

Although, in the early days, there was little indication of the massive investment that would be poured into South Africa's nuclear programme, there were already hints of the direction it might take. For example, in August 1961, an indiscreet member of the AEB, Dr Andries Visser, made public a private speech in which he suggested that the atomic energy programme should produce an atomic bomb 'for prestige and security purposes'.

Once Safari 1 got off the ground, the South Africans began to look towards the establishment of their own nuclear energy programme with a view to making themselves as self-sufficient as possible in the years to come. It is at this stage, in the mid-1960s, that the first constructive contacts were made between Israel and South Africa concerning nuclear co-operation. For South Africa, Israel had one primary advantage: a relatively advanced nuclear industry that had been working both on uranium-enrichment techniques and on the design of a nuclear bomb. For the Israelis, South Africa possessed almost unlimited supplies of uranium that it might be persuaded to part with as part of a uranium-for-technology swap. To them, this was more an investment for the future, as South Africa was not then in a position to supply enriched uranium and Israel did not as yet possess the laser enrichment technology that a few years later was to astonish the American scientific community. In the end, a technology swap was agreed, with the proviso that Israel could call on South Africa's energy resources as and when it wanted.

Israeli scientists flew to South Africa to advise on the development and construction of a new home-grown nuclear reactor, and the result was Safari 2, a small research reactor. This used low-enriched uranium – about 2 per cent U-235 – which was supplied by the United States and, like most of the uranium used in Safari 1, was made into fuel rods by the British. Safari 2 went critical in 1967, for the first time showing the world that South Africa had established an independent technological infrastructure.

While the scientific relationship between Israel and South Africa had now been established, it needed additional impetus to push it beyond the minor-league level on which it was then operating. The push came from Professor Ernst Bergmann who visited South Africa during September 1968. It had been Bergmann, first as Scientific Adviser to the Israeli Ministry of Defence and then as Chairman of that country's Atomic Energy Commission, who had brought Israel into the nuclear age and had begun the development of the bomb. In a lengthy speech before members of the South African Institute of International Affairs at Jan Smuts House in Johannesburg, Bergmann reviewed the level of scientific achievement and co-operation between the two countries:

In general I have found that, in nuclear physics, the two countries are verging on not only similar, but almost identical lines, and it is no secret that today, in the theatre of nuclear physics in which the instrumentation is extremely expensive and every experiment is equally expensive, there are indications of a move towards international collaboration . . .

It is difficult to indicate . . . whether South Africa or Israel is the more highly developed. I think that in both countries the development is uneven, and there are many areas in which Israel undoubtedly can learn from South Africa . . . There are areas in which Israel has been forced to be more progressive and in which, perhaps a country like South Africa could learn from her.

I would like to say that I have been impressed by the similarity between our two countries in the field of science . . . I have discussed with many of my colleagues whom I have met in this country and with whom I have created some personal and professional links, the question as to whether, in view of the circumstances, a collaboration between the two countries might not be of some value. I was glad to find a very enthusiastic response and the willingness to think about the exchange of professors, the exchange of graduate students and the exchange of information, and in going back to Israel, I will do my best to further and perhaps formalize such contacts between the scientists of our two countries. Because, in the last analysis, I think we can formulate the common problem in the similarity of our two countries by saying: 'Neither of us has neighbours to whom we can speak and to whom we are going to be able to speak in the near future. If we are in this position of isolation, perhaps it might be best for both countries to speak to each other.'

Bergmann was true to his word and did everything he could to further co-operation between the two countries. The political will had always

been there and this was now backed up by the wholehearted support of
the scientific community.

The experience gained in running Safari 1 and building Safari 2 proved
a vital investment in skilled manpower and expertise that, over the
next fifteen years, would form a major component in translating the
Afrikaner dream of a nuclear deterrent into a reality.

Since the 1957 co-operation agreement between the United States
and South Africa, there have been exchanges of personnel on a large
scale, making this the latter's most important source of foreign
expertise. By mid-1977, more than 155 American nuclear technologists and scientists had visited South Africa to provide assistance and
training, and ninety South Africans had gone to the United States to
receive training and practical experience. In addition to assistance and
the supply of equipment and material already mentioned, US
companies have, with the approval of their government, exported
nuclear materials to South Africa: plutonium, iron-55, cadmium,
thorium, depleted uranium, cobalt-60, carbon-14, caesium-137,
chlorine-36 and strontium-90.

In addition, the US Department of Energy has confirmed that, on
27 and 30 August and 6 September 1958, the US and South Africa
jointly mounted a series of nuclear explosions in the Indian Ocean.
Described as 'weapons-effect tests', they involved small bombs of the
one- to two-kiloton class and gave South Africa a first-hand
opportunity to observe fallout patterns in the Indian Ocean.

Along with Israel and the United States, Britain played a central
role in training and advising South African scientists. Among those
present at the formal inauguration of Safari 1, at which Prime Minister
Verwoerd unmistakably declared South Africa's interest in the
military uses of nuclear technology, was the then chairman of the
British Atomic Energy Authority, Sir William Penney. His successor,
Sir John Hill, exchanged visits with Abraham Roux, President of the
AEB, in 1970 and 1972, and in late 1974, two South African scientists
visited the British nuclear plant at Risley.

Britain has also been a source of recruitment of scientists and
technologists for the South Africa nuclear programme and, in this
respect is probably even more important than the United States. As
recently as 1979, the South African Electricity Supply Commission
(ESCOM) advertised in the British press for staff to run the Koeberg
power station and, at the same time, for South African engineers to
take a course in nuclear reactor science and engineering at Imperial
College, London, with fees paid by ESCOM. Although the British

government officially discourages any links in the nuclear field with South Africa, industry in the United Kingdom has paid little more than lip-service to this. The South Africans are still able to borrow senior scientists from the Central Electricity Generating Board (CEGB), which runs Britain's nuclear industry, and these scientists, all of whom have signed the British Official Secrets Act, are allowed to go to South Africa quite freely and return with no loss of status. Some who have gone to work for ESCOM have decided to stay and were given glowing references by the CEGB.

South African scientists have been able at least twice to develop their understanding of nuclear weapons and their effects with US and British co-operation. In 1958, US nuclear tests in the South Atlantic were monitored by a joint team from South Africa and the United States, and in 1967, it was reported in South Africa that some of the country's scientists were collaborating closely with British scientists from the Harwell Atomic Research Institute in monitoring French nuclear tests in the Pacific.

All this international aid paid early dividends for South Africa and gave an indication of the potential of her nuclear programme. In October 1964, the AEB announced that they had perfected a new method of carrying out the first step in the manufacture of nuclear bombs – the production of uranium tetrafluoride – and in a statement describing the process, they said that the Republic 'must be able to supply nuclear-grade materials in the forms most suited to the demand'. The new method had been developed by a team working under the leadership of Dr R. E. Robinson, head of the AEB's Extraction Metallurgy Division and director of the government's metallurgical laboratories. It used silicon tetrafluoride, a waste product of the fertilizer industry, and uranium ore as its starting point. The uranium tetrafluoride that was produced could be converted into either pure uranium for use in nuclear power stations or into gaseous hexafluoride, to be fed to an enrichment plant to make nuclear explosives or enriched fuels.

Although the process represented a large step forward for the South Africans, it was extremely expensive and not very efficient, and the AEB began to look around for another process that would do the job cheaper and better. It was known that the West Germans had been experimenting with a new technique, and the South African government set about getting the technology.

Just how the South Africans achieved their objective of obtaining a more efficient enrichment process was not revealed until September

1975, after the safe in the office of the South African ambassador to West Germany had been broken into. Documents from the safe that fell into the hands of the African National Congress (ANC) revealed that South Africa had agreed a technology-for-uranium deal with West Germany that had given her the ability to make nuclear weapons.

In a coup unprecedented in the history of the ANC (an organization noted more for its political activism than for its sophisticated intelligence-gathering apparatus), the documents included correspondence between the West German government, West German firms, and the South African government and the AEB, which detailed a relationship that had begun soon after the start of Safari 2 and had continued for nearly ten years. The close liaison between the two countries had given West Germany a consistent supply of high-grade uranium and other raw materials, and South Africa the vital expertise to develop a uranium-enrichment plant.

The West German/South African connection had not been entirely hidden for, in March 1967, the South African *Digest*, published by the Department of Information, had confirmed that West Germany had become closely involved in the country's nuclear programme: 'South African nuclear scientists and technologists have been and are being trained at research establishments in West Germany while others frequently pay visits to such institutions when they come overseas.'

The following year, according to the ANC-held documents, a three-man committee headed by Dr H. J. van Eck, Chairman of the Industrial Development Corporation, had been set up by the AEB to look at ways of establishing a uranium-enrichment plant. For the South Africans, who had already proved that they could build their own reactors, it was a logical step that had, potentially, a natural twofold benefit. First, for a country with enough of the mineral to service its own needs for the foreseeable future, a uranium-enrichment plant would overcome the annoying and politically vulnerable necessity of having to go outside the state for enriched reactor fuel. Second, a functioning enrichment plant would provide the necessary raw material for South Africa to develop a nuclear bomb.

The problem facing the AEB had been where to find a country that would be prepared to help with the technology and the finance for such a project in the face of international criticism of both the South African apartheid regime and its refusal to sign the nuclear Non-Proliferation Treaty. Ideally, of course, South Africa would have liked to have done a straight deal with Israel but, at this stage in their relationship, both were out on a limb. Israeli scientists had been working frantically to develop an enrichment process, having failed to find a country that would supply the knowledge direct, and their revolutionary laser technique was still two years away. Approaches from the AEB to Israel had proved unproductive: the Israelis, in 1968 at a very sensitive stage in their atomic programme, had been unwilling to give what information they had to South Africa with the consequent possibilities of security leaks. (This has been the pattern of the nuclear relationship. Israel supplies South Africa with information and technology only after Israel has moved on to the next stage of its nuclear programme. South Africa is thus always second best and never a potential rival.)

South Africa had found a willing collaborator in West Germany, but the delicacy of the operation had meant that public announcements had had to be kept to a minimum, and the previously acknowledged exchange of nuclear knowledge had now become so sensitive that even South Africa's new ambassador to West Germany had been advised not to mention it in public. In December 1968, Donald Bell Sole, due to take up his position as ambassador to West Germany at the beginning of 1969, had submitted a draft of the speech that he intended delivering when presenting his credentials to the current ambassador, J. K. Uys. The incumbent's comments (made in a letter to Sole written on 19 December) are illustrative of the new nature of nuclear co-operation between the two countries:

. . . I should be grateful if you would permit me to comment on the inclusion in the speech of a reference to nuclear energy and the production of uranium . . . As you know, the East Germans have for many years accused the Federal Republic of South Africa of co-operation in this particular field and of secretly producing atomic weapons. I fear that the reference to nuclear energy – even though you specifically mention the peaceful uses of such energy – and South Africa as a major uranium producer, and the fact that you specifically express the hope, as South Africa's governor on the IAEA [International Atomic Energy Authority], to be able to give special attention to this aspect of the relations between us, could be seized upon by our enemies as further proof of the collaboration of which we have been accused for so long. This we should avoid. Moreover, from the German side it may prove difficult to prepare a proper reply in this connection for inclusion in the Federal President's answer at the presentation-of-credentials ceremony, especially as both your speech and the President's reply will be published in the official bulletin which enjoys wide circulation. I feel that the less said in public at this stage about this aspect of our relations with the Federal Republic, the more success we shall be able to achieve behind the scenes. It is therefore strongly recommended for your consideration that the particular paragraph in the speech be omitted.

The advice had been well taken and Sole had omitted all references to either country's nuclear plans from his speech. But it was Sole who had acted as front man and who had been the prime mover in extending the relationship beyond the mere exchange of ideas into the direct supply of technology from West Germany to South Africa.

In 1969, there had been three uranium-enrichment processes currently in use: gas diffusion used by the Soviet Union, the United States, Britain, France and China; the gas centrifuge used by Britain, the Netherlands and West Germany; and finally, the jet-nozzle system. The latter had been invented by a Professor Becker of the Society of Nuclear Research (GFK), Karlsruhe, a company that is 90 per cent-owned by the West German government. It had been this system that South Africa had had its eye on.

In March 1970, GFK had concluded an agreement with the STEAG company of Essen, a fuel-economy concern controlled by the Federal government, for a joint development programme of the jet-nozzle enrichment system. At the same time, GFK had assigned the exclusive world rights for industrial use of the process to STEAG. Four months later, on 20 July 1970, Vorster had announced in a speech before the South African Parliament that his scientists had 'succeeded in developing a new process for uranium enrichment', a process he claimed as 'unique in its concept'. Vorster had added that South Africa's 'sole objective in the further development and application of the process would be to promote the peaceful application of nuclear energy'.

There have been repeated allegations that the West Germans had directly supplied to the South Africans the technology that had enabled them to develop the enrichment process. Such a judgement, while politically convenient for some, is not necessarily borne out by the facts. Certainly several South African scientists had visited the Karlsruhe research plant and an intermittent exchange of scientists had taken place for several years, but the South African enrichment process differed significantly from that developed by the Germans.

There is no doubt that West Germany's willingness to train some of South Africa's atomic scientists must have helped that country along the road, although South Africa already had considerable expertise; for some years, South Africa had had a seat on the board of the IAEA and its scientists in the nuclear field were respected throughout the world. As with all developments in the field of science, there had certainly been some degree of co-operation but, in that regard, the

United States and Britain had been as much involved as West Germany.

The ANC revelations, which have never been denied either by South Africa or West Germany, made little impact. Certainly there were headlines in newspapers around the world for some days, and analysts concluded that South Africa was several steps closer to an independent nuclear capability, but there was no suggestion of any action to be taken by any international body against either country. As a result, the traffic in information and technology between the West and South Africa has continued unhindered.

For some years after the announcement of their newly developed uranium-enrichment process, South Africa had guarded its nuclear facility closely and had denied international agencies the right to inspect the relevant plants, on the ground that other countries might steal the process. They had probably been right – as was revealed in April 1975 when the head of the South African Energy Agency, A. J. A. Roux, and its general manager, W. L. Grant, had presented a paper entitled 'The South African Uranium-Enrichment Project' to the European Nuclear Conference. In the paper, Roux and Grant had stated that the distinguishing feature of the process is a separating element which, in effect, is a 'high-performance stationary-walled centrifuge', referred to as an 'Advanced Vortex Tube Process'. The process had a uranium separation factor of 1.025–1.030 (compared to 1.004 of gas diffusion, 1.2–1.5 for centrifuge, and 1.015 for conventional gas-nozzle), low material inventory and, consequently, short equilibrium time and high-energy consumption and operation at a very low cost. Altogether it was a very sophisticated process for its time and well ahead of anything the West Germans had currently had available for their own enrichment programme.

The South African government had been sufficiently encouraged by these advances to authorize in 1971 the investment of $112 million in the construction of a pilot enrichment plant at Valindaba. This plant has been at the centre of South Africa's nuclear programme since the beginning of the 1970s, and is where the primary research into nuclear weapons has been conducted. Ironically the name 'Valindaba', which comes from the African Sotho dialect, means 'about this we do not talk'.

Although the overall strategy of the AEB had still been billed as peaceful, the adding of an enrichment facility which avoided outside monitoring had led many foreign observers to believe that South Africa was heading directly towards regular production of weapons-grade material for use in nuclear weapons. Some support was given to this in February 1979, when Dr Frene Ginwala, an official of the ANC research department, produced a document during a UN seminar in London that allegedly showed contingency plans for exploding nuclear devices along South Africa's borders. The plan, which the ANC claimed had been obtained secretly, had been drawn up by the AEB in 1972 and concluded that a ten-kiloton device could be exploded almost anywhere along South Africa's borders without doing any serious seismic damage. The ANC suggested that the AEB study had limited itself to discussing the detonating of bombs over black areas, while assessing the fallout dangers only for white areas. The main conclusion of the AEB report was that tactical nuclear weapons could be a very effective force in the eventuality that large areas of the white population might need to be defended from surrounding black unrest.

At the same time as Valindaba had been given the go-ahead, the Uranium Enrichment Corporation of South Africa (UCOR) had been set up to look into the further development of the enrichment process and its possible commercial uses. Although the Valindaba plant had been constructed using finances generated within South Africa, the Republic had had to go outside to seek the cash to develop a commercial enrichment plant (which the AEB estimated would cost some $1,320 million) to come on line by 1984 and generate an additional $375 million per annum in foreign exchange earnings through the sale of enriched uranium.

For the South Africans, finding investors for their fledgling nuclear industry had proved a serious problem. Initial approaches had been made to the British/Dutch/West German URENCO consortium; however, they had refused on political grounds and – the primary reasoning behind all the other rejections – they had been even more concerned about the large investment coupled with the eight- or ten-year lead time before the plant could possibly come on line. The necessary capital commitment over such an extended period had been considered an unacceptable risk, given the inherent instability of the South African government.

An approach to the West Germans via STEAG had initially met with more success. They had been prepared to invest in the enlarged plant, provided they would have the right to process uranium through it. In the end, though, an unexpectedly cautious West German government had vetoed the deal. Finally, a compromise had been arranged whereby STEAG would help finance the development of an expanded Valindaba facility in conjunction with the Shah's Iran. This deal fell through when Ayatollah Khomeini took power. As a result, the development programme has been cut back, and the plant, now expected to be completed in 1985, will deliver, instead of the original 5,000 tons separative work units (swu) each year, only 200 tons swu, enough to service South Africa's peaceful and military nuclear programmes, but not enough to generate any export earnings.

In August 1976, a contract was signed between the South African ESCOM and a French consortium consisting of Framatome, Alsthom and SPIE Batignolles for the building of two light-water pressurized water power reactors, each with a 922-megawatt capacity, to be built at Koeberg on the coast north of Cape Town. They will use 3 per cent enriched uranium which was originally going to be supplied by the United States. An enrichment services contract had been signed in 1975 between the two countries, but the advent of the Carter administration in the United States led to an almost total reassessment of America's nuclear policy. Carter decided that no uranium would be exported to South Africa unless it agreed to sign the nuclear Non-Proliferation Treaty, but doing so would have brought with it the right of outside agencies to inspect the South African plants and closely monitor the production and ultimate destination of all uranium. The South African government refused to sign and President Carter refused to deliver the enriched uranium.

South African reluctance to sign the treaty was understandable. Throughout the period during which the government had been examining ways of exploiting nuclear energy to serve peaceful needs, the AEB (with the full approval of the government) had also been examining ways of developing a nuclear bomb.

Israeli scientists had been regular visitors to both Safari 1 and the subsequent home-grown Safari 2 which Israeli technology had helped to develop. In addition, there had been a steady exchange of personnel – with a far larger Israeli presence in South Africa than vice versa. However, such an exchange of knowledge and personnel is not unusual in the nuclear field. The worldwide community involved in the research and development of nuclear energy is a fairly small one (for example, only 2,000 people are employed by the AEB on nuclear programmes in South Africa), and in an evolving science, the regular exchange of ideas is expected and encouraged. Both South African and Israeli scientists also regularly visited Europe and the United States to train, exchange ideas and gather useful information for their own countries. However, both Israel and South Africa were different from the other members of the nuclear club. All the others were signatories of the Non-Proliferation Treaty, which meant that, in spirit at least, there was some control over their activities and a willingness to allow some form of monitoring.

The scientific relationship between South Africa and Israel has never, in the twenty years of close co-operation, been acknowledged by any official statement. The private position is very different. Their alliance became so close that, as early as 1966, the South Africans offered Israel the chance to conduct a nuclear test on or near South Africa. Although this was about the time when Israel was developing its first atomic bomb, Prime Minister Levi Eshkol declined the offer. Israel did have a problem, however: it had consistently maintained that it would not be the first country to introduce nuclear weapons into the Middle East, and a test of one of its nuclear devices would definitely violate that agreement, although after the 1973 war, when it was known to both the United States and the Soviet Union that Israel certainly possessed a nuclear capability, some of the need for secrecy had been removed.

The problem was resolved for the Israelis by Vorster's visit in April 1976, when he and Israeli Prime Minister Yitzhak Rabin discussed their joint nuclear programmes. Vorster announced in Israel on 12 April that a joint ministerial meeting would take place at least once a year to review economic relations and to discuss scientific and industrial co-operation on the basis of 'South African raw materials and Israeli manpower in joint projects'. To the outside observer, it might have made more sense to have slightly restructured the agreement, as it was South Africa that had the vast pool of cheap labour, while Israel was already beginning to feel the adverse effects of simultaneously maintaining a war economy and a developed industrial society. But the agreement related in this instance to the exchange of nuclear materials and information as well as arms and general trade. What had previously been an almost *ad hoc* relationship was now firmed into a straight technology-for-uranium deal also taking into account arms deals and joint projects, and most importantly perhaps, Vorster repeated the offer of South African territory for Israel to test a nuclear device.

For the Israelis, the offer was tempting. The argument over Israel's bomb in the basement had surfaced and there was considerable pressure to exploit the nuclear option publicly and thus remove much of the budgetary burden of heavy expenditure on conventional weapons. Such a radical alteration in Israel's defence posture was obviously a major step to take, particularly with an untested nuclear capability. In reality, of course, there was little doubt in the minds of Israel's nuclear experts that the devices they had been working on for so long would work perfectly on the day; but the benefits of an actual test – the measuring of yield, fallout, delivery system – would be considerable and should enable the scientists to carry out further refinements which would be essential if Israel were to have a credible first-strike capability that could eliminate neighbouring Arab states without, at the same time, wiping Israel off the face of the earth.

For South Africa, too, the offer, if taken up, had several advantages. By 1976/77, it had produced barely enough enriched uranium to make one nuclear device. According to the UN Disarmament Agency, to produce weapons-grade high-enriched uranium of more than 90 per cent U-235, the amount of separative work needed is approximately 200 swu/kg. Using that figure and the available information on South Africa's enrichment project, the UN estimated that by mid-1977 the Republic had produced around 20 kilograms of enriched uranium. Depending on the design sophistication, the minimum amount of high-enriched uranium required for a 20-kiloton device can range between 15 and 25 kilograms. Consequently, by 1977 the South Africans could have produced, at most, one nuclear bomb – and even that is very problematic given that, first time around, the bomb design would not be very sophisticated and would undoubtedly call for a higher proportion of enriched uranium.

At the same time as it was being estimated that South Africa barely had the capability of producing a single nuclear device, the CIA (in one of its more memorable public mistakes) revealed that Israel had between ten and twenty nuclear weapons 'available for use'. The leak came in March 1975 at an informal cocktail party hosted by the CIA for 150 Washington members of the American Institute of Aeronautics and Astronautics (AIAA). The invitation to the party said that 'the CIA will provide an unclassified briefing to AIAA members on CIA intelligence functions in support of US policy for a peaceful world', and that there would be, among other things, refreshments and a question-and-answer session. The man charged with providing the briefing was Carl Duckett, then the CIA's Deputy Director for Science and Technology, who became so relaxed during the question-and-answer session that, in response to a question about Israel's nuclear capability, he responded that Israel 'has ten to twenty nuclear weapons'.

Like Israel, South Africa has consistently denied that it has a nuclear weapons programme, but there remains enough uncertainty in the eyes of the world, and particularly in black Africa, to act as a serious deterrent against any major assault on the Republic. An Israeli nuclear explosion on South African territory would further fuel the ambiguity over South Africa's status as a member of the nuclear club, while allowing South Africa time to develop its own independent capability.

The first the world knew that South Africa had finally decided to go public with its nuclear capability came when, on Saturday, 6 August 1977, the acting chief of the Soviet embassy in Washington, Vladillen Vasev, called at the White House with an urgent personal message from Brezhnev to Carter. According to Soviet intelligence, the message said, South Africa was secretly preparing to detonate an atomic explosion in the Kalahari desert. The Soviet premier asked for Carter's help in stopping the detonation. The Brezhnev message, still in its original Russian, contained the text of a broadcast due to be made public two days later by the official Soviet news agency, Tass, reporting South Africa's preparations. On that day, Tass issued a statement made somewhat bland by Soviet jargon and later quoted in *Pravda*, which said in part:

> The possession of nuclear weapons by the racist regime of Pretoria would constitute a most direct threat to the security of the African states; it would lead to a sharp escalation of instability and tension in southern Africa and would increase the nuclear threat to all mankind . . . The manufacture of nuclear weapons in the Republic of South Africa would have the most serious and far-reaching implications for international peace and the security of peoples.
>
> The leaders of the Soviet Union feel that the most urgent and effective efforts on the part of all states, the United Nations and international public opinion are needed in order to prevent the production of nuclear weapons in the Republic of South Africa and to avert the danger of the proliferation of such weapons.

The United States began to look into the matter; meanwhile, in an example of pecking-order diplomacy presumably decided by the USSR's interpretation of which country had most influence, the Soviets delivered the same message that had gone to Carter to France on 7 August, to Britain on 8 August and, the following day, the West Germans were apprised of the situation. By Wednesday, 10 August, the four allied powers had all made preliminary soundings in Pretoria and all were apprehensive.

According to a fascinating study prepared by the Stockholm International Peace Research Institute (SIPRI) and published in early 1978, both the United States and the Soviet Union confirmed the construction of a test site in the Kalahari through reconnaissance satellites, and SIPRI concluded that it had been observed by two Soviet Cosmos satellites and one US Big Bird during July and August. Through an analysis of satellite ground tracks (the paths traced out by a satellite over the surface of the earth), SIPRI maintained that the US satellite had been launched from the western test range of Vandenberg Air Force Base on 27 June 1977, and had made four passes over the nuclear test site on 4, 8, 15 and 26 July when there had been minimal cloud cover. The satellite had been programmed to fly over the test site at exactly the same time each day and had thus been able to get a detailed idea of work in progress. Because of the flight patterns of Big Bird, SIPRI suggested that the United States may have already known about the planned test before the Soviets sent their message on 6 August. In any event, Big Bird again overflew the test site on 2, 6 and 13 August. In both July and August, the satellite overflew the site when the sun was at an angle and cast long shadows, thus throwing any ground abnormality into sharp relief for easy interpretation.

The first Soviet satellite, Cosmos 922, had been launched from Pelsetsk on 30 June 1977 and had made two passes over the test area, on 3 and 4 July, during its thirteen-day orbit. After its recovery and the analysis of data, a second satellite, Cosmos 932, had been launched on 20 July. This differed from the earlier area surveillance Cosmos in that it was designed to make a close analysis of a specific target. It is presumed, therefore, that the first Cosmos noticed something new and strange appearing in the Kalahari, and the second Cosmos was able to get definitive photographs and other information in the four passes it made over the site during July. It was recovered on 2 August, giving the Soviets four days to analyse its findings before they asked the United States for help.

The reaction of the British government to the information was indicative of the world response at the time. In a prepared statement, the Foreign Office said:

> If it were evident that the South Africans are completing work on the production of nuclear weapons and are preparing for a test, it would be an extremely grave state of affairs which the British government would strongly condemn. Like many other governments, including the Soviet government, it is our policy to guard against any non-nuclear state acquiring a nuclear explosive capability.

Such political rhetoric did not impress the South Africans; their early response to international pressure to abandon the site was, first, to proclaim innocence and, second, to tell anyone who asked that it was none of their business.

Two days after the news of the possible test surfaced, South Africa's Foreign Minister, Pik Botha, alleged that the USSR was whipping up emotions before the UN conference in Lagos that was due to take place the following week: the Soviet statements were pure propaganda and they were simply 'fabricating ammunition', Botha claimed.

By Thursday, 11 August, the basic analyses from satellite reconnaissance and other intelligence and diplomatic sources were prepared for submission to President Carter. At a meeting the following Sunday, he ordered a full response to be sent to Brezhnev to confirm the Soviet assessment of an imminent South African nuclear explosion. Frustrated by apparent South African intransigence, Carter recalled US ambassador-at-large Gerard Smith from holiday and ordered him to go to Paris on 17 August to see President Giscard. Smith was a veteran of many nuclear negotiations, but on this occasion a bit of old-fashioned political pressure was all that was required. The United States made it clear to the French that, if this test were to be allowed to go ahead, the whole balance of power in southern Africa would be threatened; the United States, the envoy pointed out, would look very unfavourably indeed on any ally that did not do its utmost to prevent the explosion from taking place.

For the first time since the crisis began, France was forced to drop her relaxed and uninvolved posture. Giscard's government was uniquely placed to apply pressure on South Africa exactly where it hurt most, in the nuclear programme. It was a French consortium that was supplying the two giant Koeberg reactors near Cape Town, and South Africa was, at this stage, relying on France to sell them both the power stations themselves and the fuel to run them. After two days of increasingly acerbic conversation, the French were able to persuade South Africa to abandon the test, and on 21 August, Carter was able to announce at a news conference that:

> South Africa has informed us that they do not have and do not intend to develop nuclear explosive devices for any purpose, either peaceful or as a weapon; that the Kalahari test site, which has been in question, is not designed for use to test nuclear explosives; and that no nuclear explosive test will be taken in South Africa now or in the future.

Not only did the last part of the promise not preclude a test outside South Africa's territory, but two months later, in an interview with ABC TV in the United States, Vorster stated: 'I am not aware of any promise that I gave to President Carter . . . I repeated a statement which I have made very often that, as far as South Africa is concerned, we are only interested in peaceful development of nuclear facilities.' The US government quickly countered by revealing a letter that Vorster had written to Carter on 13 October 1977 which said that

'South Africa does not have nor does it intend to develop a nuclear explosive device for any purpose, peaceful or otherwise . . . and there will not be nuclear testing of any kind in South Africa.'

If the intention had been for the Israelis to detonate their first nuclear bomb, then it failed. Equally, if the intention of the South African government had been to impress upon a hostile world their new-found prowess, then the signal was unclear. Some sceptics have suggested that the whole crisis was nothing but a sham, with the South Africans building what looked like a nuclear-test-related construction in the Kalahari, knowing in advance the sort of furore and publicity such an action would generate. However, intelligence sources in Washington insist that they have since received independent confirmation that a test *was* planned, and similar supporting evidence has come from Israel.

What is perhaps most surprising about the whole event was that the South Africans, who can be very sophisticated in playing world politics, so obviously underestimated the reaction from the superpowers when word leaked out. They must have known, from their work with the United States on satellite monitoring in the early 1970s, that the Kalahari site would be spotted, although they might perhaps argue that it was mere chance that sent a Cosmos flying over it during the crucial three weeks. And there remain the overflights by Big Bird several days before Cosmos: it has never been explained why Big Bird did not pick up any signs of an imminent test. The construction necessary takes several weeks to complete, and by late July it must have been obvious for any satellite to see. It is possible, of course, that the United States knew what was happening and intended to turn a blind eye – until the USSR's Cosmos inconveniently came along.

South Africa's refusal to sign the Non-Proliferation Treaty, coupled with suspicions about its developing a nuclear weapon, have hampered its nuclear programme. One of the two French-supplied nuclear power stations at Koeberg was due to come on line in 1982 but, it was announced, had been delayed for a year, following the refusal by the United States to supply the enriched uranium essential for the plant. To counter this mounting political pressure from abroad, South Africa made a determined effort to produce its own enriched uranium from the plant at Valindaba.

In 1981 it was announced that South African scientists had perfected an enrichment process that produced small quantities of 45 per cent enriched uranium-235. While this was seen as a useful step forward, only 3 per cent enriched uranium was needed for the Koeberg station.

The problem was not one of quality but of quantity: the Koeberg station would need 100 tons of 3 per cent enriched uranium to start producing energy – and that would take years under present production methods. However, the 45 per cent enriched uranium is currently being used to keep running another power station located at Pelindaba. ('Pelindaba' is a Zulu word meaning 'the talking is over'.)

In 1982 it was generally assumed that South Africa would have to postpone the opening of the Koeberg power station for several years until either the international embargo on enriched uranium was relaxed or the Valindaba facility began producing sufficient supplies. In fact, in early 1983, the South African government announced that Koeberg would reach full power by May or June of that year. (However, this was later revealed to be grossly misleading. *See* below.) The mystery remains as to where South Africa has obtained the enriched uranium for the plant. US intelligence is convinced that it came from China. Although the Chinese vehemently deny any such deal, the Americans firmly believe that they sold South Africa, through intermediaries, all the uranium it needs. Whoever did the supplying, it appears that international embargoes have little effect and that South Africa's nuclear development continues apace.

Contrary to the South African government's announcement, Koeberg is now expected to come on stream in January 1984 – one year late. The problem is not the lack of enriched uranium; rather, the delay is due to a sabotage attack on the nuclear plant which occurred on the night of 18/19 December 1982 (well before the government's setting of the May or June date). The attack caused at least $22.4 million damage (about 1 per cent of the cost of the building of the plant) and some estimates put the damage as high as $112 million.

The fact that both South Africa and Israel now possess nuclear weapons is of considerable concern to the African continent. While neither country can be expected to admit to a nuclear capability openly, the element of uncertainty will not necessarily deter the enemies of either from launching a conventional attack. The temptation to exercise the nuclear option will always be present, and keeping the bomb in the basement is entirely dependent on peace in an unstable region.

Prime Minister Botha once told a cheering crowd in Cape Town that his country could produce enough arms to counter terrorism: 'If there are people who are thinking of doing something, I suggest they think twice about it. They might find we have military weapons they do not know about.'

10 The Indian Ocean Flash

The 'garden' route from Port Elizabeth to Cape Town along South Africa's southern coastline is one of the most beautiful drives in the world and one of the great attractions for tourist-conscious South Africa, which has done much to promote its charm. One moment the road sweeps alongside the dark and forbidding majesty of the South Atlantic, the next it rises up to run through lush valleys that provide some of the richest farming in the Cape. However, if the casual visitor were to drive south of Cape Town, he would see some equally spectacular scenery along the road that runs down the west side of False Bay and eventually stops at picturesque Simonstown.

When South Africa was a British colony and, later, when defence agreements existed between South Africa and the West, Simonstown was one of the more popular ports where sailors could have a relaxing run ashore. More recently, it has become the headquarters of the South African navy and, as the service has expanded, so Simonstown has rapidly developed into a massive harbour, complete with dry docks and small manufacturing industries.

Early in September 1979, a small and very specialized fleet of vessels put out from Simonstown and headed south-east. After a week's steady steaming, the fleet was apparently hidden in the vast and empty wastes of the southern Indian Ocean, and during the early morning of 22 September, having reached its designated position at 3.00 a.m., a nuclear device was fired into the atmosphere, to explode some eight kilometres above the earth.

South Africa had officially joined the nuclear club.

There were a number of things which conspired against the South African fleet's mission being kept secret. The CIA maintains a strong and effective intelligence arm in the country, working both overtly from the American embassy in Johannesburg and covertly within various South African agencies, including the armed forces. The CIA knew that the fleet had left Simonstown at the beginning of September and, although the purpose of the trip was not known, they tracked it to the southern Indian Ocean, around the Prince Edward Islands.

This is an area known as the 'South African anomaly', where the radiation belts circling the earth reach sea level. It is avoided by all aircraft and shipping because of its high radiation levels, and it is an ideal spot to escape detection: it is deserted, nothing would be detected from an explosion in the atmosphere, and any increase in radiation – provided the detonation was small – would be obscured by the high level already prevailing in the area.

It was already known that a British nuclear scientist, Douglas Torr, had been working in the area conducting tests using three converted Hastings bombers, ostensibly meteorological research for the South African government. More important, however, was the data culled by one of three US Vela satellites, hovering over an area roughly 3,000 miles in diameter, encompassing the southern end of Africa, the Indian Ocean, the South Atlantic and a bit of Antarctica. Launched in 1970, the Vela had been circling the globe as part of a scheme to monitor the nuclear test ban treaty of 1963; it was equipped with extremely sophisticated radiation and electromagnetic sensors able to detect nuclear blasts. Although these were apparently turned off or inadequate to register the small explosion of 22 September, its optical sensors registered a double pulse of light, characteristic of a nuclear explosion.

The information gathered by the satellite was immediately relayed back to earth; however, although the Carter administration including the President himself, was made aware of the satellite's recordings, no public announcement was made. It was almost a month later before the news was leaked to John Scali, a former State Department official working for ABC News, who broadcast it to the world.

Under the terms of the Non-Proliferation Treaty of 1978, the United States was not only responsible for monitoring compliance with the treaty but also for attempting to renegotiate the existing nuclear 'agreement for co-operation' between itself and South Africa. The United States had been trying to persuade the South African government to sign the treaty, but, after these negotiations had been deadlocked for over two years, the Carter administration introduced an official ban on nuclear exports to South Africa.

Reports of a possible detonation of a nuclear warhead by South Africa and (it was suspected) Israel could have been severely embarrassing to the US government. Under the terms of the treaty, the United States would be forced to convene a series of meetings with its allies to introduce some form of economic sanction against South Africa, and possibly against Israel. For the European allies, introducing sanctions against South Africa is almost unthinkable, given the important contributions that country makes in vital raw materials as well as gold and diamond production . . . and of course, for any American president to introduce sanctions against Israel would be a very high-risk gamble indeed. In addition, there would have been world criticism against the United States for having (before the official ban) helped South Africa get the bomb through the supply of nuclear materials.

In an attempt to calm the growing tide of speculation about the mysterious flashes of light, Carter appointed a special committee convened by Dr Frank Press, Science Adviser to the President and Director of the Office of Science and Technology Policy, to examine the evidence and determine whether or not what the Vela had seen had been a nuclear explosion. The committee met three times over a six-month period, finally wrapping up its investigations in April 1980.

The committee of nine was composed of some of the most reputable scientists in the field of nuclear physics, including a number of Nobel prizewinners. The chairman was Dr Jack Ruina from the Department of Electrical Engineering at the Massachusetts Institute of Technology. According to the hitherto unpublished official report of the investigation, their brief was to:

1 Review all available data from both classified and unclassified sources that could help corroborate that the Vela signal had originated from a nuclear explosion and suggest any additional sources of data that might be helpful in this regard.

2 Evaluate the possibility that the signal in question was a false alarm resulting from technical malfunction such as interference from other electrical components on the Vela platform.

3 Investigate the possibility that the signal recorded by the Vela was of natural origin, possibly resulting from the coincidence of two or more natural phenomena, and attempt to establish quantitative limits on the probability of such an occurrence.

The brief was therefore an extremely broad one which should have taken into account virtually every eventuality.

The scientific community was eager to present evidence for or against the nuclear theory and, only weeks after the event, two distinct camps emerged – and this was to remain the case. The first were those who believed both South Africa and Israel, as morally and politically bankrupt regimes, were capable of anything. It suited those opposed to either government to spread the idea that one or both of them had developed a nuclear capability; then, should this theory become accepted, it was hoped that world outrage, followed by sanctions, would fall on both countries. The second group comprised those in either government or intelligence for whom firm evidence would be a serious embarrassment. This included substantial elements in both the CIA and the Defense Intelligence Agency where large numbers of serving members have been consistently sympathetic to both countries, which are seen as bastions against Communism.

The first evidence that was considered was that obtained by the Vela satellite. Since its launch in 1970, the Vela had been directed to monitor forty-one nuclear explosions. In every case, these had been registered accurately and the information transmitted back to the United States. In August, all the satellite's sensors had been checked, and they had responded correctly to signals from earth. The Vela records a nuclear explosion through two light sensors called bhangmeters, located on either side of the satellite's body. In an atmospheric nuclear explosion, a huge quantity of energy is released into the atmosphere surrounding the device so nearly instantaneously, and into such a small volume, that extremes of temperature and pressure are attained and a fireball is created. The dynamics of the fireball are such that there are two distinct peaks of light occurring within a second of each other. The ball generates a pulse of light that disappears briefly when the shock wave blots it out, then reappears as a second pulse of light that is exactly ninety-nine times more intense than the first. Indeed, it is now possible to measure the size and yield of a bomb from the size of the peak and the gap between the two pulses. In this instance, the pattern indicated a three- to four-kiloton bomb – relatively small by today's standards, about 10 to 40 per cent of the size of most bombs tested by countries in the nuclear club. As a fail-safe, the Vela was equipped with two monitors which, through their positioning, would be activated at fractionally different times. A comparison of both the signal received and the gap between the two bhangmeters registering it could inform the scientists that it definitely *was* a nuclear explosion and not some passing freak of nature.

On every previous occasion, the Vela had performed perfectly; this time, the scientists had no evidential reason to doubt that a bomb had been detonated somewhere in the atmosphere. In their report, the committee agreed that the Vela readings were consistent with observing a nuclear explosion – but, although the signals looked right, there was a variation in the level of intensity that each bhangmeter registered. The panel compared twelve previous monitorings by the same Vela satellite: in each case, the two sensors measured similar light intensity within a defined limit. The 22 September measurement was well outside that limit, although it still retained the characteristics of a nuclear explosion. They then argued that, if the source of the 22 September signal was close to the satellite sensors, the relative intensity of the light signal registered on the sensors would be wider apart than if the satellite had picked up a signal from an object far away. In other words, an object passing close to the satellite would be in view of one bhangmeter for a longer time than if it were further away.

The problem – assuming that this explanation was correct – was to identify the phenomenon that could have caused the bhangmeters of the Vela to register the exact double-pulse image of a nuclear explosion. One of the first reports to arrive in support of the Vela sighting was submitted by the Institute of Nuclear Science in Wellington, New Zealand. The Institute issued a background advisory to say that they had found traces of radioactive fallout in recently collected rainwater samples, which were described as 'evidence of extremely low-level radioactivity consistent with a detonation in the Southern Hemisphere in the past three months'. The report added, 'Further measurement and analysis of three elements in the sample – barium-140, cerium and yttrium – is being undertaken before the interim results can be confirmed.' That confirmation never came. The New Zealand National Radiation Laboratory, which was not as specialized as the Institute, was unable to trace any radioactivity, but nor was the Institute able to reproduce the results of the first test. Officially, the initial test results were blamed on testing equipment that had been contaminated with radioactivity and incorrectly cleaned; however, many people felt this explanation was unsatisfactory.

Another promising lead came from the vast radio observatory at Arecibo, Puerto Rico. By chance, on 22 September, scientists at the laboratory were using one of the biggest telescopes in the world, to look into the same area of space where the Vela picked up its signal. The Arecibo scientists were hoping to monitor an Atlas Centaur rocket, launched from the United States, piercing a hole in the ionosphere. Looking through the telescope, the observers noticed a ripple moving through the layers of the ionosphere, some three hours after the Vela picked up the flash in the South Atlantic. To the scientists, it had the unmistakable look of the aftermath of a nuclear explosion, with the ripple appearing at the right time and from the right direction.

However, the committee argued that the ripple effect was not only the signature of a nuclear explosion, but it could also be attributed to

earthquakes, heavy electrical storms or other major natural disturb-
ances. The US Weather Bureau reported that at the time of the
sighting there had been a heavy electrical storm some one hundred
miles to the east of the sighting, and the committee took the view that
this could well have caused the ripple in the ionosphere. They also
argued that the telescope's distance from the sighting made the value
of the observation doubtful. These arguments were not greeted with
enthusiasm by the Arecibo scientists who felt that, if the sighting of
their long-range telescope was to have no evidential value, they might
as well give up and go home. According to those present, as the
Arecibo witnesses gave their evidence, the meeting grew 'stormy', and
so began the polarization of the scientific community into the believers
and non-believers.

Lewis Duncan, one of the Arecibo scientists who saw and analysed
the event, has remained convinced that it was an explosion. The
observation, he said, was 'striking and quite unusual' in that it moved
from south to north, whereas a natural disturbance always heads
towards the nearest pole and not away from it. Most ionospheric
ripples are caused by magnetic storms at the earth's poles and travel up
to the equator, while on this occasion, the ripple may actually have
crossed the equator, moving at speeds of 650–700 metres a second.

Despite the more obvious contradictions, the committee ruled that
the Arecibo sighting was not confirmation of the Vela information.
Duncan replied by describing the panel as 'an exercise in distrac-
tion . . . It surprised me that people have tried as much as they have to
discredit [the sighting],' said Duncan.

Convinced that the anomalies in the Vela data were sufficient to
eliminate a nuclear explosion from the list of possible explanations,
the committee turned to the alternatives; these included ordinary
lightning, superbolts of lightning, sunlight reflections from other
satellites and sunlight reflected from meteoroid particles passing by or
ejected on impact with the satellite.

Both lightning and superbolts generate a flash almost 400 times less
intense and 100 times shorter in duration than even a one-kiloton
explosion; they also produce only single light peaks, compared with
the double peak received by Vela. In addition, the committee's final
report stated:

Meteoroids of sufficient size are too rare and travel too rapidly
through the field of view to generate the observed time sequences.
Unusual astronomical signals would have been observed by other
sensors. Other satellites are too distant to reflect enough light to
trigger the Vela bhangmeters. For these reasons, except for

meteoroid impacts, all have been ruled out as likely causes of the signal.

Instead, the committee decided that the most likely cause of the Vela sighting was a tiny particle of matter hitting the satellite and bounding off. The fragmentation of the particle might have caused the light image and given the impression that it had been received from some distance. Although they plumped for the exploding meteor theory, in the final report they failed to rule in favour of any particular explanation, suggesting rather that the sighting be classed as a 'zoo event' – one of those unusual phenomena observed by man in nature for which there is no rational explanation.

It is interesting that the White House committee has been the only group, among a number that eventually studied the flash, to conclude that it was *not* a nuclear explosion. In every other case, eminent scientists and others have concluded that a nuclear device *had* been exploded in the atmosphere. Given the sensitivity of the Carter administration concerning the monitoring of nuclear explosions and the potential embarrassment that would have been caused by the committee concluding that an explosion had occurred, it is perhaps not altogether surprising that the results came out as they did. There is no doubt that, had the panel waited for the results of the other studies that were being conducted in tandem with their own, they might well have felt compelled to reverse their judgement – even if that had meant going against the wishes of the President.

Even before the report was published, critics had begun to attack its weak conclusions. The Defense Intelligence Agency and the Department of the Navy both concluded that there had been a nuclear explosion, and the scientists who had designed and built the Vela at the Los Alamos Scientific Laboratory stated (perhaps understandably) that the Vela could not possibly have made a mistake, arguing that the fireball of a nuclear explosion has an unmistakable signature, no matter what its size or composition. However, the most detailed voice of dissent came from the Naval Research Laboratory (NRL), which put together a team of seventy-five at the specific request of the Carter administration to examine all the evidence relating to the alleged blast. The NRL did give a preliminary report to the White House committee, but this had been dismissed as being too thin on facts and too fat on supposition.

The NRL eventually submitted its complete 300-page report to the White House on 30 June 1980, and it concluded that there had indeed been a nuclear explosion somewhere near the Prince Edward Islands in the Indian Ocean. The only new evidence that the NRL cited was a hydracoustic signal, picked up at the right time and from the right direction, that was directly comparable with others that have been received from overt tests in the Pacific, according to the NRL's Director of Research, Alan Berman. The NRL searched the records for thirty days either side of 22 September to find out whether some natural phenomenon had been giving off the same message, but none appeared. After Berman had submitted his report, the White House issued a detailed rebuttal, suggesting his analysis was at fault and that the hydracoustic signal was merely a reflection, not a direct sound.

In the midst of all these allegations, South Africa continued to issue strong denials. At first, South Africa tried to blame the explosion on an accident aboard a Soviet nuclear submarine operating in the relevant area, but this was in turn denied by both the Soviets and the Americans. In Pretoria, the Chairman of the AEB, Jacobus de Villiers, described allegations that his country had joined the nuclear club as 'absolute nonsense'. Then Foreign Minister Pik Botha suggested that the United States 'should ask Father Neptune what is going on in his kingdom. I say to you, stop displaying this nervousness. You are frightening your friends and appeasing your enemies.'

However, the Senate subcommittee on nuclear proliferation revealed that the Defence and Naval attachés from the South African embassy in Washington had made a search, via the National Technical Information Service, through all literature on nuclear explosions and their seismic detection, and this search took place two months prior to the Indian Ocean flash. While current information was obviously extremely helpful, South Africa had already gleaned considerable experience of the monitoring methods employed by the Western powers. As well as the three US nuclear tests in 1958, over a fifteen-year period up to 1967, South Africa had helped to monitor nuclear tests conducted by both the United States and France. This included data collection by satellites, ground analysis and flying aerial surveys, and if there were any holes in the West's monitoring system, South African scientists would have been bound to spot them.

Inevitably in such a sensitive matter, other interested parties conducted their own independent investigations and these have all remained classified: in every case, the conclusion has been that there *had* been a nuclear explosion. The Pentagon, in a private report submitted directly to Carter in mid-1980, concluded that a small nuclear device had been detonated in the air above the Indian Ocean, with an artillery piece used as a launcher (such as the howitzer smuggled to South Africa by SRC). The CIA went even further: in a classified report submitted to the National Security Council on 20 June 1980, the CIA suggested that the blast had indeed taken place, and that it was a direct result of co-operation between Israel and South Africa.

The first linking of South Africa and Israel to the explosion came on 21 February 1980 from CBS correspondent Dan Raviv. To back up his story, Raviv quoted from a book entitled *None Will Survive Us: The Story of the Israeli Atom Bomb*, written by two Israeli journalists, Eli Teicher and Ami Dor-on, which, although a novel, factually detailed the story of Israel's progress towards nuclear power. In 1980, they had submitted the book to the Israeli censor, who refused to pass it for publication. Although the book ends in 1974, it deals in considerable detail with Israel's nuclear weapons programme. Dan Raviv interviewed the authors who were able to tell him in detail about the 1979 explosion, and to bypass the censors, Raviv flew to Rome to broadcast the substance of the two journalists' allegations.

According to the authors, the 1979 explosion was a nuclear test conducted by Israel with the help of the South Africans. This appeared to be the first definitive account of the mysterious explosion, particularly as the primary sources for the book were Eliyah Speizer, member of the Knesset, and his close friend, who is heavily involved in Israel's atomic energy programme, Shimon Peres. However, since Raviv first broadcast his story, the present author has been told categorically by very senior members of Israel's intelligence community that the explosion was not an Israeli bomb. What *is* admitted is that there *was* a nuclear explosion and that Israel *has* helped South Africa develop its nuclear programme by supplying both personnel and nuclear technology.

It is, of course, rather difficult to distinguish between an 'Israeli' and a 'South African' bomb. It is certainly true that South Africa has developed her own deterrent on her own soil, but the work has been done with the help of Israeli scientists and Israeli technology. It is also true that, under their current agreements, there is a sharing of technical knowledge. It is thus inevitable that South Africa would have passed on the results of the test and any conclusions the scientists may have made to Israel.

For the South Africans there was little to be lost by conducting a test in the South Atlantic. If undetected, they would have the satisfaction of knowing that their own device worked; if detected, they could always deny responsibility and maintain the air of uncertainty that is so important if the bomb is to remain a deterrent. Additionally, relations with the Carter administration were such that little damage could be done to their dealings with the West if, by any chance, the test plans had been discovered.

For Israel, the problems were rather different. Relations with Carter over the Palestinian question were certainly strained, and the Israeli government did not wish to aggravate the situation. If Israeli scientists were discovered taking part in a nuclear test with South Africa, the political fallout would have been disastrous. The debate within the Israeli administration – whether or not to bring the bomb out of the basement – has not yet been resolved and the Israeli strategists are content to leave a cloud of uncertainty hovering over the Middle East.

There seems little doubt that there *was* a nuclear explosion in the Indian Ocean, although complete proof is never likely to be supplied by South Africa or the Western intelligence agencies who have conducted their own private assessments. On the evidence available, it also seems certain that Israel helped in the development of the bomb but was not represented when it was exploded. South Africa has shared the results with them . . . and both nations are now fully fledged members of the nuclear club.

11 Summary and Conclusions

Israel and South Africa see themselves as being in a fight for survival, and their security can be measured by their success in intimidating their enemies and persuading their friends to continue providing support in the face of growing world opposition.

For Israel, survival can be measured in days. Should the Arab nations combine to attack it, there is some doubt whether the phenomenal feats of arms carried out during the 1967 and 1973 wars could be achieved once again. Since 1973, the Arabs have substantially rearmed – in many cases with front-line American equipment – and Israeli defence chiefs worry that they may have lost the qualitative edge that gave them military superiority.

South Africa is placed rather differently. The combined might of its armed forces is greater than the total of the conventional forces available to African nations south of the Sahara. The idea of any black African nation launching a ground attack against South Africa is either suicidal or unthinkable, and both the South Africans and the countries of black Africa know it; any threats to the contrary can be viewed as simple rhetoric.

The real threat to both nations comes from the influence of underground guerrilla movements and increasing international pressure to give some of the central authority to the disenfranchised. In Israel's case, the PLO has proved a particularly successful adversary, cleverly changing its image from the terrorist movement of the 1960s and early 1970s to that of a more mature and moderate organization seeking a political settlement of the Palestinian question. The declining political influence of Chairman Yasser Arafat is likely to give the more militant members of the organization a new lease of life. If the PLO becomes more aggressive, the Israeli government can match or beat anything they have to offer. Under Shamir, it is unlikely that there will ever be any formal agreements leading to the establishment of a Palestinian state on the West Bank.

This intransigence has lost Israel many friends in the world and even the United States is beginning to lose patience with a country that has hitherto received its unqualified support. It may be that Israel's thrust into the Lebanon in 1982 forced the PLO to become the new Diaspora, spread all over the Middle East with no central power base. Unless Yasser Arafat is able to maintain the momentum of his diplomatic efforts and assure the continuing financial and political support of the Arab nations, it is possible that the PLO could become more extreme. There will remain, however, the problem of the Palestinians. Some settlement sooner or later is inevitable, but at present, it is impossible to be optimistic. The more pessimistic students of the Palestinian question are now talking of a bloody civil war within the next ten years, as the Palestinians on the West Bank attempt to wrest a political franchise from the Israeli authorities. So far there has been no sign of this and the broad mass of the Palestinian population has remained quiescent under Israeli rule.

Israel, like South Africa, has been tarred with the pariah brush. Pressure from the Eastern bloc and the more liberal groups in the West has pushed Israel to the unacceptable fringes of Western democracies, along with South Africa. Nevertheless, Israel remains a basically democratic society (excepting the Palestinians) with a remarkably free press. None the less, until there is a settlement of the Palestinian question, Israel will remain a political outcast and it will be increasingly difficult for her allies to support her openly.

The same situation has already arisen in South Africa where, because of the country's apartheid policy, a total arms embargo and partial economic embargo have been imposed, but the problems for the Pretoria government are somewhat different from those facing the Israelis. The main underground guerrilla group, the ANC, despite considerable support from the Soviet Union and liberal groups in the West, has failed to make any real impact on the South African political scene. Unlike the PLO, the ANC has insisted on a selective approach to armed attacks within South Africa: civilian targets have been generally avoided, for fear of heavy casualties among the black population, and there have been only occasional attacks on soft civilian targets, such as power stations or bridges. The ANC has now been operating since 1912, and at the present rate, there is no possibility of it becoming powerful enough to institute change in South Africa. However, government officials are well aware that the current relative stability is very finely balanced and could be destroyed by another Sharpeville or Soweto. There is general recognition within South Africa that the rigid interpretation of apartheid will have to disappear. Already there have been changes in the policy, but they have not been sufficient for the watching world, and South Africa's status as an outcast will not alter until there is a black government in Pretoria.

There has been much criticism of Israel for building such a close relationship with South Africa, and every aspect of their friendship has caused concern, from arms exchanges to the supply of nuclear technology. Both countries see the issue as part of their fight to survive, and the linking of Zionism with apartheid by the UN in 1975 gave an almost official stamp to a connection that had been developing since the founding of Israel in 1948. While the UN arms embargo remains largely ineffective and black nations continue to trade with South Africa, little can be done to alter what has become one of the most significant strategic alliances of the past ten years. This alliance has grown in an atmosphere of secrecy and, for the Israelis, something close to shame. Neither country is prepared to admit how interdependent they have become, and yet this will affect for ever the balance of power on the African continent, the stability of the Middle East and the influence of both countries on the development of the Third World.

Of course, certain sections of the world have actively encouraged the development of the relationship. If the Cubans are the tool of Soviet foreign policy, so the Israelis can act out the wishes of US administrations. It is fortunate for South Africa that both Israel and the United States see South Africa as an essential feature of Western security. In addition, there has been a growing dependency between Israel's need to win political and economic influence on the African continent and the need of the United States to counter the seemingly inexorable march of left-wing revolution in the region. South Africa, too, would like to see such a close ally as Israel increasing its influence among the very nations that are most opposed to apartheid and white rule in Africa.

While the United States and Europe may be happy for Israel to move closer to South Africa politically and act as a conduit for Western arms and technology, the alliance has dimensions that were never envisaged by the US State Department or the British Foreign Office. If Israel and South Africa continue along their current path, within the next decade they will be virtually self-sufficient in arms production. This will make South Africa almost invulnerable to outside military pressure and, if the early promise of large arms exports bears fruit, then economic independence will follow. For Israel, an independent military machine, secure from the vagaries of US defence policy, must be a high priority. Israeli defence planners are well aware how the perception of strategic balance could, in the future, move in favour of the Arabs.

A secret CIA analysis prepared in 1983 suggests that, by the 1990s, Israel will no longer be a strategic centre for the United States. Current and future administrations in Jerusalem are viewed as being increasingly militant and unreliable, and the positive aspects of having a close ally in that part of the Middle East will be far outweighed by the need to be linked with the land-rich nations of the Arabian Gulf and Africa. The CIA believes that, as new methods of cultivating desert areas are refined, so tiny Israel will shrink in significance. While such a hard-nosed view has not yet become official, the Israelis see perfectly clearly the direction of US foreign policy. A close alliance with South Africa places the two most powerful nations at either end of the African continent effectively under the same umbrella, with a joint foreign policy and similar trading ambitions. Apart from these two nuclear powers being allies – neither of whom has signed the Non-Proliferation Treaty – the alliance is of the most profound significance for the world.

An independent Israel, fighting alone, represents a far more serious threat to the Arab nations and to the Palestinians than an Israel controlled in some measure by the United States. The chances of a settlement of the Palestinian question are reduced as US influence wanes, while the prospects for war must increase. In the next confrontation – and most senior Israelis believe another war is inevitable – the possibility of Israel unleashing her nuclear weapons must be heightened. At the other end of the continent, South Africa, with the help of Israel, has now achieved a military strength far beyond anything available to its potential enemies. It is highly unlikely that any African nation will confront South Africa in a conventional war, but there will be continuing increased support for guerrilla movements opposed to white rule. With the black African nations in an effective pincer between South Africa and Israel, their freedom to develop economically and to take independent political action will be severely restricted. Israel's major diplomatic push into black Africa, which has already resulted in Zaïre and Liberia reopening diplomatic relations, can only benefit South Africa.

Attempts to isolate either country by mobilizing the African bloc vote in the UN will fail. As each African country increases its trading relationship with Israel and as more African leaders are guarded by Israeli-trained bodyguards, so anti-Israel action becomes increasingly unlikely. Equally, those same African leaders must be susceptible to Israeli pressure to stop public attacks on South Africa. As their joint arms industry develops, so the two countries will expand their sphere of influence to more Third World nations – particularly in Africa and

Latin America. This, in turn, will make any international action against either of them more difficult – which, of course, has been one of the primary strategies behind the growth of the relationship.

The direct result of their political, economic and military alliance has been a strengthening of South Africa's and Israel's positions in the world. Each owes to the other a new-found feeling of security resulting from a military machine backed up with nuclear weapons that few will dare threaten. Both countries are stronger than at any time in the past ten years, and anyone who might confidently have predicted substantial political change in either country in the near future will be wrong.

Glossary of Acronyms

AEB (South African) Atomic Energy Board
AEC (US) Atomic Energy Commission
AEI (South African) Atomic Energy Institute
AIAA American Institute of Aeronautics and Astronautics
AMC (US) Army Materiel Command
ANC African National Congress
Armcom (US) Army Armament Command
Armscor (South African) Armaments Development and Production Corporation
AWACS Airborne Warning and Control Systems
BOSS (South African) Bureau of State Security
CEGB (UK) Central Electricity Generating Board
CROTALE Land-based mobile anti-aircraft missile
EEC European Economic Community
ESCOM (South African) Electricity Supply Commission
FN Fabrique Nationale (of Belgium)
FNLA Fronte Nacional de Libertacao de Angola
GFK (West German) Society of Nuclear Research
HARP High Altitude Research Project
IAEC International Atomic Energy Commission
IAF Israeli Air Force
IAI Israeli Aircraft Industries
IDF Israeli Defence Force
IISS International Institute for Strategic Studies
IMF International Monetary Fund
IMI Israeli Military Industries
Iscor (South African) Iron and Steel Corporation
ITAR (OMC's) International Traffic in Arms Regulations
MAAG (US) Military Assistance Advisory Group

MPLA Movimento Popular de Libertacao de Angola
NAAA National Association of Arab-Americans
NIDR (South African) National Institute for Defence Research
NIS (South African) National Intelligence Service
NRC Nuclear Regulatory Commission
NRL (US) Naval Research Laboratory
NSSM (US) National Security Study Memorandum
NUMEC Nuclear Materials and Equipment Corporation
OAU Organization of African Unity
OMC (US State Department's) Office of Munitions Control
OPEC Organization of Petroleum Exporting Countries
PAC Pan-African Congress
PLO Palestine Liberation Organization
ROLAND French-manufactured land-based mobile aircraft missiles
RPV Remotely Piloted Vehicle
SAAF South African Air Force
SADF South African Defence Force
SAS (UK) Special Air Services
SATO South Atlantic Treaty Organization
SGM Société Général des Minerais
SIPRI Stockholm International Peace Research Institute
SRC Space Research Corporation
STOL Short Take-off and Landing (aircraft)
SWAPO South-West Africa People's Organization
SWASU South-West Africa Specialist Unit
UCOR Uranium Enrichment Corporation of South Africa
UNITA Unicio Nacional de Independencia Total de Angola
ZANU Zimbabwe African National Union
ZAPU Zimbabwe African People's Union

Selected Bibliography

ADAN, Avraham. *On the Banks of the Suez*. Arms & Armour Press, London, 1980.
——*Africa South of the Sahara*. Europa Publications, London, 1983.
AMERICAN JEWISH COMMITTEE. American Jewish Yearbook. Jewish Publications Society of America, 1981.
BARBER, James; BLUMENFELD, Jesmond; HILL, Christopher H. *The West and South Africa*. The Royal Institute of International Affairs, London, 1982.
BHATIA, Shyam. *India's Nuclear Bomb*. Vikas Publishing House, Sahibabad, 1979.
COUHAT, Jean Lavayle. *Combat Fleets of the World 1982/83*. Arms & Armour Press, London, 1982.
CROKER, Chester A. *South Africa's Defense Posture*. Sage Publications, Beverly Hills, 1981.
CURTIS, Michael; GITELSON, Susan Aurelia. *Israel in the Third World*. Transaction Books, New Jersey, 1976.
DALY, Lt.-Col. Ron Reid. *Secous Scouts: Top Secret War*. Galago Publishing, Alberton, 1982.
DAVENPORT, Elaine; EDDY, Paul; GILLMAN, Peter. *The Plumbat Affair*. Futura Publications, London, 1978.
DUPUY, Col. T.N.; ANDREWS, Col. John A. C.; HAYES, Grace P. *The Almanac of World Military Power*. Presidio Press, San Rafael, Calif., 1980.
EL-KHAWAS, Mohammed A.; COHEN, Barry. *The Kissinger Study of Southern Africa*. Lawrence Hill & Co., Connecticut, 1976.
EPSTEIN, Edward J., *The Diamond Invention*. Hutchinson, London, 1982.
EVRON, Yair. *The Role of Arms Control in the Middle East*. IISS, London, 1977.
FORD, Gerald R. *A Time to Heal*. W. H. Allen, London, 1979.
FREEMANTLE, Brian. *KGB*. Michael Joseph, London, 1983.
GLICK, Edward. *The Triangle Connection: America, Israel and American Jews*. George Allen & Unwin, London, 1982.
GOLAN, Matti. *The Secret Conversations of Henry Kissinger*. Bantam Books, New York, 1980.
——*Shimon Peres, a biography*. Weidenfeld & Nicolson, London, 1982.
GREENWOOD, Ted; RATHJENS, George W.; RUINA, Jack. *Nuclear Power and Weapons Proliferation*. IISS, London, 1976.
HANKS, Robert J. *The Cape Route*. Institute for Foreign Policy Analysis, Washington, 1981.
HUSSEIN, Farooq. *The Impact of Weapons Test Restrictions*. IISS, London, 1981.
INTERNATIONAL DEFENCE AND AID FUND. *The Apartheid War Machine*. IDAF, London, 1980.
INTERNATIONAL INSTITUTE FOR STRATEGIC STUDIES. *Strategic Surveys, 1970–1982*. IISS, London.
——*The Military Balance, 1975–1982*. IISS, London.
JACKSON, Henry F. *From the Congo to Soweto*. William Morrow, New York, 1982.
KISSINGER, Henry. *Years of Upheaval*. Weidenfeld & Nicolson/Michael Joseph, London, 1982.
KONIG, Barbara. *Namibia: Ravages of War*. IDAF, London, 1983.
LUSTICK, Ian. *Arabs in the Jewish State*. University of Texas Press, Austin, 1980.
MADDOX, John. *Prospects for Nuclear Proliferation*. IISS, London, 1975.
McKNIGHT, Allan. *Atomic Safeguards*. Institute for Training and Research, New York, 1981.
——*The Middle East and North Africa, 1982–83*. Europa Publications, London, 1983.
MORRIS, Roger. *Uncertain Greatness*. Quartet Books, London, 1977.
MUSHKAT, Mari'on. *Violence and Peace Building in the Middle East*. K. G. Saur, Munich, 1981.
NARMIC/AMERICAN FRIENDS SERVICES COMMITTEE. *Automating Apartheid*. NARMIC, Philadelphia, 1982.

O'BALLANCE, Edgar. *No Victor, No Vanquished*. Barrie & Jenkins, London, 1979.

PERLMUTTER, Amos; HANDEL, Michael; BAR-JOSEPH, Uri. *Two Minutes Over Baghdad*. Corgi Books, London, 1982.

PERES, Shimon. *From These Men*. Weidenfeld & Nicolson, London, 1979.

PERRY, Charles. *The West, Japan and Cape Route Imports*. Institute for Foreign Policy Analysis, Cambridge, 1982.

PIERRE, Andrew. *The Global Politics of Arms Sales*. Princeton University Press, Princeton, N.J., 1982.

POMEROY, William J. *Apartheid Axis*. International Publishers, New York, 1971.

PRANGER, Robert J.; TAHTINEN, Dale R. *Nuclear Threat in the Middle East*. American Enterprise Institute, Washington, D.C., 1975.

PRETTY, Ronald T. *Jane's Weapons Systems, 1982–83*. Jane's Publications, London, 1982.

PRINGLE, Peter; SPIGELMAN, James. *The Nuclear Barons*. Michael Joseph, London, 1982.

RAY, Ellen; SCHAAP, William; VAN METER, Carl; WOLF, Louis. *Dirty Work 2: The CIA in Africa*. Lyle Stuart, New Jersey, 1979.

RICHARDSON, Doug. *Naval Armaments*. Jane's Publications, London, 1981.

ROGERS, Barbara; CERVENKA, Zdenek. *The Nuclear Axis*. Times Books, New York, 1978.

SACHER, Howard M. *A History of Israel*. Alfred A. Knopf, New York, 1981.

SALINGER, Pierre. *America Held Hostage*. André Deutsch, London, 1982.

SPEIGEL, Steven L. *The Middle East and the Western Alliance*. George Allen & Unwin, London, 1982.

STEVEN, Stewart. *The Spymasters of Israel*. Ballantine Books, New York, 1980.

STEVENS, Richard P.; ELMESSIRI, Abdulwahab M. *Israel and South Africa: The Progression of a Relationship*. New World Press, New York, 1976.

STEWARD, Alexander. *The World, the West and Pretoria*. David McKay, New York, 1977.

SIPRI. *World Armaments and Disarmament*. Taylor & Francis, London, 1978–83.

STOCKWELL, John. *In Search of Enemies*. Washington, 1978.

STUDY COMMISSION ON US POLICY TOWARDS SOUTHERN AFRICA. *South Africa: Time Running Out*. University of California Press, Berkeley, 1981.

VILLIERS, Les de. *South Africa: A Skunk Among Nations*. International Books, London, 1975.

——*Secret Information*. Tafelberg, Cape Town, 1980.

WEEKS, Col. John. *Jane's Infantry Weapons, 1982–83*. Jane's Publications, London, 1982.

WEISSMAN, Steve; KROSNEY, Herbert. *The Islamic Bomb*. Times Books, New York, 1981.

WESTERN MASSACHUSETTS ASSOCIATION OF CONCERNED AFRICAN SCHOLARS. *US Military Involvement in Southern Africa*. South End Press, Boston, 1978.

WILKINS, Ivor; STRYDOM, Hans. *The Super Afrikaners*. Jonathan Ball, Johannesburg, 1978.

WILSON, Harold. *Final Term*. Weidenfeld & Nicolson/Michael Joseph, London, 1975.

WILSON, Michael. *Jane's Avionics, 1982–83*. Jane's Publications, London, 1982.

YAGER, Joseph A. *Non Proliferation in US Foreign Policy*. Brookings Institute, Washington, 1980.

Notes

Chapter 1: Mutual Security

p. 5   'General Smuts is written': *South Africa Jewish Chronicle*, 22 September 1950, p. 1.

—'rise of the . . . Nationalist Party': Martyn Adelberg, 'The future of the Jewish community in South Africa', *South Africa International*, January 1982, vol. xiii, no. 3, p. 434.

—'in a gesture of solidarity': Azim Huzain, 'The West, Israel and South Africa, a strategic triangle', *Third World Quarterly*, January 1982, vol. iv, p. 69.

p. 7   '*Eretz Israel*': Howard M. Sacher, *A History of Israel*, Alfred A. Knopf, New York, 1981, p. 716.

—'The reverse has also': David Frank, 'Marching from Pretoria?', *Jerusalem Post* (weekly), 10 December 1976.

—'A fourth of the South African': Sacher, *op. cit.*, p. 716.

p. 8   'In a shrewd move': Richard P. Stevens & Abdulwahab M. Elmessiri, *Israel and South Africa*, New World Press, New York, 1976.

p. 9   'When Hendrik Verwoerd': Stephen Cohen, 'Such good friends', *New Republic*, May 1981, p. 15.

p. 10   'South African exiles': SAPA report, 22 November 1982.

p. 11   'United Nations condemned': *Britannia Yearbook 1974–75*, p. 440.

p. 12   'the Jews in South Africa': Adelberg, *op. cit.*

—'emerging black African nations': *Israel's Programme of International Cooperation*, Israeli Ministry of Foreign Affairs, 1971, p. 57.

p. 13   'the Israeli secret service': CIA study captured by Khomeini revolutionary guards at the US embassy, Tehran, and released to the author.

p. 15   'direct result of the insolence': Susan Aurelia Gitelson, 'Israel's African Setback in Perspective', *Jerusalem Papers on Peace Problems*, Hebrew University of Jerusalem, May 1976, p. 19.

—'Jews in South Africa had been unstinting': 'Relations between Israel and South Africa: special report of the Special Committee Against Apartheid', UN General Assembly, Document A/31/22/Add.2, p. 27.

—'Masterminded by . . . Eschel Rhoodie': K.H. Katzen, 'The Jewish connection', *Johannesburg Star*, 23 September 1979.

p. 16   'In his book': Les de Villiers, *Secret Information*, Tafelberg, Cape Town, 1980, pp. 101–5.

—'Israel might interrupt the flow': 'South Africa: vital oil flows', *Africa Confidential*, 5 January 1983, vol. 24, no. 1, p. 1.

—'The UN General Assembly': General Assembly Resolution 3379, 10 November 1975.

p. 17   'a remarkably successful visit': 'The Israel–Africa connection', *New Africa*, April 1977, no. 68, pp. 41–3.

p. 18   're-established diplomatic relations': 'Doe tells why he wants to stop Qaddafi', *The Times*, 25 August 1983, p. 24.

—(*See* ref.) 'parachute training': 'Israel's African connection', *Newsview*, 12 January 1982, pp. 24–5.

Chapter 2: A Marriage of Money

p. 19 'According to the International Monetary Fund': *Directory of Trade Statistics*, IMF, Washington, July 1982.

p. 20 'In his absorbing book' *et seq.*: Edward J. Epstein, *The Diamond Invention*, Hutchinson, London, 1982.

p. 23 'in January 1968': *American Jewish Yearbook*, 1969, p. 454.

p. 24 'Transvaal Coal Owners Association': *Washington Post*, 31 October 1979; *Johannesburg Star*, 19 February, 1978; *Financial Times*, 20 February 1978.

p. 25 'Simcha Ehrlich visited': *Business Week*, 22 May 1978, p. 48.
—'Finance Minister Owen Horwood': *Christian Science Monitor*, 16 December 1980.
—'after Vorster's visit': Foreign trade statistics: import/export 1978–81, Israeli Central Bureau of Statistics.

p. 26 'E. Raviv, detailed': *Israel–South Africa Trade Bulletin*, March 1982, p. 6.
—'preferential access to both the EEC': *Business Week*, 22 May 1978, p. 48; *Guardian*, 15 February 1978, p. 3.

p. 27 'According to Dr Tamir Agmom': *Financial Times*, 10 October 1977.
—'Piet Kieser': *Israel–South Africa Trade Bulletin*, *op. cit.*, p. 4.

p. 28 'Israel has been swift': Information supplied to the author by Eric Marsden, January 1984.

Chapter 3: The Military Alliance

p. 29 'As a legacy of its colonial days': A very good overview of South Africa's security is provided by Robert S. Jaster in 'South Africa's narrowing security options', *Adelphi Papers*, no. 159, International Institute of Strategic Studies, London.

p. 30 'the Sharpeville massacre in 1960': Les de Villiers, *South Africa: A Skunk Among Nations*, International Books, London, 1975, pp. 50–55.
—'a shape of black militancy': 'South Africa: time running out', *Report of the Study Commission on United States Policy Toward Southern Africa*, Foreign Policy Foundation, Inc., University of California Press, Berkeley, 1981, pp. 168–205.

p. 32 'Brigadier Penn has confirmed': quoted in 'Twin outposts of imperialism', *Sechaba* (journal of the ANC), April 1982, pp. 21–2.
—'the Israeli Uzi': 'The Israeli connection', *Economist*, 5 November 1977, pp. 90–1; *Resister*, August–September 1981, pp. 20–1; *New York Times*, 30 April 1971.

p. 33 'after the end of the war': Peter Hellyer, 'Israel and South Africa', United Nations General Assembly Special Committee on Apartheid, Document A/AC.115/L.396, 14 October 1974, p. 7.
—'When the arms embargo': Chester A. Croker, *South Africa's Defense Posture*, The Washington Papers, No. 84 CSIS, Georgetown University, Washington, 1981, pp. 41–51 (published in the same year by Sage Publications, Beverly Hills, Calif.). A particularly detailed analysis of the South African Defence Force appears in *The Apartheid War Machine* by the International Defence and Aid Fund, London, April 1980.

p. 35 'The South African government': Jewish Telegraph Agency, 20 January 1970, quoted in Hellyer, *op. cit.*, p. 13.

Chapter 4: South Africa, Israel and the Nuclear Howitzer

Unless otherwise stated, the information in this chapter comes from four main sources: (1) documents submitted to the Senate staff study subcommittee convened to investigate the SRC case, including previously classified material such as statements gathered by the FBI and submissions made by the CIA; (2) the subcommittee report, *The Space Research Case and the Breakdown of the United States Arms Embargo Against South Africa*; (3) information supplied privately by members of the subcommittee; (4) the results of a brilliant investigation into SRC by Sam Hemmingway and William Scott Malone of the *Burlington* (Vermont) *Free Press*.

p. 38 'The South African invasion': John Stockwell, *In Search of Enemies*, Washington, 1978, pp. 50–84.

p. 42 'In the 1973 Yom Kippur War': Edgar O'Ballance, *No Victor, No Vanquished: The Yom Kippur War*, Barrie & Jenkins, London, 1979.
—'Arms deals in Israel': *Newsview*, 12 January 1982, p. 8.
—'one retired general said': Conversation with the author in Washington, July 1982.

p. 43 'As early as 1969': Mohammed A. El-Khawas & Barry Cohen, *The Kissinger Study of*

Southern Africa, Lawrence Hill, Westport, Conn., 1976, pp. 84–5.

p. 44　'the SADF was operating': Stockwell, *op. cit.*; International Defence and Aid Fund, *op. cit.*, pp. 57–61.

p. 46　'Fortress South Africa': William Gutteridge, 'South Africa: a strategy for survival', *Conflict Studies*, June 1981, no. 131, p. 18.

Chapter 5: Israel and the Fortification of South Africa

p. 72　'Major-General Neil Webster': Quoted in Stevens & Elmessiri, *op. cit.*, p. 188.

p. 73　'3,000 young blacks': *Economist Foreign Report*, 19 March 1981, pp. 3–5.
　　　—'The collapse of support': *Keesing's Contemporary Archives*, June 1976, p. 27775.
　　　—'The Bill also said': *Ibid.*
　　　—'As Julius Nyerere': Kenneth L. Abelman & Albion W. Knight, 'Can South Africa go nuclear?' *Orbis*, Fall 1979, p. 640.

p. 74　'Ministry of Defence': 'Pretoria prepares for total war', *Financial Times*, 29 February 1980.

p. 75　'note to Secretary-General Kurt Waldheim': *Washington Post*, 8 November 1977.
　　　—'South Africa's defence expenditure': *Strategic Survey*, International Institute of Strategic Studies, pp. 76–82; information supplied to author by Eric Marsden, Johannesburg correspondent on the *Sunday Times*, London.
　　　—'Finance Minister Owen Horwood': *Financial Times*, 13 August 1981.
　　　—'Armscor was formed': International Defence and Aid Fund, *op. cit.*; *Afrique defense*, October 1979; *Financial Times*, 22 August 1980.

p. 76　'South Africa is now self-sufficient': *Paratus*, November 1982, pp. 18–19.
　　　—'the Israeli electronics industry': *International Defense Review*, 1982, vol. 1, pp. 59–65.

p. 77　'the main thrust of their weapons development': *Strategy Week*, 24–30 November 1980, pp. 8–10; *International Defense Review*, August 1982, pp. 1001–7; *Military Technology*, MILTECH 20, pp. 26-30.

p. 78　'a highly effective technological and training edge': Private conversation with Israeli official, Tel Aviv, November 1982.

p. 79　'As the 1975 Defence White Paper': Pauline Baker, 'South Africa's strategic vulnerabilities: the citadel assumption reconsidered?' *African Studies Review*, September 1977, vol. xx, no. 2, pp. 84–99.

p. 80　'Marcia Friedman': United Nations Special Report of the Special Committee Against Apartheid, Document A/31/22/Add.2, paragraph 51.
　　　—'Friedman was correct': Privately confirmed to the author, November/January 1982/83.
　　　—'There are only about one million': *Economist Foreign Report*, 19 March 1981, p. 3.
　　　—'It was General Magnus Malan': *Financial Times*, 29 February 1980.

p. 81　'A major recruiting drive': *The Military Balance 1982–1983*, International Institute of Strategic Studies, London, pp. 70–1.
　　　—'not mere tokenism': *Newsweek*, 29 September 1980, p. 14.

p. 82　'chief Gatsha Buthelezi': *International Herald-Tribune*, 25 April 1979.
　　　—'Selous Scouts': Lt Col. Ron Reid-Daly, *Selous Scots, Top Secret War*, Galago Publishing, Alberton, 1982.

p. 83　'altering the conscription laws': *International Herald-Tribune*, 26 March 1982.

p. 84　'The State Security Committee': *Washington Post*, 30 May 1980, p. A20; *South African Foundation News*, October 1983, p. 2.

p. 85　'a function of total war': *Ibid.*
　　　—'South Africa claimed to have killed': Conversation with South African security police, November 1982.

p. 86　'Israel has supplied the Iranian regime': Documents released to the author by the People's Mojahedin of Iran, 16 October 1981.
　　　—'complete surprise to the PLO': Information supplied to author by Israeli officials in November 1982. *See also* Raphael Israeli, *The PLO in Lebanon: Selected Documents*, Weidenfeld & Nicolson, London, 1983.
　　　—'including the ANC': *The Citizen*, 1 December 1982, p. 10; *South African Forum Position Papers*, 1983, vol. 6, no. 10, p. 3.

p. 87　'headed by James Angleton': Stephen Talbot, 'The CIA and BOSS: thick as thieves' in *Dirty Work 2: The CIA in Africa*, edited by Ellen Ray *et al.*, Lyle Stuart, Secaucus, N.J., 1979, p. 260.

p. 88　'National Intelligence Service': William Schaap, 'The CIA and BOSS', *Covert Action Information Bulletin*, Winter 1983, pp. 52–6; *Guardian*, 8 February 1980.

p. 89 'ANC leaders based in Mozambique': *Sunday Times*, London, December 1982, p. 19.
—'to pre-empt cross-border strikes': *Paratus*, January 1982, p. 27.
—'Israeli counter-terrorist experts': *Tel Aviv New Outlook*, March/April 1983, pp. 31–5.

p. 91 'The Mossad has managed': Confirmed in conversations in Tel Aviv, Pretoria and Washington.
—'A secret study': Conversation with State Department official who prepared report, Washington, July 1982.

p. 92 'As Amiram Nir': ISSOP, June 1982, pp. 2-11.

p. 93 'more than fifty': Figures vary, but this estimate was supplied by sources close to Israeli intelligence and supported by diplomatic sources in South Africa and Israel.
—'with Israeli fencing': *Economist Foreign Report*, 2 November 1977, pp. 1–2.

p. 94 'farms have been abandoned': Information from Eric Marsden.
—'Hendrik Schoeman': *Ibid.*
—'the Coatsee recommendations': *South African Digest*, 30 May 1980, p. 1.

p. 95 'A research paper': Information from Eric Marsden.

p. 96 'Under a joint project': *Rand Daily Mail*, 15 December 1981.

p. 97 'Defence Minister, Ariel Sharon': Conference paper issued as Israeli Government press bulletin, Jerusalem, 15 December 1981.

p. 98 'a Memorandum of Understanding': Charles R. Denton, 'United States/Israeli arms deals with "certain countries", 1981–1982', unpublished research paper.
—'some 4,000 Israeli experts': *Christian Science Monitor*, 24 May 1982.
—'Mobuto . . . was sent to Israel': *Newsview*, 12 January 1982, pp. 24–5.

p. 99 'Sharon went on a rapid tour': *The Times*, 17 May 1982; *New York Times*, 19 June 1982.
—'made a tour of SADF positions': BBC Monitoring report, 15 December 1981.
—'Israel will hand on to Zaïre': *Rand Daily Mail*, 1 December 1982.

p. 100 'a secret plan': *Observer*, 23 January 1983.
—'Sharon again visited': *The Times*, 20 January 1983.
—'the Arabs were furious': *New Africa*, June 1982, pp. 38–9.

p. 101 'the Senate Foreign Relations Committee': Conversation with Saleh Abdul Rahini of TransAfrica, Washington, 31 August 1982.
—'a good and dependable friend': *New Africa, op. cit.*, p. 38.

Chapter 6: The Arms Business

p. 102 'Foreign Minister Moshe Dayan': *Washington Post*, 8 November 1977.
—'Israel had already supplied': *The Middle East*, June 1982, pp. 8–9.

p. 103 'South Africans secretly formed': *African News*, 7 June 1982, pp. 3–5.
—'British intelligence was naturally': The first reports of the arms shipments were leaked to the *Sunday Times* and published on 27 May 1982. MI6 supplied an astonishing amount of detail and their colleagues in the CIA were equally indiscreet.

p. 105 'Italian socialist deputy Falco Accame': Details supplied by Accame in conversation with *Sunday Times* Rome correspondent, Tana de Zulueta, October 1982.

p. 107 'large consignments of arms from Bulgaria': *Sunday Times*, London, 4 March 1983.

p. 108 'Commodore Dieter Gerhardt': *The Times*, 28 January 1983. Additional information on Gerhardt's precise role and the damage he did was supplied to the author by Israeli officials, February 1983.

p. 109 'senior officers from the army': Example given to the author by a Western diplomat in Tel Aviv in November 1982.
—'Journalists in Israel': Told to the author by Yossi Melman, an Israeli journalist, then working for Israeli Radio.
—'an export drive': South African *Sunday Tribune*, 5 December 1982, p. 9.

p. 110 'IAI, the biggest division': *Armada International*, January 1980. Background figures on arms exports are found in *World Military Expenditures and Arms Transfers*, published annually by the United States Arms Control and Disarmament Agency.
—'overhaul the armour on the tanks': *Military Technology*, MILTECH 20, pp. 26–36.

p. 111 'they needed special steel': *Economist*, 5 November 1977, p. 90.
—'An interesting device': *International Defense Review*, January 1982, p. 66.
—'The Merkhava Mark 1 tanks': *International Defense Review*, August 1982, p. 1006.
—'the 150 Centurion tanks': *Middle East International*, n.d., pp. 19–20.

—'for Israel to supply': Conversations with Israeli officials and Western diplomats in Tel Aviv and Jerusalem, November 1982.

p. 112 'Helicopters play an increasingly': Rosalin Ainslee, *Israel and South Africa: An Unlikely Alliance*, Centre Against Apartheid, July 1981, UN Document No. 81–18876, p. 13.

—'superior Israeli electronics': Conversation with Israeli defence officials, November 1982.

p. 113 'At the recent arms show': *Paratus*, November 1982, p. 19.

—'Remotely Piloted Vehicles': *International Defense Review*, August 1982, p. 1004.

p. 114 'South Africans have already taken delivery': *New Africa*, August 1983, p. 29. (An Israeli-supplied RPV was shot down over Maputo in July 1983.)

—'A crack anti-terrorist unit': *Defence and Foreign Affairs Daily*, 20 December 1978.

p. 115 'The Arava's EW capability': *Jerusalem Post* (international edition), 17–23 June 1979, pp. 11–12.

p. 117 'South Africa has already purchased': Brenda M. Branaman, *South African–Israeli Relations*, Congressional Research Service report no. 81–174F, 30 July 1981, p. 8. Figures supplied by IISS, London. NB: Before any Kfirs can reach South Africa, US approval would have to be granted; this has not happened so far.

—'following the lead of the Israelis': *Defence and Foreign Affairs Daily*, 15 December 1980.

p. 118 'Code-named the Lavi': *Aviation Week and Space Technology*, 10 January 1983, pp. 20–24.

p. 120 'a senior member of the board': Details passed to the author, April 1983.

—'Before 1970, five of the eight': Col. Norman L. Dodd, 'The South African Navy: Guardian of the Ocean Crossroads', *US Naval Institute Proceedings*, September 1976, p. 96.

p. 121 'Botha, then Minister of Defence': *Keesing's Contemporary Archives*, 29 May 1981, p. 30888.

p. 122 'The result was the Reshef': *Jane's Fighting Ships*, Jane's Publishing, London; Doug Richardson, *Naval Armament*, Jane's Publishing, London, 1981.

—'Israel would supply South Africa': *Economist*, 5 November 1977, p. 90; *Armed Forces*, October 1982, pp. 6–9.

—'While the initial order': Original information supplied by Israeli officials and confirmed by Western diplomats in Tel Aviv.

p. 123 'Following the sinking': *The Times*, 19 February 1982; *Johannesburg Star*, 20 February 1982.

—'The possibility of a joint South African–Israeli development': *Aviation and Marine International*, February 1980; *Strategy Week*, 24–30 November 1980, pp. 8–9; *Armada International*, January 1980, p. 26; *Economist*, 5 November 1977, p. 90.

p. 124 'the submarines of neither navy': *International Defense Review*, August 1982, p. 1007; *Defence and Foreign Affairs Daily*, 12 December 1979, pp. 1–2.

—'There have been reports': *Register*, August–September 1982, p. 1; *Sechaba*, April 1982, p. 21. The allegations appear to be entirely unsubstantiated and are ridiculed by defence experts.

Chapter 7: The US Lobby

p. 127 'More than $100 million': *US News and World Report*, 29 March 1982, p. 41.

—'A number of laws': *Ibid.*

p. 128 'On 6 February 1974': Les de Villiers, *Secret Information, op. cit.*, p. 73.

—'de Villiers reported': *Ibid.*, p. 66.

p. 129 'In 1959, he had teamed up': *Columbia Journalism Review*, November/December 1979; *The Nation*, 19 April 1980, pp. 455–8.

p. 131 'In the six months from': Information filed at the Justice Department by the firm of Smathers, Symington and Herlong, under the Foreign Agents Registration Act.

—'Rhoodie hired Donald de Kieffer': *Washington Post Magazine*, 25 May 1978, p. 21.

—'advised to approach Sydney Baron': *The Nation*, 14 April 1979, pp. 390–3.

p. 132 'When Gerald Ford ran': *Ibid.*, p. 392.
     —'cash went into the campaign': *Congressional Quarterly Almanac.*
p. 133 'The *Times* is backed': *Washington Notes on Africa*, Summer 1982, pp. 1–3.
     —'South Africa paid': Information on file with the Justice Department and supplied to
     the author.
p. 134 'they appointed John P. Sears': Information filed at the Justice Department by Baskin
     and Sears, under the Foreign Agents Registration Act.
p. 135 'During the war in the Lebanon': Information supplied to the author by a State
     Department official, April 1983.
     —'Jews only make up': *American Jewish Yearbook*, 1982; Edward Glick, *The Triangle
     Connection: America, Israel and American Jews*, George Allen & Unwin, London, 1982,
     pp 95–107.
p. 136 'On the eve of': Glick, *op. cit.*, p. 98.
p. 137 'The Arabs, on the other hand': *Wall Street Journal*, 29 July 1982, p. 10.
p. 138 'The Senate was due to vote': *New Republic*: 17 February 1982, pp. 1–8; 19 May 1982, pp.
     12–15; 16 June 1982, pp. 18–23.
p. 139 'The Moral Majority and the Israelis': *New York Times*, 30 November 1982; Institute of
     Jewish Affairs research report no. 14, October 1982; *Washington Notes on Africa, op.
     cit.*; *Africa News*, 16 October 1981.
p. 140 'The South Africans had discovered': *Washington Post*, 9 November 1978.
     —'The alliance of the right': *New York Times*, 8 February 1981, p. 25; *New Yorker*, 20
     July 1981, pp. 78–89.
     —'the Christian League': *The Nation*, 19 April 1980, p. 458.
p. 141 'According to Falwell's spokesman': *Congressional Quarterly*, 22 August 1981, p. 1526.

Chapter 8: Israel and the Bomb

p. 145 'Recommended by Albert Einstein': Shimon Peres, *From These Men*, Weidenfeld &
     Nicolson, London, 1979, pp. 123–42.
p. 146 'There are those who say': *Ibid.*, p. 132.
p. 147 'in early 1957': 'Israeli Nuclear Armament', UN General Assembly Document No.
     A/36/431, 18 September 1981, pp. 13–17.
p. 148 'Ben-Gurion flew to Paris': Matti Golan, *Shimon Peres: A Biography*, Wiedenfeld &
     Nicolson, London, 1982, pp. 95–6.
     —'In early December 1960': Amos Perlmutter, Michael Handel & Uri Bar-Joseph, *Two
     Minutes Over Baghdad*, Corgi Books, London, 1982, pp. 26-7; Steven Weissman &
     Herbert Krosney, *The Islamic Bomb*, Times Books, New York, 1981.
p. 149 'Ben-Gurion was extremely angry': This information and some other material relating to
     Israel's nuclear programme comes from an unpublished manuscript written by two Israeli
     journalists, Eli Teicher and Ami Dor-on (*see* p. 195), both of whom have extremely good
     connections with the political establishment. They have not released the manuscript;
     none the less, the author has been able to obtain significant unpublished sections. Factual
     material in the excerpts quoted in this book have been corroborated, but reported speech
     has been reproduced here without comment.
p. 150 'General Moshe Dayan': Amos Perlmutter, 'The Israeli raid on Iraq: a new proliferation
     landscape?', *Strategic Review*, Winter 1982, pp. 24–43.
     —'bomb in the basement': *Ibid.*, p. 37.
p. 151 'the Dimona reactor': Study on Israeli nuclear armament, Department of Political and
     Security Council Affairs, UN Centre for Disarmament, New York, 1982, pp. 10–11;
     Weissman & Krosney, *op. cit.*, p. 24.
p. 152 'The decision was made' *et seq.*: A number of major studies have been done on the
     NUMEC case, including the following: David Burnham, 'The case of the missing
     uranium', *Atlantic*, April 1979, pp. 78–82; John J. Fialka, 'How Israel got the bomb',
     Washington Monthly, January 1979, pp. 50–7; Howard Kohn & Barbara Newman, 'How
     Israel got the nuclear bomb', *Rolling Stone*, 1 December 1977, pp. 38–40; *New York
     Times*, 6 November 1973, p. 3; *Washington Star*, 6 November 1977, p. A1; Peter Pringle

& James Spigelman, *The Nuclear Barons*, Michael Joseph, London, 1982, pp 293–8.

p. 154 'Helms was also told': Information supplied to the author by the IISS, October 1982; *see also* Fialka, *op. cit.*, p. 51.

p. 157 'It is interesting to note': *New York Times*, 17 November 1982.

—'According to an article': Kohn & Newman, *op. cit.*

p. 158 'the "Plumbat Affair" *et seq.*: The definitive work on this astonishing operation was written by Elaine Davenport, Paul Eddy and Peter Gilman, *The Plumbat Affair*, Futura, London, 1978.

p. 161 'The same process had been researched': Robert J. Pranger & Dale R. Tahtinen, *Nuclear Threat in the Middle East*, American Enterprise Institute, Washington, July 1975, pp. 12–15.

p. 162 'President Richard Nixon': Teicher & Dor-on, *op. cit.*

—'Golda Meir acted': *Ibid.*

—'according to a *Time* magazine article': *Time*, 12 April 1976, pp. 39–40; Perlmutter, *Strategic Review, op. cit.*, p. 37.

p. 164 'The United States, anxious both to keep': Edgar O'Ballance, *op. cit.*, pp. 174–6; Henry Kissinger, *The Years of Upheaval*, Weidenfeld & Nicolson/Michael Joseph, London, 1982, pp. 581–91.

—'confirmation . . . came from the President of Israel': *Washington Post*, 3 December 1974.

—'Since the 1973 war': *New York Times*, 15 March 1976; Fialka, *op. cit.*; *Washington Post*, 15 March 1976 and 31 July 1975; Pranger & Tahtinen, *op. cit.*, p. 15.

—'Seven countries have so far': Pringle, *op. cit.*, p. xi.

—'An alliance of Pakistan': Weissman & Krosney, *op. cit.*

Chapter 9: Atoms for Apartheid

p. 166 'nuclear race: uranium': *Uranium 1981*, Atomic Industrial Forum Inc. (Wisconsin), 1981, pp. 22–4.

—'According to Atomic': Information supplied to the author from diplomatic sources in South Africa, November 1982; Barbara Rogers, 'South Africa gets nuclear weapons – thanks to the West' in *Dirty Work 2: The CIA in Africa, op. cit.*, p. 274; *South Africa's Nuclear Capability*, World Campaign Against Military and Nuclear Co-operation with South Africa, n.d., p. 19.

p. 167 'developing a cuise missile': Jack Anderson, *Washington Post*, 8 December 1982, p. B15. This article and an earlier one in 1980 have been used as the primary sources for every piece of speculation on the alleged cruise project. There has been absolutely no confirmation.

p. 168 'D.F. Malan': T.D. Moodie, *The Rise of Afrikanerdom*, University of California Press, Berkeley, 1975, p. 248.

—'In their excellent study': Adelman & Knight, *op. cit.*, pp. 633–47.

p. 169 'the South African Atomic Energy Institute' *et seq.*: *Ibid.*; *South Africa's Plan and Capability in the Nuclear Field*, UN Centre for Disarmament, New York, 1981, p. 4; Richard K. Betts, 'A diplomatic bomb for South Africa?', *International Security*, n.d., p. 92.

p. 171 'In a lengthy speech': Professor Ernst Bergmann, 'South Africa and Israel – different countries with common problems', speech before the South African Institute of International Affairs, Johannesburg, 13 September 1968.

p. 172 'Britain has also been': *The Citizen*, 29 November 1982, p. 13.

p. 173 'South African scientists': *The Middle East*, June 1980, p. 10.

—'All this international aid': Barbara Rogers and Zdenek Cervenka, *The Nuclear Axis*, Times Books, New York, 1978, pp. 157–220. This is the definitive study of the early development of South Africa's nuclear programme.

—'Just how the South Africans' *et seq.*: 'The nuclear conspiracy', *Sechaba*, November/ December 1975. The stolen documents were the basis of the book, *The Nuclear Axis, op. cit.*

p. 176 'Vorster had announced': A.R. Newby-Fraser, *Chain Reaction: Twenty Years of Nuclear Research and Development in South Africa*, Atomic Energy Board, Pretoria, 1979, pp. 92–4.

p. 177 'the head of the South African Energy Agency': A.J.A. Roux & W.L. Grant, 'The South African uranium enrichment process', paper presented to European Nuclear Conference, Paris, April, 1975.

p. 180 'South Africans offered': Teicher & Dor-on, *op. cit.*
—'Vorster announced in Israel': Rogers & Cervenka, *op. cit.*, pp. 326–7; *The Middle East*, June 1980, pp. 10–11.

p. 181 'CIA . . . revealed that Israel': *Washington Post*, 15 March 1976.
—'Like Israel, South Africa': Dr M. Hough, 'The political implications of the possession of nuclear weapons for South Africa', *Strategy Review*, Institute for Strategic Studies, University of Pretoria, May 1980, pp. 7–11.

p. 182 'to be made public two days later': Statement by Tass, quoted in *Pravda*, 9 August 1977.
—'According to a fascinating study': Stockholm International Peace Research Institute, *SIPRI Yearbook 1978*, Taylor & Francis, London, 1978, pp. 69–79.

p. 183 'Two days after the news': *Rand Daily Mail*, 22 August 1977.

p. 184 'South Africa has informed us': *Washington Post*, 27 September 1977, p. A2; Rogers & Cervenka, *op. cit.*

p. 185 —'However, intelligence sources': Information supplied to author, Washington and London, 1982.

p. 186 'The problem was': Information supplied by Eric Marsden.
—'US intelligence is convinced': *International Herald-Tribune*, 14–15 November 1981; *Financial Times*, 26 November 1981.

Chapter 10: The Indian Ocean Flash

p. 187 'A small and very specialized fleet': *The Middle East*, June 1980, pp. 8–12; *Newsweek*, 5 November 1979, pp. 64–5.

p. 188 'This is an area': *The Middle East, op. cit.*, p. 11.
—'the Vela had been circling' *et seq.*: 'Ad Hoc Panel report on the September 22 event', Executive Office of the President, Office of Science and Technology Policy, Washington, D.C., n.d. This is the most detailed account of the sighting.

p. 192 'These arguments were not': *Science*, 1 February 1980, vol. 207, pp. 504–5.

p. 193 'The Defense Intelligence Agency': *Aviation Week and Space Technology*, 11 August 1980, pp. 67–72.
—'Naval Research Laboratory': *Science*, 29 August 1980, pp. 996–7.

p. 194 'The Senate subcommittee': *Washington Post*, 14 November 1975, p. A1.

p. 195 'the CIA suggested': *Washington Post*, 16 September 1980, p. A25.
—'The first linking': See note for p. 149. Raviv subsequently had his press credentials withdrawn by the Israeli government.

Index

The Sonnets

∽

Warwick Collins

The Friday Project
An imprint of HarperCollins Publishers
77–85 Fulham Palace Road
Hammersmith, London W6 8JB
www.thefridayproject.co.uk
www.harpercollins.co.uk

First published by The Friday Project in 2008

A catalogue record for this book is available
from the British Library

ISBN 978-1-90-632178-9

Typeset by Maggie Dana
Printed and bound in Great Britain by Clays Ltd, St Ives plc

Mixed Sources

Product group from well-managed
forests and other controlled sources
www.fsc.org Cert no. SW-COC-1806
© 1996 Forest Stewardship Council

FSC is a non-profit international organisation established to
promote the responsible management of the world's forests. Products
carrying the FSC label are independently certified to assure
consumers that they come from forests that are managed to meet the
social, economic and ecological needs of present or future
generations.

Find out more about HarperCollins and the environment at
www.harpercollins.co.uk/green

To Chris Owen

Chapter 1

My Lord Southampton, at the lake that day, removed his garments, wading in silence to deeper water. In hungry dawn his slender frame, already bearing scars and calluses of fearful games and hunts, seemed to pause and flicker. A heron stood on the neighbouring bank, observing the edge of the shallows. Against that human figure a bird's shadow, hovering over water, preparing to strike at waiting fish, would not have seemed more ghostly or more pale. There my lord waited, hardly moving, suspended in the heron's eye, as though lost in invisible thought.

I, standing on the shore, observed how light became flesh, seeming to pause and thicken. Water covered his thighs, his lower back. From the bank I considered him as he walked further into the lake, until it lapped his shoulder blades. I continued to observe him as he waded deeper into that periphrastic calm. The liquid line rose until, once level with shoulder and neck, he began to swim, both languidly and strongly.

Out there he seemed impalpable. Only his head appeared, floating on the surface. Under the dawn light he moved alongside his own reflection, touching ghost to liquid ghost, leaving a soft wake which formed and glimmered like an arrowhead.

Instead it was I – the watching man, the unquiet one – who took up my usual position, holding the reins of both our nervous horses. Part of that mind which lives in shadow now became alert. I remained con-stantly fretful – the silent waiter at the water's edge.

Standing between the horses in that calm, with a warm and breathing beast on each side of me, I sensed the shudder of their animal spirits. Both seemed tense. My own gelding stood still, occasionally reaching down to feed. But beside me the stallion stamped and neighed softly, dancing on his hooves, restless as any child who wants to play. He was in perpetual motion, never still. I felt him strain, then call forth his challenge. His long whinny reached out across the tranquil earth and water. Holding their reins, I listened for that thread of silence which the horses could perceive. And then I heard, as though in answer, another horse's call, as clear as a bugle note, from half a mile away; from some dark stretch of woodland, some invisible valley. Strange sound! It might as easily have come from a mythical, hidden underworld.

During those times when the London theatres were closed, curtailed by plague, I too was nervous, aware of my own vulnerability. My scribbling of plays had no market, and I could not even work upon the stage. It is true that poets often live at the edge of starvation – vulnerable as song birds to winter's cold – but those days were the worst.

By some strange alchemy, my lord's very confidence rendered me more sensitive. On his behalf sometimes I felt we were overlooked, or that another party spied on him. Sometimes I heard a horse neigh, far away, and once I saw three riders on a hill – distant, pricked out

by light – observing us in what seemed like lucid concentration.

He began to swim now, languidly and strongly, into
the deeper part of the lake, so that the shadow of his
body dissolved in the water. Only his head appeared,
like a bust, floating on the milky surface. I stood a little
back from the bank's edge, ever-watchful.

Though he was my patron, I continued to chafe at
his recklessness. For these were dangerous times, with
many eddies of insurrection around our Protestant
Queen. His family retained their allegiance to the
Catholic Church. In their midst, he moved with peculiar ease, and feared nothing.

Out on the water, my lord turned, treading water,
and looked back towards the silent land. Could he perceive me, soberly coloured against the darker earth?
Even at that distance, I could see there was amusement
in his expression. He called out, 'Will you not swim,
Master Shakespeare?'

I did not answer.

'Come, gentle man,' he sang out. 'Swim with me.'

I, the nominative, smiled to myself and answered, 'I
prefer to keep a watch, my lord!'

'Come,' he repeated. 'The animals will not run far. If they do, we'll catch 'em.'

Alas, he thought my concern was with the horses. Around us lay an unsettled land. The woods had spies in them, and there were those whose loyalty was to the other great families – a number of whom did not wish him well. Yet he regarded himself as invulnerable. If I were not here, he would have let the horses wander and have happily chased them for a morning, naked and alone, without a thought for himself or for those who might see him in a state of nature.

Out on the lake my lord still swam. Now he turned and sang out to me in his clear, melodious voice, 'Come, live with me, and be my love, and we will all the pleasures prove.'

I observed him laugh at his own joke – knowing that he quoted Christopher Marlowe at me, and aware that it fretted at my profession of poet and incited my jealousy. He enjoyed reminding me that our great Marlowe also vied for his patronage. Perhaps, too, he relished the suggestion that Marlowe would be more responsive than I to his playful overtures. And since my patron, though young, was a man of subtlety and mischief, his remark reminded me that Master Marlowe was invited to dine at his house that night, during which time, no doubt, we two poets would be teased like rival and delicate young mistresses.

Perhaps my lord realised that I would not abandon my lookout. He shook his head at my caution, smiled to himself, turned, and swam out further into the lake.

Chapter 2

STRANGE TO OBSERVE, yet stranger to recall, were those who called my lord ladylike, affected, languorous. Around him I observed his acolytes gather and whisper. Yet all who bore close witness to his pale beauty also observed, beneath the liquid surface, the stir of muscle and sinew. A condign will fleshed the hidden currents of the water. The searching eye, bent towards its surface, recognised fierce pride, and cold reflection. It was true that he was one of those who are unaware of how he scattered light. The effect was that all those admiring glances, falling on that surface, were reflected backwards to their source. In that way, he was like all heroes: you saw what you hoped for; he refracted your dreams.

Unaware of his own power, such grace seemed strange to him as much as to his companions. Yet to write of him as Narcissus, in truth, was also to address another. Rumours moved around him. He was there and not there, laughing at those vanities attributed to him by others. During the plague years, when the London theatres were closed, I saw my own fond hopes and circling ambitions reflected in that youthful, mirthful glass. He was both my plight and my aspiration.

As for effeminacy, in those surroundings what argument could one propose for such a creature? There were other realms, even in our own society, where effeminacy was much admired. In our theatre companies women were forbidden to act on the stage; beautiful boys and young men played the female roles, and were celebrated for their virtuosity. I myself loved their ambivalence; the flavour of the unknown and forbidden beneath the formal inhibition. Maleness might be enforced in the theatre, but not masculinity.

Our martial aristocracy, by contrast, lived by bloodlines. Twenty generations of great Pharaohs

might create inbred leaders with perfect skin and
lissom hips, but our turbulent kingdom, always on the
edge of war, gave cruel tests to its warriors, often allowing less than a man's brief span before disease or death,
the axe-man, struck them down. Their deepest truths
were brutal, simply this: all their lives hovered on the
verge of annihilation. And these, our politic-ridden
times, allowed no easy settlement into placidity or
plain repose.

If we were sometimes witness to things of grace, it
was by contrast rather than by inherence. Stare into
fire, see how the greatest heat lies like a mellow ghost
on wood or coal. So, in the harshness of our age, such a
youth, whose fair exterior floated as a fervent dream
before our eyes, was at the limit of benign possibility.

But grace itself is a form of power, carrying its own
hidden and implicit threat. If I myself survived and
even thrived in my lord's companionship, it was precisely because, beneath that surface, I never forgot the
harsh heat of his potency. I attempted to describe
something of his character in a sonnet I was writing,
addressing as its subject the nature of his attractions to
those in his circle, his reflection of their dreams:

What is your substance, whereof are you made,
That millions of strange shadows on you tend?
Since every one hath, every one, one shade,
And you, but one, can every shadow lend.
Describe Adonis, and the counterfeit
Is poorly imitated after you;
On Helen's cheek all art of beauty set,
And you in Grecian tires are painted new:
Speak of the spring and foison of the year,
The one doth shadow of your beauty show,
The other as your bounty doth appear;
And you in every blessed shape we know.
   In all external grace you have some part,
   But you like none, none you, for constant heart.

That 'constant heart' I attributed to him was not a mere conceit, or a pretty figure of speech. He was my patron, my source of life in those bad times, and every waking day I thanked my good fortune for his loyalty.

As for myself, my own beginnings had been strange. When, after several years as a travelling player, I began to try out a line or two, to help my fellow actors with a scene – bridging an awkward pause here, helping to refine a phrase there – it seemed to me no more than journeyman's work. But then, like an artisan found amongst gentlefolk, my own poor skills became more valuable. 'This ending appears too long, would you say?', or 'Could we not fit an extra scene here?' Silver-tongued, I mouthed the words, worrying back and forth upon the stage, adjusting entrances, reworking rhythms, waving my arms in emphasis, bowing, stooping to kiss imagined ladies' hands, learning meanwhile the practical difference between iambic *di dah* or trochaic *dah di*, or how to use the two long beats of a spondee to add occasional emphasis.

Here I stand, a mere grammar-school boy, risen wit, obsequious survivor, forced to rely for my living on the ancient tradition of a line of warriors. Should I plead for aristocracy or heritage? No, let the dice fall where they may. Yet here were no effete men, but soldiers, soldiers' sons, robbers, intimidators. Above the ranks of *villeins* rose the lords, greater villains all, whose hidden power lay not in virtue or principle, but the hissing edge of axe or broadsword or skull-crushing mace. In France they say *chevalier*, meaning horseman, from whose high mount, delivering painful punishment or death, a little mercy sometimes followed. Hence the code of chivalric virtue.

These were the men I lived among, who asked and gave no quarter to themselves; jealous of bloodlines, but hardly bloodless, fierce in pride, quick to anger, remorseless in revenge. In my lord's household those were the local spirits who inhabited his terrain.

Chapter 3

I REMEMBER, as though it were yesterday, my horse's heavy breathing as it strained its heaving chest against the night air. The large house loomed close. My sturdy mount cantered, jingling bridle and reins, until the stonework reared out of the darkness, with braziers burning at its entrance.

I rode through the main gate, past gargoyles and heraldic stone roses, into walled gardens. My lord's house at Titchfield had once been an abbey, confiscated from the monks by our monarch's father, granted as gift to my lord's grandfather – the first Earl of

Southampton – by Henry VIII. The buildings still retained their atmosphere of contemplation.

In the courtyard I dismounted. A stable boy, emerging from the dark, took my horse and led it away.

In my best clothes – a doublet and hose, with a rakish hat and a tattered black cloak – I stepped forward, striding towards a doorway from which there came the noise of men laughing. Passing through, I faced on my left side a great dining hall, with a long table at which were seated thirty or so guests and retainers of the house. I looked towards the head of the table where my lord presided, and bowed my head to his presence.

On his right there was an empty place. On his left sat a singular, dark, saturnine man, whose intelligent eyes surveyed me.

'Master Shakespeare!' my lord called out. Holding my attention, he indicated the vacant seat near him with a finger's tap, so that I went to my allotted place, sliding my legs under the table. 'You have not met Master Marlowe before?'

'In passing,' I replied.

Beside my patron the figure stirred its languid length, as if his wit steeled itself.

14

'Then in that passing,' Marlowe said, 'we did not meet.'

Though casual, all conversation on the great table seemed to cease.

Around me the silence seemed somehow both decisive and complete. My lord, too, considered me. I felt as though a French fencing master, contemptuously and elegantly, had flicked a fly off my cloak with the point of his sword, as though to say, 'I may choose to strike when I will.' The whole hall watched me suffer their regard. For several moments it seemed as though I were about to fall.

But I am an actor, and I know that timing is all. The performer inside me rose to the occasion, sensing the drama, even milking the moment for its worth. That same congregation noted my own answering stillness, observed me incline my head in calm acknowledgement of my rival's superior artistry. So it seemed from the first fateful meeting that we two poets were doomed to consider each other – from our different perspectives – like rivals about to engage.

'Tell me, Master Shakespeare,' my lord asked, allowing himself to throw casual extra fuel on our vanities, and playing to the gallery. 'Tell me now, according to their virtue, which of Master Marlowe's plays do you prefer?'

His directness made me smile, despite my fear. His pure thirst for entertainment was as clear as a hunter's horn on a still day. Noting at the same time how the rest of the company continued their watchfulness, hoping for sport, I too became temporarily silent, as though hunting with them.

'You are considering, are you, Master Shakespeare?' my patron said.

'My lord,' I replied, 'from all I have read of Master Marlowe, there is too much richness to easily contemplate.'

I remember the nature and depth of that silence. From its centre a small ripple of applause moved outwards at this diplomatic answer, spreading round the table. Even Master Marlowe smiled. My lord, too, seemed pleased at the *frisson*. But he persisted. 'And now that you have had time to consider your answer, what think you?'

'I believe,' I began, 'that I admire most, before *The Jew of Malta*, even before *Doctor Faustus* ... *Hero and Leander*.'

There was another silence. A small, clear frown formed on my lord's forehead. 'Come now, is this a riddle? Who here has heard of *Hero and Leander?*'

Our host turned towards the other poet. 'I believe he teases you, Master Marlowe. By citing a play that does not exist, he surely incites your retribution.'

Cold and calm, the one he addressed spoke out. 'No, my lord, what he says is true. Except this: the work in question is not a play but a poem. And it exists, as yet unfinished.'

The rival poet turned towards me, detached enquiry in those fierce, dark eyes. He asked, with a deceptive limpidity, 'And how is it, Master Shakespeare, that you have read my own unfinished work?'

But by then I had begun to gauge the feelings of that waiting audience; its liking for directness, its hunger for incisive clarities. I said, 'You are so famed, sir, that copies of it circulate.' I gestured with my hand in visible circles, so that one or two of the watchers laughed.

His next words were carefully chosen, laid out like chess pieces on a board. 'And you make it your business to read it?'

The question's coldness touched me somewhere deep. But if I am a player, I am used to contingency, to turn and pivot. So I responded, hearing myself say, 'What I most admire, I fear. And what I most fear, I admire.'

As if by instinct – though not greater skill – I had cause to believe his sword was turned; or that, passing through me, his blade found no flesh, no bone to hasp. From the long table I heard again that limpid, expectant silence, and then a rising ripple of applause.

My lord seemed pleased at this exchange. He had played on our rivalry, enjoyed his sport. His restless mind moved to other subjects. And so, to my own relief, he began to discourse with others, while the applause died down and the table settled again to its eating and interrupted conversations.

A little later, my lord touched me on the shoulder in support, signalling that constant affection for which he was both praised and slandered, whispering in my ear, 'Well spoken, sir,' while from the other side of that long table Master Marlowe looked on, saturnine and amused, keeping his thoughts to himself.

The dinner reached its end, the candles flickered.

Some of the guests lay forward on the table, drunk. My lord surveyed the scene with approval, saying, 'It seems that we are surfeited.'

I, by nature more cautious and abstemious than the others, nodded to where Marlowe also lay forward, asleep on his arms. Of the visiting poet my lord said softly, 'Let us not wake him. He rode from London, where it is said he conspires constantly with the younger Walsingham. Let him sleep.'

He turned towards me. 'Come, now, let us play a game of throw-apple, and while we may, wake certain of these diners.'

He plucked an apple from a dish of fruit in front of him, and rose from his seat. Gathering my wits, I followed him as he walked alongside the great table, shaking awake various of his guests. A number rose and stumbled after him, mumbling to themselves as though in a dream. I took hold of one of the torches that lay against the wall, lit it from the last of the burning logs, and followed the young earl out into the cold air of the courtyard.

The drunken company followed behind. A rough circle was formed, with my lord in the middle, around whom other torches burned, as further guests and servants arrived. So he waited, at the centre of the circle, weighing the apple in his hand, throwing it in the cold air, catching it, calling out his open challenge, saying, 'Who can keep this from me?'

He peered around him at the faces of his companions, lit by the light of the encircling flames. The guests and servants stared back at him, hoping for entertainment. Choosing his time, my lord threw the apple towards me.

In that moment, it seemed to me, time slowed. The cold air brought sobriety, lifting the fumes of the wine. Above me, the apple seemed no more than a star-gleam; then, falling towards me, it expressed its unexpected mass. I caught it as deftly as I could, surprised by the sudden weight of it, in my spare left hand – the one not holding a torch. Around me other hands applauded the speed of my catch.

My lord wiped his lips with the back of his wrist, flexed his shoulders, began his charge like a boar towards me. His speed and determination seemed almost devilish. I waited until he was almost upon me,

then flicked the apple over his charging head, watching it sail through the air, upwards, glinting like a
planet, until one of the sturdier servants caught it.

There was another burst of applause. With fear-
some dexterity my lord turned and pursued the apple to
its catcher. The same servant, holding the apple,
appeared intimidated by his ferocious charge. Even so,
he managed to throw it over his lordship's head in
time. Another guest caught it. (And so it seemed to me
that, as I watched the game, I observed the circle from
above, the apple sailing through air, the scion of the
house chasing with absorption and ferocity, almost
under its shadow, panther-like, moving so fast from
thrower to catcher that beneath each glimmering flight
he seemed to be gaining ground on the flying prey.)

It happened that one of the greater guests, a powerful Seneschal, a renowned warrior, caught the apple a
moment before the charging youth – closing on him at
speed and calculating its upward trajectory – snatched
it in the very act of rising again from his hand.

'Huzzah!' our host called out in triumph. Holding
his prize aloft, he backed into the middle of the circle,

to rising roars. There he took a wolf bite of the apple, to further approbation, while among the gathered others, I watched in smiling approval.

Chapter 4

MY LORD BURNED WITH A CONTINUOUS, dense energy. He was one of those who needed little sleep. When he rested, he slept instinctively and deeply, like an animal. After we had thrown the apple, he approached me and said, 'Master Shakespeare, I wish to speak with you about certain matters.'

It was already past midnight. In his chambers during the early hours, he paced up and down. I stood still and silent, leaning against the wall, not daring to interrupt his fervent movement. Eventually he turned towards me. 'Is Master Marlowe older than you?'

'Hardly,' I answered, surprised by this odd question. 'By only a few months, I believe.'

'Yet you openly acknowledge him your superior?'

'My superior in art,' I said. 'The worthier pen.'

'You say so freely.'

To which I answered, 'Every scribbler in our land is in debt to his great peroration, his mighty line. Where he leads, we others follow.'

'You truly admire *Faustus?*' he asked.

'Marlowe *is* Faustus,' I replied. 'They say he necromances spirits, that he is on speaking terms with Mephistopheles.'

He smiled at that, saying, 'This ... other work that you mentioned at our table –'

'*Hero and Leander,*' I said.

'*Hero and Leander.* What is it, precisely?'

'A poem about love, dwelling much on masculine beauty. It is said that he intends to dedicate it to you.'

His face lit up. He was addicted to praise.

'To me?'

'So it is said.'

'Yet it is unfinished.'

I smiled. 'So it is said.'

He looked at me searchingly. 'And you do not mind ... a rival for your praise?'

'He has a worthy subject.'

He paused and considered me. 'You are honest. You see coldly and clearly, and yet I believe you burn hot inside.'

I would not deny it. So before him I said, as though in affirmation of a fact, 'I see clearly and burn hot.'

That night, after I left my lord's rooms, I attempted to give some further shape to the thoughts I had earlier that day – that his youth and beauty incited dreams in the observer. Earlier that morning, when he emerged from the lake, there was one more witness than those I had already described. In the dawn mists, a figure was collecting brushwood in some dense, nearby scrub. At first I thought it might have been a boar, rooting in the undergrowth. Despite the low-lying vapour, I could begin to make out an elderly crone, bent-backed, in a grey hood. She had been dragging a sack of brushwood backwards from a thick covert where she had been collecting sticks for firewood.

The foliage was so dense there that it would have been difficult to lift the sack under the immediate oppression of the overhanging boughs. Once she was out of its entanglements, she intended to lift her load onto her shoulders. So she emerged from the thicket backwards, like some strange animal, hauling her load, wheezing and gasping, at precisely that place on the shore where my lord, unconscious of any other human witness, was approaching after his swim in the lake. I supposed that, suspecting a meeting, I could have warned her of his emergence from the water, but the comical nature of our situation touched me and stimulated my curiosity.

Perhaps the elderly crone heard the jingle of horses' bridles, or the splashing of my lord's feet as he neared the shore, for she seemed suddenly aware of others in her vicinity. She turned round, perplexed, and was faced with an entirely naked youth emerging like a god from the elements.

Her face, I do recall, was a picture. It was a wonder-ful old countenance, wrinkled and shriven, but with a clear, bright, and intelligent eye. I know enough of age to appreciate that the inhabiter of that bag of bones was the same being who had danced with graceful feet on the common in her youth.

For a brief moment her eye surveyed the figure that had risen from the waters – heavy, pale shoulders, long fair hair, the nub between the slender legs – with the purest appreciation.

Why should either of them have been offended? It is true that he, at first as startled as she, tensed a little from the unexpected meeting; but seeing almost imme-diately that his witness offered no offence and appeared appreciative of his form, he relaxed, and even lowered the lid of his eye in the form of a rakish wink. For a moment, all that old woman's Christmases seemed rolled into one. She cackled with pleasure, allowed her eye one more appreciative traverse of his figure, and then – modesty imposing itself at last – turned away to lift the sack onto her back. It seemed she shook with laughter as she slowly disappeared into the mist.

I handed my lord his clothes. When he had dressed, we rode back through the morning towards the great house.

Chapter 5

I HAD BEEN WORKING on the idea of composing a sequence of poems or sonnets addressed to my patron. The sonnet itself had a complex history. According to a prevailing fashion, it was addressed by a poet to a mistress, often one who was out of reach, after whom he yearned, or at least affected to do so for the sake of the fulsome compliments he would bestow upon her. It was a convention which had emerged in part at least from the troubadour tradition of France, and since we English tended to ape French fashions, it had its adherents amongst the nobility. Great ladies found it amusing to be addressed thus, in appropriately lofty language, by one who remained suitably distant and chaste. I had one obvious difficulty in my own circumstances: my patron was a master, not a mistress. Yet precisely because of this, the convention imposed its own interesting construction. It reminded me of the convention in a theatre, whereby a man would play a woman's role. By the same processes, perhaps, it stimulated rather than repressed the imagination.

If a man, rather than a woman, were to be the object of those high-flown praises, a more subtle tone was required – of fervent infatuation which was, at the same time, ironic. And since my master was himself both intelligent and someone who enjoyed praise, I began with the advantage of a most discerning subject for my poetry.

Until then I had mainly drafted certain thoughts in the form of individual lines and brief passages of description or argument. But now, reaching my rooms, I attempted to write a sonnet which would perhaps function as a keystone to my efforts. With a clean page before me, I began by praising my master's beauty as though he were my beloved mistress, at the same time asserting that my love was not physical, but spiritual.

A woman's face, with Nature's own hand painted,
Hast thou, the master-mistress of my passion;
A woman's gentle heart, but not acquainted
With shifting change, as is false women's fashion;
An eye more bright than theirs, less false in rolling,
Gilding the object whereupon it gazeth;
A man in hew all Hews in his controlling,
Which steals men's eyes, and women's souls amazeth.
And for a woman wert thou first created;
Till Nature, as she wrought thee, fell a-doting,
And by addition thee of me defeated,
By adding one thing to my purpose nothing.
   But since she prick'd thee out for women's pleasure,
   Mine be thy love, and thy love's use their treasure.

If it were a sonnet which would form the key to the others I would write, there were certain ways in which I would attempt to make it stand out from the other sonnets I intended to compose. I deliberately chose to use eleven syllables to the line, as opposed the usual ten. In addition, I left a clue to the identity of my patron in the phrase:

A man in hew all Hews *in his controlling,*

The mysterious word 'Hews', with a capital letter, as though it were a name, would be opaque to the merely casual reader. But since my patron was Henry Wriothesley, Earl of Southampton, whose initials were HWES, an anagram of Hews, it would give a clue to the identity of the fair young man. It happened too that certain of those tradesmen, builders and merchants who had cause to address my lord, or wrote him bills, often altered his name to 'Henry, Earl Wriothesley of Southampton'. Thus 'Hews' would act as a vernacular reference to my patron.

I chose the moment carefully to show the poem to my lord. We had been riding through the nearby forest that early summer morning. He dismounted from his horse in order to walk to the edge of a nearby decline, so that he could survey the surrounding country. As I walked alongside him, I drew the paper forth from my clothes. Taking it from me, he read it with studied amusement. I watched him raise his eyebrows at the last few lines, read them again, and then laugh the louder.

'Most excellent,' he said. 'I am thy spiritual love, but Nature pricked me out for women's pleasure.' He smiled again. 'I should be desirous to see more.'

I asked him whether he had noted the hidden reference to his name in 'Hews'.

My patron said, 'If these are dangerous times, as you counsel me, then it is right that living persons should not be mentioned. And since these are private poems, for our own enjoyment, Master Shakespeare, I believe all your references to me as your patron should be hidden to an outside view. If you will accept those conditions, pray continue as you will.'

He returned the paper to me. 'Will you make a copy of this, in your own hand, so that I may keep it?'

It became our custom. When I had finished a

poem, I would copy it; keeping the overwritten and amended original for myself, giving the fair version to him. As for the content, perhaps I could do better in due course. But the tone – part infatuation, part irony, directed at a mysterious and unidentified beautiful youth – seemed well set for our enterprise. In due course I would arrange the poems in a different order, but meanwhile they would steadily accrue.

Chapter 6

THAT SUMMER, GRANTED MY LORD'S PERMISSION, I
began to sing his praises in those effusive and extrava-
gant terms so dearly beloved of my countrymen. For
there was another circumstance which propelled me
towards such orisons to beauty, and my lord towards
receiving them with a good grace. It happened that in
our kingdom we were ruled by a Queen, a veritable
lion-hearted Empress, and in our pleading for her
mercy and her favour we all of us sounded like troubadour poets singing of our love. It happened too that the
very form or construction of my sonnets – soliciting the
favours of a fair subject – rhymed with the prevailing

fashion among courtiers. And so I proceeded from one to the next, gaining greater confidence as each one was well received by my patron.

When in disgrace with fortune and men's eyes,
I all alone beweep my outcast state,
And trouble deaf heaven with my bootless cries,
And look upon myself, and curse my fate,
Wishing me like to one more rich in hope,
Featur'd like him, like him with friends possess'd,
Desiring this man's art, and that man's scope,
With what I most enjoy contented least;
Yet in these thoughts myself almost despising,
Haply I think on thee, – and then my state,
Like to the lark at break of day arising
From sullen earth, sings hymns at heaven's gate;
    For thy sweet love remember'd such wealth brings,
    That then I scorn to change my state with kings.

I continued to sing my calculated songs throughout that summer, piling verse on verse, page on page, making each time a fresh copy for my lord. With the form established between us, I began to exceed myself in gallantry, making the object of my praises the subject of love itself. Though my poem was addressed to a handsome youth, I strove as best I could to reflect some universal desire.

Shall I compare thee to a summer's day?
Thou art more lovely and more temperate:
Rough winds do shake the darling buds of May,
And summer's lease hath all too short a date:
Sometime too the eye of heaven shines,
And often is his gold complexion dimm'd;
And every fair from fair sometimes declines,
By chance, or nature's changing course, untrimm'd;
But thy eternal summer shall not fade,
Nor lose possession of that fair thou ow'st;
Nor shall Death brag thou wander'st in his shade,

When in eternal lines to time thou grow'st:
So long as men can breathe, or eyes can see,
So long lives this, and this gives life to thee.

I burnt my nightly hours as he inferred, confined to my small room, bent over my formal rhythms, counting the beats on my fingers, feeling for that thread of sense which would hold together the discreet observations and soaring praises they would contain. Sometimes several days, or even a week, would pass without a single line that I deemed worth showing to him. At other times, in the course of a night's labour, I would find several pages of some worth had piled one upon the other. So, often laboriously and occasionally swiftly, I began to accumulate my efforts.

Who will believe my verse in time to come,
If it were fill'd with your most high deserts?
Though yet, heaven knows, it is but as a tomb

Which hides your life, and shows not half your parts.
If I could write the beauty of your eyes,
And in fresh numbers number all your graces,
The age to come would say, 'This poet lies;
Such heavenly touches ne'er touch'd earthly faces.'
So should my papers, yellow'd with their age,
Be scorn'd, like old men of less truth than tongue,
And your true rights be term'd a poet's rage
And stretched metre of an antique song:
   But were some child of yours alive that time,
   You should live twice, – in it and in my rhyme.

The introduction of a child of his own making who would perpetuate that beauty was accidental and felicitous, though perhaps with my poetic senses now attuned to his particular circumstances, I presaged some future development.

Chapter 7

THERE WERE TIMES when my lord seemed to regard me with a certain wry amusement for my pains. In conversation one day, he deliberately switched the subject from the sonnet he had been reading towards another subject perhaps closer to his heart. At the time he was staring at the floor, as though gathering his thoughts. Now he turned to peer once more at me with his green eyes, flecked with gold. 'My mother has spoken to you again?'

'She has.'

'And on the usual subject?'

'The usual,' I said.

'And you take her side, as always.'

'Her side is your side,' I replied, and added, 'She speaks for you.'

He turned away. 'Damn me, if she does.'

I said, 'There are matters which await you. That is all she says.'

'Yes, yes, matters!' This was fierce and fast. He seemed compelled to continue, for the rest of what he wished to say now streamed forth. 'It is time, perhaps, that you knew something further of me, of my closer circumstances ... '

'Your closer circumstances?' The phrase rang oddly, and I was at a loss as to this new departure.

He said, 'You know, for example, that my father died when I was eight.' I nodded, nervous at his apparent continued excitement. Now, with an effort, he seemed to compose himself sufficiently to explain. 'After my father had been buried, my Lord Burghley became my legal guardian. When I was still no more than a child, my great guardian caused me to sign a contract, promising to marry his granddaughter, Elizabeth de Vere, on pain of which refusal, on reaching my majority, I would pay a fine – a terrible fine, almost equal to the value of my entire estate. You know of this?'

It was common gossip, so I said, cautiously, 'I have heard rumours, nothing more.'

'Then,' he insisted, 'you have heard of the disposition of my Lord Burghley?'

I said only that I knew that he had the disposition of a lawyer, and the reputation of a courtier.

'And what else have you heard of him?' he asked.

'That he is our Queen's closest advisor, and the strongest voice in the Privy Council.'

'Yes, yes, that is his political suit. But have you ever seen the man, in person?'

'No, my lord.'

'He is the coldest creature that ever walked upon this earth. He regards all art, all painting, all poetry, as vanity. The theatre in particular he considers both impious and seditious. They say he is not of the Puritan party, yet he has a puritan's instincts. Whatever he touches, becomes ice. If he walks through summer, winter follows. And yet it was he who replaced my dead and lamented father – *in nomine patris.*'

'In your maturity,' I tentatively suggested, 'You will grow away from him.'

'If only it were so!' He seemed a little calmer now, staring at the floor, but still biting his fist, his attention set in some other realm. 'Even from a distance, from London, he still controls my household. My mother too is fearful of him.'

'Why, my lord?' I asked.

He raised his eyes again to mine. 'If I do not marry the one he has chosen for me, my mother too shall be ruined by the catastrophic fine that my Lord Burghley, in his wisdom, shall apportion on me.'

He remained unusually excited. I did my best to calm him, saying, 'Your mother thinks more of an heir from you than of your inheritance.'

'Yes, yes! He blackmails her too, though at a remove. His reach is great. His claws are in everyone.'

I was about to say something more, but my lord continued, 'And then, of course, there is my tutor, Master Florio.' He paused, raised his eyes towards the ceiling, adding with emphasis, '*Master Florio.*'

I attempted emollience. 'Master John Florio. A

most eminent Italian scholar, to whom you owe your own achievement in learning.'

'A fine tutor, and in that respect I perhaps am willing to accept your description. But we should not forget one thing – that he writes regularly to his own master.'

'His own master?'

'My Lord Burghley, who appointed him.'

I halted, silenced in part by the strange complexity of my patron's circumstances. 'Perhaps he writes to apprise my Lord Burghley of your great advances in learning.'

He laughed at this, with a dismissive air. 'No, no, my dear Master William. He writes of my predisposition to marriage, of my carousing in certain company. And so, Master Florio, instructed by his master, admonishes me for my behaviour. Amongst his lessons he coldly arranges certain threats against me. Why, the man's an Italian, of passionate mind. Yet he passes on the current of my Lord Burghley's coldness as though it were his own.'

I smiled at this, and said, 'Machiavelli too was a Florentine,' then added, 'In Master Florio's favour, he imposes upon himself the same discipline he would exert upon you.'

'What discipline is that?' he shot back at me.

'He constructs a dictionary of Italian and English, a great and noble undertaking – '

'In his own interest – '

'And in my interests, too,' I said, 'for I find in his other translations of Italian works a rich source of stories and quaint dramas. It is, I admit, my own concern, but he is generous to me with his translations – '

'And no doubt you are grateful to him, as you should be. And I am grateful to him, too. But why should a man play double if he is, as you say, of so single a mind? Why should he serve two masters if one master is enough?'

'It sounds as though his other master – my Lord Burghley – is difficult to refuse.'

'Don't you see? He admires his master, just as Signor Machiavelli admired his prince ... ' He paused, then burst out, '*He is Lord Burghley's flea!*'

I allowed the first clean wave of his anger to pass me by, swiftly and uncomfortably. 'How can you be certain that what he writes is anything more than praise of you? You yourself received your Master's degree from Cambridge at the age of sixteen. He has good reason to be proud of his pupil.'

But he objected, 'You are too generous. You take every other's part. I believe you' – he struggled for words – 'complicate matters.'

'My lord, it is in my nature to seek for wider motive.'

'Then, speaking of wider motive, let us return to my mother. She would arrange some further slip of a girl to marry me, and because I hesitate – '

'She would accept your direct refusal,' I said. 'If you proposed another match – '

He turned away in anger. 'Another girl, another victim of the great imperative ... ' His voice became fierce again, ironical. '*Why, marry and produce an heir.*'

I could not help but smile at his retort.

'You laugh at me, Master William?' he asked.

I replied, as gently as I could, 'No, sir, I do not laugh. I merely play the devil's advocate, as you have asked.'

He considered me for several moments. Who knows what he saw, or for what he searched. Perhaps he observed something genuine in my perplexity.

Calmer now, he appeared to ease a little. He said, 'I am not like you, William – so silent, so determined upon your life. You resemble nothing so much as one of those steel springs inside a lock. Tonight I will go to bed and sleep, and dream. And you, to some further vigil at the board?'

It was true. I observed in my mind's eye another appointment, until the early dawn, with a sheet of paper and the little flame. 'That is how I choose to burn my hours.'

'Yet it is I who have no other cause, more weighty than to be myself.'

I said, as gently as I could, 'That is enough.'

'Oh, it would be,' he said, 'if I knew the meaning of myself.'

'You will learn it.'

'How?' he asked, with genuine puzzlement.

I smiled at his earnestness. 'It will grow into you. You will grow into it.'

'Will I?'

'You will.'

'You make a pun upon your name.'

'You made it first. I merely follow you. Your will is your own.'

'Damn these circumstances, though. In many respects you are kindness itself. Yet still you press me.'

'I do not press you. I remind you.'

'Of my duty.'

'Of yourself.'

'And you will teach me to be myself?'

'I will attempt to remind you, from time to time, of what you may be.'

Chapter 8

*B*UT OUR RELATIONS WERE SUCH that my patron was apt to remind me of what I should be, too. One day while out riding, he said, 'I should like to show you at first hand how my Lord Burghley attempts to influence me. Two years ago, when I was merely seventeen years, my guardian engaged one of his secretaries, a Master John Clapham, to write a poem in Latin, dedicated to me, called *Narcissus*.'

'A poem called *Narcissus*?' I was incredulous, I must admit. Rumours had moved around him, suggesting vanity, but here was a source of its direct propagation by an interested party. Even then, I could not help but smile. I had a vision of some ambitious young secretary, at the behest of his master, scratching out a poem in orotund Latin, addressed to a youth who would not obey the dictums of his enraged protector.

From the depths of his clothes my patron withdrew a large, portentous document that seemed almost like a will or testament. He said, 'I have brought it for you to consider. An entire poem which urges me, in formal Latin, to cease from my vain preoccupations with myself. Its clear implication is that I should marry the young woman who waits so patiently and unhappily for me.'

My consternation that such a poem had been written was due, in part at least, to my patron's assertion that his guardian despised art. Perhaps I began to see a little more deeply into Lord Burghley's soul. Art was permissible if it served a political purpose, and especially if it served his own. Setting these thoughts aside, I said, 'The poem mentions you directly?'

'No, not in so many words. It is dedicated to me, but it extemporises *ad infinitum* on a young man who might be thought to resemble me.'

'Why did the poet – my Lord Burghley's secretary – not have the courage of his convictions, and make you its direct subject?'

He laughed. 'For good reason. The poem is happy enough to omit certain details of my circumstances – that the marriage contract was signed when I was a child, before I had even met my intended, or that she is the granddaughter of my guardian, so that the person who will benefit from the arrangement is my Lord Burghley.'

'I shall look forward to studying it,' I said, accepting the proffered document from his hand. A question struck me. 'Are there others such as you for whom Lord Burghley acts as guardian?'

I witnessed a somewhat rueful smile. 'It seems that, as a reward for his continuing labours for Her Majesty, for some twenty years my Lord Burghley has held the position of Master of the Court of Wards. All those infants and children who inherit large estates and who lose their father are placed in his care. It would seem to be a habit of my guardian to contract his wards to an approved marriage which benefits him. If they refuse, the marriage contract will place such a heavy fine upon them that their estate will pass to him or his chosen beneficiaries in perpetuity.'

I had a vision of my Lord Burghley – industrious, cold, puritanical – exploiting the properties of small and defenceless children, offering them the choice of unhappiness in an arranged marriage – or, as an alternative, if they did not obey him, an impoverishment of their birthright.

As though my patron understood the line and direction of my thought, he said, 'My guardian has used his position to make himself one of the richest men in the land. Amongst his many properties, he has built a magnificent palace for himself at Theobalds, and another great house in Covent Garden.'

We rode on in silence for a while. Mulling over my patron's account of his arranged marriage, I became curious as to whether he and his betrothed had ever met.

He smiled at my enquiry. 'When I was old enough to consider more seriously the fate which had been arranged for me, I took it upon myself to travel to my betrothed's parents' house with the intention of meeting her, and making her acquaintance. Lord Burghley's daughter Ann had married the Earl of Oxford, Edward de Vere. My betrothed, Elizabeth de Vere, was the product of their marriage. Perhaps I was foolish in announcing my visit beforehand. My betrothed's parents, when I entered their house, hid her from me. At first they told me she was unwell, and indisposed to a meeting. Perhaps they hoped that my patience would wear thin and I would depart. I began to perceive that their daughter's own voluntary acquiescence in the marriage was something to be doubted, but this only redoubled my determination. In the circumstances, I was forced to wait impatiently for several days. Eventually, out of persistence, I was permitted to meet my intended.'

'You spoke with your betrothed?'

'During the meeting, she was not even permitted to speak to me directly. Any question I might put to her, however courteous, her mother answered on her behalf. It was only by accident that one day, while I walked in the grounds of the house, in the greatest perplexity at my predicament, I caught sight of my betrothed in a distant part of the garden. She was seated on a bench, attended by her elderly nurse. I made my way there as quickly and discreetly as I was able. The beldame, who at first was inclined to keep me at bay, took pity on two such youthful creatures, and allowed us to converse in a private corner of a nearby arbour, while she kept a nervous watch.'

I was fascinated by the oddness of the arrangement – the image of two youthful creatures sworn to each other against their will, for the greed or benefit of others. I could not help but compare it with my own marriage, to a woman eight years older than me, my own Anne Hathaway, and with the fact that our own marriage ceremony was arranged somewhat in haste on account of her pregnancy.

My curiosity led me to enquire, 'You were not drawn by affection towards your betrothed?'

He smiled. 'From what I saw of her, I believe I could have liked her, but I do not love her or feel any special affection for her. Yet I found that she too, once allowed to express herself, had an independent disposition. And in the course of our conversation I discovered that she felt nothing but sympathy for me about my own predicament. It seemed that in her heart my intended was as set against marrying me by arrangement as I was against marrying her.'

'So you found yourselves in cautious agreement?'

He smiled. 'It was a strangely happy meeting. When two people find something in common, it often happens that a bond of sympathy forms between them. We were able to talk only briefly, because the beldame was growing nervous that some other party might observe us in discussion. When the old woman saw my betrothed's mother emerge from the house to look for her daughter, she fell into a panic, and insisted that we two should separate immediately.'

'Yet it seems you and your betrothed parted on amicable terms.'

'Before I slipped away, my intended said she would write to her grandfather, Lord Burghley, complaining, in courteous terms, that some account of her own feelings should be taken in the matter.' He smiled again. 'I should like to have seen the letter.'

I looked at the sheaf of pages he had given me, each covered in a neat but somewhat laboured hand, and carefully placed it in my own clothes for safekeeping.

That night, seated at my board, I studied the poem more carefully. My own grammar-school Latin was rigorous enough to enable me to get at the meaning. I had been trained in rhetoric, in study of the Latin masters such as Ovid, Terence, Mantuan, Tully, Horace, Sallust. But where once, in my younger days, I had been more than capable of discriminating between various styles, and imitating them, in my life as a player I had forgotten some of the finer points of the Latin verse I had studied in my youth.

Even so, I could see in the poem before me that although the Latin itself was grammatical enough, the verses themselves were the most lamentable doggerel it had ever been my misfortune to read. Conceit after laboured conceit rolled forth ceaselessly, mixed with wooden references to a vague, mythological past which was imperfectly and hastily resurrected for the purposes of the present. I had a vision of Lord Burghley poring over this work in progress, nodding his sage head in approval at the sentiments, perhaps inserting a phrase of his own here or there in order to strengthen a point – since it is ever the view of those in authority that they are superior in art over those who merely write.

As I endeavoured to understand the meanings and conceits, smiling to myself at the clumsy metaphors and plodding locutions, I believed I could even perceive in certain places the interdiction of Lord Burghley's hand – in the form of a sharper phrase here or an argument there. In the young scribe's attempts at rhetoric there was at least a certain heartfelt attempt at metre and rhythm, though when clearly overlain by his master's instructions and interpolations the verse was utterly devoid of any music.

There is nothing that I enjoy more than 'turning' a work to new advantage. I wondered whether I could satirise the earnest homilies in *Narcissus*. Since my desire was to entertain my patron, I could perhaps accept in light-hearted fashion the charge of narcissism on his behalf. But instead of arguing that his youthful self-absorption was the enemy of propagation, I would

continue to sing that the very beauty of my patron was
the chief reason why he should reproduce himself and
perpetuate his line.

Several nights later, with the laboured conceits of
Narcissus still echoing in my mind, I began to draft a
poem on the subject which, though it lacked the usual
formal precision at which I aimed, nevertheless
expressed the sincerity of my anger. The first draft ran:

Lord of laughter, you showed me Narcissus,
A poem whose heart is hollowed by power;
Falsely addressed, it pretends to kiss us,
Telling of beauty, Cupid's sweet bower;
Yet cold hearts form cold minds, eyes lose their sight;
Stealing our childhood, it counsels good faith.
Framed by deceit, the sun's fatal glower
Reversing all virtue, makes permanent night.
In hell's own smithies, Authority labours,
Shadow on shadow, reversing the year;
And what is more wretched, than making wretched,

When, lacking all mercy, he sheds no tear?
  Then punish him not for what he may say;
  A mind without light can never see day.

I showed the poem to my patron while we were out riding. He read it carefully as his horse walked companionably alongside mine. Raising his eye from the page he laughed out aloud in fierce delight. 'A most sincere and clear castigation of my Lord Burghley.' But when his mirth had subsided, he added, 'That is its virtue, but also its danger.' As though demonstrating his own skill at recalling, my patron read the poem to himself a second time, raised his face into the sunlight and, without a prompt, repeated the entire work verbatim. It was a feat of repetition which even I, an actor, could appreciate. But then, having memorised the poem, he touched his forehead lightly with his forefinger, and said, 'It is better preserved in here.' Saying this, he proceeded to tear the page into a dozen small pieces. At the same time he said, 'If this were to fall into the hands of Lord Burghley's spies, and my guardian were to set eyes upon it, you may be certain he would order a warrant for your arrest on the charge of sedition.'

I observed the pieces drift down to the surface of the stream along whose banks we rode, and settle there.

I said, 'I have not named my Lord Burghley directly.'

'You have named the poem he authorised,' my patron replied. 'That is enough, since it carries his imprimatur. Furthermore, he would prosecute you for also naming Authority in the abstract and attempting to undermine her. I believe, sir, that in these times your well-being, and perhaps your life, would be forfeit within a few months of his taking sight of any such document.'

I watched the pieces float on the stream and observed how the fingers of paper, becoming water-logged, slowly began to sink into the river's darker depths. As though interrupting my contemplation, my lord said, 'My dear Master Shakespeare, you are my mentor in art and in life, but in politics, I believe I have certain things to teach you. From this day onward, I most earnestly hope that everything you write in your sonnets should be couched in ambiguity. Your hiding place should be language itself. If you are ever arraigned or indicted for your works, your defence must be that every word or phrase of yours may be capable of a different interpretation, or may be viewed in a different light.'

'You forbid me to address any matters politic?'

'No, that is my point. With regard to my Lord Burghley, or other matters of high authority, I advise you merely to hide your direct meaning.'

'Even though it places a severe constraint on the writing?'

'There is no restriction that cannot be overcome with subtlety,' he said. 'Ambivalence of meaning is a gift of yours. It must become not merely a clever conceit, but the source of your future safety.'

'Now you lecture me on my nature,' I replied, 'as I lectured you on yours.'

'Precisely so. Any poem of yours which moves, by aberration, into perfect clarity, I will attempt to persuade you to censor, for your own sake.'

I absorbed the weight of this peroration. But a part

of me was still disturbed by his peremptory action. I said, 'I believe that Master Marlowe would have openly authored that poem.'

My patron smiled. 'It is in Marlowe's nature to challenge all who pose in authority. He lives by his own calling. But you, sir, should aim to preserve yourself for as long as you may. Only live birds sing.'

'Only ambiguous birds, it seems,' I said, a part of me still stinging with mortification at the loss of my draft.

Chapter 9

*M*Y WOUNDED FEELINGS at his treatment of my poem were not long-lived. As my hurt cooled, I began to see the sense of my patron's objection. He had permitted me to write verses praising him in exaggerated and ironic terms, and had cautioned me in favour of complex ambivalence for my own protection. The thought occurred to me, not for the first time, that what at first appears a restraint may also be a spur to greater invention.

There had been an example of it in my own work. In the English language the pattern of speech settles almost naturally into the double beat, the iamb – a short beat followed by a longer beat, *di dah*. In my plays, following Marlowe, I had used five of these iambs to make up a line, the iambic pentameter, containing ten syllables. My sonnets were also predominantly ten syllables, but differed in having a rhyming scheme at the end of each line. Before attempting a sonnet I should have believed my sonnets' usual rhyme scheme of alternative lines, ending on a rhyming couplet, would have restricted the composition and rendered it more difficult. But on those quiet vigils when I worked at the board, as often as not the rhyme itself would suggest the next sentence, and so what seemed at first an impediment was transformed into a source of invention.

Meanwhile, I transmitted my anger at my patron's treatment by his guardian into more abstract form:

Tir'd with all these, for restful death I cry
As to behold desert a beggar born,
And needy nothing trimm'd in jollity,
And purest faith unhappily forsworn,

And gilded honour shamefully misplaced,
And maiden virtue rudely strumpeted,
And right perfection wrongfully disgraced,
And strength by limping sway disabled,
And art made tongue-tied by authority,
And folly – doctor-like – controlling skill,
And simple truth miscall'd simplicity,
And captive good attending captain ill:
    Tir'd with all these, from these would I be gone,
    Save that, to die, I leave my love alone.

My patron had requested me to be ambivalent, and no doubt would be appreciative of my listing of the catalogue of calumny directed against him and his reputation. But since he was a remarkably perceptive and intelligent soul, he would have noticed in the line: 'And art made tongue-tied by authority', an ambiguous reference to a certain incident of tearing up one of my sonnets and allowing the pieces to drift down onto the surface of the river. Yet, in his favour, I would be foolish to deny that a part of my joy in labouring at my verses for one such as he, who was so confident in his own sincerity, was that he would appreciate subtle irony at his own expense.

So I continued to work upon my sonnets in earnest, turning and re-directing the intended meaning of *Narcissus*, labouring during the night hours at my board, producing one paean to my patron after another. And in the process of committing myself to my labours, I began to fall in love not so much with the idealised creature I addressed there as with the form of the sonnet itself – that almost perfect amalgamation of precise structure and living animate being.

The process of writing even a single sonnet was a difficult and demanding performance. Often I would toil with little or no result. Yet sometimes, in the course of my labours, a line or phrase, emerging from shadowy intuition, would appear beneath my pen, and in a trance of concentration I would examine its unexpected beauty. Perhaps paradoxically, it was only when such a phrase or line was written down that I could view it from every angle, considering it for its hidden beauties and ambiguities. Sometimes, because I mistrusted my judgement in the full heat of invention, I would set aside a poem and take it out later, on another occasion, when I was more able to peruse with a cold and objective eye the deeper meaning of what I had written. At other times, sensing some imminent victory, I would press ahead, like a horseman leaping an obstacle without knowing what lay on the other side. When I asserted there was something animate in the sonnet, during the height of composition it seemed to me that I was controlling a living creature in almost a literal manner, a being whose inner life required all my wit and attention to give it its proper form and motion.

Sometimes these imaginings, far from granting me sleep, pursued me to my narrow cot, where I lay sleepless while my mind brimmed with thoughts and images. Partly for the entertainment of my patron, I recorded my nightly obsessions with my labours:

Weary with toil, I haste me to my bed,
The dear repose for limbs with travel tired;
But then begins a journey in my head,
To work my mind, when body's work's expir'd:

For then my thoughts – from far where I abide –
Intend a zealous pilgrimage to thee,
And keep my drooping eyelids open wide,
Looking on darkness which the blind do see:
Save that my soul's imaginary sight
Presents thy shadow to my sightless view,
Which, like a jewel hung in ghostly night,
Makes black night beauteous and her old face new.
  Lo! thus by day my limbs, by night my mind,
  For thee, and for myself no quiet find.

Chapter 10

*T*HERE WAS ANOTHER PRESENCE in that great house, one who hardly stirred from his rooms because of his labours, whose wife and several children I had seen mostly at a distance. The following day, I knocked upon his heavy door with its brass knocker. From inside a voice marked with an Italian accent rang out. 'Who calls?'

'Shakespeare!' I responded.

Sounds of footsteps followed across the floor, both impatient and dragging, as though it might be a wounded beast, or as if he were lugging some imperishable weight. With an aggravated growl, a wooden bar was swung aside. The oak door widened and grinned open.

Facing me was a tall, thin man in his late forties; scholarly, intense, with fierce and brooding eyes. His harried gaze fixed on mine.

'Master Shakespeare, the poet,' he announced. There was something cynical, both agitated and mocking, about his demeanour.

'Master Florio, the scholar,' I replied. 'I shamelessly seek a volume to study.'

'Which volume, now?' He examined me. 'Speak, if you dare.'

'Why, a volume of your own fine work. Who else's?'

Master Florio smiled at my importunity, but relented. As though quoting some private text, he said to himself, 'Thou art a flatterer.' To which I said, 'No better and no worse.'

He stood aside and let me pass. Inside the sullen gloom his rooms were a scholar's den, with manuscripts piled high on chests and chairs. The remaining furniture was submerged beneath piles of written documents.

He glanced around at this confusion with something like approval, and said, 'You seek inspiration for your verses? You wish to rob my resources for your own?'

'Precisely, sir,' I said. 'Most ably put.'

He smiled again at my audacity, seating himself once more at his desk. He waved his hand in the general direction of the small back room where he stored his works. 'You may look through my volumes. But in return for my generosity, you will forgive me if I continue with my labours.'

I bowed. 'You are kindness itself.'

He called for his wife, pronouncing 'Lucia' in the Italian manner. A door opened and a handsome dark-haired woman appeared, in her middle twenties, with a small child held on her hip.

'Lucia,' my host repeated. 'Show Master Shakespeare to the little cell.'

In answer to his instruction, Lucia nodded. She set down the child, turned and led me through a bedchamber strewn with children's clothes, opening another door. There I found a tiny cell with a single window, piled high with so many volumes it was almost impossible to stand.

She waited behind me, and said, 'It is not very inviting, sir.'

'Oh, it is inviting to me, madam.'

I noticed a volume that interested me and pulled it down from a high pile of books, blowing dust off it as I did so. '*The Discourses*, by Signor Niccolò Machiavelli,' I said. 'You have read him?'

She hovered in the doorway. 'I was told he was an evil man.'

'Evil? No. A sweet and kind man. But he who advises tyrants must place himself in the tyrant's mind.' Saying this, I could not help but think of her husband in the next room.

'That was his sin?' she asked, inquisitive. 'Placing himself in another's mind?'

'Sympathy was his sin, madam. Honesty and lucidity were his means. Peaceful governance was his intention.'

She half smiled at these unfamiliar descriptions. 'My husband says – '

But I was swift to intercept. 'Your husband is Signor Machiavelli's countryman, madam. In such matters he is like all of us; when we consider our close compatriots, we underrate our native genius.'

She contemplated this, and smiled. 'No man is a prophet in his own land.'

'Exactly so.' And so she disappeared, nodding and closing the door.

I found myself alone in that monk's cell, surrounded by books. But I was happy enough, sniffing the scents of ancient wisdom. Balancing Signor Machiavelli upon a high pile of other works, I leaned against the nearby wall and began to read, running the tips of my careful fingers along the page, mouthing the words as I concentrated on the line.

That evening I sat at my board with the intention to address a certain theme in a sonnet. Though it was summer, the clear nights dissipated heat. For warmth, I had gathered around my shoulders the pelt of a sheep. Beside me, a single candle guttered and shed a faint light.

Since my lord's full name was Henry Wriothesley, Earl of Southampton and Baron of Titchfield, some consideration was commonly made for the difficulty of pronunciation of his family name. For greater ease, even on formal occasions, Wriothesley was pronounced 'Rye-ose-ley', though it was more common still to pronounce it 'Rosely'. The combination of 'Rose' in the pronunciation of his name, and the heraldic roses which decorated his house, tempted me to compose on the subject of roses in my verse.

I scratched with a quill on a sheet of parchment, paused, counted beats on my fingers, mouthed a phrase silently to myself, put quill to paper, withdrew, hesitated, and wrote:

From fairest creatures we desire increase,
That thereby beauty's Rose might never die,

The poem began to take a clearer shape:

From fairest creatures we desire increase,
That thereby beauty's Rose might never die,

But as the riper should by time decease,
His tender heir might bear his memory:
But thou, contracted to thine own bright eyes,
Feed'st thy light's flame with self-substantial fuel,
Making a famine where abundance lies,
Thyself thy foe, to thy sweet self too cruel.

The following day, in the rose garden, I watched
my lord mime the beat and then express aloud the final
words:

Thou that art now the world's fresh ornament
And only herald to the gaudy spring,
Within thine own bud buriest thy content
And, tender churl, mak'st waste in niggarding.
Pity this world, or else this glutton be,
To eat the world's due, by the grave and thee.

Reclining on a bench in that walled garden in the sunlight, having finished the sonnet, he raised his attention from the page and whispered to himself, 'Damn me, it's beautiful.'

Seated opposite him, my back against a wall, I inclined my head in acknowledgement. He stretched out his arms in languor, speaking with the rasp of sleepiness, 'Yet you do my mother's bidding, and chide me again for not marrying.'

I nodded.

He raised his face to the warm sunlight, and appeared to be thinking, for his eyelids fluttered. Then he opened his eyes, as though caught with an idea. 'Yet still, if my childlessness inspires such verse – why then, it must be continued!'

Something of his fire spread to me. I responded warmly to the idea, like a tutor to a favourite pupil. 'A fine conceit.'

My lord, charged with enthusiasm for his own idea, rose to his feet, and began walking up and down in an agitated state. 'So, then, let us have some more verses on this subject. Why, I believe I shall be angry if you do not pile more chastisement on my state. And if you do not chide me, sir, be certain that it will be I who chides you, for not doing your sacred duty.'

That night, seated in front of the board that served as my writing desk, I paused again. Beside me, the window was open. In the cool, starlit night I could hear a dog barking, and, further away, the scream of a vixen. I hesitated on my bench, whispered something to myself, and began again to scratch the surface of the paper with my quill.

When forty winters shall besiege thy brow,
And dig deep trenches in thy beauty's field,
Thy youth's proud livery, so gaz'd on now,
Will be a tatter'd weed, of small worth held:
Then, being asked where all thy beauty lies,
Where all the treasure of thy lusty days;
　　To say within thine own deep-sunken eyes,
　　Were an all-eating shame and shiftless praise.

The room seemed to become darker as I, engrossed in my own labour, set down the remainder of the poem, working as fast as I could, attempting to pin the thought like a live thing to the page. At times the poem seemed to draw away from me, and my corrections and crossings-out filled the page. For some time I worked, in a trance of concentration, until the sonnet was complete. Afterwards I stood at the small window of my cell, breathless, as though my mind had been voided by the effort. The following day, I listened while my lord completed the lines.

How much more praise deserv'd thy beauty's use,
If thou could answer, 'This fair child of mine
Shall sum my count, and make my old excuse,'
Proving his beauty by succession thine!
This were to be new-made when thou art old,
And see thy blood warm when thou feel'st it cold.

We were seated in our usual place in the garden, a corner protected from the prevailing winds. My lord set down the page he had been reading on the grass beside him. Folding his hands behind his head, he addressed the air above him. 'Such felicity! I believe you should show both of these sonnets to my mother. She will be forever in your debt for chastising me so ... beautifully.'

I remember looking about me, over the garden walls at the summer woods behind, at the country with its rolling meadows and woodlands, its nearby silver stream.

Observing my attention, my lord said, 'The colours of autumn already fall upon us. Soon it will be winter.'

I looked upwards and around me, at sunlight slanting through the nearby elms. Perhaps the beauty made my lord talkative; after gazing around at the countryside, he said, 'If I were without my duties, I should like, above everything, to return to my cell in St John's, in Cambridge, and burn candles and read volumes of Latin and Greek.'

'You do not fear solitude?'

He smiled. 'The greatest solitude I feel is when my

relations are gathered at Christmas feast-day, and as the head of the family, and heir, I must act as *paterfamilias*. That is what I fear most – what is owed to others. Why, I prefer my books.' He looked up at the falling sunlight. 'You do not believe me?'

'Oh, I believe you, my lord. I believe every word you say.'

He gave me a strange look. 'Perhaps you do. Yet you smile.'

'I smile because I should like nothing more than to be in the bosom of my family.'

'Your family?' he asked.

'In Stratford,' I replied. 'I should like above all to sit at the head of the table, and carve the meat.'

He smiled, but he insisted, 'And yet you live in exile, in a cold room, in my house in Hampshire, and seem to ask for nothing in the way of comfort except a supply of ink and parchment.'

'You misunderstand me, I think, if you believe I complain about my lot. I am a player and a scribbler, freely chosen.'

'You do yourself a disservice,' he said. 'You are called by some a great poet. You have dedicated both

Venus and Adonis and *The Rape of Lucrece* to me. I have seen your worth.'

'I have also been called an upstart crow, who can hardly beat out a verse. And here I am, exiled from London by the plague, twice removed from that simple life that I desire.'

'We strike a melancholy note, between us. I wish to be a monk, and you – '

'To plunge myself into simple, unthinking human life.'

If he seemed amused by my earnestness, it was fleeting. 'I believe that in our aims, we swim past each other like fishes. I should give an arm to be like you – '

'Like me?'

He seemed to choose his words. 'Detached from this world, yet always observing.'

'And I should give an arm to be like you.'

'And what is that?' he asked. 'What does it mean "to be like me"?'

I struggled for expression. 'Living and breathing the world's rich scents.'

There was a moment's silence between us, after which he said, with a sigh, as though contemplative,

'My mother continues to instruct you regarding my behaviour?'

I nodded.

He smiled. 'I believe my mother would gladly exchange you for me.'

'Why so?' I asked.

'She admires your sober devotion to your work, and contrasts it with my dissipation and irresponsibility.'

I said, 'She loves you entirely and magnificently.'

'Not for myself, though. For what I owe. For what I should be.'

I did not comment. We considered peaceably the sloping shadows of the trees.

Chapter 11

THE FOLLOWING MORNING I leaned against a wall in the anteroom of my lord's mother, the Countess, staring out of the window at the autumn day.

The door to her room opened. I had expected her to open it herself, but instead her bailiff, a heavyset man, walked out carrying a bundle of sealed letters. His somewhat ursine body and short legs gave his gait a distinctive roll. Halting before me, he said, 'Master Shakespeare?'

I bowed my head indulgently.

'Her Ladyship would see you,' he said. 'She expects you.'

I thanked him. When he had passed on his way I walked towards the door of the inner chamber and knocked. Soft footsteps approached from the inside. The latch was raised soundlessly, the wood swung back. My lady was still strikingly beautiful.

'Master Shakespeare,' she said.

I bowed my head again, with greater sincerity than to her bailiff.

She drew back and I entered the room. Closing the door, she turned towards me, leaning upon it. 'My son sends me your verses.'

'They are nothing, madam. Sonnets merely.'

'Yet he commends you on your worth.'

'He is my patron, madam. In these hard times I am doubly grateful.'

'The London theatres are still closed by plague?'

'Except for a brief month at midwinter, my lady, when the cold seems to damp the fever. And then the entertainments are nothing more than masques and pantomimes.'

She hesitated. Her next statement seemed carefully framed. 'I hear you see much of my son.'

'He flatters me with his companionship.'

'His companionship?' She seemed to muse upon the word. There was a change of tone, a kind of insistence. 'You see much of him?'

Her question caused me to pause, to consider the weight of implication.

'Come now, Master Shakespeare,' the Countess said. 'It is time we discussed these matters. I do not hold it against you if you speak your mind. I am a woman with experience of this world.'

Perhaps something of the shock at such direct questioning showed on my face. I began, 'Madam, it is not my nature – '

'To be so disposed,' she said, 'towards young men?'

'No,' I answered. She considered me carefully, without speaking. Then she smiled ruefully. 'I do believe you ... Yet he has other companions who ... are so disposed.'

'Feckless youth, madam,' I responded. 'Puppies in a litter. You will not hold that against him.'

'Well turned, sir. He will not marry, though. You do not think these things are ... related?'

I am not as bold as Marlowe, perhaps, but in the theatre I am used to a certain latitude in human affairs, so that sometimes I am driven to express an imp of general truth. 'Madam, if I may speak for myself, and with utmost sincerity, I see no connection between the quality of a man's soul and the private uses to which he puts his body.'

I saw a sudden blaze of feeling behind her eyes, but could not tell whether it was disapproval, or some other, more complex, emotion. Before her husband died, there had been a great scandal, in which he had accused his long-suffering wife of adultery, apparently without reason; but her blameless life as a widow since his early death seemed to have allayed the ghost of that accusation. She approached me now across the room. It was almost as though she dared me to proceed further with my thoughts. Under that impassioned gaze, it occurred to me that she was not so much questioning my words as testing my own sincerity.

'Continue, sir,' she said, as though challenging me.

'I merely apply my general beliefs to a singular matter,' I replied.

If she seemed to disapprove of my homily, it was

alleviated at least by a trace of humour. 'I sometimes forget, sir, that you are from the theatre.'

'Indeed, madam,' I replied.

'Where women are played by principal boys.'

'There are not many puritans on the stage, madam, I willingly concede.'

'Is that so? They do not gather there?'

'It is true, madam, that I have not seen many puritans clustering thickly in the theatre.'

Any amusement at my response seemed to occur entirely in her eyes, if it occurred at all. Since she continued to consider me directly, for my part I would continue to press my small advantage. Attempting to ameliorate, I said, 'Your son may sow wild oats, madam. But he is not idle.'

'Idle?'

'His tutors speak of a most gifted mind. He has the discipline of a scholar. And all who see him joust and play know that he has the frame and determination of a warrior.'

'Scholar and warrior,' she said, as if with disapproval, though she seemed a little more composed. 'Mere occupations. This house needs an heir.'

She turned away. Now it was my concern to choose my words carefully. 'I believe he has a fine and generous soul, madam. He will not disgrace you.'

That was when she turned towards me again, burning. 'Then perhaps you know something of him which I do not?'

Her eyes were on me, her attention concentrated. But observing something of my own perplexity, she appeared to soften once more. 'Forgive me. I make apology for my impatience. You, of all his companions, are the most consistent in his education upon necessity.' She seemed to breathe more slowly. 'Yet how is it that you do not irk him with your own constant reminders?'

'He turns me to his account, madam,' I said. 'He says if his childlessness is to be the source of such fine, high-minded verse, why then, he shall be obliged to honour it by living his life as it is.'

She smiled at that, despite herself, and said, 'He has a courtier's tongue, too, amongst his other attributes.'

'That, too,' I said.

'Which very attribute he could be employing to woo a bride.'

'He is hardly yet twenty, madam.'

She considered me a little slyly, still searching, I suspected, for advantage.

'And you, sir? In years, you are ... ?'

'Twenty-nine, madam.'

'Have you no offspring?'

'Three.'

'Ah, three.' She considered this new knowledge. 'And – forgive my enquiry, sir – what age were you when you fathered your firstborn?'

My mind drifted backwards. 'When I was seventeen or eighteen, madam. But surely – '

'And at your last child?' she insisted.

'Some twenty years of age, I believe. Yet I do not see – '

'Do you not, sir? My son is already as old as you were at your third child. I have no other children, and he has a duty upon his house.'

Perhaps because I sensed only too well her noble

obsession with the extension of her line, I felt power-less in the face of such a will. There were shadows of her own life, too, which I had no inclination to disturb. And so I attempted to maintain my expression, remaining equivocal, saying merely, 'I am your ally, madam.'

She raised her hand for me to kiss, and said, 'I have other matters to attend.'

'Then I shall depart,' I replied. 'And I thank you for your audience.'

Out of respect, I moved backwards towards the door. When I turned to depart, she had seated herself at her desk and was already concentrating on her corre-spondence.

I closed the door softly.

That night I sat at my own hard board, the flicker-ing light of the little flame on the white face of the paper, writing feverishly. Through the open window I could see the moon shining on a dew-laden field. But I was oblivious of my surroundings. Occasionally I had recourse to a cup of wine. Sometimes, if my thoughts flowed well, or I found some hidden virtue in a phrase, I smiled to myself, nodded, dipped my quill in inky darkness, and began again to scratch the paper.

Look in thy glass and tell the face thou viewest
Now is the time that face should form another;
Whose fresh repair if now thou not renewest,
Thou dost beguile the world, unbless some mother.
For where is she so fair whose unear'd womb
Disdains the tillage of thy husbandry?
Or who is he so fond will be the tomb
Of his self-love to stop posterity?

A few days later I was walking with the Countess, side by side, along the great flagstones of one of the interior passages. She was reading aloud, apparently absorbed, as she continued the sonnet to its conclusion.

'Thou art thy mother's glass and she in thee
Calls back the lovely April of her prime:
So thou through windows of thine age shall see,
Despite of wrinkles, this thy golden time.'

She paused before enunciating the last two lines:

'But if thou live, remember'd not to be,
Die single and thine image dies with thee.'

She halted, lowered the page, turned and smiled at me.

'Who could resist such measured and unswerving advice?'

'Your son, madam,' I said. 'Only he.'

'And he is the only one who should heed it.'

'That is the world's way.'

'Then what is it holds him back?'

'The rites of spring, perhaps.'

'But we approach winter once more.'

In our walk along the corridor, we were passing by a window that overlooked the main courtyard. My attention was distracted for a moment by a movement outside.

'What holds you?' the Countess inquired.

Out of politeness, I halted so that she, turning around me, might have a better view. Following the direction of my gaze, she looked out through the same window, onto the courtyard, where a small retinue was moving across the cobbles.

At its head was a heavy old man, sitting on a great piebald horse. Several other riders followed at a respectful distance. Amongst them was a dark-haired, younger woman.

Following my gaze to the head of the column, my lady said, 'My Lord Hunsdon, the Lord Chamberlain. He visits us for several days.'

I nodded. At the same time, I could not help but

continue to stare out, transfixed. Perhaps my lady noticed this unswerving attention, for she looked out at the little train again.

'Who is the lady, madam?' I asked.

'Why, Master Shakespeare, I believe you are smitten.'

Sensing her amusement, I replied, 'You forbid my further interest?'

'An Italian whore,' she said, 'since you ask.'

I added, as lightly as I could, 'Handsome, even so.'

'Handsome indeed,' she said, looking out again on the scene unfolding in the courtyard. 'She is fathered, as I remember, by one of the Queen's musicians, and has come to be his lordship's mistress. For colour, his lordship married her to a minstrel, so that he may continue to have her as he wishes – respectably.'

'The minstrel to whom she is married?' I asked. 'He rides beside her?'

'The young man? I believe so.'

'He seems even younger than she.'

'A mere stripling, as you say. But that is his purpose. The greener to his role. Meanwhile, the old boar will visit his sow as he wishes.'

Under the circumstances, perhaps, it was as much information as I could expect. My mind was already attempting to absorb the implications. With some reluctance I removed my attention from the sight of the procession, and so found myself facing her ladyship again. Her eyes were like lights. She seemed both agitated and amused by my interest.

I said, 'My Lord Hunsdon has his own players, for whom I have acted and penned the occasional entertainment.'

'Indeed. And so you have a proper interest in him, not merely in his whore.'

'I have an interest in many things, madam.'

The Countess smiled. 'And so you do, sir.' Her voice, which until now had been almost flirtatious, became commanding. 'Meanwhile, be so good as to maintain your interest in my son's duty. Now, I must attend to my own.'

Without waiting for my bow, she moved on. I observed her depart down the passage. As soon as she had disappeared, I felt it safe to return my attention once more to the procession.

In the courtyard, the dark lady dismounted. She

was statuesque, with raven hair and a complexion that suggested something of her Italian ancestry. She looked round the courtyard imperiously. Nervously, the young man, her husband, approached and seemed to speak with her. But she hardly appeared to notice him, treating him almost as she would a servant.

Chapter 12

*I*T HAPPENED THAT I STRONGLY DESIRED to speak with my Lord Hunsdon, my former theatre patron, that venerable soldier and cousin of our Queen. For the next few days I attempted to engineer a meeting. But, howsoever I approached him, he seemed engaged in discussion with one or another of the visitors who seemed to throng the house. Two days later I saw him in the rose garden, strutting broad-shouldered like a raven in an empty field. His hands were on his hips, while he walked restlessly backwards and forwards, seeming deep in thought.

For several moments I considered, then stepped out

firmly towards him. As I approached, my Lord Hunsdon continued to pace. When I was nearly upon him,
he raised his attention. An emotion touched his venerable face, briefly, like a fly on the face of a bull. Then,
almost immediately, he resumed his walking. It was as
though he were lost in a dream of contemplation,
unwilling to be distracted from his thoughts. So I continued to walk past him without stopping.

It was only when I was about to leave the rose-
garden that my Lord Hunsdon, as though waking from
his reverie, called out, 'Master Shakespeare!' I halted
and turned. He beckoned me back imperiously. As I
approached, he said, 'Come, sir. You cannot avoid me
so easily. I see everything, y'know. And what I do not
see is not worth consideration.'

I made a brief bow. 'Your all-seeing lordship.'

'And tell me now,' he said, 'what mischief do you
practise while the London theatres are closed?'

'I write verses, my lord, and work on a play.'

'Southampton keeps you?' he asked slyly.

'Most ably,' I replied.

'Now,' he said, drawing closer, 'now listen, damn
you. I heard of a play you wrote, a most excellent play,

that was recommended by a woman acquaintance.'

Speaking thus, he waved his arm towards a recessed part of the garden, where the same dark-haired woman I had previously observed now sat at a little distance in an arbour in the fleeting sunshine.

Following my gaze, my Lord Hunsdon said, 'One of my minstrels, Miss Bassano, now married to another, Master Lanier. You have met the young couple?'

'No, my lord.'

'Well, never mind, sir. She has read an actor's copy of your work and speaks most highly of it. Now, if I remember the title of it, let me see, now, the title of it, the name of it tips my tongue, it tips my tongue. Ah yes, dammit, yes, dammit, it comes now: *The Taming of the Shrew.*'

I nodded, saying, 'Written recently, perhaps a year ago.'

'And why did you not bring it me? Why not?'

'I waited my opportunity to speak to you in person.'

'Yet we speak now, and it is I who mention it you, courtesy of a lady.'

'You are most kind.'

'All-seeing, sir. All-seeing – though I am almost

blind in one eye. Have you seen the younger Walsing-ham?'

'No, my lord.'

His bold eyes considered me. 'That damn fox. He's here. I'm damned if I've seen him, though. Slinking through the brush. No sooner sighted than departed.'

While he talked so animatedly of Walsingham, I looked over at the arbour, where it seemed Mrs Lanier was quietly observing us. Meanwhile my Lord Hunsdon continued, 'When you are in London, bring a copy of it to me, do you hear? When the theatres open, it will be our first performance. Damn me, *The Taming of the Shrew*. There's a saucy title for you. Damn me.'

'Thank you, my lord. But I see you were preoccu-pied before I came. And therefore, with your kind per-mission, I will absent myself, and will leave you to your thoughts.'

'Yes, yes ... If you see a fox, pray, report him to me.'

'At the first sight,' I said.

'And we will set our hounds after him.'

'He shall not brush us off, my lord.'

A smile spread on his old face. 'Heh, heh, damned

fine. Be off with you, you punning vagabond. And bring that play to me.'

He nodded once, out of courtesy, then began to walk up and down again. And so I knew that I was dismissed, and could return to my life again. I bowed to him. But before departing, I allowed myself one last glance at Emilia Lanier, seated calmly in the arbour.

Chapter 13

*E*ACH DAY FOLLOWED ANOTHER. One morning I was walking along one of the passages of the great house, inclining my head occasionally to people who passed, thinking to myself; how shall a man be smitten by a woman who is called behind her back a whore, who is Lord Hunsdon's mistress, who has been a paramour of several others of the great, all before she has reached the age of twenty-three?

During these ruminations I greeted several other people, embracing certain retainers from other great houses – scholars, tutors, secretaries, scribes, members of the scratching professions – and various others with whom I had in common an itch to exchange gossip. I had found, though I was in a provincial court, that there was a constant ebb and flow of guests to and from this great house. For while London was in plague the court itself was dispersed, as much as we poor players. And so one might find, in the antechambers and halls, great men conspiring in little corners. There was one in particular for whom I kept an eye upon, for reasons of my own.

It happened that one day a group of several men passed me in a corridor. I recognised red hair, almost albino eyes, and bowed more deeply to one in particular than to the others.

'Sir Thomas,' I said, raising my head. Sir Thomas Walsingham was a cold, interior man, younger kinsman of Sir Francis, the Queen's great spymaster, who had died several years before. He had inherited the family reputation for intrigue. Now he turned slowly, as though he recognised me. This compelled me to turn with him, so that we were like two objects circling one another, earth and moon.

'Why, Master Shakespeare,' he said.

The three stalwarts who accompanied him until

then had stood back while we conducted our manoeu-
vre. As we came to rest, so they, like other moons,
lined up behind the curve of his shoulder. It did not
pass my notice that all three were muscular and heavy,
that each had the build of a torturer.

Walsingham opened his account, in his usual
manner, saying, 'I have a riddle for you, sir, which I
would dearly have you answer. What bird is it that
singeth most sweetly for his supper?'

'A poet, I believe.'

Behind him his retainers stirred a little. He turned
to his companions with a mocking, portentous movement, saying, 'A bird of wit.'

'You employ greater wits than I,' I said.

'Master Marlowe?' he enquired. 'Indeed, but Master
Marlowe hath a complex tongue. And sometimes, he
being so witty, we his companions do not entirely know
what he sings.'

The other men smiled at this allusion.

We were in a place that was open to observation by
others, and so he pointed to a recess which lay out of
sight of the main passage. In a single body, we moved
there, I perhaps a little uncomfortably, but carried by

the general will. Out of sight of the passing traffic, Walsingham turned to me again and spoke *sotto voce*.

'I look upon you for a favour, sir.'

'A favour?' I asked, surprised.

'Indeed, I would request that you deliver a message.'

At the same moment he indicated one of his henchmen who, from the depths of his clothes, produced a sealed letter and held it out to me. Without touching it, I read the name of the person to whom it was addressed.

Walsingham said, 'A simple letter, intended for my Lord Southampton.'

I was now alarmed. To hide my consternation, and to gather a few precious seconds, I said, 'I feel certain, sir, that if it is from you, he should receive it from you directly.'

'Unlike you, sir, I do not make his acquaintance every day.'

It seemed to me there was an element of insinuation in what he said. The silence floated between us.

'Even so,' I smiled to allay as best I could. 'I do believe it would better come from you.'

Walsingham's expression became colder. He said, 'Your scribbling, now. It keeps you and your young family?'

'We survive, sir.'

'Indeed,' he said, 'you survive.'

He gestured to another of his henchmen, who produced from one of his deep sleeves a small purse. 'Then perhaps we may add to your good fortune. Twenty gold florins for a small mission, nothing more. A letter, sir, to a patron you would see in normal course.'

'I am grateful for your interest,' I said. 'But I deduce that, for twenty florins, the message must be one of importance. And since, therefore, I am not of importance myself, but a simple scribbler, why, I assume that twenty florins and I shall not be suited.'

The atmosphere between us, which had been cold, now grew colder still. The letter and the bag of florins continued to be held out towards me, like temptations. For what seemed to be an unconscionable time, four pairs of cold eyes regarded me. Then Walsingham nodded to his henchmen again, and both offerings were summarily withdrawn.

Now my tempter said, 'I perceive that you and Mr

Marlowe, whom you hold so highly, must be different men.'

'That may be so, sir.'

'Master Marlowe hath strong opinions, and involves himself in the movements of the day.'

'He is a greater man than I,' I said.

'My compliments to my Lord Southampton, on choosing trustworthy friends.'

Delivered coldly, this seemed more criticism than compliment. After that, he turned his back to me and departed, his henchmen following him like faithful dogs.

I observed him grow smaller, and felt a shadow had passed across my life, like a wave that washes back from striking a sea wall, subverting other waves. With it came the terrible intuition that if I had accepted the bribe once, I would forever be in the society of conspirators and torturers.

Chapter 14

THOUGH I ATTENDED upon my Lord Southampton during the day, and bent to my poor verses at night, throughout that winter I hunted for one presence. My Lord Hunsdon visited several times, accompanied by his retinue. So it was that one morning I was walking across a courtyard, engaged in my own thoughts, when I heard, through a window, the virginals being played. The keys were being struck with such thoughtful precision and dexterity that I halted, like an animal enchanted, and leaned against the wall, listening to the beautiful notes.

Following the sound, I made a detour from my

intended course, and entered the building through a side door. It was not a part of the great house that I normally visited – an old granary or chapter, used for dancing lessons, or the practising of music. At first I found myself in a passage, hearing the faint notes of the virginals as though still a little way off.

I followed the notes, like a man following a scent. Eventually I arrived at a place where the sound was loudest. Raising my hand, I pressed on the door; a room like a small hall opened before me.

At the end of the room, Emilia Lanier was seated at the keys. She paused when I entered, turning towards me slowly.

'Play on, madam,' I said, remembering a line on which I had been working, feeling for the scansion in some recess of my memory. 'If love be the food of music,' I said, 'play on.' That didn't sound quite right. I resolved to work upon it.

She looked at me, then turned back to the instrument and with her light fingers perpetuated the air.

While the notes sang, I walked into the room, sat down on a bench a few feet away from her upright back, leaning against a neighbouring wall. Closing my eyes I entered that state of contemplation which is the province of devout monks and lovers. And there I remained, for how long I do not remember, lost from grace until Emilia Lanier finished her tune, turned towards me, and smiled.

I said, 'I believe I owe you my gratitude.'

'For what, sir?' she asked.

'For speaking to my Lord Hunsdon favourably, about a play of mine – *The Taming of the Shrew.*'

'It is a fine play,' she said, 'on the outside very crude and fierce; and on the inside ... subtle.'

'My Lord Hunsdon is now here in this house again?' I asked. 'I have not seen him.'

'He has departed on a journey to a military outpost which he says is too cold and bitter for my temperament. He leaves me here to wait his return.'

I smiled. 'In honour of your temperament, madam, which, by contrast, is warm, and sunny, and perhaps inclined to generosity.'

'Towards those whom it admires.'

So we continued, bantering happily. And so it struck me, not for the first time, that in each profession there is a nobility; even in harlotry. Though I might be the companion and mentor of a great lord, and think myself a gentleman, yet there was something between us that was like music. She brought my plays to Lord Hunsdon's attention. She carried a certain beauty of thought to that gruff old soldier, that Warden of the East Marches. And she played the virginals with such sympathy of feeling that sometimes I thought that we were performers both, and that in our lives our only purpose was that we should play our roles as best we might.

We continued through the morning, she playing and I listening, talking alternately, as though old friends. When she finished playing and stood up, I followed her example and we two faced each other. Emilia held out her hand towards me with a graceful, formal precision. Carefully, I took her hand in mine. She did not resist, but at the same time she said gently, 'My Lord Hunsdon is your former patron. And he would be your patron again.'

'Indeed, madam,' I said, 'and it is you who put him in mind of me, for which I am eternally grateful.' I leaned forward and kissed her hand, but she said softly, 'I do not ask for recompense.'

I raised my eyes to meet hers. 'Recompense is deserved, madam, even if not asked for.'

She considered me with amusement. 'You would do well to listen to what I say.'

'I listen to your music, madam,' I said, 'And my heart answers.'

Emilia continued to regard me. Then she pulled her hand – still gripped in my own – gently but firmly away from me. Having disentangled herself, she placed her own two palms around my left hand, and drew it gently towards her face. It seemed she was about to kiss my hand. A thrill passed through me, for she seemed to be signalling that she returned my desire. I observed her progress. As she brought my left hand to her lips, I watched in fascination. She opened her mouth, her lips touched my hand, and then I felt a searing pain as she bit into me savagely.

I heard my own cry of agony and pulled my hand away, staggering backwards to the neighbouring wall. There I crouched over my wound, nursing my bleeding hand with my other. I brought it to my mouth to lick away the blood, meanwhile watching her observe me almost considerately.

I began to protest. 'Madam ... '

But she, by contrast, seemed to have returned to her original composure. Now she calmly said, 'I warned you to listen to what I say.'

'It seems I did not hear,' I said.

'Then listen to me now. Do not bite the hand that feeds you.'

With my free hand, I reached into my sleeve for a kerchief and began to wind it around my bleeding paw. Using my teeth and free hand, I attempted to tie a knot. Between these attempts to bind my wound, I conducted a brief conversation with her, beginning, 'You are loyal to your master.'

'No, I am loyal to you. You should not mortgage your destiny to a merely furtive pleasure.'

'A merely furtive pleasure! As you are his mistress, madam, I believe I will stand being lectured by you on furtive pleasures.'

'My Lord Hunsdon has married me to a young man in his employ. I am become respectable.'

'Becoming is not being,' I said.

'Do not be bitter,' she said.

'Bitten, more likely, madam.'

'I bit your left hand,' she said, 'so that you may continue to write with your right.'

'How kind you are, madam,' I rejoined, 'Praise be I am not sinister.'

The initial pain and shock of her bite had partially subsided. I had more or less succeeded in tying my kerchief with a knot. I even began to see some small vestige of humour in my situation. Holding up my bound hand, I said, 'Truly, madam, my Lord Hunsdon hath no need of a hound to protect him, if he has you.'

'I protect you, sir, as well as him.'

'Then you bite your own master.'

'I will continue to protect you – against your will, if necessary.'

Raising my bound hand, I said, 'And I will continue to wear this as a keepsake. Now,' – I made a mock furtive glance towards the door, as though planning my escape, and with an actor's relish I began to sidle sideways along the wall, towards the door, saying – 'if you will be kind enough to allow me an avenue of safe passage, I hope that you will not consider protecting me again.'

She watched my antics with hardly suppressed

amusement, even raising a hand to her mouth to hide a smile.

I reacted to her gesture with mock fright. 'Careful, madam ... '

By then I had reached the door. Still with my back to it, I carefully edged through the opening, and exited stage right, slamming the door closed behind me in comical relief.

Inside the room I heard her burst into loud laughter. Then she must have paused briefly, because silence ensued. But mirth must have overtaken her once more, because she burst into loud laughter again.

I do not know what further changes took place inside the blessed music room, how many swift changes of mood may have passed, except that another period of silence followed. I moved down the passageway, towards the outside of the building.

Perhaps she sat down at the virginals. Perhaps she considered the keys for a while. By the time I was outside, passing by the window, I heard her begin playing again, though this time the tune was 'Greensleeves', that popular and sentimental lament.

Can one play music with irony? I do not know. But I believe I heard it then – something of bitterness and amusement imparted through those fingers. It seemed to me that just as I had overacted my departure for her amusement, so now the melodious strains signalled a response – as though she too, for my own entertainment, mocked her own sadness.

Her music followed me as I made my way across the quadrangle. I paused for a moment, looked down at my wounded hand, glanced once more at the open window, hoping, perhaps, to see her again, then shook my head and walked on.

Chapter 15

THAT NIGHT I ATTEMPTED TO WRITE, but could not. I sat with my quill in my right hand, my wounded left hand resting on the table, staring forward into the darkness. It was not the pain itself but the shock of her admonishment. What she had done burned me too deep and close for objective consideration. Instead I sat at my board and, after a certain time, unable either to compose or to dissemble, I fell asleep upon my duty.

I lay there until light began to pour in through the small window. In luminous dawn, my hand burned still. Before my lord's household stirred, I took it upon myself to leave my room and walk down to the small stream that passed the main house a hundred paces away. There I bathed my wound, and put on a fresh covering of cloth. But I was still in agitation. It seemed to me that any truth which is inflicted from the outside is like a poison to the unwilling. I resolved to find her when I could and make my apologies, the interval having granted me at least the beginnings of sincerity.

When I had bathed and dressed my hand I walked to the rose garden, where early mists lingered. There my restlessness continued. I must have walked up and down for the best part of an hour, preoccupied, moving back and forth, my wounded hand clasped by the other behind my back. I was so absorbed I did not hear the sound of a retinue approaching, the faint tinkle and fret of a harness, until I was hailed directly by a half-familiar voice. 'Master Shakespeare!'

I turned round. My Lord Hunsdon was seated on his heavy piebald horse, with several mounted retainers halted behind him. When I had gathered my senses I recalled that he had a reputation for travelling by night. It was said that since no one else travelled the roads during the dark hours, he would not be noticed as he went about his duties of inspection. It was also reported that he liked nothing more than to appear at some outpost or stronghold in dawn's early mist, before anyone was much awake, in order to catch sentries unawares and make his private assessments. If so, it seemed to have become a habit of his old age. Now he had surprised me, with my hand still bandaged from his mistress's attentions.

In dawn's early mist I observed him slowly dismount and walk towards me with his old horseman's barrel roll. 'You seem preoccupied, Master Shakespeare.'

I nodded in greeting and distant agreement.

Halting in front of me, he took hold of my bandaged hand, firmly but gently, and raised it to his closer view. 'Why, I believe you are wounded.'

I inclined my head again.

'I am a soldier, sir, and expert upon such matters.' He raised his wise old eyes to mine. 'The cause, tell me now, the cause?'

'A hound, my lord.'

'A hound? He should be whipped.'

'A faithful female hound,' I said. 'Who merely did her duty.'

My Lord Hunsdon's eyes stared calmly into my own. Their expression reminded me of the eyes of a pike when one looks over a riverbank, and sees – firm and unflinching – yellow eyes regarding you. At the same time, I detected a faint and somewhat steely glimmer of amusement in his expression.

'Beware of female teeth,' he said at last.

'Indeed, my lord.'

'Behind them there are strong emotions.'

While he talked, he was busily engaged in undoing the bandage. The wound was exposed.

'It no longer bleeds,' he said.

'Then I believe I am forgiven,' I replied.

His pike's eyes, rising again, looked into mine. 'This hound ... forgives you?' He paused a second time for his own calm consideration and amusement. 'Good. Forgiveness purifies. Give it air, sir, is my advice.'

'I will, my lord.'

It seemed he had extracted as much entertainment as he desired from my condition. Now he lowered his voice. 'I return to collect my mistress, and to pay my respects to our Countess.'

I said nothing, grateful above all that he had seen

fit to change the subject. He continued, 'You shall visit me in London, when the theatres open.'

'Thank you, my lord.'

The glint of amusement hovered in his expression. He leant towards me again, and whispered in his throaty voice, with what seemed to me a certain degree of theatrical relish, 'And keep away from faithful female hounds.'

Then he nodded, turned, remounted his horse, and at the head of the retinue rode into the main court of the house. I watched him depart.

Of what strange components is loyalty compounded? My own disloyalty had been noticed, calmly exposed and, it seemed, jovially and liberally forgiven, with no more than a soldier's considered warning. And what was perhaps strangest of all was that in the very act of forgiveness my old patron had reclaimed my life-long adherence to him, to his causes and his heirs.

Chapter 16

UNTIL THEN I HAD FELT UNABLE TO WRITE. It was not merely the literal pain of Emilia's bite, but rather that she had forbidden my love in the name of my art – as though I myself were not sufficient curator of my own meagre talent. Since my Lord Hunsdon had also forgiven me, I felt moved to compose a private valediction of our love, if only because sometimes the expression of a feeling acts to relieve the writer of some more morbid anguish. As I have found in the past, intense emotion sometimes drives the pen with a certain lucid force. After a period of concentration, I managed to write:

If I hear music in the painted day,
Drawing myself towards those fateful sounds,
And all my thoughts move outward to the lay,
Like lines of scent on which run faithful hounds,
Then I must hide my thoughts in careful praise
Which, praising you, fall short of what I feel.
If I should moan your loss, make better days
The sad account of my most bitter meal:
Your fingers on the cloth, touching their hem,
Press me to sit and watch your subtle hands;
The singular white thoughts which rise from them,
Graceful as hinds towards that hidden land.
   O, let me sit beside you while you play,
   Allowing thoughts to alter night for day.

When I had finished the poem, I read it through
several times to check the beat and rhythm. The piece
was flawed in certain places, and needed further work,
but at least it expressed the glimmer of something that

128

I felt. I was satisfied that I had caught my sense of anguish, although briefly and imperfectly. In that respect, it had served its cathartic purpose. Raising the page, I held it to the candle flame and watched as that soft and savage form lovingly devoured it. So, it seemed to me, I cleaned my mind of my forbidden love, though in truth I could not persuade myself that some ashes did not remain.

Chapter 17

*O*VER THE NEXT FEW DAYS I felt a sense of exalta-
tion, knowing that any danger of reprisal from my Lord
Hunsdon had passed. Now I looked about me at the
cold winter countryside beyond the walls of the garden,
the shadows of the great bare oaks which overhung the
meadows.

Something still agitated me. I was about to sink
into my thoughts, return to my pacing, when I heard a
faint tune, a scent of music, from the virginals.

Glancing around, I listened, then began to walk
towards the sound. It came through the same window,
from the same room in which Emilia last played.

Perhaps a benign fate was granting me one final opportunity to make apologies before she departed with her master.

So I hurried towards the room, entering by the usual side entrance. Travelling along the passage, I paused at the door, and opened it.

A dark-haired young woman was playing at the keys, but it was not Emilia. She halted at my sudden entrance, turning her head towards me.

I said, 'Madam Florio.'

'Clearly, sir, from your expression I see that you did not expect me.'

'I apologise for interrupting you. I expected ... another.'

'Emilia?' she smiled.

'Perhaps.'

'How strange. She asked me to play this morning, though she did not say for what purpose. As she is my friend, I could think of no good reason for not granting her wish.'

'I believe she is about to depart.'

'Why, yes, Lord Hunsdon has returned for her.'

Out of the window I could see, in the main courtyard, Emilia on my Lord Hunsdon's arm, and the train
of baggage horses being assembled behind them. I
observed beauty beside her wise, old beast.

To Lucia, I said, 'Madam, may I ... listen?'

Lucia smiled. 'Of course.'

I sat down on the nearby bench, though somewhat
thoughtfully.

She, as one who was constantly ministering to
others of her family, had little time to feed herself, and
had set a half-eaten apple down beside on the side of
the instrument. She hesitated again before striking the
keys. To encourage her, I said, 'If food be the music of
love, play on.' No, that didn't seem quite right, either.

Lucia smiled at me. She paused, a little self-con-
sciously, in front of the keys, then began to play. At
first her notes seemed to falter. She halted, turned to
look at me. I nodded and smiled further encouragement. She returned to the keyboard, composed herself,
inclined her head once in rhythm, and commenced
again.

Now she seemed to pick the theme. Her fingers

started to skip, she began to play with lightness and elegance. I watched her fingers nimbly moving over the keys.

In my room that night, I wrote:

How oft when thou, my music, music play'st,
Upon that blessed wood whose motion sounds
With thy sweet fingers, when thou gently sway'st
The wiry concord that mine ear confounds,
Do I envy those jacks that nimble leap
To kiss the tender inward of thy hand,
  Whilst my poor lips, which should that harvest reap,
  At the wood's boldness by thee blushing stand!

In my Lord Southampton's rooms that evening, my host sat in his chair by a great fire, reading aloud, taking up the theme:

To be so tickl'd, they would change their state
And situation with those dancing chips,
O'er whom thy fingers walk with gentle gait,
Making dead wood more bless'd than living lips.
Since saucy jacks so happy are in this,
Give them thy fingers, me thy lips to kiss.

My lord paused for a moment, then raised his attention from the page. "'*Since saucy jacks ...* " John Florio, her husband, my tutor, is a "jack", is he not? And if he is happy with her fingers, why, you may be happy with her lips.' He smiled at his analysis. 'A most rich and lewd conceit.'

But now, as other matters impressed, his expression sobered and then seemed to darken. He rose from his chair and paced up and down, saying, after several moments, 'I also have something for you to read.'

He walked over to a pile of documents upon his writing desk, picked up one, raised it, identified it with a brief examination, and handed it to me, accompanied by the words, 'Consider it carefully.'

For several moments I studied the stern and dominating hand – the hand of a scholar – disciplined, upright, rigorous. It was written with a brisk economy in which I recognised the authentic style of Master Florio.

My lord, meanwhile, continued to pace and discourse. 'I told you that damned spy was writing his reports of me. I became intrigued to find out how he magicked his messages to his master. Several days ago, I observed him ride out from this house, as though taking the air. I registered carefully the direction in which he departed and, after a suitable interval, rode after him. He crossed the stream and entered the woods, then proceeded perhaps a furlong into their fastness. Out of caution, I dismounted and walked my horse. In a clearing I observed him meet three other horsemen, and pass what seemed a document to them. While they talked amongst themselves, I retreated into hiding. When the three horseman had conducted their business with Master Florio, they returned by the way they had come. I took another path, which I calculated would take me to a place ahead of them on their journey. And there I waited for them.'

As he talked, I envisaged the scene.

Chapter 18

MY LORD SAT ON HIS HORSE, in the little valley, his chosen defile, facing down the empty track, steep slopes on either side. Ahead of him, hidden by a tongue of woodland, a horse neighed. Then three riders turned the corner. They were covered in dark cloaks and hoods.

The waiting youth, controlling his restless stallion, considered them as they rode towards him. There was something calm and forbidding about him, this warrior's son – not least in the manner his horse quartered back and forth, dominating the pathway – which caused the three horsemen to pause on the path in front of him. There they halted.

It seemed to the solitary rider that the horseman in the middle of the three was the leader of that troupe. Heavy, broad-shouldered, his powerful war-horse took several steps forward, while his companions hung back as though in deference. In an authoritative voice he called out, 'I request that you stand aside, sir.'

The young earl did not move. Instead he said coldly, 'Announce yourself, and name your companions.'

There was a moment's pause between the confronting parties, as though the three horsemen were deciding whether to risk riding past their questioner. Then their leader sang out again, deep and cold, 'We are Lord Burghley's men, on the business of the Privy Council.'

'Show your livery,' demanded our solitary rider.

'Who asks?' demanded their leader.

'Henry Wriothesley, Earl of Southampton.'

The three horsemen whispered a few words among themselves. Then something else passed between them, something lighter, a note of sly mirth. It seemed that the single rider was transformed from a warrior into a nubile youth, swimming in a lake. One of the three horsemen was heard to say, 'Ask him to quote you a pretty verse.' Another said, 'Perhaps he will swim naked for us.' More laughter passed between them, moving backwards and forwards like a ripple of water, while the single rider watched them dispassionately.

Then the leader, asserting his status once again, unfastened his riding cloak, showing Lord Burghley's vertical green and black striped livery. Observing this, Southampton said, 'I must warn you that you trespass my estates.'

'This is a lawful common path.'

'That may be so. But you have upon your persons a document which is rightfully mine. And therefore – one such thing following another – I must proclaim you common thieves.'

There was another ripple of laughter between the three. At the same time, perhaps because animals have superior senses, a certain restlessness seemed to spread among their horses. Their leader said, 'We have no such document, except what is lawful.'

My lord said casually, as though stating a point of law, 'I have given you my warning.'

There was another brief animation of restless horses. Then the leader of the three said, 'And we have received it.' Placing his hand on his sword-hilt, he said, 'Now stand aside.'

But, despite the proclamation, the young earl stood his ground, observing his opponents calmly, announcing as though across the breakfast table, 'It seems enough has now been said between us, all diplomacy exhausted.'

So saying, he spurred his horse forward. The stallion pranced merrily, dauntless and bold. At first it seemed as if he were going to ride past his opponents and return to his house. But as he drew abreast the left-hand side of the three horsemen, he reached out casually, as though in greeting, or to tap a shoulder, except that his fingers lightly spread around the nearest horseman's chin and neck. At the same time, the young earl's fingers gripped like talons, he spurred his own mount forward, hauling his armed opponent backward off his horse, so that he fell heavily into the dust of the common path.

There followed an *affray*, or what the French sometimes call a *mêlée*, of plunging and screaming horses. The two remaining horsemen were still too close to each other to lay about them with their swords. In the confusion, my Lord Southampton's fist, in its heavy riding glove, struck the side of the face of a second rider, who also tumbled into the dust.

The two remaining riders circled each other, though the earl was without armament. His armed opponent, at last with sufficient space to use his sword arm, swung his weapon backwards, ready to strike, and manoeuvred to come alongside. But if one horseman was ready to strike, the other was armed with cunning. As the swordsman attempted to come within striking distance, so the earl swung his stallion to face the other, always keeping his own body a sword's length from disaster, while the two stallions pranced like rivals in love, baring teeth, angry as their riders. At the same time as the earl held himself distant from sword-strike, he urged his horse forwards, driving the other horse backwards towards a grove of oak trees at the side of the defile.

For a time the two stallions screamed and bit and reared in that small valley, the earl manoeuvring the other horse constantly backwards, deliberately cutting and driving, until the leader's horse struck a tree trunk, crushing the rider's leg, causing him to cry out in anguish, and in turn causing his frightened horse to rear and throw him off.

The horseman regained his feet and backed away, limping, towards a nearby grove of trees. My lord dismounted from his horse and followed him. The leader retreated until his back touched the trunk of one of the trees, as though for security.

There the two faced each other. But if the earl intended to speak, the other man now pre-empted him. 'My Lord Southampton, I give you fair warning that any man who touches a person in the livery of Lord Burghley, strikes at the authority of the Privy Council.'

My lord held out his hand, opened his palm, saying, 'The document.'

At this demand, the jaw of the leader hardened. 'I acknowledge no property of yours.'

My lord reached his hand into the other's clothes, deftly hauling out the sealed document hidden in his livery. He raised the paper to the other's eyes, saying, 'You do not acknowledge this?'

'That letter is sealed and is addressed to my Lord Burghley.'

'Why then, if he spies on me, I shall return the compliment. I hereby confiscate this article.'

White-faced, defiant, the horseman said, 'I will report your action to my master.'

My lord stowed the document in his own clothes. He removed one of his heavy riding gloves. Holding the glove in his right hand, he said, 'What you will report to your master is also this.' Then he struck his opponent so hard across his face with the glove, his head was forced sideways.

Under the sunlight in the clearing, there was an intake of breath as the leader absorbed the full weight of the insult. He was motionless at first, then slowly returned his white face and burning eyes to face his tormentor. Face to face, my lord seized the other's right hand with his left, placed the glove in its palm and said, 'Take this to your master, and speak thus: "If you wish to take issue with me, then do so to my face, and not behind my back, like a common thief."'

The leader could do nothing but observe as his assailant turned and walked back to his horse, mounted, swung his leg astride, and rode away.

Chapter 19

*I*N HIS ROOMS THAT NIGHT, I observed my host walking up and down. Anger made him light. He paused to say, 'I believe Lord Burghley will receive my message before another day is out.'

He interrupted his pacing to turn towards me so that he could judge my response. 'How do you answer?' he said.

'My lord,' I began, unsure how to proceed, 'I do not know the consequences.'

'My dear Master William, I do not pretend to know the consequences either – except this, that I have challenged my great, cold guardian to show his open hand.'

'You think he will answer your challenge?'

'I am certain of it. But he will answer in his own time, and in his own manner. I am no longer a child, to be intimidated. It is time to open my account with my Lord Burghley.' He pointed to the letter in my hand. 'But now, sir, we come to the missive itself, for which I risked my own safety. Perhaps you would be so kind as to remind me of its contents.'

I hesitated. He had begun pacing again. Now he observed my hesitation, stopped and made a brief ironic gesture for me to read out loud. So I cleared my throat and began:

To the Right Honourable William Cecil, Baron of Burghley
My Most Esteemed Lordship –
I write in mixed exasperation and anger to inform you that I can make no further impression upon our youthful charge who, despite my most earnest entreaties that he should conduct himself soberly and chastely, yet ignores my advice and good offices, and continues in his ways. He loses himself in masques and feasts, and carouses to excess. In

addition, he keeps the lowest company, in the form of a certain actor and sometime writer of vulgar plays called William Shakespeare, who in turn fancies himself a poet. I most earnestly believe the said Shakespeare's influence is harmful upon our subject, being full of silly ditties of love, which distract our impressionable youth from his proper actions and considerations. In the course of my own duties as tutor, I have seen certain of these supposed sonnets in my Lord Southampton's chambers, and would have made a copy of some of them to act as evidence for your eyes, except that they are of such airy nonsense that I would not deem them suitable for your most esteemed consideration.

To keep a closer watch on this rhyme-maker, I offer him the use of my small library, so that at least while he pilfers my scholarship for his own purposes, he is not in the company of our young charge. Meanwhile, the account of my generosity is that the aforesaid rhymer plagues me with questions about Florence, and Genoa and Venice, and other such places, which he conceives as the settings of scenes or plays, for he has only the vaguest idea of geography in that region. Why, he thinks Milan a seaport and that Bohemia hath a coast!

I remain convinced that this magpie must be dismissed,

so that our charge may be brought to sobriety, towards
which end I will bend my intentions.

Meanwhile, Your Worshipful Lordship,
I remain, Yr. mst. humble servant,
Johannes Florio, Scholar

I finished reading. My ears burned at the various
charges of being a bumpkin, though in my circumstances I should have become used to the charges by
now. I was shaken out of my reverie, however, by my
patron, who had stopped stalking and was now considering me with a calm but fervent expression.

My lord said, 'A nimble jack indeed, whose hand is
truly turned against his own master.'

I could not find it in myself to disagree. 'It seems he
disappoints your trust.'

'Indeed,' he replied, gazing up at the ceiling,
announcing, in exasperation, and as though to a wider
audience, 'Master Florio disappoints our trust.'

Now he began to pace up and down again, attempting at the same time to withhold his rage. 'By all that reasons, I should dismiss the traitor from my livery.'

While my patron raged and reflected, I thought not so much of Florio himself, but of his wife and young family, turned out of employment and set upon the road. And so it happened that, despite the excess of insults that had been directed at me, I tempered my opinion.

'That would be justified, certainly,' I said. 'But would it be the wisest course?'

'Why would it not?' he asked.

'Is it not better to know the identity of Burghley's man, than not to know?'

'In what manner? His guilt has been established.'

'Knowing his identity, one may use him as a conduit, to convey whatever message one wishes to convey.'

My lord, who had been pacing rhythmically, halted now, though somewhat cautiously and reluctantly. 'Cleverly argued. But then I am baulked of my desire for honest retribution.'

'Revenge may be enjoyed in its own time.'

He observed me for several moments. 'So be it. Then let us turn our attention to other matters which interest us.'

'Which other matters, my lord?'

'Let us consider the subject of your poem.'

'Which subject in particular?'

'Madam Florio, playing upon the virginals.' He turned towards me. 'You find Master Florio's wife to your liking?'

Perhaps, in answering his question as fully as I did, I tried to deflect him from what I suspected he might now intend. I said, 'One of her brothers is the poet, Samuel Daniel. Her father is a music master, as is her other brother. She is now the wife of a great scholar. And she seems to have absorbed the best influences from each, for she writes verse, she plays music, and she has a scholarly application. Yes, she is to my liking.'

To which he replied, 'On all these points I am in agreement. Which, adding each to each, would make her seduction all the sweeter.'

'Seduction?'

'From Latin, *seducio, seducere*. As Master Florio would tell you. To lead to oneself.'

'You would seduce her?'

'Or you would.' He paused. 'One or another way, I will have my revenge on Master Florio.'

My lord returned once more to his angry pacing, locked in his own thoughts, while I observed him, my expression equivocal.

Chapter 20

THAT NIGHT I LAY ON MY BED, staring up at the ceiling, fretting, sleepless by turns, eyelids leaning against the night, my thoughts far distant.

The next morning I stood outside the door of the room which held the virginals, from which sweet music could be heard within.

Pausing there, I listened to the notes, then smoothly pushed my entrance, expecting what I saw, seeing what I expected – Lucia practising on the instrument, her fingers dancing over the jacks.

Becoming aware of me, she turned briefly, regarded

me, smiled trustingly, then pursued the shimmering and rapid movements of her hands.

I stood in the doorway, until she halted her playing and looked up, guileless, at her interloper, who now advanced towards her across the floor. His calculated footsteps, hollowing their tones, echoed his heart. Immodest, shameless, he sat down on the empty bench beside her.

She said, 'You see, sir, how you have encouraged me in my practice.'

'You need no encouragement, madam,' I said. 'If music be the food of love, play on.' The sentence scanned well, and sounded in tune, at least. Even so, my words seemed false.

Meanwhile she would insist, babbling on, sweetly disingenuous, 'I have had several children, and had forgot my musical studies. Now I find myself able to return. You see how it is.'

My expression was sympathetic, but perhaps distracted. So it was she who, noticing some silence at my core, said, 'Sir, it is you who seem preoccupied.'

I could not answer, lost in my own thoughts. It was her innocence that silenced me. When finally I raised my face, I knew I must give her some warning, some alert, and felt compelled to measure out the danger. So I began, 'I am obliged to forewarn you, madam.'

'Warn me?' she asked, curious at first, displaying no immediate alarm.

'Yes,' I confirmed.

'Of what?'

'Of a danger.'

'To whom?'

'To yourself.'

Her eyes opened wider. 'To me?'

'To you.'

'Of violence?'

'No, madam. A suit of passion. Aimed at you.'

'From whom?'

'From me.'

She was silent for several long moments, during which time I returned to my own thoughts.

I expected that she might begin to play. But suddenly, as though by swift election, Lucia was standing, looking down on me, her expression in sweet and deep turmoil. Almost before I knew it she had parted her knees, was seated astride my legs, facing me. She placed her hand round the back of my head, pulled my face to her neck, murmured softly and passionately, 'I knew it, oh, I knew it, from the way that you looked at me, I knew. Oh do not be ashamed, do not be ashamed ... '

I was about to object, but just as I raised my face from the warmth of her neck, she smothered my words with her lips.

My hands, which were about to push her away, stuttered, seemed to hesitate; then, of their own volition, they tightened around her waist and held her. Our embrace was fierce and urgent. She reached down with her hand, raised her dress, freed me from my cloth, positioned herself, rose up and down on me. Carried away, she seemed about to cry out, until my hand closed gently but firmly over her mouth.

I had heard a sound in the passageway outside, distinctive steps. We both turned, frightened as deer, while footsteps in the passage outside approached the door. They seemed to pause outside. After a while they passed.

Lucia let out a gasp, rising from me. She pulled her dress back into decency. I followed suit. Facing one another, both of us poised on the cusp of our passion, it was she who said, 'Do not be ashamed, I beg you.'

'I am sorry, madam, I took advantage of your kindness towards me – '

'No, no, no – ' she said.

But I insisted, 'Return to your playing, I beg you. I should not have compromised you by visiting you alone. I will depart now.'

Yet she seemed determined upon a final throw, 'No, you are wrong, women do not retreat in matters of love. I should have risked ... ' She breathed out, 'I should have risked everything.'

Struggling to control myself, I bowed and left. In the passage outside, I looked up and down, relieved at not being seen. I leaned against the door, breathing deeply for a few moments, before departing. Inside the room, I could envisage how sweet Lucia listened, eyes wide with passion, to my retreating footsteps. I imagined her returning to the virginals. Shy as leaves, I could imagine how her fingers touched the jacks. But she seemed in too much turmoil to play.

Chapter 21

*T*HAT NIGHT I PUT MY FACE IN MY HANDS, in deepest thought and abject misery, recalling the episode in which I had been both actor and merciless observer. It was not the act itself, but my own motives, from which I recoiled most deeply. When I raised my face from my hands, I attempted to compose myself. I sat down at the bench. My board at least was a small consolation. I reached for my quill, dipped it in ink, paused, then began to write. After a time I halted, hesitated, looked at the first and second lines, crossed them out, began again, and so on, half a dozen times, until the black beginning took its shape, and the rest of the piece followed.

The expense of spirit in a waste of shame
Is lust in action; and till action, lust
Is perjur'd, murderous, bloody, full of blame,
Savage, extreme, rude, cruel, not to trust;
Enjoy'd no sooner but despised straight,
Past reason hunted, and no sooner had,
Past reason hated, as a swallow'd bait,
On purpose laid to make the taker mad:
Mad in pursuit, and in possession so;
Had, having, and in quest to have, extreme;
A bliss in proof, – and prov'd, a very woe;
Before, a joy propos'd; behind, a dream.
 And this the world well knows; yet none knows well
 To shun the heaven that leads men to this hell.

When I finished the poem, my vision became progressively darker, until it seemed the final lines blackened into deep night.

Chapter 22

MY LORD AND I were each in chairs seated close to a roaring fire. After his first reading of the verse, he flung down the written page, crying out, 'Damn this. Damn this. I feel I should apologise. Not only to you, but to her.'

I continued to stare into the fire. But he, as though seeking some displacement, agitated beyond measure, seized a strong brass poker and turned the logs energetically.

After a few seconds, I said, 'You are not to blame. It was I who took advantage of her.'

But he, contradicting my equivocation, said, 'No, not so. The blame is mine alone.'

'Even so – ' I began.

'Even so,' he said.

'Even so, my lord, the error being mine, perhaps we should no longer use an innocent woman to serve our purposes against Master Florio.'

He rose from his chair and began to stalk the room. After a while he paused. 'I am properly admonished. Let us, as you suggest, cease this deployment.'

But I said, 'It is not so easy, now.'

'Why not?' he turned, and I saw something there – some continuation of his former ferocity – that frightened me.

Pressing on, I said, 'There is Madam Florio. She is unleashed. She has no fear. She will have her say.'

'Then we are not alone.'

In answer, I merely returned his stare, allowing him to reach his own conclusion. After a brief interval, he shook his head at life's complexity, then continued pacing. After another pause he said, 'Now that we have put this matter aside, I consider also my Lord Burghley.'

'You have received word from him?' I asked.

'No, but I believe he stirs.'

'You have heard a report, perhaps?'

'The Privy Council extends the closure of London theatres for another year.'

'Even though the plague decreases?'

'I sense his cold hand in the decision. He would happily starve them unto death; or, failing that, drive them to destitution.'

'But if he is as cold, as calculating as you say, why would he act so passionately against so small and distant a threat?'

At this, my lord turned away. 'Oh, he is mortally insulted. He will consider where to strike. Perhaps he believes he has found my weakness.'

Turning his own attention once more to the flames, he continued to strike at the logs with the iron.

Chapter 23

I WALKED DOWN THE PASSAGEWAYS OF THE HOUSE,
nodding to passers-by, as if in a dream, when Lucia
turned a corner. She walked towards me, tall, slender,
graceful, her demeanour open. Drawing broadside, she
gave me a searching, powerful glance. I continued
walking, not looking back, not daring to invoke that
haughty strength. I heard nothing but my own deep
breathing, rocked by the naked power of that look, like
a small boat in another's wash. That night at my board
I wrote:

∞

O! call not me to justify the wrong
That thy unkindness lays upon my heart;
Wound me not with thine eye, but with thy tongue:
Use power with power, and slay me not by art.
Tell me thou lovest elsewhere; but in my sight,
Dear heart, forebear to glance thine eye aside:
What need'st thou wound with cunning, when thy might
Is more than my o'erpress'd defence can bide?
Let me excuse thee: ah! my love well knows
Her pretty looks have been mine enemies;
And therefore from my face she turns my foes,
That they elsewhere may dart their injuries:
Yet do not so, but since I am near slain,
Kill me outright with looks, and rid my pain.

Eating a midday meal in the great hall, I gnawed my meat, distracted by half-considered thoughts, dipping my other hand into the great earthen pot. My fingers, industrious, located a large potato which, splitting in two halves with my knife, I ate both swiftly and greedily. So poets wolf their food, unconscious of their feeding. Thus engaged, I glanced absently down the table, until I saw – my fuller sight returning – something that struck me dumb.

My mind, as though distant, observed, ensconced at the other end of the table, the image of beauty incarnate. Lucia herself was not eating, but instead observing her own children, her expression calm and direct. Her husband Florio, that high-minded scholar and hater of poets, was engaged in feeding an infant – seated on his knee, pretty face upraised amongst the brood of four lusty children – with tender ministration. Amongst this family scene she seemed pale, composed, yet not unhappy. She did not look my way.

I wiped my mouth with the back of my hand and rose from my bench. I walked down the length of hall, acknowledged Florio (though he barely acknowledged me) and moved briskly by him. Nothing, not a glance, passed between Lucia and myself. Perhaps she knew I intended then to crush our affair before it started. She, no doubt sensing my hardened will, merely looked away. Outside the dining hall, I drew in deep breath, was about to step forth when I was hailed from behind.

'Master Shakespeare!'

My lord approached me with his hand on the shoulder of another man, whom I recognised immediately.

'Our friend Master Marlowe has deigned to visit us. He takes temporary refuge from London.'

Master Marlowe and I bowed to one another in mock courtly ritual. My patron asked, turning to address me, 'Have you eaten?'

'I have.'

To Marlowe, my lord said, 'He scribbles unceasingly. He bolts his food and retires to his room.'

Marlowe shrugged laconically.

'Come, Master Marlowe, you will sit in his place.'

Marlowe smiled. The two of them entered the dining hall like old friends. But I watched them depart in an agony of apprehension, for there is nothing, perhaps even love, that makes a poet so jealous as another who threatens to cut off the light of his praise and sustenance.

Yet in addressing my rival, it was also something of a relief not to write of my own love, of my fiercest and obsessive passion. Sometimes a simple change of tone breathes light into a writer's circumstances. I could at least approach the task of writing about my fellow poet with a measure of irony.

In my room that night, I worked at my board, addressing my lord once more, scratching busily with my pen, pausing occasionally to read what I had written, then bending to my work again.

O! how I faint when I of you do write,
Knowing a better spirit doth use your name,
And in the praise thereof spends all his might,
To make me tongue-tied, speaking of your fame!
But since your worth – wide as the ocean is, –
The humble as the proudest sail doth bear,
My saucy bark, inferior far to his,
On your broad main doth wilfully appear.
Your shallowest help will hold me up afloat,
Whilst he upon your soundless deep doth ride:
Or, being wrack'd, I am a worthless boat,
He of tall building and of goodly pride.

Then if I thrive and I be cast away,
The worst was this; – my love was my decay.

Several days later, lost in thought, I walked through the garden in the main courtyard and saw my lord emerge from a doorway. He called out, 'My dear William, you have hidden yourself away.'

'You had a famous guest.'

'Master Marlowe? He is long departed. He visited but for a day. Now I wish to speak with you. There is something I should prefer to tell you in confidence. Perhaps you will be kind enough to pay a visit to my rooms this evening.'

I nodded, bowed, and we continued on our ways.

That evening, I did as he commanded, making my way along the paving stones of a passage on which a single rushlight burned. Its guttering light washed the walls. At the prospect of seeing him, I was perhaps a little lighter of heart than had been my usual diet over the last few days. As I approached the door to my lord's chambers, I heard sounds coming from within his room – the most common and yet the most unmistakable sounds. There was a high-pitched call, that might have been woman's voice, and then the deeper groan of a man. Reaching the outside of that familiar door, I was like some vessel that passes along a river bank, about to touch the shore, but not yet touching. I slowed my walk, but did not halt as I passed the door. I even smiled to myself, for it seemed my young master had a female companion.

I am after all a man of the theatre, a somewhat raffish world. And since I am of a liberal disposition, why should I not be broad-minded about mistresses? I continued to walk, to float by on my current, though my ears listened. My momentum took me past the door. By now the sounds had ceased, as if the last seconds had been spent.

Amused at my lord's proclivities, and musing to myself, I was about to turn the corner, and return to my room, when I heard behind me the sound of a door being opened. I ducked into another passage. It was a good hiding place, well away from the flame that supplied the only illumination to that corridor. After a few moments, I put my head around the corner, then pulled back again, as someone from my lord's rooms emerged into the passageway. I heard, from the rising sound of footsteps, that the figure was walking towards me, so I withdrew further into darkness. The footsteps came closer. Like some night-creature, I pulled back yet further into the black.

A feminine shape with a strangely familiar profile passed. At its recognition I felt a terrible sickness come over me. Of those brief moments I remember nothing, except my pain, as I tried to swallow. The jaw hardens, and the mouth dries, though the mind seems oppressed. It was my own Lucia, Madam Florio, who walked past my hiding place – returning, no doubt, to her family. There was something precise and composed about her footsteps, something direct and almost wilful, and a strange intuition struck me then that perhaps it was not she who had been an entirely unwitting victim.

I felt crushed, as though a stone had been placed on

my lungs. Like the animal I had become, I retreated to my room. I opened the door of my own small cell, leaned on the foot of my bed, fumbled with my hand along the shelf on which sat a few implements for eating. In my internal darkness I remember only knocking over several things which clattered to the floor. My searching, insensible fingers found a large wooden eating bowl, whose rim I gripped. I sat on the end of the bed, and was heartily sick into it.

When I finished retching, I put the bowl back on the stand, felt for my candleholder, raised myself, stepped outside the door, advanced to a nearby rush-light, lit my candle, returned to my room. The air inside seemed fetid. Ill with jealousy, I stood and opened a window, gazing out into empty darkness.

Setting the candle down so I could write on the board, I took up the quill, dipped it in ink, and for a while stared at the sheet of paper. I coughed once or twice, considered for a few moments, then began to write, hesitatingly at first:

∞

Be wise as thou art cruel; do not press
My tongue-tied patience with too much disdain;
Lest sorrow lend me words, and words express
The manner of my pity-wanting pain.
If I might teach thee wit, better it were,
Though not to love, yet, love, to tell me so; –
As testy sick men when their deaths be near,
No news but health from their physicians know; –
For, if I should despair, I should grow mad,
And in my madness might speak ill of thee:
Now this ill-wresting world is grown so bad,
Mad slanderers by mad ears believed be.

  That I may be not so, nor thou belied,
  Bear thine eyes straight, though thy proud heart go
    wide.

Chapter 24

IN THE DINING HALL, seated at the great wooden table, I ate slowly and thoughtfully. Sometimes I glanced towards the end of the table. Lucia sat there with her young family, her husband Florio opposite her. She was helping her youngest child with food. Her other children played about her.

I turned back to my eating, staring ahead, then glanced back down the table again. Florio, no doubt wishing to return to his studies, was rising from the bench, leaning over to kiss his wife, patting one of the children on the head.

I returned to my eating. After a little while, I looked down the table once more. Florio had gone. Lucia was seated amongst her children. Now she answered my look with a direct stare. Deliberately, after holding my eyes, she moved her gaze towards a window that overlooked the garden outside. Even though I did not understand her full meaning, I gave a single nod, took in a deep breath, returned to my eating.

Outside, in the open air, I looked round at the empty gardens, glancing down one bare wall, then another. My attention halted and fixed on a point some fifty paces away where I could see the opening of an alcove, whose interior could not be seen from where I stood. I made my way towards it, glancing about me at the vacant spaces, before turning into the arbour.

Lucia rose from her seat. Before I could speak, she said, 'I know that it was you who saw me departing from my Lord Southampton's rooms.'

I felt an urge to draw back my hand to strike her, or perhaps to strike at my own fierce jealousy. But she pre-empted me, saying, 'Is that what I must do, sir, to gain your attention?'

Her expression was unflinching and defiant. I felt

the agony return. 'What would you have me do?' I asked.

Fiercely she answered, 'Meet me.'

'Where?'

She swept her arm around, towards the surrounding country. 'Spring has come. The trees are full of leaves.'

'Nature will hide our shame?'

'I have no shame,' she replied.

'And what of my Lord Southampton?'

'That is my own affair.'

I might have remonstrated with her, but she was implacable. Instead I indicated with a gesture the shallow hillside. 'Behind that hill is a woodland, and in that wood is a glade surrounded by several dense thickets. I sometimes walk there in the afternoon. It helps my composition.'

She looked up towards the hill. 'I will find an excuse to leave my duties. And I will find you, if you are to be found.'

I turned back to her. 'Now we must go. This place is more dangerous for you even than for me.'

But she seemed unafraid. 'Go first,' she said calmly, 'and I will follow when you are gone.'

That night I lay on my bed, the flame of the candle beside me. My mind was filled with the images of my love, and the peculiar circumstances by which, having attempted to prevent her husband from being dismissed, I was now the victim of my own charity. Meanwhile, I had struggled to express my own feelings through the only means that seemed open to the expression of my thoughts. I had begun the poem in fierce anger and exasperation at my plight, but what emerged in the course of a night of labour was more like pleading. Beside me, on the board, another page had been filled with verse.

Lo, as a careful housewife runs to catch
One of her feather'd creatures broke away,
Sets down her babe, and makes all swift dispatch
In pursuit of the thing she would have stay;
While her neglected child holds her in chase,
Cries to catch her whose busy care is bent

To follow that which flies before her face,
Nor prizing her poor infant's discontent:
So runn'st thou after that which flies from thee,
Whilst I thy babe chase thee afar behind;
But if thou catch thy hope, turn back to me,
And play the mother's part, kiss me, be kind.
  So will I pray that thou mayst have thy Will,
  If thou turn back and my loud crying still.

I turned on my side and blew out the candle. In the dark I heard, as though beside me, the sounds of a woman crying out in pleasure. In my mind's eye, in that shadowy limit between sleeping and waking, Lucia and I rolled in the undergrowth, turning over and over languorously. It seemed to me that much of that spring and early summer passed like that dream, half way between darkness and light, one foot in heaven and another in hell. And so for several months I cuckolded Florio while my lord, in a manner of speaking, cuckolded me.

Chapter 25

I NOW HAD TWO RIVALS FOR MY MISTRESS – her own husband and my lord. Yet I continued to visit Master Florio's rooms in pursuit of his stored volumes on Italy, whose city states seemed increasingly appropriate as settings for my plays – despite his jibes about my ignorance. His own work, in the form of manuscripts, lay about the place, and since he gave me access to his scholarship – if only on the grounds that when I was in his rooms I would not be diverting my lord with my wasteful sonnets – I also perused his finished manuscripts for scholarship or learning of which I could make use. I noticed that in one of his own works John Florio had written that his ideal of feminine beauty was dark: dark hair, dark eyebrows, dark eyes. His own wife epitomised those views. Lucia was dark in those ways that he described, and since I felt a touch of spite or irony towards one who was so dismissive of poets, I used the theme as a constant to describe my beloved in the sonnets I was writing so fervently in the quiet secrecy of my room:

In the old age black was not counted fair,
Or if it were, it bore not beauty's name;
But now is black beauty's successive heir,
And beauty slander'd with a bastard shame:
For since each hand hath put on Nature's power,
Fairing the foul with Art's false borrow'd face,
Sweet beauty hath no name, no holy bower,
But is profan'd, if not lives in disgrace.
Therefore my mistress' brows are raven black,
Her eyes so suited, and they mourners seem

At such who, not born fair, no beauty lack,
Sland'ring creation with a false esteem:
   Yet so they mourn, becoming of their woe,
   That every tongue says beauty should look so.

The tensions of living in that house, and pursuing my dark love, released a flood of composition and work in me. Writing about my beloved seemed to me a counterpoint to writing of my patron. In my lord's case, the agreement between us was that I would create a set of flowering praises based upon chaste love, according to the traditions of the sonnet. But this convention of continuous praise also acted as a kind of constraint on my writing. In composing upon my mistress I could do almost the opposite. I could list her attributes – even those which were not beautiful – with a realistic, fervent relish. The elegant inversion was that however beautiful my lord might be, I had no physical passion for him. However unremarkable my dark lady might be, my feelings towards her were suffused with fiercest and most holy desire. And what was stranger, perhaps, was that I could be certain that that most high and intelligent being, my patron, would approve of my disquisitions upon her charms.

My mistress' eyes are nothing like the sun;
Coral is far more red than her lips' red:
If snow be white, why then her breasts are dun;
If hairs be wires, black wires grow on her head.
I have seen roses damask'd, red and white,
But no such roses see I in her cheeks;
And in some perfumes is there more delight
Than in the breath that from my mistress reeks.
I love to hear her speak, yet well I know
That music hath a far more pleasing sound:
I grant I never saw a goddess go; –
My mistress, when she walks, treads on the ground:
*   And yet, by heaven, I think my love as rare*
*   As any she belied with false compare.*

However much I might attempt to separate my patron and my beloved in my mind, I could not help myself complaining of the affair between them. So my verse continued to pour out from me, taking this or that attitude, exploring this or that conceit. Beneath all my imagery lay a continuous excitation and pain. We each of us lived under the same roof, after all, and whereas both her husband and my lord could consort with my love in that household – the first by right as a husband and the second as *seigneur* in the privacy of his own apartments – I myself was forced to live on the periphery, like a scavenger or crow, pleading for assignations in the furthest gardens or nearest woodlands, which were difficult to achieve. For though my mistress could be seen openly carrying messages or documents between Master Florio and his young charge, she could not be seen to visit my own rooms. Addressing my lord, and the circumstances of our mutual love, at certain times I gritted my teeth and tried to make the best of it, attempting to place his own coupling with my beloved in a more detached frame.

Take all my loves, my love, yea, take them all;
What has thou then more than thou hadst before?
No love, my love, that thou mayst true love call;
All mine, was thine before thou hadst this more.
Then, if for my love thou my love receivest,
I cannot blame thee for my love thou usest;
But yet be blam'd, if thou thyself deceivest
By wilful taste of what thyself refusest.
I do forgive thy robbery, gentle thief,
Although thou steal thee all my poverty;
And yet, love knows it is a greater grief
To bear love's wrong than hate's known injury.
   Lascivious grace, in whom all ill well shows,
   Kill me with spites; yet we must not be foes.

Every hour of every day I struggled to keep a sense of perspective, and tried not to hate my patron. For even while he extended like an angel the hand of protection over me, gave me food and warmth and enough payment for my efforts to at least send to my own family in Stratford, yet the fact of his commingling with my beloved burned into my soul. I could not prevent my own bitterness from entering my verse, and addressing my mistress in wounded terms:

So, now I have confess'd that he is thine,
And I myself am mortgag'd to thy will,
Myself I'll forfeit, so that other mine
Thou wilt restore, to be my comfort still:
But thou wilt not, nor he will not be free,
For thou art covetous, and he is kind;
He learn'd but surety-like to write for me,
Under that bond that him as fast does bind.
The statue of thy beauty thou wilt take,
Thou usurer, that putt'st forth all to use,
And sue a friend came debtor for thy sake;
So him I lose through my unkind abuse.
　　Him have I lost; thou has both him and me:
　　He pays the whole, and yet I am not free.

And so the dance proceeded. Despite the double pain of knowledge and acquiescence, my mind continued obsessively to churn the theme, searching for different perspectives. Because my love for her was fierce and overwhelming, she was the one I could not forgive, and the one about whom my writing was harshest and most brutal. In my lord's case, it seemed to me that when one as fair and attractive as he was wooed or pursued by one as formidably alluring as my mistress, he was bound to succumb. So, while my hurting heart turned like an animal in its cage, my mind constructed further sonnets of praise to my patron:

Those petty wrongs that liberty commits,
When I am sometimes absent from thy heart,
Thy beauty and thy years full well befits,
For still temptation follows where thou art.
Gentle thou art, and therefore to be won,
Beauteous thou art, therefore to be assail'd;
And when a woman woos, what woman's son
Will sourly leave her till she have prevail'd?

190

Ay me! but yet thou mightst my seat forbear,
And chide thy beauty and thy straying youth,
Who lead thee in their riot even there
Where thou art forc'd to break a twofold truth,—
  Hers, by thy beauty tempting her to thee,
  Thine, by thy beauty being false to me.

Chapter 26

THROUGH THAT YEAR and into the winter, my mind continued to turn in its agony, even searching for hidden compensations in my circumstances:

That thou hast her, it is not all my grief,
And yet it may be said I lov'd her dearly;
That she hath thee, is of my wailing chief,
A loss in love that touches me more nearly.
Loving offenders, thus I will excuse ye:
Thou dost love her, because thou know'st I love her;

And for my sake even so doth she abuse me,
Suffering my friend for my sake to approve her.
If I lose thee, my loss is my love's gain,
And losing her, my friend has found that loss;
Both find each other, and I lose both twain,
And both for my sake lay on me this cross:
    But here's the joy; my friend and I are one;
    Sweet flattery! then she loves but me alone.

There were other aspects of my circumstances that fretted at me, and to which I gave certain licence. I was entering my thirtieth year, and my patron and rival in love was not yet twenty. I could not help but compare our respective ages.

When my love swears that she is made of truth,
I do believe her, though I know she lies,
That she might think me some untutor'd youth,
Unlearned in the world's false subtleties.

Thus vainly thinking that she thinks me young,
Although she knows my days are past the best,
Simply I credit her false-speaking tongue:
On both sides thus is simple truth supprest.
But wherefore says she not she is unjust?
And wherefore say not I that I am old?
O! love's best habit is in seeming trust,
And age in love loves not to have years told:
　Therefore I lie with her and she with me,
　And in our faults by lies we flatter'd be.

However much I tried to balance the competing claims of the players in our drama, sometimes the strains were too much to bear, and I released my emotions in a stream of vitriol. In our common slang 'hell' was a synonym for the female sexual parts. In that respect I visited my own favourite hell as much as I could, and with an enthusiasm that over-rode all other considerations.

Two loves I have of comfort and despair,
Which like two spirits do suggest me still:
The better angel is a man right fair,
The worser spirit a woman, colour'd ill.
To win me soon to hell, my female evil
Tempteth my better angel from my side,
And would corrupt my saint to be a devil,
Wooing his purity with her foul pride.
And whether that my angel be turn'd fiend
Suspect I may, but not directly tell;
But being both from me, both to each friend,
I guess one angel in another's hell:
    Yet this shall I ne'er know, but live in doubt,
    Till my bad angel fire my good one out.

My lord had once said of me that I see clear and burn hot. Yet my mistress had dragged me out of my vaunted detachment, hauled me to my own hell. Sometimes, in moments of repose, my equilibrium would return. In order to assuage some sense of spirit, during her absence I began yet another sonnet.

196

For several days I had been tempted to write about the cost to the spirit of living so recklessly in the physical world, arguing that the very act of love and courtship was a poor return for the soul's investment. The body itself would soon grow old and be eaten by worms. By turning away from that vain world, could not one buy better terms than to lose oneself entirely in the infernal delights of passion? Could not one feed oneself internally by contemplation, study, writing – perhaps by constructing some immemorial lines on the fallibility of all things physical?

Poor soul, the centre of my sinful earth,
Fool'd by these rebel powers that thee array,
Why dost thou pine within and suffer dearth,
Painting thy outward walls so costly gay?
Why so large cost, having so short a lease,
Dost thou upon thy fading mansion spend?
Shall worms, inheritors of this excess,
Eat up thy charge? Is this thy body's end?
Then, soul, live thou upon thy servant's loss,

And let that pine to aggravate thy store;
Buy terms divine in selling hours of dross;
Within be fed, without be rich no more:
  So shalt thou feed on Death, that feeds on men,
  And Death once dead, there's no more dying then.

It is one thing to write sonnets advocating ascetism and the inner life, another to live out that life with dedication. Soon I was drawn once more into that self-absorbed cycle of passion and repletion. Every thought has its counter-thought, and the vehemence of my mind was such that every counter-thought could be explored with equal ferocity and rigour. My prick, that dumb lover, too often led my spirit:

Love is too young to know what conscience is;
Yet who knows not conscience is born of love?
Then, gentle cheater, urge not my amiss,
Lest guilty of my faults thy sweet self prove:

For, thou betraying me, I do betray
My nobler part to my gross body's treason;
My soul doth tell my body that he may
Triumph in love; flesh stays no further reason;
But, rising at thy name, doth point out thee
As his triumphant prize. Proud of this pride,
He is contented thy poor drudge to be,
To stand in thy affairs, fall by thy side.
   No want of conscience hold it that I call
   Her 'love' for whose dear love I rise and fall.

It did not matter to me that we were both married, had good and faithful spouses, that I had three children by mine and she four by hers, the fact was that we broke our bed-vows constantly.

In loving thee thou know'st I am forsworn,
But thou art twice forsworn, to me love swearing;
In act thy bed-vow broke, and new faith torn

In vowing new hate after new love bearing.
But why of two oaths' breach do I accuse thee,
When I break twenty? I am perjur'd most;
For all my vows are oaths but to misuse thee,
All my honest faith in thee is lost:
For I have sworn deep oaths of thy deep kindness,
Oaths of thy love, thy truth, thy constancy;
And, to enlighten thee, gave eyes to blindness,
Or made them swear against the thing they see;
   For I have sworn thee fair; more perjur'd I,
   To swear against the truth so foul a lie!

Chapter 27

IT HAPPENED THAT MY LORD and I would ride out for exercise on most days, especially if a winter sun showed through. If I feared for his safety against the greater forces in the land, it also sometimes seemed to me that his precocious and scholarly mind moved ahead of my own. One day, while we rode together, he said, 'I sometimes am tempted to believe that life is nothing more than a comedy, a comedy of errors.'

'In what manner?' I asked.

'I think of my Lord Burghley, of his effect upon me. What if another guardian had been appointed after my father's death? I would not have been engaged by arrangement to Elizabeth de Vere, and the great fine that threatens me would now not overhang me. I would not have a tutor by the name of John Florio, or his wife living within my house. And I would not be engaged with his wife upon matters which set me at odds with a certain suitor of hers called Master Shake-speare, for whom I am happy to act as patron.'

We now seldom mentioned directly the subject of our mutual mistress. In truth I did not mind this much. In our silence was complicity, and perhaps a certain respect for the rights of the other. Besides which, he read my sonnets, continued to praise them avidly for their force and cogency, and through them at least knew enough of the turmoil of my mind.

Tentatively I asked, 'Of what aspect in particular do you think?'

I expected him to raise the matter of Florio, and perhaps of Florio's wife, but instead he answered, 'I think of the manner in which my Lord Burghley, having received my insult to his supervision of me, has not yet seen fit to respond. I think of his patience, while he waits his opportunity, and how each day he increases his threat by the act of withholding.'

'You do not think perhaps that we are subject to a false alarm?' I asked.

He smiled on me, kindly, but a little pityingly, as though perhaps I did not understand matters of honour between noblemen. 'You think that this is much ado about nothing, do you, Master Shakespeare?'

'You know the mind of my Lord Burghley better than I,' I conceded.

He smiled again, but said nothing, and so we continued on our journey in silence.

In winter the fires warmed the halls of that former monastery. We, its denizens, were often out upon our errands and obligations. Sometimes the freezing sea winds would cross the lea, cutting through clothes, touching the bone, chilling the fastnesses of garden. There we reclined, in fitful sunshine. So, exposed to fate, we found ourselves arrested in false calm, throwing no shadows, but filling the shallow industry of days. I myself, no less active by night than day, limned my private hours with furtive labour. So time passed, ending in exhausted sleep.

But just as storm clouds rising in the west appeared from nothing, a single speck or spark in the horizon's blue, so Lord Burghley's threat and presence lay across that house, bringing winter's cold to winter's fitful sunlight. The seasons changed in slow course. In spring, the white flowers we called snowdrops rose from the fields as pale as ghosts. We lived in a dilapidated sun, which brought us light, but kept us from the warmth.

I continued to work upon my plays, hoping for that time when the threat of plague would be lifted from the theatres, and I could earn my living once more from entertaining the restless London crowds. If nothing else, the forced interval allowed me to review my own past work, to consider my own salient weaknesses and occasional strengths.

As I laboured on new schemes and plays, it seemed to me that if there was an emptiness in my own drama, it lay with schemers, machiavels, and birds of ill passage. Their drive towards evil I failed to understand.

My answer was to clothe them in darkness, in grand mystery, removing their motive, and by so doing magnify their intent. By dissolving their motive, I both solved and resolved their ambition.

If I am a countryman, lover of earth and women, respecter of the seasons, sceptical of religion and all abstractions, my lack of a grand design means that I cannot help but offer sympathy to every character. In my own mind each living thing that moves upon the world strives to perfect itself. If I make a common thief he shall be the finest thief that I can imagine – the most wicked and full of pathos. Thus my emerging characters, conforming to no special design, and almost by the accident of my own lack of a philosophy, seem to stand out from their surrounds, becoming the agents of nothing but themselves.

My great peer and rival, Marlowe, by contrast, gave his darkness motive. Faustus sold his soul for worldly goods, Tamburlaine for an earthly crown. Darkness was a poetic sublime, always present; darkness as deft line on hourglass day, darkness as faint image in stained glass, darkness as incarmined rose. Darkness was close with him, was in certain respects his familiar. In other aspects I could match him, perhaps even overcome him – in subtlety rather than strength, in the complexity of an individual's inner life, in the myriad motives within that individual's deepest self. But I would never match the almost voluptuous movement of his soul towards ultimate perdition. And perhaps that was why I would never write a play to match the hell-conjuring *Faustus*, that great and wilful supplicant of eternal damnation.

It seemed to me – who did not know Marlowe well – that he was drawn towards darkness as others were drawn towards light. He was the great Lucifer of our drama – atheist, philosopher, diplomat, spy, lover of men, goad of authority, implacable in his confidence and arrogance. Beneath my own amiable rivalry and admiration was a deeper fear: that he could entrance the mind of my patron, encourage him to stare over the precipice, entice him not so much to hell as to a romantic self-destruction. So I watched nervously as the great poet visited my lord's house occasionally through the seasons, conferred at length with my patron, and mysteriously came and went.

Winter mists moved across the land and, pale as ghosts, were blown across winter fields. By simple fervour of mind, it sometimes seemed to me, I held the world at bay. My own thoughts were delicate deer on mind's horizon. I used to live with an ear to the line of communal earth, surviving like a ghost myself, outside London, writing my work in the recesses of a great house, absorbing information where I could about the political movements of the day, hoping one day to return to the stage.

Chapter 28

WHILE WINTER HAD LASTED, it at least had held one advantage. The removal of foliage from the trees meant that one could survey the land more easily. It became correspondingly more difficult for horsemen or watchers to hide in our proximity. When I travelled with my lord to his early morning swims at the lake, I could look about the land, knowing that no horsemen were concealed in the neighbouring bare woods.

Yet when spring returned, and foliage appeared once more on the trees, I again became nervous. Even when golden sunshine dappled the earth, and the birds began to sing, I surveyed the surrounding country, the rolling hills, the verdant woods, searching for any sign of the horsemen who had haunted us the previous year. For the time being I could see nothing, only our companionable shadows. Our horses trotted, neighbourly and calm, side by side along the beaten track. Light fell in palpable, bright sentences through the early foliage of trees.

My apprehension remained with me. Yet it was only when I was riding on my own that I became most fully aware of the danger. On one occasion my lord was away for several days in London attending to his duties at court; and so, after a night of working at my board, followed by brief, fitful sleep, the following morning I saddled and rode out into the countryside alone.

Several furlongs from the house, I turned around a corner of hillside, and observed unexpectedly three bulking shadows beside a small stream, three horses drinking shadow. In that clearing the horsemen who sat on their animals' backs were armed as if for war, with chain mail and with long swords sheathed in scabbards. They were in restful state, turning to observe my approach while their horses drank and they talked casually amongst themselves. But unlike my Lord

Southampton, who might have challenged them, interrogating their presence in his woods, I shrank back from the sight of them, not wishing even to draw close. Instead I swung my horse as deftly as I could down another path, which, to my good fortune, led along a gully and so removed me from their immediate sight. Nervously, I strained to hear whether, curious at my sudden diversion, they would follow me. Perhaps they suspected I was the indigent poet and playwright who accompanied the young earl and who – according to Master Florio – led him astray. On my own, without my lord's protection, I was someone they could kill easily, as easily as snapping the spine of some small bird or animal. There would have been no evidence either, just a dead man lying in the forest leaf-litter and a nervous horse cropping the grass nearby. Perhaps my playwright's mind was too filled with the images of murder.

Carefully, while following the path along that gully, I swung my horse onto the mossy verge, where its hooves would make less sound than on the stony path. It seemed to my alarmed mind that those three horsemen were less likely to hear me break into a canter, then a gallop, as I rode fast through the woodland towards the protection of the great house. Only when I came within sight of its chimneys, and could be viewed from its windows, did I consider myself safe, at least on that day. A part of me was still fearful, was listening to the sound of hoofbeats behind me. But no sound came. I slowed my horse to a trot, and then to a walk, as my swiftly pounding heart subsided.

Chapter 29

DESPITE THE THREAT FROM HORSEMEN, it was still my custom, waiting for my love, to seat myself on a rudimentary bench in a certain clearing in the woods a mile or so distant from the house. One day, positioned there, I was lost in contemplation. A breeze moved the grass and the leaves on the trees. Glancing up, I caught sight of a figure approaching along the path, in a hood and dark cloak. When the figure drew closer I saw that it was Lucia, now standing tall and slender in front of me, the hood still covering most of her face.

I stood up and faced her. Tenderly I drew back the hood, drawing in my breath sharply. The side of her face was a dark, heavy bruise. I shuddered with horror, but Lucia looked with fierce calm into my eyes.

'It is my husband. He has found me out.'

'My sweet – ' I began, but she interceded.

'I need no sympathy. It is less than I expected. In his own country there is a law that a man may kill his wife out of passion if she is faithless.'

'He has spied on us?' I asked.

'No,' – still with that peculiar, settled calm, as though speaking of the weather – 'not on us. On my Lord Southampton.'

My turmoil took a different shape.

'You should beware,' I said. 'Your husband has the ferocity and discipline of a scholar.'

'Oh, he is rigorous,' she said. 'Yet he will not harm me any further in my lord's household. It would shame his master.'

But I persisted, 'What would happen if he should discover us?'

She replied, with apparent unconcern, 'He would have killed me for certain. Not only for my unfaithfulness, but because he despises poets above everything.'

Despite our circumstances, I could not help but smile. At the same I time felt obliged to mitigate my mirth. 'Forgive me, my sweet. This is no time for levity at our predicament.'

But she was smiling too, rare and beautiful. 'Oh, it is the very time for mirth. To him, the work of poets is nothing but a useless absurdity. He says of your poems that they are the "lost labours" of love. I believe he has used precisely this phrase to my Lord Southampton in admonishing him for wasting his time on such things.'

'The lost labours of love,' I repeated. 'He hath the tongue of a poet himself.' Some of my mirth left me. 'He is certain of matters ... between you and my lord?'

She swallowed and nodded.

I stroked her hair, and said tenderly, 'Then I can risk your life no longer.'

She stared back at me. 'I do not regret one moment, my one and only love.'

I returned her tender stare. 'And what of his lordship?'

'I will continue. It is now the only thing which keeps my husband in employment.'

I marvelled again at her perspicacity. 'If your husband were dismissed, my Lord Burghley would surely employ him.'

'No. His use to my Lord Burghley is as a spy. Without that he would lack all utility.'

'But his scholarship – '

'My Lord Burghley makes a distinction between a scholar and a poet, it is true. But he finds no other use for scholars than to pursue his ends.'

'Yet you protect your husband, even though – ' I could not help but look at the brutal bruises on her face.

'He is a good father. He needs me for the children.'

'That will be your life?'

'Now that our love is over, I will protect my family as I know best.'

Bereft of words, I put my arms around her, and held her close to me, crushed my face to her neck, felt the agony overcome me.

Chapter 30

THE LIFE OF A POET IS STRANGE; haunted by fear, ransacked by loathing at the workings of this false world, yet also sometimes steeped in admiration for those who are able to walk its crooked paths without being corrupted. While I burned with jealousy at my love's continuation with my Lord Southampton, at the same time I perceived something admirable in her steadfastness to both him and me, which did not cause me to lose my desire, but if anything increased it. I worked at my table, writing a line of verse, pausing, writing another.

Thine eyes I love, and they, as pitying me,
Knowing thy heart torments me with disdain,
Have put on black and loving mourners be,
Looking with pretty ruth upon my pain.
And truly not the morning sun of heaven
Better becomes the grey cheeks of the east,
Nor that full star that ushers in the even,
Doth half that glory to the sober west,
As those two mourning eyes become thy face:
O! let it then as well beseem thy heart
To mourn for me, since mourning doth thee grace,
And suit thy pity like in every part.
   Then will I swear beauty herself is black,
   And all they foul that thy complexion lack.

Chapter 31

I CONTINUED TO FREQUENT THOSE WOODS and glades where we had made love, haunted them like a spectre. Above me the raucous crows cawed. One day, staring at the ground in deepest thought, in the distance I heard the faint neighing of a horse, the jingle of a bridle, then sounds of footsteps, feet sloughing in leaf-litter. In my reverie I heard, closer now, yet still as though in some distant part of me, a hoof stamp as a waiting horse fed on grass. I was too preoccupied to notice, until a gloved rider's hand was laid firmly on my shoulder.

I looked up to face my lord, looking down on me.

'Master William,' he said. 'Thou should not be too morbid.'

He looked around at the landscape, at the crows, maddened in the treetops. 'I have seen you sitting here on several occasions now. It suits your mood?'

I shrugged, but did not answer.

My lord pointed behind him to where two horses stood, patiently grazing. 'I thought perhaps I might find you here. I have brought a spare mount, so that I may invite you to ride with me.'

'Ride?'

'Let us go to the coast. It is only a mile or two, and we will be alone. I want to speak with you on an important matter, away from this place and its damned conspiracies.' He gestured with his arm to indicate the direction of the house and its grounds.

So it was that, despite my reluctance to leave my accustomed post, I agreed to accompany him. We both mounted our horses, turned away and rode, through wood and meadow, until we reached the coast of the Solent. There we paused, and looked out upon the green sea, towards the louring island, where the gulls spun in the sun and wind like flakes of gold.

My lord dismounted at a small wood on the edge of the water. I followed suit. We tethered our horses to the stunted oak trees along the edge of that wind-shriven shore, and together we walked towards the small beach where the breeze sang over the sand. There we stood looking out over the sea.

My lord said, 'I like to see the breeze upon the Solent, the boats moving under sail, and behind them the sun falling about the hills of the Isle of Wight. When I was a child, I would imagine the island was some foreign country.'

Several large stones or boulders stood nearby. My lord sat down on one of them. He seemed curiously weary at first, not inclined to speak. Then he said, 'As you know, I have been to London in the last few days, to attend to my duties as a peer. Our capital is aflame with reports and rumours. The Privy Council, under my Lord Burghley, has issued a warrant for the arrest of Christopher Marlowe and Thomas Kyd, on charges of atheism and heresy.'

At first I was struck silent by the news. These were my brothers in the scribbling arts, my most admired peers. I recall stammering, 'Why? Our two greatest dramatists – '

My lord interrupted me, speaking in cold, clipped

sentences which perhaps hid his own anguish. 'Marlowe has protectors and is on bail, but Kyd is arrested. They say that Kyd has already been racked, and that Marlowe will soon follow.'

Horror touched my insides. I said, 'Kyd is made of sweetness. He is called "sporting Kyd". He would not willingly offend against anyone.'

'Broken-backed, on his bed, crying his confession.'

I put my head in my hands. My lord said, 'Marlowe is made of harsher stuff. They say he defies the Privy Council to arrest him, that as a spy for the Walsinghams he yet knows about certain things which under torture he would reveal. There are matters which would perhaps bring down some of the great with him, including perhaps the younger Walsingham, who inherits the mantle of the old spymaster.'

A sudden anger gripped me. 'Who drives this?' I asked. 'Who is so motivated to destroy a few harmless songbirds – ?'

'My Lord Burghley,' he interrupted me. 'Our great, puritan Lord Burghley, chief minister in the Privy Council, who, if he could, would abolish all the arts, save the art of conspiracy. My Lord Burghley, to whom my tutor Master Florio is in thrall, sends out his cold message to me, his ward, to mend my ways and to desist from the company of poets.'

The pattern of it became clearer. In my confusion I enquired of my youthful master, as though he might hold the answer to these unfolding events, 'And what will you do now?'

To my surprise he smiled at me, a strange soft smile, as though he foresaw his own destiny.

'I am the third Earl of Southampton. My grandfather, the first Earl, was a greater statesman than Burghley. You think I shall be intimidated?'

'Even so, my Lord, would you not do well to proceed cautiously.'

'In what manner?' he asked.

'Perhaps,' I suggested tentatively, 'it would be better if I should leave your house.'

'Only the fearful proceed cautiously,' he replied. 'As for your proposal, sir, I have this to say: do what you do best, Master Shakespeare. Continue to sing like a bird. And allow me the task of responding to my Lord Burghley, one thing for another, measure for measure.'

What he said had been asserted with peculiar confidence. And not for the first time on that strange and melancholy day, I perceived perhaps that the youth was changing into the man.

I persisted as best I could in my concern. 'Is Marlowe entirely beyond our help? What I mean, my lord, is that I would leave your house if you felt you could offer him protection in my stead.'

He stood up and faced out to sea. But he seemed distracted. I said, 'Marlowe needs your protection more than I do.'

'You have spoken well,' he replied at last. 'But I doubt if he would accept my offer. Besides, now that Kyd and Marlowe are both disarmed, I believe I have a duty to protect you.'

Something in his answer caused me to pause. 'Marlowe is gone, too?'

'I believe it in my bones.' He still stared out to sea.

For myself I could not help a touch of irony at his certainty, 'You foresee the future, perhaps?'

If he noticed my sarcasm, he ignored it. Instead he said, 'It is dangerous, dangerous beyond the point of recklessness, for Master Marlowe to threaten to expose his master Walsingham if he himself should be tortured.'

'Why? What alternative has he?'

He shook his head at my naïveté. 'Cannot you see? My Lord Burghley has arranged circumstances so that either Walsingham or Marlowe will be revealed. Like a skilful hunter, he drives them both towards the same trap. The younger Walsingham will only survive if Marlowe dies.' He turned towards me. 'My Lord Burghley has set the pieces of his machinery in position. The engine of events will now take its course.'

I should have kept quiet, but his confident assertions seemed to goad me. I said, 'You know something more than you have said, perhaps?'

A sound like a sigh escaped him. 'There is a rumour now abroad that a certain great poet, while staying in a low tavern at Deptford, entered an argument with his companions over who would pay the bill of fare.'

He continued speaking in his low, calm voice, and while he talked the place that he described became vivid for me, and my mind constructed the scene.

Chapter 32

CHRISTOPHER MARLOWE SAT in a tavern with several companions. Even my lord's mention of their names caused a shudder to run through me – Ingram Frizer, Robert Poley and Nicholas Skeres – the very same stalwarts and torturers who accompanied the younger Walsingham when he accosted me in a passageway of my lord's house.

The four of them sat round a table, throwing dice, until the turn passed to Master Marlowe himself. He slipped the two cubes into a little cup, rattled them, and threw them on the table, saying, 'Fate obeys me tonight.'

The dice passed on to Poley, who shook them and threw casually. While the dice passed around the table, Frizer spoke in a soft, insinuating voice. 'It is said, Master Marlowe, that you threaten to expose our master Walsingham if the Privy Council have a mind to put you on the rack.'

'Indeed, Master Frizer,' Marlowe replied. 'Since torture searches one's innards, it would be difficult not to say what one knows, or not to intimate what one has seen.'

'And what has one seen?' Frizer asked.

'One has seen, for example, our master Walsingham's interest in certain young men, and one has witnessed his subsequent enjoyment of them.'

It was Frizer's turn to throw the dice. At the same time he said calmly, 'One should not throw stones in a glass house, so it is said.'

'You misunderstand me,' Marlowe replied. 'I do not criticise our master. On the contrary, I praise him. I merely state what I have seen.'

'Even so,' Frizer persisted, 'it is said that, since you have the same tastes, the pot should not call the kettle black.'

Marlowe observed the dice, smiling ironically, replying, 'They that like not tobacco and boys are fools.'

Around the table the other men smiled to themselves. At the same Frizer, softly insistent, said, 'You have not answered my question.'

'What question is that?' asked Marlowe.

'You intend to speak of what you have seen?'

'That is precisely the point, Master Frizer. Under torture these fine distinctions will cease to matter. All will be revealed. That is the thought which properly exercises our master Walsingham.'

'And you think this will save you?' Frizer asked.

Marlowe appeared outwardly calm while he threw the dice again. 'Our master will strive to save himself, and therefore he will strive his utmost to save me.'

The others continued to pass around the dice. At that stage, perhaps, Frizer glanced over at the somewhat burly landlord, who was dipping tankards in a bowl of water, wiping them with a rag, and setting them up on a shelf. The landlord nodded and, taking his time – as though in answer to Frizer's look – walked over to the doorway. He closed the wooden door and set the heavy crossbar down firmly across it.

Perhaps Marlowe noticed the arcane communication between Frizer and the landlord, for he commented, 'I have a sense, Master Frizer, that you are a denizen of this locality.'

'I am a citizen of Deptford, it is true.'

'Our master Walsingham prizes the citizens of Deptford,' Marlowe said. 'He informed me of it personally.'

'How did he express himself?'

'He told me,' Marlowe added, throwing the dice again, 'that they were the scurviest knaves in the kingdom, and if he ever wanted as mean and low a torturer's assistant as he could find, why, Deptford was the place to find him.'

Having secured the door, the landlord approached the table casually behind the speaker, standing silent, as though witnessing the throw of dice. Suddenly, without warning, he seized Marlowe from behind and pulled him backwards. At the same time, as though animated by the same impulse, Poley and Skeres leapt up from their seats and seized the poet by each of his arms.

Marlowe struggled, kicked and twisted, but he

could not break their grip. The fiercely struggling group moved back until they struck one of the walls. Frizer followed them, carrying one of the chairs. There they forced their victim into a seated position.

Frizer reached into his pocket and pulled out a dirty leather bundle. From it he unsheathed a knife with a long blade.

He advanced on Marlowe, saying, 'Our master Walsingham asked me to say one thing to you – that the eye is what it sees.'

With this, he plunged the knife into Marlowe's right eye, into the brain. The dying man gave a terrible scream, his body shuddered, his feet kicked spasmodically. The others held him until his struggles had ceased, and he was finally still.

Together they laid the body out on one of the long stout tables, even though Marlowe's legs still twitched.

Now Frizer rose – smooth, insinuating Frizer – addressing the landlord, enquiring, 'Tell me what you saw.'

The landlord said, 'I gave a reckoning of what was owed, but this gentleman lying here saw fit to debate the bill. And I said, who should settle it but him? And when it was pointed out what was owing, and that he should pay it, he pulled out a knife, so that what happened, happened.'

'And what might that be?'

'In the struggle which followed, that same knife entered his eye by accident.'

'You swear by this?' Frizer asked.

'On my life,' the landlord said.

Frizer withdrew a bag full of coins. 'And these pieces of silver?'

'I never saw them in my life.'

Frizer placed the money in the landlord's palm. The landlord's heavy fist closed over them.

'You see them now?' Frizer asked.

'To my eye, they are invisible.'

'Remember, if a word of this passes out, we will all swing together.'

'Of that I have no doubt,' the landlord said.

Chapter 33

WHEN THE DETAILS OF HIS STORY had been recounted, my Lord Southampton placed his hand on my shoulder. I shuddered, since I was still in the tavern of my own imagination.

For long afterwards, I would hear different accounts of the same event, all conflicting, all agreeing on only one thing – that Marlowe had been killed in a brawl in Deptford. A certain darkness, it seemed to me, lay over that part of London.

My lord said quietly, 'It is time we returned.'

That night I wrote at my board by the light of a single candle:

Was it the proud full sail of his great verse,
Bound for the prize of all too precious you,
That did my ripe thoughts in my brain inhearse,
Making their tomb the womb wherein they grew?
Was it his spirit, by spirits taught to write
Above a mortal pitch, that struck me dead?
No, neither he, nor his compeers by night
Giving him aid, my verse astonished.
He, nor that affable familiar ghost
Which nightly gulls him with intelligence,
As victors, of my silence cannot boast;
I was not sick of any fear from thence:
    But when your countenance fill'd up his line,
    Then lack'd I matter; that enfeebled mine.

When I had finished, I leaned back and stared past the candle into the blackness. At the same time, I could not help but whisper softly to myself, 'The better poet died. The lesser poet survived.'

Chapter 34

ALMOST ANOTHER YEAR PASSED, and during that time I remained like a nervous creature in my patron's household, hoping that my Lord Burghley's cold hand would not reach towards me too, and pluck me out. I continued to work in my cell through the autumn and the following frozen winter, writing and arranging my sonnets, attending to my plays, sometimes stepping out into thin spring sunshine for brief exercise.

I was fortunate to be absorbed by my labours. The acceptance that my love affair with my mistress was at an end was cruelly underlined by her continuation of relations with my patron. I could not blame her directly, for she herself had been entirely honest in the matter. She would persist with him, not least for the sake of her husband's position. Sometimes, though, my bitterness turned directly towards my lord, whose serene detachment over my predicament at times seemed to me like coldness, even heartlessness. It was only because I trusted him, and he trusted some sincerity in me, that I could write a poem which, though full of praises, yet had a vicious sting in its tail.

> They that have power to hurt and will do none,
> That do not do the thing they most do show,
> Who, moving others, are themselves as stone,
> Unmoved, cold, and to temptation slow;
> They rightly do inherit heaven's graces,
> And husband nature's riches from expense;
> They are the lords and masters of their faces,
> Others but stewards of their excellence.
> The summer's flower is to the summer sweet,
> Though to itself it only live and die;
> But if that flower with base infection meet,

The basest weed outbraves his dignity:
  For sweetest things turn sourest by their deeds;
  Lilies that fester smell far worse than weeds.

A part of me desired to provoke him into some denial of heartlessness, or at least to account for his imperious detachment. Yet instead of reacting against my strictures on his coldness, he absorbed my criticism equably and without argument. So we continued in our own relations without further direct discussion of his perpetuation of relations with Madam Florio. It was as though he understood my tortured frustrations, but at the same time regarded them as peculiarly my own, and was unwilling to pander to them. I sensed too that he considered his greater responsibility lay in protecting me, and for that at least I continued to remain unfailingly grateful.

Perhaps I also misunderstood him, or at least the direction of his mind. For he was changing too, turning away from the more obvious pleasures of the world. It appeared to me that he was sinking deeper into his own thoughts and preoccupations. It was not so much that he had tired of constantly acting a single role – that of a glowing and gilded youth – but rather that he was in the process of growing into something else. By various means the heavy fine which hung over him now began to exert its effect. Perhaps he perceived that as the time of his payment approached, he would be forced by circumstances to live less magnificently.

I gained the impression that he calculated that he would be able to pay his fine in full, while at the same time keeping the main body of his lands and estate. The consequence was that on reaching his majority, he would be obliged to live more frugally. In anticipation of that fact, he had already begun to shed the trappings of earthly arrogance and power. The virtuous respond to their strictures by shriving their souls.

Perhaps he also perceived my perplexity at the changes in him. Our closer and more intimate discussions took place usually on horseback, when we were out of earshot of those in his house, such as John Florio, who might spy upon him. One day, as we rode through the country, he handed to me, without speaking, a parchment on which certain sentences had been scribbled in his hand. At the time we were on level terrain, and while my horse walked beside his, I was able to read the jottings. The first paragraph was set out in verse:

Rising each day, we think of the fallen.
Sleeping by night, we dream of the risen.
When the dawn is like a funeral pyre
I think of him in the time-honoured days –
Of one who was braver, more arrogant
Than ever hero lived, or wielded sword –
Fearless in confrontation, unflinching
In deed

The farewell he had begun seemed to end there. Another verse was begun below that, as though he were trying for a different metre and expression, following that of the person he mourned:

Brave, arrogant Marlowe, our much-lamented dead,
Had swept all before him, his over-reaching mind
Forming our new theatre, the tragic hero's tread
Stamping his impression on the public boards.

With something of a surprise, I saw my own name mentioned next, as though by contrast.

Calm, philosophic Shakespeare, far less bold
Moved beneath the surface, like some private spirit
Tightening his metre, rescinding rhetoric;
Though force might be lost, made up in subtle beauty.
To his task he brought an actor's precision,
Could turn and pivot with perfect timing,
Making rhythm dance, creating new forms
Of myriad diversity.

Beneath that was a final set of jottings, as though my patron were following his thoughts to some form of conclusion:

Though he may not possess Marlowe's thunder
Or his infernal sense of the sublime,
Yet by living within his creations
They emerge like true beings on the stage.

There the lines ended. They were not poems so much as private musings, thoughts caught on the wing. Yet though they were somewhat rough, I could see in them the clear workings of my patron's mind. His consideration of the difference between the single beacon of Marlowe's genius and my own more pragmatic and varied talents seemed to me perceptive and not unfair.

At some level I believe Marlowe's death had affected my patron deeply, for the most profound changes occurred in him after the news of the great poet's decease. I did not know of the full nature of the companionship between them, and could not be certain if perhaps Marlowe had been his lover. If it were so, my patron had responded to his companion's death not by ostentatious lamentation, but with that cold and private solitude with which the strongest amongst us receive the worst news. My sense of intuition at the depth of his loss made my respect for him, if anything, the greater.

Chapter 35

My PATRON INSISTED that I stay under his protection for as long as I wished. But one day in late spring two horsemen rode up a shallow hillside overlooking the Earl of Southampton's great house.

Smoke poured from the chimneys. With the house behind us, we two riders approached the summit of that shallow hill – that hill which had become familiar to me in a previous summer, when leaves covered my assignations. Reaching the brow, my host turned his horse so that he faced me.

'Well, Master Shakespeare, I shall miss your company. But since the worst of the plague is over, and the theatres open again, it seems you are called once more to London.'

He was silent, patting his horse's mane.

I said, 'Lord Hunsdon has settled his theatre company for the new season. He calls it "The Lord Chamberlain's Men". I believe I will have employment there.'

'He charges you to write new plays?'

'I have several new plays for his eyes,' I replied, 'written during the plague years, while I enjoyed your patronage.'

'Remind me of them,' my lord requested.

'*The Taming of the Shrew, Richard III, Love's Labour's Lost.*'

He smiled at this, looking up at the sky as though in private enjoyment.

'So it is true,' he said finally aloud. 'You stole one of your titles from Master Florio, as he rightly maintains.'

'I am a magpie, my lord. Whatever shines, I will pilfer.'

He paused in amused contemplation. 'Your motto, then, is that the end justifies the means. All's well that ends well.'

'Precisely phrased,' I said.

Slowly, his expression became more serious. 'I have considered what best I might do to proceed against my Lord Burghley. For the time being, I will obey your advice, and keep Master Florio under my roof. Amongst other things, I owe it to his wife.'

I nodded my appreciation. He continued, 'But I have also considered, most calmly and carefully, how best I might strike back against my guardian. To that end, I have taken the trouble to purchase, for a round thousand pounds, a share in your name in Lord Hunsdon's company. I hope and believe that it will secure you against an uncertain future.'

My breath left me in contemplation of his act. It was an enormous sum. I said, mumbling incoherently, 'But you can ill afford – '

'I will survive,' he said, 'even after I have paid my great fine to my guardian. But afterwards, I will have the satisfaction of knowing that every success you make, every great and small entertainment, every poem or play that registers its force or felicity upon the mind of the public, will offend my Lord Burghley to his deepest soul.'

Tears started involuntarily in my eyes. I spoke, or stammered, 'A poet's life is no longer than a songbird's. If I could thank you for keeping me alive ... '

He seemed amused at this flood of emotion, and merely shrugged. Then he paused, and added, 'No gratitude is necessary, sir. Which of us truly knows his own future? Now, be gone with you. And do your work.'

I attempted to smile, but the tears were pouring uncontrollably down my cheeks. To hide my embarrassment, I started my horse. And so it was, approaching early summer, I rode away from my lord, blinded by both grief and gratitude.

When I turned to wave my final goodbye, he had already swung his horse and was riding back to his house, which for so long had been my home and refuge.

Chapter 36

I look back now, at the end of my life, upon those times. During the plague years of 1592 to 1594, when the London theatres were closed, almost an entire generation of my fellow playwrights perished, amongst them Robert Greene, Thomas Kyd and Christopher Marlowe. Others, such as George Peele and Thomas Nashe, died not long afterwards of poverty.

On that late spring day, when my lord had announced the gift of an investment that would bolster me against the vicissitudes of my calling for the remainder of my life, I gave him in return a folded letter, which he acknowledged merely with a nod, and tucked into his clothes before he rode away.

In the course of my final message to him, I thanked him from my heart for his courtesy and generosity. At the end of that letter, like a *post scriptum*, I included one final poem. He had been utterly steadfast to me, through every adversity, through the attention of greater poets and the turmoil of our own passionate rivalry over a certain dark lady. And so it happened that the poem I passed to him on that day was my own paean to Platonic love.

Let me not to the marriage of true minds
Admit impediments. Love is not love
Which alters when it alteration finds,
Or bends with the remover to remove:
O, no! It is an ever-fixed mark,
That looks on tempests and is never shaken,
It is the star to every wandering bark,
Whose worth's unknown, although his height be taken.
Love's not Time's fool, though rosy lips and cheeks

Within his bending sickle's compass come;
Love alters not with his brief hours and weeks,
But bears it out even to the edge of doom.
  If this be error, and upon me prov'd,
  I never writ, nor no man ever lov'd.

In that final year I had not often seen my beloved, only in brief glimpses on her duties with her family, when she appeared both preoccupied and distracted. She seemed to have returned to her role as mother of her four children, a distant and remote figure inhabiting the same household. As my departure to London drew nearer, I did not attempt to write to her, since it would have risked her husband's wrath. But one day, as we passed one another in the rose garden, without speaking or embracing (for we might have been overlooked) I took the opportunity to hand to her a fair copy of a poem which I kept about my person. Hardly pausing, she slipped it carefully into her sleeve, though she smiled briefly at me – the first smile she had given me for many months – before walking on.

The poem would form the last of my sequence of a hundred and fifty-four sonnets. Its subject was desire itself. Despite every anguish and impediment, passion lived amongst us, not by sweetness and delight, but by the deepest and purest designs of our being. In one as sceptical as myself, I would choose to end my stream of sonnets on the subject of the perpetual fever of love, not as the harbinger of peace or wisdom, but expressed in the form of its own fire.

The little Love-god lying once asleep
Laid by his side his heart-inflaming brand,
Whilst many nymphs that vow'd chaste life to keep
Came tripping by; but in her maiden hand
The fairest votary took up that fire
Which many legions of true hearts had warm'd;
And so the general of hot desire
Was, sleeping, by a virgin hand disarm'd.
This brand she quenched in a cool well by,
Which from Love's fire took heat perpetual,

Growing a bath and healthful remedy
For men diseas'd; but I, my mistress' thrall,
   Came here for cure, and this by that I prove,
   Love's fire heats water, water cools not love.

Biographical Note

*H*ENRY WRIOTHESLEY, the third Earl of Southampton, became a leading soldier and military commander who participated in numerous campaigns. He was a close ally of Queen Elizabeth's favourite, Robert Devereux, Earl of Essex. In 1598 Southampton, shortly before his twenty-fifth birthday, secretly married one of the Queen's maids of honour, Elizabeth Vernon, who was pregnant with his child. The marriage, which enraged the Queen (her maids of honour were meant to be maids) was considered a happy one, and produced several children. In 1601 Southampton was imprisoned in the Tower for his role in Essex's unsuccessful *coup* *d'état* against Elizabeth. Essex was executed. Southampton was eventually released from imprisonment on the accession of James I and restored to court. In 1624 Southampton died of fever while on military expedition in the Low Countries; his eldest son died with him, also of fever, in the same campaign.

William Shakespeare died peacefully in 1616, in Stratford-upon-Avon.

Afterword

ANYONE WHO ATTEMPTS TO WRITE on the subject of Shakespeare's sonnets approaches these great and mysterious works with considerable trepidation.

My own chief interest in writing *The Sonnets* was not so much to attempt to explore the social or physical world in which Shakespeare lived, as the landscape of his mind – the mind that produced his unprecedented body of work and which is, to some extent, revealed to us most directly in the poems themselves.

Given this background, it seemed to me that my approach should be to attempt to create a narrative frame for as many of Shakespeare's sonnets as could reasonably be incorporated (eventually some thirty-two of the poems were used) and to allow those sonnets – each reproduced in full – a leading role in creating that 'colour'.

In the course of working on the narrative of *The Sonnets* there were, however, two clear exceptions to the direct use and quotation of Shakespeare's poems.

Towards the beginning of the book, the Earl of Southampton tells Shakespeare of the marriage contract which his guardian Lord Burghley persuaded him to sign while a child, promising to marry Burghley's granddaughter, Elizabeth de Vere. Shakespeare is incensed at the way the poem *Narcissus* – written at Burghley's behest by his secretary John Clapham – has been deliberately constructed to apply pressure to Southampton to marry. The 'sonnet' which Shakespeare then writes in partial response is my own invention:

Lord of laughter, you showed me Narcissus,
A poem whose heart is hollowed by power;

Falsely addressed, it pretends to kiss us,
Telling of beauty, Cupid's sweet bower;
Yet cold hearts form cold minds, eyes lose their sight;
Stealing our childhood, it counsels good faith.
Framed by deceit, the sun's fatal glower
Reversing all virtue, makes permanent night.
In Hell's own smithies, Authority labours,
Shadow on shadow, reversing the year;
And what is more wretched, than making wretched,
When, lacking all mercy, he sheds no tear?
   Then punish him not for what he may say;
   A mind without light can never see day.

Southampton tears up the sonnet on the grounds
that it is likely to endanger Shakespeare's life if it
should ever fall into Lord Burghley's hands. By so
doing, I hope I made it reasonably plain to the reader
that the poem is not one of Shakespeare's own surviving sonnets.

The second and only other use of an imitation
sonnet occurs during the narrative sequence when

Shakespeare encounters and is rejected by Emilia Bassano. He then finds an answering love in Lucia Florio. My purpose in suggesting this change of loves was to parallel the more recent scholarly view that John Florio's wife appears a more likely candidate for the role of dark lady than the traditional candidate of Emilia Bassano. During this narrative sequence Shakespeare makes a pass at Emilia, who says she is faithful to Lord Hunsdon. When Shakespeare persists with his suit, she bites his hand to emphasise her point. Later, when Shakespeare meets his former (and future) patron Lord Hunsdon, the wily old nobleman enquires how Shakespeare received the wound to his hand. Shakespeare replies that he was bitten 'by a faithful female hound'. Both men know they are talking about Emilia.

Since (perhaps unsurprisingly) there appeared to be no sonnet entirely appropriate to the circumstances of that change of loves, I constructed an imitation sonnet which was aimed to express Shakespeare's regret at his unrequited love for Emilia Bassano. It seemed to me that I should attempt do my best to include at least an oblique reference to a hound or faithful hound.

The Sonnets

If I hear music in the painted day,
Drawing myself towards those fateful sounds,
And all my thoughts move outward to the lay,
Like lines of scent on which run faithful hounds,
Then I must hide my thoughts in careful praise
Which, praising you, fall short of what I feel.
If I should moan your loss, make better days
The sad account of my most bitter meal,
Your fingers on the cloth, touching their hem,
Press me to sit and watch your subtle hands;
The singular white thoughts which rise from them,
Graceful as hinds towards that hidden land.
    O, let me sit beside you while you play,
    Allowing thoughts to alter night for day.

As with the first imitation sonnet, I tried to signal to the reader that the poem did not survive (in this case Shakespeare burns it immediately after writing it) and that therefore it was my own construction.

259

The only other verses I have attempted are a few pieces of doggerel which Southampton writes in order to give passing voice to Marlowe's death. Since they are obviously not from Shakespeare himself and do not raise any questions of authorship, I shall not reproduce them here or discuss them further.

Finally, I am strongly aware that the fact that I have used Shakespeare's sonnets for the purposes of my own narrative necessarily affects the way in which such sonnets are read. For those readers who are interested to look at certain individual sonnets again, outside the impulsion of the novel's own narrative, and in the order in which Shakespeare himself arranged them, I have drawn up a list of the pages on which each occurs and, alongside them in darker letters, the number of that sonnet in Shakespeare's 154-sonnet sequence. (For the purposes of this book, I used an Oxford University Press edition of the sonnets, but many other editions are available, too.)

The Sonnets